U.S. History

DeMYSTiFieD®

DeMYSTiFieD® Series

U.S. History
DeMYSTiFieD®

Stephanie Muntone

New York   Chicago   San Francisco   Lisbon   London   Madrid   Mexico City
Milan   New Delhi   San Juan   Seoul   Singapore   Sydney   Toronto

Contents

How to Use This Book

The important questions a historian asks are "What happened?" and "Why did it happen?" This book should help you to answer those questions on the topic of U.S. history—that is, from the arrival of the Indians on the North American continent up to the end of the Cold War in 1991.

History students are often confused by a wealth of information being thrown at them at once—names, dates, presidents, and acts of Congress following one another in a bewildering array. The easiest way to sort out the confusion is to think about how events connect with one another. History is a long story of causes and effects. For example, the Missouri Compromise led indirectly to the Civil War. Provisions of the peace treaty signed at the end of World War I created the conditions that led to World War II. And so on. It's much easier to remember events when you understand how they relate to one another.

This book tells you the political, social, and cultural history of the United States in a narrative format, emphasizing the key ideas so you will understand why they are important—why congressional leaders compromised on slavery, what caused a major wave of migration or immigration, or why the Civil Rights movement began when it did. Each chapter deals with an important era or event in history, such as the Civil War or the Great Depression. Chapter topics can overlap in time, but the order of topics is basically chronological. The book is divided into three major sections:

- Part 1 begins with the first arrival of human beings in North America and ends shortly after the ratification of the U.S. Constitution.

- Part 2 covers the United States in the nineteenth century, including the Industrial Revolution, the Civil War, Reconstruction, and the Gilded Age.
- Part 3 narrates the course of U.S. history in the twentieth century, including both world wars, the Great Depression, and the Civil Rights movement.

Each chapter ends with a 10-question quiz, and each section ends with a 50-question exam. There is also a 100-question exam at the end of the book. The questions are all multiple-choice, similar to the sorts of questions used on standardized tests. Many of the questions ask you about causes and effects: Why did this event happen? What happened as a result of that decision?

You might try taking the chapter quiz first, before reading the chapter. This will tell you which sections of each chapter you already know well, and which sections you need to study further. Read and study the chapter, then take the quiz again. Keep working on each chapter until you can answer at least 9 of the 10 questions correctly.

Take each section exam after you have mastered the corresponding series of chapters, and take the final exam once you have mastered the entire book. Check your work against the answer key; if you answer at least 92 of the 100 questions correctly, you can consider that you have mastered the subject satisfactorily. Go back and study any areas of the book that cover questions you did not answer correctly.

If you are using this book as a course companion, follow along at the same pace your professor is taking. Use the book for extra tutorial and practice in addition to what is covered in class. If you are using the book as a substitute for taking a course, or to prepare yourself for an exam, then allow yourself time to get the most out of it. Allow three months, one month for each section of the book. Read the narrative, take the quizzes, and make a list of questions on aspects of U.S. history that aren't clear to you. Use the sources recommended in the bibliography, or similar titles in the library or bookstore, to find the answers. When you're done with the course, you can use this book, with its comprehensive index, as a permanent reference.

Introduction
Understanding the Themes of U.S. History

History, like a great work of literature, has themes—major motifs and concerns that arise again and again over the course of time. Understanding these themes helps the student make sense of history. Themes show connections—causes and effects that can help you understand not only what happened, but also why it happened. Themes show you the important factors that shape the course of history for a nation, a region, and a continent.

Geography

The history of any nation is inseparable from its geography—its position in relation to other nations, its climate, its topography, its natural resources, whether or not it has a seacoast, the location of its major rivers, and similar factors. The United States is so large that regional geographical differences have also played a role. Here are some examples of how geography has affected U.S. history:

- The United States is vast in its physical size and population, which means it can muster an enormous army. The Atlantic and Pacific oceans form a safety zone on both coasts. These two factors made the United States all but invulnerable to invasion and conquest until the mid-twentieth century, when attack from the air became technologically possible.

- Westward expansion is a major theme in U.S. history. So many immigrants continued to cross the Atlantic that it was natural for the settlers to expand further and further westward to occupy what seemed like unlimited fertile land.

- Climate is one reason why slavery existed in the South as long as it did. The South has the appropriate climate for growing labor-intensive crops on a large scale: tobacco, cotton, and rice. Climate is also the reason for the livestock and grain industries in the Great Plains.

Imperialism

Imperialism refers to the conquest of lands beyond a state's own borders. Through the centuries, great imperial powers have acquired their empires in one of two ways. Some nations have invaded and conquered lands far from their own home base. Britain is one example of this type of imperialism; at its height, the British Empire included colonies in North America, the Caribbean, Africa, Australia, and India. Other nations have simply expanded their state borders, thus developing a vast nation-state that is one contiguous landmass; the Soviet Union/Russia, China, and the United States are examples of this type of empire. The United States has acquired a few colonies or territories outside its borders, but for the most part, U.S. imperialism took the form of westward expansion on the North American continent. Throughout U.S. history, almost all national leaders have concentrated on expanding the nation's size rather than on colonizing or annexing other nations.

This is partly a question of geography and climate. The United States has such a vast quantity of fertile land, and is so rich in important natural resources such as gold, silver, and coal, that it has only rarely found it necessary to seek such resources elsewhere.

Religion

Religion is a powerful emotional force that can work to unite people who think alike and divide people who think differently. Throughout history, a great many wars have been fought over the issue of religion—or at any rate, leaders have used religious differences as an excuse to go to war.

Religion has been a major bone of contention throughout U.S. history for the simple reason that, unlike most other countries, the United States is not culturally or ethnically homogenous. It is and always has been a nation of immigrants who come from many nations and who represent all religions known to humankind. This underscores the enormous importance of the First Amendment: that Congress may neither establish a state religion nor interfere with the free exercise of religion—any religion. It is significant that the authors of the Constitution listed this as the very first individual freedom, suggesting that they regarded it as the most important of all.

The United States was founded after the great era of religious wars and has never fought a war over this issue. However, religion has been a divisive social and political issue since the 1600s. The Salem witch trials, anti-Catholic bigotry leveled against Irish immigrants, and the 1925 Scopes trial are only a few highlights of the religious divisions that have plagued and continue to plague American society.

Racism

Black/white racism is and almost always has been a defining factor in U.S. history. Race was at the bottom of the single most important issue that decided that history from 1776 until 1865—chattel slavery in the South. Racial apartheid continued—openly in the South, more covertly in the North—until the Civil Rights era, 100 years after the Civil War ended.

Slavery was a contentious issue in the First Continental Congress; a reference criticizing it as an institution had to be removed from the Declaration of Independence before the southern colonies would agree to vote for independence. From then until the election of President Abraham Lincoln and the secession of the southern states from the United States, it was the most bitterly contested issue in the growing nation. Southerners were determined to maintain it for their own economic benefit; northerners were determined to eradicate it for the same reason—in addition to racist beliefs in African inferiority on the southern side, and outrage over such beliefs on the northern side. However, the North was hardly free from racism.

From 1776 until at least 1968, when federal troops finally completed the work of Reconstruction, African Americans were second-class citizens at best. Suspicion and hostility between African and White Americans is a major theme throughout this book.

Other groups besides Africans have suffered from racism. The core group that considers itself "American" has consistently discriminated against any group it considers something *other* than American—the Irish, the Chinese, and the Japanese, to name only a few examples.

Racism against American Indians is perhaps the worst example of all, given that they were here first. Americans of European descent always considered the Indians to be a foreign population, not American at all, and not capable of assimilating into the mainstream European-American or Anglo-American culture. On their side, the American Indians showed no desire to assimilate; however, they would cheerfully have agreed to maintain separate tribal societies had the United States kept its many promises to leave them alone.

Immigration

The United States is probably the most culturally and ethnically diverse nation in the world. Its population is entirely comprised of immigrants—even Native Americans are not actually native to this continent. Every single person in the United States is either an immigrant or the descendant of immigrants, and this has been true throughout its history.

The first wave of immigrants to settle what later became the original United States was primarily northern European—English, Dutch, Swedes, and Germans. The first Africans arrived on the Atlantic coast in the early 1600s. The next major wave of immigrants was largely Irish and Central European. The third major wave came across both oceans: Chinese came across the Pacific, while Italians, Slavs, and Jews crossed the Atlantic. The most recent major wave of immigration continues to pour into the United States from Latin America.

Federalism

A federal government is one in which the power of government is shared between the states and the national government. Each of the 13 original British colonies had its own state government. In 1776, the colonies became states and began writing their own constitutions. In 1789, the U.S. Constitution gave shape to the national government. Each state is represented in Congress, and the president and Supreme Court represent all the people.

U.S. history has been a long tussle between the power of the White House and the self-governing power of the individual states. State governments are independent on a number of issues, such as the legal age for drinking, the qualifications for legal marriage, and the requirements for a driver's license. The federal government is responsible for passing laws that apply equally to all the states.

If a state disagrees with a federal law, it will pass its own law overturning it. If the federal government considers a state law illegal, it can send federal troops to occupy the state and force obedience. This happened during Reconstruction and again during the Civil Rights era.

PART I

Settlement and Colonization: Ratification of the U.S. Constitution

Settlement and Colonization of North America

Four groups of people settled and colonized the land that became the United States of America. The first were Asian nomads, who later became known as "Native Americans" or "American Indians." Thousands of years later, they were followed by the Europeans: first the Spanish, then the French, and finally the British.

Native American tribes eventually settled all parts of North and South America, including the islands that could support human habitation. Their cultures were diverse, but in some important ways they were all alike. Common elements of American-Indian culture included respect for the land, making what was needed by hand, hunting and gathering food, and maintaining an oral rather than a written culture.

While European monarchs vied with one another to establish strong nation-states in Europe, they also began sponsoring voyages of exploration beyond the known world. The purposes were fourfold: trade, conquest and expansion, religious conversion, and curiosity. The primary reason for their stupendous success can be summed up in one word: guns.

Europeans had been trading with Asia for a long time, but the overland routes were problematic. Going over land, goods could not be transported any faster than a horse could walk; ships, by contrast, could move much more quickly, and a single ship could carry far more goods than a team of horses. In addition, the overland routes were dangerous; traders were constantly vulnerable to robbery and attack, weather caused problems at most times of the year, and geographical features such as mountains created obstacles to a smooth passage. All these factors ate into profits and led the traders to look for water routes to Asia, since transport of goods by water was much easier, more efficient, and less hazardous.

The second motive was conquest and expansion. European nations tended to have an aggressive foreign policy, constantly attacking one another in order to acquire valuable territory and expand their power bases. A larger population meant more revenue for the Crown in taxes, more income for the Church in tithes, and more soldiers in the army. Therefore, three of the most powerful branches of society—the court, the clergy, and the military—were united in their desire to explore the seas and lands beyond Europe in the hope of establishing colonies that would make the country richer and stronger than its neighbors.

The third motive, religious conversion, was a product of the universal Christian belief that non-Christians were heathens and that it was a Christian's duty to convert them, thus saving their souls from eternal damnation after death. Just as a nation is politically and economically stronger when it has a larger population, a church is stronger when it has more believers; therefore the European churches were eager to send missionaries to Asia, Africa, and the Americas to bring more souls into the fold.

The last motive, and a very powerful one, was a sense of adventure and curiosity—the urge to find out what lay beyond the horizon and the willingness to take the risk of finding out. This urge has characterized human beings since the beginning of civilization, and is responsible for all scientific discoveries and technological achievements. Just as the twentieth-century explorations of outer space could not have been accomplished without the fundamental human desire to see and learn about the unknown, the sixteenth- and seventeenth-century voyages of exploration could never have happened if a number of brave souls had not taken the plunge and risked boarding the ships.

Although the Chinese had invented gunpowder centuries before, there were no guns elsewhere in the world that could match those that the Europeans had developed by the 1500s. One of the most important axioms in understanding history is that in any conflict, the side with the greater firepower generally wins. The Asians had much less sophisticated guns than the Europeans, and the Americans had no guns at all. This is almost certainly the main reason that the Europeans were able to impose their will on the peoples of the other continents.

CHAPTER OBJECTIVES

- Identify the four major groups of people who settled and colonized North America.
- Identify the reasons that each group came to North America.
- Evaluate the accomplishments of each group of people.
- Describe the major differences between Native American and European cultures and the effects of these differences.

Chapter 1 Time Line

BC

- **circa 38,000–15,000**   Land bridge across Bering Strait links Asia and North America, making human migration possible.

- **circa 11,000**   Age of oldest human remains ever discovered in North America.

- **circa 11,000–9,000**   Bering land bridge disappears permanently under water.

- **1500**   Corn, native to Mexico and South America, is first grown in the North.

- **circa 100**   Anasazi culture takes shape at present day "Four Corners" in Southwest.

AD

- **circa 1100**   Iroquois Confederacy founded in Northeast.

- **1492**   Christopher Columbus and his party sail from Spain to the Caribbean islands.

- **1516**   Smallpox epidemic decimates America-Indian population.

- **1539**   Hernando de Soto explores the Southeast; many hostile encounters with Indian tribes.

- **1565**   Pedro Menendez de Áviles founds St. Augustine on the Florida coast.

- **1584**   Sir Walter Raleigh explores the Atlantic coast and claims the Virginia territory for England.

- **1585–1590**   Establishment and disappearance of colony on Roanoke Island.

- **1607**   London Company establishes Jamestown colony near Chesapeake Bay.

The First Peoples

Archaeologists believe that the first people to settle the Americas came here from Asia, walking across a land bridge between Siberia and Alaska. These Asian nomads followed herds of animals on which they depended for food. Eventually, these people settled all habitable regions of North and South America and the Caribbean islands. Groups were small and widely scattered, and each one eventually developed a tribal identity, language, and culture all its own.

No one knows when these first Americans arrived. The oldest human bones ever found in North America are 13,000 years old, but other archaeological evidence suggests that human habitation goes back much farther than that. Archaeologists continue to gather and study the evidence.

This map shows human settlement in North America at the time the first Europeans began to explore the continent. You can see the diversity of America-Indian tribes and the places where they settled.

The early American cultures had two major characteristics: diversity and unity. Both characteristics were related to the land, the climate, and natural forces.

Diversity

Across all America Indian tribes, culture was dictated by the climate and natural resources in the area where the people settled. Native Americans hunted local animals, ate local fruits and vegetables, and made their houses of whatever natural materials were easily found in the area.

Except for nomadic tribes, America Indians did not travel very far beyond what they considered to be their own territory. Tribes of the Mississippi delta, for instance, would never journey upriver to communicate or trade with tribes at a distance. Therefore, cultural exchange among Native Americans remained at a minimum, and tribal identities remained distinct and individual.

Native American Tribes Before the Arrival of the Europeans

Unity

All Native-American cultures were (and remain) united by certain shared characteristics. The most important was respect for the physical environment. American Indians depended entirely on the land for their food, clothing, and shelter, so they treated it with care. Native-American religious rituals for many tribes involved prayers for good weather, harvests, and hunting. American Indians believed that nature was not to be mastered, but to be served and maintained.

Compared to Europeans, American Indians were not technologically advanced. They made everything they needed, but they did not invent machines.

The tools and weapons they made were relatively crude and unsophisticated, because their needs were simple. Ancient American-Indian pottery and woven baskets remain both beautiful and functional to this day.

Politically, most North American Indian tribes were democratic. Because tribes were small groups of people, it was easy to consult everyone's opinion and consider it in making decisions. Most Native-American cultures were matriarchal; the women of the tribes held important positions as heads of families. However, chiefs were male, and in theory if not in fact, councils of men made most tribal decisions.

Tribes that lived near one another communicated and traded on a regular basis. These groups of tribes formed nations—tribal associations based on similar linguistic, religious, political, and cultural characteristics. Democracy in pre-Columbian America reached its most sophisticated form among the tribes of the Iroquois Nation of the Northeast. The Seneca, Cayuga, Oneida, Onondaga, and Mohawk tribes were prone to quarrel. During the 1400s, tribal leaders agreed that it was time to form a regular council in which conflicts could be settled peacefully. They agreed to form a confederacy. Elders and chiefs chosen by popular vote from each of the five tribes would meet to discuss issues of importance to their people. The founders of the council agreed that all decisions were to be made based on the welfare of the people. Chiefs could be removed from the council for committing crimes.

THE MYTH

Native Americans are, as their name says, native to North and South America.

THE FACTS

The term *Native Americans* came into common use in the late twentieth century, in an attempt to correct Columbus' mistaken belief that he had reached India in 1492. Under that assumption, he and his crew members called the islanders "Indians," and the name "American Indians" has stuck to them ever since.

However, "Native Americans" is also a misnomer. As far as archaeologists have been able to determine, human beings are not native to the Americas. The first settlers of this land arrived thousands of years before the Europeans or Africans, but still, they are not native to this continent. Like all subsequent immigrants, they came here from somewhere else.

A sixth nation, the Tuscarora, joined the Iroquois Confederacy during the 1700s. In the colonial period, the Confederacy provided a powerful bulwark against British expansion. Although its power to affect national policy waned after the American Revolution, it continues to meet to this day.

The European Voyagers

The first Europeans to reach the Americas were Norsemen. Around the year AD 982, Erik the Red discovered Greenland and established a Viking settlement there. In the year 1000, his son Leif Erikson landed on the eastern coast of Canada. However, the Norsemen did not pursue their ventures into the Western Hemisphere.

The Spanish Explorers

Trade Routes to the East

The race for American colonies and the continuing cultural exchange between the Americas and Europe began in the early sixteenth century following Christopher Columbus' arrival in the Caribbean in 1492. Columbus, an Italian sponsored by the monarchs of Spain, had sailed forth in charge of a fleet of three ships looking for the elusive trade route to India and China. He reasoned that since the world was spherical, one should be able to reach the East by sailing west. There was only one flaw in his theory—the Americas and the Pacific Ocean lay between Europe and Asia. Europeans were ignorant of the existence of this great landmass.

In four voyages to the Caribbean, Columbus claimed Cuba, Hispaniola, Antigua, and the Bahamas for Spain, establishing a base of operations for the Spanish explorers who followed him. The islands are called the "West Indies" because Columbus never realized that he had not in fact reached India; the misnomer "Indians" has stuck to the earliest inhabitants of the Americas ever since.

Power and Religion

European monarchs realized that by sponsoring explorers like Columbus they could establish colonies and expand their power bases abroad. Missionaries of the Catholic Church were also pleased at the discovery that there were whole societies of people to convert to their faith.

Spain soon sponsored more voyages to the West. In 1513, Vasco Nuñez de Balboa crossed the Isthmus of Panama and became the first European to see the Pacific Ocean. In 1519, Ferdinand Magellan of Portugal sailed westward past the southern tip of South America. Magellan was killed in a fight in the Philippines, but several of his crew members returned safely to Spain, having circled the globe. They established beyond doubt that it was possible to reach the East by sailing west.

Wealth and Greed

Between 1519 and 1531, the Spaniards defeated and wiped out the mighty Aztec and Inca armies of Mexico and Peru. The great wealth they seized fired the imaginations of explorers such as Juan Ponce de León and Hernando de Soto, who sailed to North America in search of similar wealth. These men are known to history by the romantic name of *conquistadors*, a word that celebrates their adventurous spirit and undoubted bravery while minimizing the fact that they were motivated by greed and behaved brutally to those whose lands they invaded.

Ponce de León led the first party of European explorers to reach the North-American mainland. They landed near present-day Tampa Bay, Florida, in 1513. Hernando de Soto followed Ponce de León in 1539. He and his party penetrated deep into the heart of the southeastern United States, killing, kidnapping, and robbing the numerous American-Indian tribes they encountered on the way. In 1541, De Soto and his party became the first Europeans to see and cross the Mississippi River. At the same time, Francisco Vasquez de Coronado, Gárcia López de Cárdenas, and Juan Rodriguez Cabrillo were exploring the Southwest and the California coast. At one time, Spain claimed almost two-thirds of the present United States.

In 1565, Pedro Menendez de Áviles finally established the first Spanish colony in North America. He and his party founded the city of St. Augustine, Florida. The Spaniards began to settle Texas in the late 1600s and California in the mid-1700s. Their influence can still be seen in the Spanish place names, the architectural styles, and the predominance of Catholic churches in these areas.

The French Explorers

While the Spaniards sought fairy-tale riches in the New World, the French explorers began with a more practical motive: the expansion of the fur trade. Giovanni da Verrazano in 1524 and Jacques Cartier in 1535 were the first Frenchmen to explore any part of North America. However, the French did not attempt to establish American colonies until 1603, when a party of fur-traders traveled west to Canada. Samuel de Champlain went with the party as their mapmaker. He mapped the St. Lawrence River and the northern Atlantic coast. Champlain founded the towns of Port Royal and Quebec. He established friendly relations with the Huron and Algonquin tribes. This friendship led to an alliance of forces during the French and Indian War. (See Chapter 4.)

In 1615, Champlain became the first European to see the Great Lakes. This area became the hub of the French fur-trading industry. As the French prospered, they began exploring further south. They settled parts of Ohio and sailed all the way down the Mississippi River to the Gulf of Mexico, where Robert Cavelier, Sieur de la Salle, founded the colony of Louisiana.

The French fur-traders explored as far west as South Dakota. They built forts and trading posts along the rivers, but did not try to set up permanent governments or colonies beyond those they had established in the east. Instead, they tried to cooperate with the local tribes, who were able to provide guidance and advice.

The British Explorers

Trade Routes

Like Christopher Columbus, the British wanted to find a way to sail west to Asia. The search for the elusive "Northwest Passage" was the motive for early British explorations.

In 1497, John Cabot landed on the coast of Maine, becoming the first European since Leif Erikson to see North America. Cabot never returned from a second voyage. His son Sebastian followed him in 1508, and reached the entrance to what would later be named Hudson Bay. In 1609, Henry Hudson found the mouth of the Hudson River and followed it north to Albany before he and his party realized that it would not lead them west. On a second voyage, Hudson drove his crew further and further west through the network of islands north of Canada; finally, terrified for their lives in the frigid, unknown waters, Hudson's crew marooned him and turned the ship back east toward safety.

Power

Realizing that Spain and France were establishing a foothold in the Americas, England joined in the competition for colonies. Its first success was the Chesapeake Bay colony of Jamestown, founded in 1607. By 1638, England had founded seven colonies along the Atlantic coast. As the American population grew, the colonies began to expand westward, carrying out the commands of their royal charters to continue exploring and expanding their territory. These

British colonies, in the end, would become the first of the United States of America. (See Chapter 2.)

Clashes between the Native Americans and the Europeans

Clashes between the American Indians and Europeans were inevitable. The two groups of people were different in every possible way. The Native Americans had settled the land thousands of years before the arrival of the Europeans, and naturally considered that it belonged to them. They did not keep written records; their culture was primarily oral. They respected the land and adapted their needs and lives to suit what it could provide. They did not share either languages, religion, or social customs with the Europeans who invaded their lands during the Age of Exploration.

The various groups of Europeans shared a common religious, linguistic, and cultural heritage. They had developed sophisticated weapons. They had a conquering mentality that differed greatly from the mentality of the American-Indian tribes, who had found that there was room enough for all to settle, with fights over territory being very rare.

Europeans believed themselves to be racially superior to the Native Americans. They based this prejudice on a number of factors. First, the tribes had no technological know-how; to European eyes, their clothing, architecture, and weapons were primitive. Second, their physical characteristics were not European. Third, they did not read or write, and Europeans viewed literacy as a mark of education, intelligence, and high social status. Last, the Native Americans were not Christians. Europeans were educated to believe that their own faith was the only true one and that all nonbelievers were heathens. European explorers and settlers felt that this supposed superiority gave them the right to enslave the Indians, convert them to Christianity, and take control of their lands.

Tribal customs dictated hospitality to visitors. The Native Americans never anticipated that the white men would steal their lands and their liberty. When they learned their mistake, they fought fiercely. However, the Europeans were bound to triumph in the struggle. Bows and arrows were of little use against European guns. In addition, the Native Americans had never been exposed to diseases such as smallpox, and therefore had no immunity to them. The germs traveled westward with the explorers, and American Indians sickened and died by the thousands. Some historians estimate that about 85 percent of the North American population died between 1500 and 1550, as a direct result of the European conquest.

When the Europeans began to establish colonies, more clashes arose. Native Americans and Europeans were now fighting for possession of land. Despite the tenacity of their struggles, the tribes gradually began giving way to the superior weapons and organization of the Europeans. They were slowly but surely driven away from their ancestral lands.

CHAPTER 1 QUIZ

1. **The first people to settle North America are today known as "American Indians" because _____**
   A. they originally came from India.
   B. they arrived in North America long before any other groups of people followed.
   C. the first Europeans to reach the Caribbean thought that they had reached India.
   D. they settled every area of the Americas that was fit for human habitation.

2. **_____ is an important historical figure because he initiated the cultural exchange between Europe and the Americas.**
   A. Leif Erikson
   B. Christopher Columbus
   C. Samuel de Champlain
   D. Henry Hudson

3. **In the late 1400s, _____ became the first European nation to sponsor a western voyage of discovery.**
   A. France
   B. Great Britain
   C. India
   D. Spain

4. **The original motive for French exploration was _____**
   A. the expansion of Christianity into the New World.
   B. the kidnapping, enslavement, and transportation of Native Americans.
   C. the expansion of the profitable fur trade.
   D. the desire to expand the French power base by establishing colonies.

5. One powerful motivating force behind the European conquest of the Native Americans was the European _____
   A. belief in racial superiority.
   B. desire to study American-Indian language and culture.
   C. interest in making treaties with tribal governments.
   D. desire to find trade routes to the Far East.

6. Columbus believed that he landed in India in 1492 because _____
   A. he had been sailing for several weeks.
   B. he did not know of the existence of the Americas.
   C. he did not realize that he could reach the East by sailing west.
   D. he believed what the Native Americans told him when he landed.

7. The first explorer to see mainland North America after Leif Erikson was sponsored by _____
   A. France.
   B. Great Britain.
   C. Portugal.
   D. Spain.

8. The French established the hub of their North American fur-trading base in _____
   A. Louisiana.
   B. Ohio.
   C. the Great Lakes region.
   D. Canada.

9. The most important common characteristic of all Native-American tribal cultures is that _____
   A. their chiefs are female.
   B. they speak the same language.
   C. they constantly make war on each other.
   D. they treat the land with respect.

10. The Native Americans did not possess any _____ that could compete effectively with those of the Europeans.
    A. maps
    B. religions
    C. diseases
    D. weapons

Chapter 2

The British Colonies

Of the European nations that established a presence north of Latin America, the British were the most successful. The British colonies are those that ultimately became the United States of America. These original thirteen colonies were founded for a variety of reasons, including religious freedom, economic opportunity, the desire for self-government, and escape from debt.

The Protestant Reformation that had begun in Europe in 1517 had created a new desire for religious self-determination. This was often impossible to achieve in Europe, where the subjects were bound to worship according to the preference of the monarch. One reason for Europeans to sail to the New World was to escape from such rules. In the New England colonies, however, the oppressed quickly became the oppressors; the Puritans forced their religious beliefs and practices on everyone in the colony, just as the Catholics and later the Protestants had done in Europe. When religious tyranny led to judicial murders in Massachusetts, the era of theocracy was broken; the other Atlantic coast colonies built the free exercise of religion into their constitutions.

The New World offered almost unlimited economic opportunities. Fertile farmland was to be had for the asking. All the new towns and villages needed blacksmiths, innkeepers, ministers, midwives, and teachers. Settling new colonies also meant a chance for political power; governors and other officials were needed to fill positions of authority.

CHAPTER OBJECTIVES

- Identify the thirteen British colonies established along the Atlantic coast of North America.

- Identify who founded each colony and the motives for its creation.

- Describe similarities and differences among the colonies.

Chapter 2 Time Line

- **1584**   Sir Walter Raleigh explores the Atlantic coast and claims the Virginia territory for England.

- **1585–1590**   Establishment and disappearance of colony on Roanoke Island.

- **1607**   London Company establishes Jamestown colony near Chesapeake Bay.

- **1619**   Twenty African servants arrive in Chesapeake colony; they are the first Africans to come to North America.

- **1620**   *Mayflower* reaches Cape Cod Bay; Pilgrims, religious separatists, settle Plymouth Colony, sign Mayflower Compact.

- **1629**   Puritans found Massachusetts Bay Colony by royal charter.

- **1632**   Lord Baltimore establishes the colony of Maryland on the Chesapeake.

- **1636**   Roger Williams establishes the colony of Rhode Island and Providence Plantations.

- **1638**   Religious dissenters found the colony of Connecticut.

- **1700s**   African slave trade is firmly established in the British colonies.

Economic Opportunity

Virginia

In 1583, Sir Humphrey Gilbert sailed west to establish a colony on Newfoundland. He never returned to England; historians believe that his ship went down with all hands on the return voyage. Gilbert's half-brother, Sir Walter Raleigh, made the next attempt. Raleigh explored the Atlantic coast and claimed the territory of Virginia, named in honor of Elizabeth I, the "Virgin Queen." This territory was much larger than the present-day state of Virginia; it included West Virginia, Maryland, and the Carolinas.

Raleigh felt that the Virginia territory was ideal for a colony. The climate was mild, rivers and game were plentiful, and the soil was fertile. His favorable reports aroused enough enthusiasm that he was able to return to Virginia in 1585 with a small group of people who were prepared to settle the new colony. They landed on the island of Roanoke, off present-day North Carolina. Most gave up the attempt to subdue the wilderness after struggling for about a year. Raleigh, however, was too stubborn to accept defeat. He recruited about 100 people for another attempt, and put John White in command of the group. White saw his charges settled on Roanoke, then returned to England for supplies. He was unable to return to Roanoke until 1590. When he did return, there was no trace of the colony he had left. To this day, historians do not know what became of the settlers of Roanoke.

The British were still convinced that they would succeed in settling America. King James I issued the Charter of 1606, licensing the Plymouth Company to settle the coast from Maine to Virginia, and the London Company to do the same from New York to South Carolina. These joint-stock companies were made up of investors who agreed to share in the expenses of the voyages in return for equal shares of the profits (if any). The London Company lost no time in sending its first shipload of willing men and women to America. They settled on a river leading to the Chesapeake Bay and named their colony Jamestown, in honor of the king. John Smith, a strong-willed and capable man who had been by turns an adventurer, a murderer, a soldier, and a pirate, was chosen the first president of Jamestown.

The Jamestown colonists were fortunate to find the local Algonquin tribes friendly and helpful. The Algonquin showed the British how to grow and cook corn, and dry and grind it for flour; corn was native to the Americas but unknown in Europe. The Algonquin chief Wahunsonacock (called Powhatan by the English) had a daughter aged 10 or 12 called Pocahontas, who would later marry Englishman John Rolfe and travel to England. Her friendliness to the settlers helped to maintain good relations between the Algonquin and the British. Both sides trusted her, and she argued for the release of British prisoners of the Algonquin (although many historians doubt the legend that she threw herself across John Smith's body to save him from being killed).

The winter months of 1609–1610 proved to be bitterly cold, and the English were still unable to fend for themselves in this strange new country. They felt no scruples about raiding the Algonquin villages for food and supplies, thus creating ongoing hostility between the two groups.

Georgia

Georgia was founded in 1732, much later than the other British colonies. Its origins lay in a specific reclamation project for the poor of England. People who were heavily in debt could emigrate to Georgia and make a fresh start. With laws that forbade alcohol and slavery, Georgia failed to attract many immigrants at first. It did not begin to prosper until the 1750s.

New York and New Jersey

New Netherland was the one Atlantic coast colony founded by the Dutch, who purchased Manhattan from the local Native Americans. This island at the

THE MYTH

The Dutch swindled the unwary Lenape or Delaware Indians out of Manhattan Island in exchange for either a handful of cheap jewelry or a sum of money worth $24, depending on the source.

THE FACTS

The official deed of the transaction between Dutch negotiator Peter Minuit and the Lenape has not survived. However, an official letter to the Dutch government written in 1626 specifies that Minuit purchased Manhattan for trade goods of the value of 60 guilders. In 1846, a historian noted that 60 Dutch guilders equaled $24 U.S., and people have repeated this story ever since without taking inflation into account. $24 in 1626 had the same purchasing power as $1,000 in 2010.

The reference to "trade goods" means that Minuit bought Manhattan on the barter system rather than paying cash. Bartering was common at the time, for both large and small purchases. The Dutch gave the Lenape large quantities of useful items—cloth, tools, and kitchen implements—and perhaps beads and trinkets as well.

The "swindle" was not a matter of money or goods—it was the product of a serious cultural misunderstanding. The Lenape did not understand the notion of "owning" land outright. They thought they were accepting gifts in exchange for sharing the use of the land with the Dutch. The Dutch, of course, thought of it as a straight business transaction—goods for land.

confluence of the Hudson and East rivers was a perfect location for trading, and thus an ideal place for the new Dutch city of New Amsterdam. This was the beginning of a long history of European immigration to what was to become New York City. It was not exclusively a Dutch colony, but attracted settlers from many nations.

In 1664, the English invaded New Amsterdam; its governor Peter Stuyvesant surrendered without a fight, and the colony was divided into two sections. One was renamed New York; the other, across the Hudson River, was called New Jersey.

Religious Self-Determination: The New England Theocracy

Plymouth

The settlers of Jamestown had been practical people who traveled westward in search of financial opportunity and adventure. The groups who settled Plymouth and the Massachusetts Bay Colony had entirely different motives in sailing west.

Until 1517, there was only one Christian church in Western Europe—the Roman Catholic Church. This religious unity was broken when Martin Luther founded the Lutheran Church. Frenchman Jean Calvin favored a much stricter form of Protestantism, called Calvinism after its founder. In England, Parliament created the Anglican Church, also called the Church of England.

Two distinct forms of Anglicanism eventually developed. A high Anglican service was similar to a Catholic mass. Low Anglicans, frowning on this similarity, preferred to worship along the spartan lines favored by the Calvinists. Churches were plain and unadorned, services were conducted in the language of the people, and attendance was mandatory. During the week, it was forbidden to dance, sing, or play cards. Clothing was as plain as possible. These low-church Anglicans were called Puritans because they wanted to purify the Anglican Church. The Pilgrims were the most extreme among the Puritans.

Because English society was strictly conformist, religious separatists soon found themselves ostracized. Many Pilgrims fled to Holland, where their habits of worship were tolerated. However, they did not like the Dutch culture and customs, and they cast about for a better solution. The New World provided them with an answer.

In 1620, the *Mayflower* set sail from Holland, with a full company of Pilgrims aboard. Virginia was their goal, but their ship was blown off course and they landed in Cape Cod Bay, where they established the colony of Plymouth. The men in the company agreed that their first priority was to set up a government by which all could agree to be ruled. The result of this was the Mayflower Compact, an early exercise in a republican system that called for a council of male church members who would rule by majority vote. It stated, in part:

> We, whose names are underwritten . . . Do by these Presents, solemnly and mutually, in the presence of God and one another, covenant and combine ourselves together into a civil Body Politik, for our better Ordering and Preservation and Furtherance of the Ends aforesaid; And by Virtue hereof do enact, constitute, and frame, such just and equal Laws, Ordinances, Acts, Constitutions, and Officers from time to time, as shall be thought most meet and convenient for the general Good of the Colony; unto which we promise all due Submission and Obedience.

During the first winter, nearly half the Plymouth settlers died of disease, extreme cold, and a poor diet. The local Wampanoag people came to their rescue; luckily for the colonists, a Wampanoag named Squanto spoke some English, having lived in England at one time. Squanto served as mediator for a peace treaty between the two groups, who celebrated the first English harvest together.

Massachusetts Bay

In 1629 a group of English Puritans formed the Massachusetts Bay Company and sailed to America, intending to settle near Plymouth. These low-church Anglicans wished to establish a "city on a hill," as the Bible described—a moral Christian community in which every member would contribute his or her best efforts for the good of the whole population.

Like Plymouth, Massachusetts practiced a limited form of republican government. All adult men who were church members and property owners had the right to vote for representatives to the General Court—the body that made the colony's laws. John Winthrop was chosen as the first governor of Massachusetts Bay. Instead of the modern separation between church and state, the Puritans believed in making them work together. This was symbolized by the fact that the same building did duty as both a church and a town-meeting hall.

One of the first issues that the voters discussed was that of a school system. Puritans believed that Christians should devote their lives to God, and in order to do so, they must be able to read and understand the Bible. Therefore, all children must be taught to read, and young men should be properly educated to become preachers. In 1636, the General Court founded Harvard College as a school for would-be clergy.

American Pilgrims and Puritans proved to be every bit as intolerant as European Christians. All inhabitants of Plymouth and Massachusetts were required to attend worship services and to live as the churches dictated. Those who did not conform soon found themselves victims of discrimination—ineligible for office, unable to sustain a business, unmarriageable, and socially ostracized. The most shameful hour of this New England theocracy came in the 1690s with the Salem witch trials. Several young girls of the town of Salem accused various neighbors of witchcraft. Hundreds were arrested and tried before courts that accepted unsupported accusations as evidence. Nineteen of the accused were executed, despite the fact that no criminal behavior was ever proven. In the end, protests from the surrounding community put a stop to the sensational trials and hangings. This disgraceful spectacle severely weakened Puritan authority in New England from that time on.

Religious Self-Determination: The Dissenters

Some settlers of the Plymouth and Massachusetts Bay colonies soon began moving south to found new colonies. A variety of motives came into play. First, the Puritans would not permit freedom of religious worship. Second, church and government were so interconnected that religious dissenters could not fit into the community even outside church. Third, the population was growing steadily, and good farmland was becoming scarce.

Connecticut

In 1639, dissenting minister Thomas Hooker and a group of like-minded colonists founded the colony of New Haven on the southern coast of Connecticut. There they wrote a document called "The Fundamental Orders of Connecticut," which was the first formal constitution of any colonial government in North America. The Connecticut colonists soon established Yale College as a more liberal rival to Harvard.

Rhode Island

Like Thomas Hooker, Roger Williams found himself in disagreement with Puritan authorities. Williams disapproved of any relationship between church and state; he felt that the two should be separated. People should be free to worship in whatever way they pleased; membership in a particular church should not affect civil rights. Williams was so outspoken on this issue that he was banished from Massachusetts. He established the colony of Providence, Rhode Island, in 1636. When Rhode Island was granted a royal charter in 1644, Williams insisted on a guarantee of religious freedom for all the colony's inhabitants.

Shortly before Williams established his colony, a woman named Anne Hutchinson arrived in Boston in 1634. Although women could not be ordained ministers, she became an unofficial religious leader soon after her arrival. In her home, she led discussions of the Bible and of the sermons of the leading ministers of the city. These meetings were widely popular, especially among women. However, many Bostonians believed that Hutchinson's growing influence threatened the authority of the ministers. As time passed, and Hutchinson became more and more critical of the ministers who ran the city, she was arrested on a charge of weakening their authority. Hutchinson put up a spirited and logical defense of her actions, but lost her case. She found sanctuary in Rhode Island.

Pennsylvania

In 1681, William Penn received the colony of Pennsylvania as a gift from King Charles II of England. A Quaker, Penn founded his colony as an experiment in religious tolerance and equal rights for all inhabitants. Thousands of immigrants sailed to Pennsylvania, attracted by the promise of freedom and by its abundance of fertile farmland. Philadelphia, Penn's planned "City of Brotherly Love," soon became the largest city in the colonies.

Maryland

Lord Baltimore (George Calvert) envisioned a colony on Chesapeake Bay and petitioned King Charles I to grant him land there. Although he died in 1632, before the charter was signed, his son established the colony the following year and named it Maryland. The colony had been intended as a refuge for Catholic immigrants who were persecuted by Anglicans in England and the nearby colony of Virginia, but soon it was opened to Protestants as well. Settlers of both Maryland and Virginia dedicated their efforts to growing tobacco, which the Jamestown colonists had proved was a highly profitable cash crop.

Tobacco meant plantations and a large labor force to work them. At first, indentured servants made up the labor pool, but once they had worked out their indentures and become free, they began to start small farms of their own. Small and large farmers did not get along well, since each encroached on the other's economic interests. In Bacon's Rebellion (1676), the small farmers attacked local the American Indians, whose lands they wanted for themselves. They also looted the large plantations and even took over the government in Jamestown for a short time. In the end, the rebellion was put down, and the governing body of Virginia, called the House of Burgesses, declared that the Anglo-American colonists had the right to settle on Native-American lands.

This outbreak of violence helped lead to the increase in the slave trade. The first record of any African slaves in North America was in the Chesapeake Bay area in 1640. After Bacon's Rebellion, the tobacco and cotton planters of the South realized that they could not rely on the labor of indentured servants. They wanted a labor force over which they could exercise total and permanent control. African slaves fit their requirements perfectly. Because they looked different from Europeans, spoke languages that Europeans could not understand, and were not Christians, it was easy for the Anglo-Americans to justify slavery to themselves on the false grounds that Africans were racially inferior to Europeans.

Carolina

The Carolinas were originally one colony, founded in 1663 and named in honor of King Charles I. Carolina was a colony of small farms and rice plantations. Growing rice and cotton demanded so much slave labor that by 1720, slaves comprised two-thirds of the population. Knowing that they were out-

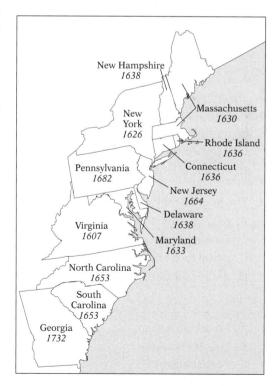

numbered and fearing possible slave rebellions, the leaders of the Carolinas made their slave codes especially harsh.

This map shows the original thirteen British colonies, with the dates of their founding.

CHAPTER 2 QUIZ

1. After 1732, British debtors could emigrate to _____ and begin again with a clean slate.
   A. Virginia
   B. the Carolinas
   C. Massachusetts
   D. Georgia

2. In the 1600s, the colonies of Plymouth and Massachusetts Bay were known for _____
   A. separation between church and state.
   B. wars of religion.
   C. lack of religious freedom.
   D. a series of judicial murders.

3. The Mayflower Compact is best described as _____
   A. a royal charter.
   B. a constitution.
   C. a set of religious commandments.
   D. an official letter.

4. The original motive for the founding of Connecticut was _____
   A. religious dissent from Puritan worship.
   B. economic opportunity.
   C. desire for a milder climate.
   D. desire to avoid contact with hostile Native Americans.

5. _____ established the colony of Rhode Island.
   A. Anne Hutchinson
   B. Thomas Hooker
   C. Roger Williams
   D. William Penn

6. The colonists justified the practice of slavery on all the following grounds
   except _____
   A. racism.
   B. economics.
   C. religion.
   D. politics.

7. Why was slavery much more widespread in the southern colonies than in
   the northern?
   A. because of the types of crops grown
   B. because of the different constitutions in each colony
   C. because the North was industrial rather than agricultural
   D. because more immigrants settled in the North

8. What was the main consequence of Bacon's Rebellion?
   A. Slavery was established throughout the British colonies.
   B. Native Americans and European settlers agreed to share the arable land.
   C. European settlers were allowed to grab American-Indian lands for farming.
   D. Harsh slave codes went into effect in the southern colonies.

9. All of the following resulted directly from the union of church and state in
   Massachusetts **except** _____
   A. Anne Hutchinson's departure for Rhode Island.
   B. the founding of Yale College.
   C. Thomas Hooker's establishment of the Connecticut colony.
   D. the establishment of the transatlantic slave trade.

10. Which best describes the government of Massachusetts in the 1600s?
    A. a theocracy
    B. a democracy
    C. a monarchy
    D. a corporation

Chapter 3

Colonial Life

After surviving the hard times of their first years in the New World, the European colonists settled down to the task of building a new society. Over the course of the next 200 years, that society became distinctly American, and no longer European.

Society centered around various institutions: the church, local politics, the business economy, and the family. Colonists lived in relatively small communities, and no one, including children, was ever idle. The tasks of building the new towns and cities, creating social and political institutions, cultivating land, and starting new businesses meant that there was something for everyone to do.

As the slave population continued to grow, the slaves developed a society of their own. They held onto what they could of their native cultures while coping as best they could with harsh conditions in a strange land. African slavery remains the most shameful aspect of U.S. history. Many historians have echoed Abigail Adams's conclusion that slavery in a society that insisted on its own independence was rank hypocrisy.

Most colonists, whatever their home culture, could agree on one thing: they did not want interference from Europe. Religious freedom had been built into the constitutions of all the colonies except Plymouth and Massachusetts, and political freedom seemed to go hand in hand with religious freedom. The British government on the whole felt the same way and left the colonies alone to govern themselves as they saw fit. Spasmodic attempts at British control resulted in the strong assertion of colonial rights. In 1688–1689, Britain had deposed an autocratic ruler and transferred much of the monarch's authority to the legislature; this revolutionary means of dealing with tyranny made a strong impression on the colonists.

CHAPTER OBJECTIVES

- Describe everyday social life and working life in the British colonies.
- Describe the conditions of African slavery, including the Middle Passage.
- Explain the major opposing influences on the American character and American society.
- Analyze the relationship between the British Parliament and the colonies.

Chapter 3 Time Line

- **1650**   Navigation Acts
- **1686**   Founding of Dominion of New England
- **1689**   Glorious Revolution; English Bill of Rights
- **1690**   Slaves present in all British colonies in North America
- **1730–1750**   Great Awakening

Family and Community Life

The family was the most important unit of society in colonial America. Communities in the New World were quite small at first, and for a long time they remained relatively small compared to the size of the same cities and towns today. Most people were related by blood or marriage to nearly every family in the village. These family relationships connected the colonists to one another in a network of close bonds.

Every member of a family contributed to its welfare. Farming jobs were divided along gender lines, with men and boys doing the heavy outdoor chores, such as plowing and taking care of livestock, while women and girls did the equally demanding indoor work of cooking, cleaning, washing, sewing, spinning, weaving, and raising children. Children were given chores to do by the age of five; even a small child could set the table, weed the garden, and feed

THE MYTH

The term *British colonists* leads many Americans to believe that the population of the British colonies was entirely or almost entirely ethnically English.

THE FACTS

British colonists means "subjects living in the British colonies." It does not mean that the people themselves came from Britain; it means that they were citizens of the British Empire, subject to the rule of the British government. The term is used to distinguish people living in the British colonies from those in the French or Spanish colonies; the term *American colonists* would apply equally to any of these groups, so historians generally use British colonists instead.

In fact, the population of the thirteen original colonies was very diverse even in the days before the huge waves of nineteenth-century immigration. Subjects of the British colonies included large groups of English, Welsh, Scots, Dutch, Germans, Swedes, and Africans. Probably all the European nations were represented to some degree, although northern Europeans were much more common at this time.

It is true that Englishmen held most of the positions of power and authority throughout the colonies. This was a natural consequence of the fact that the British government had first established the settlements. It also explains why English quickly became the common language used throughout the colonies.

the chickens. At age eight or ten, town boys were often apprenticed to masters, receiving free room and board in exchange for their labor while learning the trade on the job. Girls remained at home with their mothers, helping to take care of their younger siblings and learning how to manage a household.

In towns and cities, men worked at such jobs as printer, blacksmith, wheelwright, innkeeper, or lawyer. Businesses were small; an innkeeper might have five or six wage-earning employees, or he and his family might run the inn on their own. Urban women worked as hard as farm women at the demanding job of running a house and raising children. Some earned wages as servants, dressmakers, schoolteachers, or midwives. If an innkeeper died, his wife would often carry on the business and take control of the profits. Widows were allowed to own property; many of them became quite wealthy.

Life expectancy in Colonial times was low. It was higher for men than for women, because pregnancy made women vulnerable. Childbirth was a risky procedure in the days before modern sanitary practices. A high percentage of young women died in childbirth, or of infections contracted during childbirth, and a high percentage of children died in the first two years of life. Women frequently burned to death in their own homes, or were severely injured, when their long skirts caught fire at the open hearths where they did their cooking. Illnesses that could easily be cured today with penicillin or antibiotics killed many people of both sexes. People married in their mid to late teens, and young brides usually became pregnant very quickly; more children meant more pairs of hands to help with the work, and the more children a couple had, the more were likely to survive to adulthood. If a father of several children was widowed, he usually lost no time in marrying again so that his children would have a mother; men might go through three or even four wives in a lifetime. Widows also often remarried; since they usually inherited their husband's property and sometimes his business, they were very desirable marriage partners.

Northerners lived longer than southerners because the marshy, humid southern climate was ideal for the growth of bacteria and the spread of germs. The unsanitary conditions in which slaves were forced to live also contributed to the unhealthy atmosphere. This meant that a southern family was more likely than a northern one to include relations such as stepparents, half-sisters and half-brothers, and so on.

On a farm, of course, the working and living areas were identical. It was the same in the towns; a shopkeeper would have his business on the ground floor of the house, with the living area on the floor or floors above. The blacksmith probably lived in a house next door to his forge. At most, a city dweller would live only a few minutes' walk from his office. Family members ate together and attended social occasions and church as a group; social activities were not segregated by age and gender as they are today.

Even among the dour Puritans and Pilgrims, Colonial social life was full and fun. A birth or wedding was always cause for celebration. People also gathered for harvest festivals, holiday feasts, and other large parties. In the colonies, there was little spare time, but work was often combined with play. For example, when farmers harvested their corn, the whole village would gather for the "husking bee." Everyone would husk the cobs of fresh corn that would be dried to make flour for the coming winter. The workers sang, joked, and laughed to make the time pass enjoyably. The women of the village provided a hearty supper for the workers, and when anyone found a red ear of corn, it was used as bait in a "kissing game" among the younger people. Similarly, during the brief maple-sugaring season in the North, everyone in the community would come together to harvest the sap, cook it, and turn it into sugar and syrup. Festivities—including sampling the tasty sugar—accompanied the hard work.

The Growth of Slavery

Slavery grew rapidly as the colonies developed. The first Africans to come to America arrived in Jamestown in 1619; they were indentured servants who would earn their freedom after an agreed-upon term of labor. In 1661, the colony of Virginia passed laws stating that slavery was legal; the following year, the Virginia House of Burgesses made slave status hereditary. Massachusetts had passed laws against slavery in 1641; in 1670 these laws were amended to state that the children of slaves could be sold into slavery. By 1690 there were slaves in every colony, although there were far more of them in the South than in the North. This was a matter of economics and geography. Slaves were not in great demand north of Maryland because there were few large-scale farms or plantations. Africans who lived in the North might be laborers or house servants, many of whom were able, over time, to save money and purchase their freedom.

There were objections to slavery from the earliest days of the colonies. The Pennsylvania Quakers spoke out publicly against slavery as early as 1688. Benjamin Franklin founded the first antislavery society in the colonies. During the Revolutionary War, Abigail Adams noted how hypocritical it was for Congress to demand freedom for Americans while denying it to African Americans. However, those who insisted on maintaining slavery always overpowered those who opposed it. The abolitionist movement gained no real power or influence until the nineteenth century.

Slavers would sail to Africa to capture Africans, usually in the western region that Europeans referred to as the Gold Coast. African tribes aided and abetted the slavers by helping to capture people from tribes that were hostile to their own. The Middle Passage, as the trip across the Atlantic is known, was a horrifying nightmare for the African captives. They were crammed into the hold of the ship, where there was no fresh air or light. They were kept in chains throughout the voyage. Because the traders insisted on maximum profit, they stuffed as many captives into the ship as it could possibly hold. The slaves were laid side by side and end to end, each within a space no more than about two feet wide and six feet long. There were no sanitary facilities. Captives were occasionally taken on deck for fresh air; many threw themselves overboard to escape the terror. Many more died of disease on the way over. Still, 600,000 Africans survived the journey during the course of the eighteenth century. In some colonies, such as South Carolina, Africans soon made up the majority of the population.

Once a slaver had enough captives to fill the hold of his ship, he would sail to either the Caribbean or the North American mainland and unload his human cargo for sale at auction. Captives were robbed of all dignity during this process: buyers forced their mouths open to look at their teeth, squeezed their arms and legs to test muscle strength, and otherwise examined them as if they had been livestock. There was no attempt to keep families together; buyers purchased only the types of workers they needed. Husbands and wives, children and parents were often parted for good on the auction block—ironic considering the importance of religion and family in white Colonial society.

Some slaves were put to work as house servants, but most Africans had been imported to labor outdoors on the large farms or plantations in the Caribbean and the southern colonies. They were given the minimum amount of food needed to keep them alive and productive. They had no days off, received no pay, and worked constantly in all weathers, often under the threat of whipping, beating, or even more severe punishments for any infraction of rules. Female slaves had an even worse time than their male counterparts, because they were sexually abused. No white man would incur any legal or social penalty for raping a black woman. It was very common for a slave to bear her master's children, who of course inherited her slave status.

White colonists were always concerned about the possibility of slave rebellion. Therefore, the southern colonies, where slaves were the most numerous, passed laws that severely curtailed opportunities for slaves to bond with one another. Slaves were forbidden to meet in large groups, to marry, to leave the master's home without permission, to possess any weapons, or to learn to read or write. Despite these prohibitions, slaves frequently escaped North, where it was not too difficult to gain their freedom. The slaves escaped despite knowing that they were running serious risks of punishment if they were captured. A runaway slave would certainly be whipped, and might have their face branded, tongue cut out, or fingers or a whole hand chopped off. Slaves were considered valuable property, but they were easily replaced; therefore "troublemakers" were considered expendable.

Although slaves were forbidden so many freedoms, they somehow managed to function and even to develop a lively culture of their own. They remembered and were able to sustain and pass on aspects of culture from their distant

African homes. Jazz, for example, is based on traditional African music. Slaves were also encouraged to absorb Christianity, at least up to a point, and developed their own style of worship, with its call-and-response motif that comes straight from African culture.

Education and the Enlightenment

Two basic cultural forces have shaped the United States of America; both came into evidence in Colonial times, and they remain hostile to each other to this day. The first is the influence of the Enlightenment; the second is religious fervor.

The Enlightenment

The main ideas of the eighteenth-century Enlightenment that originated in France were these: all people were born free and equal, they had the right to make their own laws and to govern themselves, they must be free to write and speak their thoughts without censorship, and they must be permitted to worship as they saw fit. Thinkers of the Enlightenment also argued that literacy and education were desirable goals because literacy made people aware of the world around them, and able to think about it for themselves and draw their own conclusions. Education made a blacksmith the equal of an aristocrat and made it perfectly legitimate for a cobbler to criticize the king.

Colonial Americans also believed that education was very important, although they felt this way originally for religious reasons. Protestants believed that everyone must read the Bible regularly, so almost all Colonial children were taught to read. Higher education was reserved for boys, because only boys could enter professions for which education was clearly necessary, such as medicine, the law, or the ministry. However, many American girls succeeded in getting good educations at home, either because they had enlightened parents or simply through their own persistence. Abigail Smith Adams, Mercy Otis Warren, and poet Phillis Wheatley are just a few examples of women who were as well read and well educated as any man of their times.

One of the major ideals of the Enlightenment was tolerance for points of view other than one's own. The mere fact that the colonies were becoming a diverse society of immigrants from all the nations of Europe (and west Africa) reinforced the need for cultural and religious tolerance. In addition, the forces of the Enlightenment encouraged people to think for themselves, rather than blindly following the dictates of their particular church or minister.

Religion and the Great Awakening

The second great force that shaped American society and the American character was religious fervor. In the 1600s, the Pilgrims and Puritans came to America in order to establish moral Christian communities. In the 1700s, a series of religious revivals known as the Great Awakening swept the colonies.

Historians credit Jonathan Edwards of Connecticut with launching the Great Awakening in New England around 1730. Edwards was an unforgettable preacher whose dramatic and impressive denunciations of sinners terrified his parishioners into leading blameless lives. Because Edwards suggested that God could be merciful to those who sincerely repented of their sins, many people were moved to confess their sins publicly and claim to be reborn in God's love. However, since the New England Calvinist churches preached the doctrine of predestination—that God had chosen those to be saved before they were born—Edwards was taking a risk by suggesting that a person could play an active role in his or her own salvation. Church officials eventually dismissed him from the pulpit for his unorthodox teachings.

The Great Awakening continued nonetheless. Beginning in 1738, British preacher George Whitefield drew huge crowds to hear his sermons. He was a celebrity before the concept of celebrity existed, receiving regular front-page coverage in Colonial newspapers wherever he traveled. Whitefield was a powerful and charismatic speaker whose sermons inspired a surge in church membership and a wave of new congregations, many of which were Baptist or Methodist.

Politics and the Economy

The political relationship between the colonies and Britain was a mix of heavy-handed control and near-total noninterference. The inconsistency of the British approach to Colonial rule was a major factor in the colonists' desire to declare independence from Britain. On the one hand, Britain insisted on establishing and enforcing trade regulations that the colonists found too sweeping, too intrusive, and too detrimental to their own economic profits. On the other hand, Britain left the colonies alone to create and manage their own legislative assemblies and other political institutions. This was largely a matter of geography; Britain was simply too far away for Parliament, its legislative assembly, to do the everyday work of governing in the colonies.

In 1688–1689, the British Parliament carried out a landmark political event known to history as the Glorious Revolution. The harsh high-Anglican policies of King James II united both parties in Parliament against him; they agreed that James must be deposed. A parliamentary delegation invited James's daughter Mary and her husband William of Orange, *stadholder* (hereditary ruler) of the Netherlands, to rule England jointly. When they arrived in England in 1688, James II fled to France, and the Glorious Revolution was won without a shot being fired. From the passage of the English Bill of Rights in 1689, Britain was a constitutional monarchy; the monarch was the head of state, but the legislative assembly did the actual governing. This change in the form of government made a deep impression on the colonists, who were developing a tradition of their own in which the legislature, rather than the executive, was the most important branch of the government.

All the colonies had representative assemblies of some sort, and men participated in them with enthusiasm, attending sessions regularly and arguing over which laws were best for the people. However, the colonists were not represented in Parliament, the British legislative assembly. Again, geographical distance made such representation impractical. The British argued that Parliament as a whole represented all British subjects, including the colonists; the colonists argued that Parliament did not have any representatives who had lived in America or understood its particular social, geographical, and economic conditions.

One of the reasons that Britain had acquired colonies in the first place was as a market for British goods. British laws governed all trade within the colonies and between the colonies and other nations. In 1650, Parliament passed the first of the Navigation Acts, which had three major requirements. First, all European goods exported to the colonies must be routed through Britain; this allowed Britain to assess import duties, which would be added to the prices once the goods reached the colonies. Second, all Colonial trade had to be carried out on ships owned by British subjects (the colonists, of course, were all British subjects). Third, Colonial products such as tobacco, cotton, and sugar could be exported only to certain nations.

These acts constricted Colonial trade by driving up the prices of imports and by controlling exports. Traders in the colonies resented laws that cut into their profits, and ordinary people objected to paying the British duty imposed on all imported goods. The colonists reasoned that since they had not participated in the wording, creation, or passage of the Navigation Acts, they did not have to follow them to the letter. Despite British efforts to enforce the acts—including the revocation of the Massachusetts charter in 1684—smuggling was a thriving industry in the colonies. This flouting of faraway parliamentary laws presaged the revolution that was to come.

CHAPTER 3 QUIZ

1. Jonathan Edwards was required to stop preaching because he questioned the doctrine of _____
   A. predestination.
   B. free will.
   C. good works.
   D. faith.

2. Colonists objected to receiving all their imported goods through Britain because this meant _____
   A. a delay in shipments.
   B. poorer-quality goods.
   C. higher prices.
   D. fewer goods to choose from.

3. Smuggling thrived in the colonies in defiance of _____
   A. the Glorious Revolution.
   B. the Great Awakening.
   C. the English Bill of Rights.
   D. the Navigation Acts.

4. The colonists often combined work and play because _____
   A. everyone participated in the work of the community.
   B. there was little spare time for play.
   C. social activities were centered on the church.
   D. all members of the community attended.

5. Slavery continued to spread and grow through the 1700s because _____
   A. it gave rise to economic profit for those who controlled it.
   B. slaves gave up any attempt to escape.
   C. antislavery societies were founded in the North.
   D. people began to speak out against slavery.

6. **The colonists objected to attempts at parliamentary control because** _____
   A. they were not British subjects.
   B. they wanted to unite and establish their own federal government.
   C. they preferred to answer only to the monarch.
   D. they were not represented in Parliament.

7. **Widespread newspaper coverage and large crowds gave** _____ **the distinction of being the first celebrity in America.**
   A. Abigail Adams
   B. George Whitefield
   C. Jonathan Edwards
   D. Benjamin Franklin

8. **What is the source of the hostility between the force of religious fervor and the influence of the Enlightenment?**
   A. Religion requires obedience, while the Enlightenment encouraged thinking for oneself.
   B. Religion discourages education and literacy, while the Enlightenment encouraged them.
   C. Religion encourages political independence, while the Enlightenment discouraged it.
   D. Religion reinforces the need for cultural tolerance, while the Enlightenment weakened it.

9. _____ **made it next to impossible for Britain to manage the affairs of the colonies.**
   A. Geography
   B. The economy
   C. Politics
   D. Slavery

10. **The Glorious Revolution changed Britain into** _____
    A. an autocracy.
    B. a hereditary monarchy.
    C. an oligarchy.
    D. a constitutional monarchy.

Chapter 4

The French and Indian War, 1747–1763

Royal charters encouraged the British colonies to expand their territory westward. This happened gradually as birth and continued immigration increased the population. Expansion, of course, meant taking over more land—land that was already claimed by other groups. In the period before the Revolutionary War, the colonists faced two opponents in their drive westward: the Indians and the French.

Fighting the Indians was comparatively easy for a variety of reasons. First and most important, the colonists had more guns and were more ready to use them. This meant that they were generally able to dictate the terms of any fighting. Second, the two cultures did not share the same assumptions about the possession of land as private property; the Indians did not understand this point of view, and thus were unable to find an effective way to counter it. Because the Indians were highly skilled fighters, they remained a constant threat, but with no organized army, they had no chance against the colonists.

Fighting the French meant conducting a war against a similar culture whose people shared the same assumptions and the same understanding of how to seize and hold power. When both sides claimed the same land in the Ohio River Valley, Britain and France sent troops and officers across the Atlantic to conduct an all-out war. Although Colonial volunteers played a large role in the war, and Indians fought on both sides, this was fundamentally a European war, managed by European commanders.

The most important result of the French and Indian War was the deepening of mistrust between the colonies and Britain. Throughout the war, the British generals had questioned the loyalty of Colonial officers such as George Washington, ignoring the fact that all the colonists were British subjects. On their side, the colonists resented the British assumption of authority in the conduct of the war. These feelings of dislike and distrust would grow as Britain sought ways to force the colonists to help pay off the war debt.

CHAPTER OBJECTIVES

- Explain the source of the conflict between the French and the British.
- Describe the course of the French and Indian War.
- Explain the role played by the Indians in the war.
- Analyze the effects of the war.

Chapter 4 Time Line

- **1747** Ohio Company is formed
- **1752** French build Fort Duquesne
- **1755** French defeat British at Fort Duquesne
- **1756** French and Indian War begins
- **1757** William Pitt becomes prime minister of Great Britain

    French capture Fort Oswego and Fort William Henry
- **1758** British capture Forts Louisbourg and Frontenac
- **1759** British take Fort Niagara and win battle at Quebec
- **1760** Canada surrenders to British
- **1762** Treaty of Fontainebleau
- **1763** Treaty of Paris

Europeans and Indians: Conflict and Alliance

By the mid-1700s, France had claimed eastern Canada and a large central portion of the present United States. Control of the Mississippi River was key to the French fur-trading industry. The French had built the cities of Quebec and Montreal in Canada, but for the most part they had been content to build trading posts along the Mississippi and other temporary settlements wherever they were needed. The bulk of the Mississippi Valley was left to the Indians.

Three factors created a degree of friendship between the French and the Indians. The first was that, except in eastern Canada, the French had not tried to seize Indian lands or build permanent towns and cities. Second, the fur trade brought the tribes financial profits and the means of acquiring weapons and modern tools. Third, many French had followed Samuel de Champlain's example of learning Indian languages and customs. (See Chapter 1.)

In the fur trade, the Indians helped the French by keeping them supplied; they were much better than the French at hunting and trapping fur-bearing animals along the trails that were so familiar to them. The French helped the in return by trading items the Indians could not manufacture—weapons, horses, and sophisticated metal tools—in exchange for the pelts.

However, conflict lay ahead. Playing an active role in the fur trade caused two problems for the tribes. First, hunting and trapping for fur took time away from other essential chores, particularly cultivating or hunting for food. Indians suddenly found themselves having to trade for or purchase food, when for centuries they had been self-sufficient. Second, participating in the fur trade forced formerly stationary tribes to migrate. When they had decimated the fur-bearing animal population in one area, they had to move on—often into territory claimed by another tribe. This meant unprecedented contact and competition among the tribes and nations. The Iroquois Confederacy managed these issues to some extent, often brokering trades between the tribes and Europeans.

Britain, France, and Spain fought over Colonial territory just as they fought over their territorial boundaries in Europe. Spain had established itself in Mexico, Florida, California, and the Southwest; Britain along the Atlantic coast; and France over the rest of the continent. All three nations recognized that the Indians would make valuable allies. They were familiar with the land and were fierce, uncompromising fighters. They had learned to combine European weapons with guerrilla-style fighting, making themselves into a formidable enemy and a desirable ally. However, the Indians did not ally themselves with any particular group of colonists. They felt they should support whichever side best furthered their own interests.

On their first arrival, the British colonists had established cordial relations with the Indians. However, these did not last. As the Colonial population grew, the colonists needed more land. The land that was there was tribal land, but the colonists had no hesitation about taking it. Because they were stronger and better organized, they were usually successful. The Indians retaliated by fighting back—ambushing, killing, and kidnapping settlers whenever they could.

The Albany Plan of Union

Benjamin Franklin was among the first to realize that large-scale conflict over Colonial land lay ahead. Franklin considered the Iroquois Confederacy an impressive exercise in democratic rule, and in 1751 he proposed that the colonists create a similar official body for their mutual defense. When representatives from seven colonies met in Albany, New York to discuss the question, Franklin outlined an idea that became known as the Albany Plan of Union. It failed with both the Colonial governments and the British Parliament for two reasons. First, Parliament did not want to set up any institution that would rival its own authority over the colonies. Second, representatives of one colony did not necessarily trust those of another.

Franklin drew this cartoon to illustrate why his plan of union was a good idea for the defense of the colonies. As a whole animal, the snake was well able to defend itself and to attack when necessary; but its individual pieces were helpless.

The French and Indian War

The French and Indian War came about because France and Britain did not agree on the western boundaries of the British colonies. Britain's colonists believed—in many cases their royal charters explicitly stated—that they were entitled to spread out as far as they needed to. In practice, this effort to expand borders to the west meant that Britain was encroaching on territory claimed by France.

The Ohio River Valley became the first bone of contention between the two European powers. In 1749, King George II of England had given a group of settlers known as the Ohio Company a large land grant in this area. The French claimed the same land. When they built Fort Duquesne at the juncture of the Allegheny and Monongahela rivers in 1754, the governor of Virginia appointed 19-year-old George Washington to lead troops to Fort Duquesne and warn the French to leave British territory. Washington was made a lieutenant colonel and authorized to use force if the French ignored the warning.

When Washington handed the French a letter warning them to leave the area, they laughed in his face, telling him that their claim to the land was as good as the British claim. Washington assigned some of his men to build a fort, and left with others to bring back supplies. When he returned, he found that the French had taken the fort. Undaunted, the British troops built a new fort, which they named Necessity. In the ensuing fighting, the British side was defeated.

Both Britain and France saw this skirmish as a perfect opportunity to prevent the enemy from further Colonial expansion, and both sent professional troops to the colonies. At that time, the British colonies had no standing army and no trained military leaders. Washington's troops had lost the battle of Fort Duquesne because Washington had not learned the guerrilla-style warfare practiced by the Indians. Instead, he fought in the style he had read about in military histories, in which two opposing armies faced one another on open ground. The tribes had briefly allied themselves with the British, but Washington's first failure convinced them that he was a fool and that the French were better fighters. Seeing no reason to ally themselves with the side that was bound to lose, the Indians ranged themselves in support of the French.

British generals Edward Braddock and William Johnson decided to attack the French in three places: at Fort Duquesne, at Fort Niagara, and on the Atlantic coast of Nova Scotia. Braddock was killed in the charge against Fort Duquesne; George Washington took over and led the retreat to safety. The British expelled the French from Nova Scotia and claimed it for England. At Fort Niagara, the British won a great victory in September 1755 under General Johnson.

On May 8, 1756, the Marquis de Montcalm led the French troops against the British garrison at Oswego on the Great Lakes. Canadians and Indians attacked the small British frontier towns and settlements in western New York and Pennsylvania. Meanwhile, the British and Colonial forces blocked the mouth of the St. Lawrence River, which was a lifeline for the cities of Quebec and Montreal, and attacked tribal villages in the Ohio River Valley.

France gained the advantage with a successful siege of Fort William Henry on the shores of Lake George. In August of 1757, Montcalm and his troops, with their Indian allies, destroyed the fort and killed the remaining British troops. The British lost control of the St. Lawrence River when a storm destroyed many of their ships.

Because they had received better treatment from the French, the Indians allied with them through most of the war. However, experience had made them mistrustful of both sides, and they were determined to act only in their own best interests. When the tide of war turned in favor of the British in the summer of 1758, the Iroquois went over to the British side.

When reinforcements arrived, the British took back the St. Lawrence, captured Fort Frontenac in Quebec, then mounted a determined assault on Fort Duquesne. The French eventually burned the fort rather than cede it to the enemy. The English built a new fort nearby, which they named Fort Pitt in honor of British Prime Minister William Pitt. Pitt was something of a hero to the colonists, for as soon as he became prime minister, he concentrated his efforts—and the British treasury—on winning the war in the colonies.

Under the command of General James Wolfe, the British laid siege to Quebec in 1759. After a battle on the Plains of Abraham outside the city, in which both Wolfe and Montcalm were killed, the English emerged victorious. The victory was largely due to the fact that the British army had cannon and the French army had none. The French surrendered formally on September 18, 1759.

The fighting in North America ended in 1761. The 1763 Treaty of Paris granted England all of Canada and all French holdings east of the Mississippi River except New Orleans. To prevent England from gaining total control over the North American continent, France had ceded the vast Louisiana territory to Spain in the 1762 Treaty of Fontainebleau.

Effects of the French and Indian War

The French and Indian War had a number of important effects on events that would happen in the near future. First, the threat of any western attack by the French had been removed. Second, the war increased hostility and bad feeling between the British and the colonists—particularly within the military. Third, defeating France—a major military power—gave the American troops confidence and experience. Fourth, the war helped to establish bonds among troops from different colonies, while demonstrating the need for a regular American army. Fifth, George Washington gained valuable command experience and rose to prominence throughout the colonies. Last, Britain ended the war hugely in debt.

Although Washington was commander in chief of the American forces, the British officers had treated him with contempt throughout the war. These experienced generals may have resented Washington because he was young; they may have distrusted him because he was American; they may have held aloof simply because he was a stranger. To Washington, it appeared that the British did not think of him or the Colonial soldiers as fellow countrymen. Deciding that there was nothing he could profitably accomplish against these odds of distrust and contempt, Washington resigned from the army in 1759.

Before the war, colonists had tended to think of Virginia, New York, or Rhode Island as their "country." The war proved a unifying force in Colonial society by bringing together men from different colonies against a common enemy. This fostered a feeling of comradeship and made men and boys from the various colonies begin to view one another as friends and fellow countrymen—to develop a common American identity.

None of the colonies had a standing army; all American troops in the French and Indian War were volunteers. As volunteers, they assumed certain privileges that no regular troops would ever have: desertion and disobedience. Since they were not paid to fight, soldiers deserted whenever they felt they were needed at home. They were also liable to refuse to obey any orders with which they disagreed, feeling that their own opinions were as good as those of their leaders. Under these circumstances, Washington had found command an exhausting task that challenged all of his ingenuity. Probably nothing but his great personal popularity and the respect his men felt for him held the volunteers together.

Britain had spent thousands of pounds transporting, equipping, supplying, and paying troops during the war, and was now faced with an enormous war debt. In the end, Parliament decided that since the war had been fought in part on behalf of the colonists, the colonists should bear some of the costs.

CHAPTER 4 QUIZ

1. War between the French and British in the colonies arose from a disagreement over _____
   A. who would rule over the Indians.
   B. which side would ally with the Indians.
   C. territorial expansion.
   D. religious faith.

2. What role did the Iroquois Confederacy play in the fur trade?
   A. It brokered trades between Indians and colonists.
   B. It resolved disputes between French and British traders.
   C. It arbitrated disagreements between tribes.
   D. It designated places where the French could hunt and trap.

3. Which best describes the Albany Plan of Union?
   A. a royal charter for the colony of New York
   B. a founding document of the American federal government
   C. a loose association of colonies for their mutual defense
   D. a freely elected legislative assembly

4. At the start of the war, the British strategy called for launching offensives in all these areas except _____
   A. Fort Duquesne.
   B. Fort Niagara.
   C. Nova Scotia.
   D. Quebec.

5. Which best describes Indian participation in the French and Indian war?
   A. The Indians allied with the French against the British.
   B. The Indians allied with the British against the French.
   C. The Indians allied first with the French, then with the British.
   D. The Indians took no part in the conflict.

6. As a result of the 1763 Treaty of Paris, Canada ended up _____
   A. under Spanish control.
   B. under British control.
   C. under French control.
   D. under Indian control.

7. George Washington resigned from the army because _____
    A. he believed that the British commanders did not trust or respect him.
    B. he was exasperated with the high rate of desertion among the troops.
    C. he was never paid for his services to the colonies.
    D. he was ambitious to play a role in government.

8. In what way did the war help to unify the British colonists?
    A. It gave them a permanent distrust of the Indians.
    B. It provided them with a reason to fight for their independence.
    C. It united them in a common cause against an outside enemy.
    D. It encouraged the leaders to pass the Albany Plan of Union.

9. Why did Parliament decide to make the colonies assume part of the war debt?
    A. because so many Colonial troops had deserted
    B. because the war had been fought for the colonists' benefit
    C. because Britain had gained no new territory from the war
    D. because Britain had lost the war

10. The British beat the French at Quebec because they had _____
    A. cannon.
    B. more troops.
    C. better generals.
    D. loyal allies.

Chapter 5

The Road to Revolution, 1763–1774

The French and Indian War led inevitably to a second war—the American Revolution, or the War for Independence. This war did not break out overnight. Relations between Britain and the colonies deteriorated in several slow, painful stages.

The basic dispute between Britain and the colonies was over the issue of representation in government—a British principle that dated back to 1215, the year of the Magna Carta. Parliament argued that as the British legislative assembly, it represented all citizens of the British Empire and therefore had the right to expect their obedience to its laws. The colonists argued that since there were no American voting members of Parliament, the colonies were not represented and therefore did not have to obey.

Neither side was willing to give way on this issue. Parliamentary leaders chose a course of action that united the colonists against Parliament as their common enemy—they passed a series of acts legalizing taxes on various colonial imports, such as molasses, tea, and paper. The colonists retaliated with a series of acts of civil disobedience, such as the Boston Tea Party. In the end, they realized that they needed a national assembly of their own to address the problem as a matter of state. Delegates to the Continental Congress of 1774 petitioned Parliament for the redress of their grievances. Before they received a reply, the first shots of the Revolutionary War were fired in Massachusetts.

CHAPTER OBJECTIVES

- Explain the source of the conflict between Parliament and the colonies.
- Identify the parliamentary acts passed during the 1760s and 1770s.
- Describe the colonial response to these acts of Parliament.
- Explain the composition and purpose of the First Continental Congress.

Chapter 5 Time Line

- **1763** Proclamation of 1763
- **1764** Sugar Act
- **1765** **March** Stamp Act

    October Stamp Act Congress
- **1766** Repeal of Stamp Act

    Declaratory Act
- **1767** Townshend Acts
- **1770** **March 5** Boston Massacre
- **1773** **December 16** Boston Tea Party
- **1774** Coercive/Intolerable Acts and Quebec Act

    First Continental Congress convenes in Philadelphia

    Declaration and Resolves

Effects of the French and Indian War

In the French and Indian War, Britain gained vast tracts of American land and crushed France's ambitions on the American continent. However, victory brought a number of complications and problems with it.

First, the war had been hugely expensive. Britain ended the war heavily in debt, with no ready means of payment. Second, it would take some time to settle all the new British territory; therefore, it would have to be guarded against enemies who might move in and lay claim to it. This meant that Britain would have to maintain a standing army in the colonies for the first time. Third, Parliament felt that victory provided it with a perfect opportunity to strengthen its authority over the colonies.

It had never been possible for Britain to settle every problem that arose in the colonies from across the Atlantic. This geographical distance had given rise to a great deal of independence in the colonies; because most of their own leaders and officials were of British descent, they generally followed familiar British laws and customs, but they were more or less self-governing. The House of Commons had no members who specifically represented the colonies; no one living in England knew much about the circumstances and conditions in America. Again, distance was responsible for this. Frequent travel across an ocean was impossible, as was swift communication over long distances. Even if Americans had been allowed to sit in the House of Commons, there was simply no means for them to stay in touch with the colonies on a day-to-day basis.

Each colony had its own constitution and its own governor. No two constitutions were alike; a colony's laws depended on when and how it had originally been settled. Some colonial governors were locally-elected Americans; others were Englishmen appointed by the monarch. Each colony had a legislative assembly whose members were elected by those who had the right to vote—property-owning adult men, including free Africans.

The Parliamentary Acts

The Proclamation of 1763

In 1763, Parliament made three new colonies out of the territory Britain had acquired in the Treaty of Paris: Quebec, East Florida, and West Florida. All the land between the thirteen original colonies and the Mississippi River was left to the Indians, and the proclamation made it illegal for Europeans to buy any of this land from them. Parliament's hope was that this segregation of the two peoples would end the strife between the British colonists and the Indians.

The Sugar Act

Parliament's next action was to crack down on abuses of the Navigation Acts. The abuses were widespread and had gone on for many years. Colonial legislatures refused to pass laws putting a stop to smuggling, and even when governors disagreed with the legislatures, they were powerless to enforce the laws when every colonist appeared to be in league to continue the practice of smuggling and refusing to pay duty at the customhouse. This was a simple matter of economic profit.

In 1764, Parliament passed the Sugar Act, which had three main provisions. First, it called for a three-cent per gallon tax on imported molasses—an import duty had always existed, but in the past it had rarely been enforced. Second, Parliament would appoint more cargo inspectors and give the Royal Navy the right to inspect any ship in American waters. Third, captains who failed to report their cargo accurately or refused to pay the duty on it would be tried in the admiralty courts, which had no juries.

From New England to Georgia, the colonists were united in their objections. These were twofold: financial and political. Financially, paying the duty on molasses would bankrupt the merchants, and the process of inspection would drastically impede the mobility and efficiency of the small boats that shipped goods within the colonies. Politically, the objections were just as serious. The Sugar Act infringed on two of the colonists' long-held rights as British citizens—the right not to be taxed without their own consent, and the right to a trial by jury. The tradition of taxation by general consent and the right to trial by jury were specified in a document called the Magna Carta, signed by King John in the year 1215. The Magna Carta specifies and clarifies the relationship between the monarch and his or her subjects. It states that the monarch is legally bound to govern the people justly and fairly; if he or she fails to do so, the people have the right to state their grievances and have them addressed.

The colonists sent official letters to England protesting the Sugar Act. Newspaper editorials urged colonists to boycott English goods. Men and boys also expressed their displeasure with their fists; rioting between working men and men of the Royal Navy became an everyday occurrence in port cities such as Boston. In an effort to smooth things over, Parliament lowered the tax on molasses to one cent per gallon in 1766. The colonists were not entirely satisfied, but they paid.

The Stamp Act

The Sugar Act had included one item that failed to pass: the Stamp Act, which eventually passed in March of 1765. The Act required the use of an official stamp on most paper goods sold or issued in the colonies, charged a tax for the use of the paper, and appointed a stamp inspector for each colony who would issue the stamps and collect the taxes. The Stamp Act affected newspapers, legal papers, property records, and legal and professional licenses.

Passage of the Stamp Act touched off outraged reactions throughout the colonies. There was an important difference between the Sugar Act and the Stamp Act. The Sugar Act could be seen as an attempt to regulate trade, which the colonists acknowledged Britain had every right to do. The Stamp Act, however, was an outright tax, imposed on British citizens without their consent. Colonial leaders decided that it called for a united official response, since it affected all colonies equally. The Stamp Act Congress, a meeting of political leaders from nine colonies, met in New York to discuss their response; they agreed on a policy of active resistance. Sons and Daughters of Liberty, as Colonial activist groups were called, encouraged the people to damage the inspectors' property, hang them in effigy, insult them in newspaper articles, and generally harass them. Many of the inspectors resigned, afraid for their lives; all reported to Parliament that it was impossible to collect the stamp tax.

In Britain, two men presented the colonies' case before Parliament—William Pitt and Benjamin Franklin. Pitt urged repeal of the Stamp Act on the basis that taxation of the people without their consent was illegal. Franklin supported Pitt, testifying that Americans believed that if they were British subjects, they had the right to refuse taxation without representation. Parliament repealed the Stamp Act, but asserted itself by publishing a Declaratory Act insisting that all citizens in the empire were "virtually represented" in Parliament and that parliamentary authority over them was absolute.

The Townshend Acts

In 1767, Parliament tried again to raise money from the colonies. The Townshend Acts, named for the British chancellor of the exchequer who proposed them to Parliament, taxed all imported paint, paper, glass, and tea. Since the colonists had grudgingly accepted the Sugar Act as a trade regulation rather than a tax, Townshend believed they would regard the new acts in the same light. He was mistaken. The colonists were furious. Led by Samuel Adams, a political activist from Boston, they complained in print that the Townshend Acts were simply more illegal attempts to tax them. Adams sent a circular letter to the governments of all the colonies, laying out the reasons for Colonial objection. Soon there were riots in the streets of the port cities again, most notably in Boston. Conditions grew so unsafe that British officials in Boston asked General Gage, head of the standing army, to send troops to the city to help maintain order.

Protest in Boston

The Boston Massacre

The English soldiers, known locally as "redcoats" for the distinctive scarlet color of their uniforms, quickly became the most despised people in Boston. On the night of March 5, 1770, tension between soldiers and citizens erupted into what became known as the Boston Massacre. A group of colonists, including the free African merchant seaman Crispus Attucks, jeered at a group of redcoats. Suddenly an American hurled a stone, then another. A shot was fired, and moments later Attucks lay dead on the ground. In the ensuing melee, the soldiers shot and killed four more people. The next day, the Bostonians' bodies were carried to Faneuil Hall, where people paid their respects to the fallen as martyrs to a cause.

This engraving by Bostonian silversmith Paul Revere shows a highly exaggerated account of the riot, in which the British appear as brutal aggressors and the Bostonians as helpless victims. Though this was a distortion of the facts, the colonists eagerly embraced it. The engraving was reprinted and made available all over the colonies very shortly after the event. It is an excellent example of propaganda and helped to unite the colonists against Britain.

The Boston Massacre (engraving by Paul Revere)

The morning after the riot, Samuel Adams rose to his feet in the Massachusetts Assembly and demanded the "total evacuation of the town by all regular troops." Royal Governor Thomas Hutchinson realized that Adams was right and that the situation in Boston had become untenable and unsafe. He ordered the redcoats to leave the city.

Months later, the soldiers who had killed Attucks and the other rioters were tried for murder. John Adams, Samuel Adams's cousin, agreed to defend them. Defending the British was an unpopular move, but Adams stood fast on the principle that if the colonists demanded the right to trial by jury, they must be prepared to extend that right to others. Because the colonists had been the aggressors, the jury agreed that the soldiers were not guilty of murder.

The Boston Tea Party

The colonists retaliated against the Townshend Acts by boycotting British tea, which was imported from India. As a result, Britain's East India Company had no buyers for the millions of pounds of tea in its warehouses. British merchants in India, who stood to lose a fortune, begged Parliament for help. Parliament agreed to allow the East India Company to sell its tea in the colonies at a special low price, so that even with the tax, it would be cheaper than the Dutch tea the colonists regularly drank. The Americans saw this agreement as an attempt to manipulate them into paying a tax that they opposed on principle. They knew that if they bought the East India tea in order to save money, the British would have a hold over them in the long-standing quarrel over payment of taxes.

Various Colonial merchants, thinking of profits first and principles second, had agreed to sell the East India tea. The Sons of Liberty met in Philadelphia and New York in October and agreed not to accept the tea. This had the effect of making most merchants renege on their agreements to sell it. There was one crucial holdout, however—the sons of Governor Hutchinson were merchants, and held firm to their agreement to sell the East India tea.

On November 27, 1773, the *Dartmouth* sailed into Boston harbor with a cargo of East India tea. No dockworker in Boston was willing to help unload it. On their side, the Hutchinsons refused to allow the *Dartmouth* to leave the port until the tea was unloaded and the duty paid. By law, the ship could be seized in 20 days for nonpayment of duty. If this happened, the tea would be unloaded and could be put on sale. The Sons of Liberty decided to unload the tea themselves—into Boston Harbor.

December 16 was the last day of grace before the customs house could seize the cargo. That night, a crowd of 200 "Indians," with feathers in their hair and hatchets in their hands, stormed aboard the *Dartmouth*. They hacked the wooden crates of tea open and dumped them into the sea, cheered on by a great crowd of Bostonians on the docks.

The Sons of Liberty had planned well. They knew that no actual American Indians would be blamed, because they had taken no part in the hostilities between Britain and the colonists. They also knew that they needed to keep their identities secret, because they were destroying valuable property and perhaps even committing treason. The secret was well kept; to this day, historians do not know exactly who boarded the *Dartmouth* that night.

The Coercive/Intolerable Acts

News of the Boston Tea Party reached Britain in January 1774. Parliament agreed that Boston must be harshly punished, as an example to other colonies that might be tempted to defy Parliamentary authority. Parliament promptly passed a series of acts that became known in the colonies as "Intolerable Acts."

Name of Act	Provisions	Effect
Boston Port Act	Closed the port of Boston until Boston agreed to pay the East India Company for the *Dartmouth* cargo	Boston could not import any foreign goods or export to other nations
Massachusetts Government Act	Members of the legislature were to be appointed by the king instead of being popularly elected	Revoked the Massachusetts Charter of 1691; forbade town meetings for which the governor had not given permission
Administration of Justice Act	No royal official committing a capital offense could be tried in Massachusetts	Made it more likely that soldiers would get away with violence against citizens
Quartering Act	Colonists must provide food and housing for British soldiers on demand	Robbed citizens of the right to privacy and security in their own homes
Quebec Act (passed later in 1774)	Changed the system of government for Canada; disbanded representative assembly and revoked the right to trial by jury	Suggested to colonists that their own assemblies would soon be disbanded and their rights revoked

The First Continental Congress

Samuel Adams and the other Massachusetts Assembly members who were thrown out of office by the Intolerable Acts met privately to discuss their situation. They wrote to the assemblies of the other colonies, asking for their support in a total suspension of trade with Britain. Leaders from all the colonies except Georgia agreed to meet in Philadelphia in September to take steps to protect the security of colonial rights, which everyone agreed were seriously threatened by a pattern of oppression from Britain.

Leaders from each colony decided who would best represent the colony in the Continental Congress. Samuel and John Adams, the two radical leaders from Boston, were chosen to represent Massachusetts. Both men were well read and well educated; both had risen to prominence around the time of the Stamp Act crisis. Samuel Adams was a political leader and a writer of great influence; John Adams was a lawyer with a passionate interest in politics.

George Washington and Patrick Henry represented Virginia. Washington had acquired a distaste for the British during his experience of being snubbed and shoved aside in the French and Indian War. Patrick Henry was a fiery liberal who rose to his feet on the first day of Congress, exclaiming, "The distinctions between Virginians, Pennsylvanians, New Yorkers, and New Englanders are no more. I am no longer a Virginian, but an American!" John Dickinson, who had written a famous pamphlet opposing the Townshend Acts, represented Pennsylvania.

All the delegates were united in their opposition to the Intolerable Acts, which had specifically been designed to punish Boston and were harder on Massachusetts than on any other colony. By October, they had debated and approved a document called the Declaration and Resolves. This document had several provisions. First, it stated that since the colonists were not represented in Parliament, it had no authority over them; they were entitled to elect their own local governments. Second, the colonies would immediately cut off most trade with Britain (exceptions were made for the 1774 cotton and tobacco crops) and boycott all British goods until the Intolerable Acts were repealed and the standing army disbanded and sent back to Britain. Third, each colony would establish its own militia for defense against the British army.

Congress discussed two ideas: breaking completely away from Great Britain, or resolving their difference with the mother country and remaining within the British Empire. Joseph Galloway, a Quaker delegate from Pennsylvania, believed that it would be best to steer a middle course. He suggested a Plan

of Union that would give each colony control of its own affairs, with the addition of a national American assembly that was to be a branch of the British
Parliament. This American Parliament would have representatives from all the
colonies and would be headed by a president-general, to be appointed by the
monarch. The Plan of Union was narrowly rejected in a vote.

The delegates agreed to meet again in May of 1775 if they had no positive
response from London addressing their concerns. On April 19, something happened that would give them a new topic for debate. The "shot heard round the
world" was fired in Massachusetts.

CHAPTER 5 QUIZ

1. Before the Revolution, each British colony might be described as _____
   A. a constitutional monarchy.
   B. an absolute monarchy.
   C. a popular democracy.
   D. a republic.

2. _____ taxed imported paint, paper, glass, and tea throughout the
   colonies.
   A. The Sugar Act
   B. The Stamp Act
   C. The Townshend Acts
   D. The Intolerable Acts

3. What was the important difference between the Sugar Act and the subsequent
   parliamentary acts?
   A. The Sugar Act was an attempt to regulate trade.
   B. The Sugar Act was an outright tax.
   C. Parliament repealed the Sugar Act.
   D. William Pitt and Benjamin Franklin argued against the Sugar Act in Parliament.

4. John Adams agreed to defend the British soldiers involved in the Boston
   Massacre because _____
   A. he was a member of the British army.
   B. he was loyal to the British government.
   C. he believed that they had the right to a fair trial.
   D. he had participated in the incident and knew what had happened.

5. **The Sons and Daughters of Liberty are best described as** _____
    A. anarchists.
    B. political activists.
    C. official representatives.
    D. delegates to a national assembly.

6. **Why did the participants in the Boston Tea Party disguise themselves as "Indians"?**
    A. so that the Indians would be blamed
    B. so that they would escape punishment
    C. to show friendship for the Indians
    D. to show defiance to the British

7. **Parliament responded to the Boston Tea Party by passing** _____
    A. the Proclamation of 1763.
    B. the Townshend Act.
    C. the Intolerable Acts.
    D. the Magna Carta.

8. **What was the purpose of the First Continental Congress?**
    A. to raise a standing army and appoint a commander in chief
    B. to establish a unified central government for the colonies
    C. to declare independence from Great Britain
    D. to discuss opposition to the Intolerable Acts

9. _____ **was the direct target of the Intolerable Acts of 1774.**
    A. Georgia
    B. Massachusetts
    C. New York
    D. Virginia

10. _____ **is famous for an engraving depicting a highly exaggerated image of the Boston Massacre.**
    A. Samuel Adams
    B. Patrick Henry
    C. Benjamin Franklin
    D. Paul Revere

Chapter 6

The American Revolution, 1775–1783

The Revolutionary War began the morning of April 19, 1775, when someone fired a shot on Lexington Green just outside Boston. To this day, no one knows who fired this first shot of the American War for Independence. It was only the first of many shots fired over the next six years.

At first glance, no one would have thought that the Americans could possibly defeat the British army. American soldiers were volunteers who had little training and who were not being paid; the British army was famous throughout the world and had a glorious history. Its men were better equipped, better trained, and much more experienced.

The Americans had two major advantages, however—a knowledge of their own terrain and the ability to fight like the Native Americans. They had learned the value of the native method of hiding behind cover, then leaping out to take an enemy by surprise. Most of the American victories in the war were brought off by stealth. To the British, such a method of conducting a military campaign was cheating. Armies should fight fairly, facing one another across an open field. The Americans had learned the futility of this method during the French and Indian War.

The passage of the Declaration of Independence in July 1776 put new heart into the army, giving it a cause to fight for. George Washington's leadership kept the troops united under the worst of conditions; the soldiers felt such personal loyalty to their commander that there was very little desertion from Valley Forge during the winter of 1777–1778, despite the dreadful conditions.

The alliance with France in 1778 was a second and welcome boost to American morale. French and American forces finally cornered the British at Yorktown, Virginia, in 1781. Two years later, in the 1783 Treaty of Paris, Britain formally recognized the colonies as an independent nation—the United States of America.

CHAPTER OBJECTIVES

- Explain the main ideas of *Common Sense* and its effect on American readers.
- Identify and analyze the main ideas of the Declaration of Independence.
- Identify Revolutionary War battles on a map.
- Describe the course of the Revolutionary War and how it was won.

Chapter 6 Time Line

- **1775** **April 19**   Battles at Lexington and Concord, Massachusetts

  May 10   Second Continental Congress convenes in Philadelphia

  June 15   George Washington named commander of the Continental Army

  June 16   Battle of Bunker Hill (Breed's Hill)

- **1776** **January**   Publication of Thomas Paine's *Common Sense*

  July   Signing of the Declaration of Independence

  December 26   Battle of Trenton, New Jersey

- **1777** **January 3**   Battle of Princeton, New Jersey

  September   Battle of Brandywine, Pennsylvania

  October 7–17   Battle of Saratoga, New York

- **1778** **February**   American alliance with France

  June   Battle of Monmouth, New Jersey

● 1781   **October**   British surrender at Yorktown, Virginia

● 1783   Treaty of Paris

The Shot Heard Round the World

In the wake of rioting and civil unrest in Boston, Parliament replaced Governor Thomas Hutchinson of Massachusetts with General Thomas Gage, charging him to use his troops to maintain order in Boston. Gage faced two formidable threats to his authority. First, the Massachusetts Assembly members continued to meet, despite the ban imposed by the Massachusetts Government Act. (See Chapter 5.) Second, the ordinary people of Boston deeply resented the presence of a standing army in peacetime.

In response to the presence of the redcoats, the assembly members decided on two measures for their own security. First, all the towns near Boston formed their own militias, known as "minutemen" because they agreed to be ready to take up arms at a minute's notice. Many of these volunteer minutemen were boys in their mid-teens. Veterans of the French and Indian War provided them with rudimentary training. Second, the Americans began stockpiling weapons for possible use against the enemy, if necessary. Samuel Adams, prominent Boston merchant and statesman John Hancock, and the other members of the assembly agreed that the village of Concord would be a good place to store the weapons; it was close enough to Boston for the weapons to be handy for the city's defense, but far enough away to prevent discovery and capture of the weapons. Or so the assembly thought, but in fact the secret of the cache leaked out.

General Gage sent two patrols of men to Concord: one to seize the weapons, and the other to arrest Adams and Hancock. The troops began their short journey after dark; Gage wanted to keep their mission quiet, hoping to take the Americans by surprise. However, the Sons of Liberty spied on the troops and sounded the alarm. On the night of April 18, when the British crossed the Charles River and began their march toward Concord, Paul Revere warned a friend to light two lanterns in the tower of Boston's Old North Church; the people north of Boston would see the signal and know that the redcoats were on the move. William Dawes mounted a fast horse and rode hard to Lexington to warn the people and summon the minutemen from their beds. Revere crossed the Charles and followed Dawes. The townspeople along the route, roused by the shouts of the riders, leaped into their clothes and grabbed their muskets.

On Lexington Green, the redcoats and minutemen faced one another for the first time. The British officers ordered the Americans to disperse. The Americans, outnumbered by more than fifteen to one and unused to military discipline, were confused and disorderly. Some backed away. A shot rang out, then another and another. Seven minutemen and their commander were killed. Each side claimed that the other fired first. No historian has ever been able to discover the truth of the matter; no one will ever know who fired the "shot heard round the world." American author Ralph Waldo Emerson of Concord, whose grandfather witnessed the battle, coined this phrase in a patriotic poem many years later.

Satisfied with having chased the rebels away, the British marched on toward Concord. They were unable to find the weapons cache; warnings had arrived early enough for the people to hide most of them. At Concord Bridge, there was another skirmish between the two sides; it ended when the British commander ordered the redcoats to retreat to Boston. The minutemen followed them and surrounded the city, laying siege to it with the intent of starving the recoats into surrender. Reinforcements arrived from the nearby colonies as soon as the news spread; thousands of Americans marched to Boston to support the siege. Soon the minutemen outnumbered the redcoats by about five to one; the British had no choice but to wait for help from outside. Meanwhile, many Bostonians left the city; those who stayed to face the food shortages and stoppage of trade were among the bravest Americans of the Revolution.

The Battle of Bunker Hill

The Second Continental Congress met in Philadelphia on May 10, three weeks after the Battles of Lexington and Concord. The British use of arms against their fellow citizens had united the colonies, which immediately took steps for their defense. First, Congress formally created the Continental Army and ordered it to raise six companies of soldiers in Pennsylvania, Maryland, and Virginia. Second, it unanimously chose George Washington as commander in chief. With his newly appointed staff officers, Washington rode north toward Boston, arriving in early July, just in time to hear of the battles of Breed's Hill and Bunker Hill.

The Americans knew that if they had heavy artillery, they might fire on the redcoats and force them to surrender. There were French and Indian War cannon at far-off Fort Ticonderoga, New York; acting independently of one another, both the Connecticut Assembly and the leaders of Massachusetts made plans to bring the artillery to Boston. New Hampshire's Ethan Allen and his Green Mountain Boys joined forces with Massachusetts patriot Benedict Arnold and his friends; together they captured the cannon and hauled them toward Boston.

In June, British General John Burgoyne brought reinforcements to Boston and planned an attack on the Americans from the high ground overlooking the city. The watchful Sons of Liberty discovered the plan and informed the American troops. On the night of June 16, American commanders General Israel Putnam and Colonel William Prescott led a thousand soldiers to Bunker Hill, the location that gave its name to the ensuing battle. A last-minute change of plans moved them to nearby Breed's Hill, where they dug trenches and built a barricade. When the sun rose the next morning and the British saw what had happened, they fired on the Americans, who held their ground. In their scarlet and white uniforms, glittering in the morning sun, the British made easy targets for the minutemen, one of whom later remembered General Putnam's warning, "Reserve your fire until the enemy approaches so near as to enable you to see the whites of their eyes!" Many British fell, but when the Americans began to run out of bullets, they were chased out of Charlestown, which the redcoats burned to the ground. The British had gained control of the heights, but had lost more than twice as many men as the Americans.

The Colonies Declare Independence

"We have it in our power to begin the world over again." With these simple words, a pamphlet called *Common Sense* boldly suggested that America should become an independent nation as soon as possible. After Bunker Hill, many Americans had begun discussing independence; *Common Sense* convinced many more.

Born in the county of Norfolk, England in 1737, journalist Thomas Paine began working on *Common Sense* in November of 1775. His pamphlet did not specifically address the various acts of Parliament that had so angered the colonists; Paine knew little about these issues. The main argument of *Common Sense* was as follows: any system of government was at best a necessary evil, but a hereditary monarchy was the worst system of all because monarchs ruled by the accident of birth. *Common Sense* urged the Americans to adopt a new, democratic system based on merit, not on birth; if the colonies declared their independence from Great Britain and set an example of democratic rule, other nations would follow. The events of 1775 had convinced Paine that this was the right time for the colonies to take this step. Many readers agreed; *Common Sense* sold 500,000 copies in 1776—one copy for every four or five people living in the colonies.

Most Colonial assemblies declared their support for independence from Britain. Others, however, believed that reconciliation was still possible. John Dickinson of Pennsylvania was the leading conservative voice in Congress. He wrote a document called the Olive Branch Petition, a direct appeal to King George III to bring about peace between Parliament and the colonies. Congress voted to sign and send the Olive Branch Petition, but also approved a Declaration of the Causes and Necessity of Taking Up Arms. Written by Thomas Jefferson, this document closed with the words: "We most solemnly . . . declare, that, . . . we will . . . employ for the preservation of; our liberties, being with one mind resolved to die freemen rather than to live slaves."

In June 1776, Richard Henry Lee of Virginia rose in Congress and read this resolution:

> . . . that these United Colonies are, and of right ought to be, free and independent States, that they are absolved from all allegiance to the British Crown, and that all political connection between them and the State of Great Britain is, and ought to be, totally dissolved.

This resolution was America's actual declaration of independence from Britain, or would be when it was approved by the Continental Congress. The much-more-famous Declaration of Independence had a different purpose. Looking back in 1823, its author Thomas Jefferson described that purpose: ". . . to place before mankind the common sense of the subject, in terms so plain and firm as to command their assent. . . ." In other words, the delegates believed in the importance of setting forth their purposes and goals to the world, so that everyone would understand why they were rebelling and what they hoped to accomplish.

The Declaration of Independence clearly shows the influence of the European Enlightenment on the people of America. It refers to "self-evident truths" and "unalienable rights" that the Americans believed the British government was denying them. It explained that when a government was unjust to its people, the people had both the right and the duty to overthrow it. It described in detail the "injuries and usurpations" that Britain had committed against the colonists. The conclusion included the text of Richard Henry Lee's resolution.

Jefferson's elegant writing was fiercely debated in Congress for three days, during which John Adams passionately defended every sentence while others raised objections to short phrases or even long passages. The most crucial passage to be deleted referred to slavery as "cruel war against human nature itself." Southern delegates did not like this implication that slavery was morally wrong; they had no intention of abolishing an institution that brought their colonies so much economic profit. Northern delegates, despite their awareness of the hypocrisy of declaring independence for themselves while denying it to Africans, had no choice but to agree to strike the passage, since without it the southerners would not have voted in favor of independence. The seeds of the American Civil War of 1861–1865 lay in this compromise.

The amended declaration was finally approved and the Virginia resolution carried unanimously on July 2; it was made official on July 4. The British colonies were now a new country, the United States of America. John Adams accurately predicted that in the future, the anniversary of American independence would be celebrated "with pomp and parade, with shows, games, sports, guns, bells, bonfires, and illuminations, from one end of this continent to the other, from this time forward forevermore."

Battles of the Revolutionary War

The American Army

Arriving in Boston after the Battle of Bunker Hill, Washington immediately brought order and discipline to the troops camped round the city. His plan was to wait for the British to leave, as they would have to do sooner or later if they were not to starve. However, the British were prepared to wait, and the Americans grew bored. They were volunteers and did not have the professional discipline of the British regulars, nor were they being paid any salary for their efforts. They had thought that war would be an exciting adventure, not just endless weeks of waiting for something to happen. Many of them returned to their homes. By January 1776, Washington had only about 10,000 men remaining.

Women, American Indians, and African Americans all fought in the Revolutionary War. Washington had originally banned African Americans from serving as soldiers, but when Virginia's royalist governor offered freedom to any slave who would fight on the British side, and hundreds of slaves accepted, the U.S. army began enlisting free African Americans. Perhaps 5,000 of them fought in the war.

American Indians were considered valuable allies by both sides, because of their knowledge of the terrain. For their part, the tribes were willing to fight for whichever side seemed most likely to respect their own rights. The Cayuga, Mohawk, Onondaga, and Seneca fought for the British, while many Oneida and Tuscarora Indians fought on the American side.

Many American women followed their husbands to war. They camped with the troops, working hard as nurses, cooks, and laundresses. These women were in as much danger as the men, under constant threat of enemy fire. Mary Ludwig Hayes is famous for taking over a cannon at the Battle of Monmouth; Deborah Sampson disguised herself as a man and fought under the name "Robert Shurtleff" for many months before her masquerade was discovered.

Battles in the Northern Colonies

In March, Washington agreed to allow the redcoats safe passage out of the city in exchange for a promise that there would be no shooting or damage to property. The British marched south, planning to take over New York City; this would cut New England off from the rest of the colonies, allowing the British army to crush both sections in turn. Thousands of mercenaries from the German state of Hesse were sailing across the Atlantic to reinforce the British troops.

Battle of Brooklyn

General William Howe staged an attack on the Americans from the northeast in August of 1776; at the same time, other British troops opened fire behind the Americans in a surprise second attack. The Battle of Brooklyn was a great success for the British. Thousands of Americans were killed; the survivors retreated to Manhattan. If Howe had attacked again right away, the Continental Army could not have retreated safely; as it was, the Americans marched north through Manhattan and fought the British again at Harlem Heights. Meanwhile, the patriotic citizens of Manhattan set the city on fire, leaving the British surrounded by smoking ruins. Washington's army eventually crossed the river to New Jersey.

Battle of Trenton

By this time, Congress had declared independence and the Continental Army had become the Army of the United States. Christmas night of 1776 found the American army in Pennsylvania, just across the Delaware River from the British camp in Trenton, New Jersey. Despite their ragged uniforms and badly-patched boots, the soldiers were ready for action. Washington suddenly wondered if he could turn the holiday into an American advantage. If he and his men slipped back into Trenton on Christmas night and attacked the following morning, they might take the Hessians by surprise. Between the late-afternoon dusk and the following dawn, more than 2,400 soldiers had been quietly ferried back across the Delaware. American officer Alexander Hamilton noticed the bloody tracks their feet left in the snow—but he also saw grim determination on every face.

Washington's daring plan succeeded. The Hessians had celebrated Christmas until late at night and were caught completely off guard by the Americans in the morning. Nearly 1,000 Hessians were taken prisoner and their weapons distributed among the American troops. Washington's great victory made many of his men decide to re-enlist, and inspired many more to join up for the first time.

Battle of Brandywine

In January 1777, Washington won the Battle of Princeton, pushing the British out of New Jersey for good. By September, however, General Howe had swung his troops around the Americans to attack them from the rear. His goal was to capture Philadelphia, the capital of the United States and the meeting place of Congress. The battle was fought at Brandywine Creek, several miles from Philadelphia. The Americans were forced to retreat to Germantown, just north of the city. A week later, the British attacked Paoli, a town about 25 miles west of the city. By the end of September, the British were riding through the streets of Philadelphia.

Battle of Germantown

In October, Washington attacked Howe's men in Germantown. The day was foggy and the American troops, confused, panicked and ran in all directions. This was the fifth time that Howe had defeated Washington in battle. The rag-tag Colonial army gathered itself together and settled at Valley Forge for the winter. Although conditions were dreadful—deep snow, bitterly cold temperatures, little food, and no new boots or clothing to replace the garments they had been wearing for months—few soldiers deserted. In spite of the defeats and hardships of combat, Washington had somehow gained the personal loyalty and respect of every one of his troops.

The army put the time to good use. Frederich von Steuben, a career Prussian army officer who had befriended Benjamin Franklin in Paris, began working with the men, drilling them on a daily basis until they began to look as sharp and disciplined as the British regulars. In February, France formally allied itself with the United States.

Battle of Monmouth

In the summer of 1778, Washington led his troops forth into battle at Monmouth, New Jersey. This was the first time that the two armies had met in battle across open fields. When the American commander Charles Lee ordered his troops to retreat, George Washington lost his temper for the first time, swearing "until the leaves shook on the trees," according to one officer. Washington rallied his troops and continued the battle. There was no clear victory for either side, but the British had learned that the Americans were formidable opponents even in traditional European-style warfare.

Battle of Saratoga

In October 1777, the Americans pulled off a miracle by forcing the British to surrender at Saratoga, a small town in northern New York. That spring, General Burgoyne had planned to march on Albany. He would lead troops from the north, taking back Fort Ticonderoga and Lake Champlain. Colonel Barry St. Leger and his troops would approach Albany from the west.

General Benedict Arnold bribed a prisoner of war called Schuyler into giving false information to the Iroquois allies of the British. Schuyler, who could speak Iroquois, easily persuaded them to convince St. Leger's troops to retreat. Under Arnold's leadership and at the suggestion of Colonel Tadeusz Kosciuszko, who had come from Poland to help the American cause, the Americans grouped their cannon at the top of a cliff. Burgoyne's troops could not pass without marching directly through the line of fire. On October 17, Burgoyne surrendered.

Battles in the Southern Colonies

In December of 1778, the British army began a determined attack on the southern colonies. Since the American army had left the South largely undefended, British commanders Charles Cornwallis and Henry Clinton thought they could easily conquer the South and then march north, taking control of each colony as the passed through it. By the spring of 1780, the British had captured Georgia and were marching toward Charleston, South Carolina. General Clinton won a great victory at Charleston in May, capturing 5,400 American soldiers and a small fleet of ships.

By October, the British were threatening North Carolina. Under the command of Major Patrick Ferguson, they had taken up a position on a high hill. The Americans charged the hill twice and were beaten back, but a third charge was successful. By the end of the battle, all the British had been captured or killed. This loss made the British generals decide to march on to Virginia. By this time, French troops, ships, and money had arrived in the United States. Washington and the French commander Rochambeau agreed to march south to Virginia to meet the enemy.

The Americans and French soon backed General Cornwallis and his troops into a corner. The redcoats occupied Yorktown, Virginia. American and French troops headed by Washington, the French commander Lafayette, and other commanders were able to fire on Yorktown from several different directions at once. The British held out for six weeks, but they were running out of supplies and had no allies who could come to their rescue. Redcoats were dying every day from illness and starvation. In mid-October, General Cornwallis surrendered to Washington.

The 1783 Treaty of Paris

The 1783 Treaty of Paris officially ended the war. Benjamin Franklin and John Adams represented the United States in the discussions of the treaty's provisions. The treaty granted the United States its independence, and all the lands between the Atlantic coast and the Mississippi River, and between the Great Lakes and Florida. The United States also received fishing rights in the Gulf of St. Lawrence and off the coast of Newfoundland. In return, the United States agreed to repay any debt owed to Britain.

CHAPTER 6 QUIZ

1. The Americans won the Battle of Trenton because _____
   A. they were better equipped.
   B. they outnumbered the enemy.
   C. they caught the enemy by surprise.
   D. their troops were more experienced.

2. _____ played a strategic role in the American victory at Saratoga.
   A. Benedict Arnold
   B. George Washington
   C. John Adams
   D. Thomas Paine

3. Northern delegates agreed to strike a passage referring to slavery from the Declaration of Independence because _____
   A. they did not believe it was the right time to free the slaves.
   B. they supported the institution of slavery.
   C. most of them were slaveholders.
   D. they wanted the southerners to vote in favor of independence.

4. _____ asked the British monarch to resolve the dispute between the colonies and Parliament.
   A. The Declaration of Independence
   B. The Olive Branch Petition
   C. *Common Sense*
   D. The Declaration of the Causes and Necessity of Taking Up Arms

5. The British army surrendered to the Americans in _____, ending the war.
   A. New Jersey
   B. Pennsylvania
   C. Massachusetts
   D. Virginia

6. The British army marched to Concord in 1775 in order to _____
   A. take possession of a cache of weapons.
   B. lay siege to the city of Boston.
   C. fight the American minutemen on the village green.
   D. capture the men of the Second Continental Congress.

7. **What was the purpose of the Declaration of Independence?**
    A. to explain why the Americans wanted their freedom from Great Britain
    B. to free the slaves throughout the American colonies
    C. to provide the Continental Army with a cause to fight for
    D. to resolve the dispute between Parliament and the colonies

8. **In the 1783 Treaty of Paris, the United States agreed to _____**
    A. cede part of its territory to France.
    B. free its African slaves.
    C. abandon its fight for independence.
    D. repay its financial debt to Britain.

9. **What important lesson did the American troops learn from the Native Americans?**
    A. to attack stealthily and take the enemy by surprise
    B. to allow women to serve as soldiers
    C. to switch sides depending on individual interest
    D. to fight across open fields

10. **The British plan was to occupy _____ , then crush the northern and southern colonies in turn.**
    A. Boston
    B. New York
    C. Philadelphia
    D. Concord

Chapter **7**

The Articles of Confederation, 1777–1781

Shortly after the signing of the Declaration of Independence, Congress appointed a committee to begin work on a national constitution. The committee members produced the Articles of Confederation, which were debated and amended over the next year and a half before being passed in November 1777. It took until 1781 for the Articles of Confederation to be ratified by all thirteen states.

The Articles of Confederation were a very poor attempt at developing a working plan for a central government. First, they left far too much power with the states. Second, they did not create a national executive or a judicial branch. Third, they did not give Congress the power to collect taxes. All national governments must collect taxes; they are a necessary source of revenue that a nation must use to pay for services such as an army. This was especially crucial for the fledgling United States because it was at war at the time the articles were written.

Unable to force the states to help pay for the costs of the Revolution, Congress found itself with a huge war debt when the Revolution was over. When states belatedly began raising taxes to help pay the debt, the people rebelled, believing that Congress was just the British Parliament all over again. Political leaders such as James Madison and George Washington began speaking out against the articles, urging that Congress try again and this time create a stronger central government, one that had real authority to administer the states. By 1787, it was clear that this was essential if the new nation were going to succeed.

CHAPTER OBJECTIVES

- Describe the state governments created after the United States declared its independence.
- Describe the Articles of Confederation and list its provisions.
- Analyze the weaknesses of the Articles of Confederation.
- Describe the major issues that led to the decision to replace the articles with a new constitution.

Chapter 7 Time Line

- **1777**   Congress approves the Articles of Confederation
- **1781**   **March**   Articles of Confederation ratified by all states

      October   British surrender at Yorktown

- **1783**   Treaty of Paris
- **1786**   Shays's Rebellion
- **1787**   **April**   "Vices of the Political System of the United States"

      May   Constitutional Convention

The State Governments

The individual states—formerly colonies—began establishing new state governments in 1776, as soon as the United States declared its independence from Britain. By 1780, eleven of the thirteen United States had written constitutions; the other two, Connecticut and Rhode Island, had revised their royal charters.

THE MYTH

Most Americans are taught as schoolchildren, and believe ever afterward, that the United States is a democracy.

THE FACTS

The United States is now and has always been a republic—a government in which the people elect representatives to rule them. The definition of *democracy* is "a government in which the people rule themselves." True democracy is possible only in very small communities where it is practical for all the people to meet and decide on laws; the town meetings that are still held throughout New England are examples of democratic rule.

Almost all freely elected representative governments in the world are republics. The greater the possibility for voter participation, the more democratic the republic is. In the United States, the presence of free speech and a free press make for a democratic society. The expansion of voting rights from male property owners age 21 and older to all adults age 18 and over has, over time, created a government that might be described as a democratic republic.

The state governments relied on freely elected representative forms of government, in which adult men voted for their leaders.

Each state had a governor and a legislative assembly. Most early state constitutions gave much more power to the legislature than to the governor; they were determined to make the new system truly representative of the voters' needs. In Colonial times, the governor had usually represented the interests of the British Crown, while the legislative assemblies were locally elected and represented the colonists' interests. This history of opposing interests led the Americans to distrust the notion of a strong executive.

State governors and legislators were popularly elected, although voting was still a privilege rather than a right. Women, slaves, and American Indians could not vote. Each state established slightly different age and income requirements for male voters. Free African-American men could vote in most states, if they met the qualifications of age and property ownership. (See the "The Myth—The Facts," Chapter 16.)

State constitutions guaranteed freedom of religion to all varieties of Christians; some extended this freedom to anyone who professed a belief in the

Judeo-Christian God. Many of the leaders of the new state governments had been strongly influenced by the thinkers of the European Enlightenment and feared the influence of religion on the state. Many also recognized that the United States was already a land of religious plurality, where Quakers, Anglicans, Protestants of all kinds, Jews, Catholics, and others all had to live and work side by side. It made sense to ensure that no American citizen could be penalized for worshipping God according to the dictates of his or her conscience.

The National Government

As the state governments began to take shape, Congress turned its attention to designing a national government. John Dickinson of Pennsylvania was put in charge of the committee to draft a plan for this new government. Congress adopted Dickinson's plan, the Articles of Confederation, on November 15, 1777.

The Articles of Confederation did not create a modern nation-state; they created a loosely knit association of thirteen sovereign powers that were guaranteed their independence and freedom. The Articles of Confederation echoed the same fear of a strong central government that had made each state constitution limit the powers of the governor.

Legislative Powers

The national legislative body was to be called the Congress. Congress had the power to borrow and coin money, set a standard for a national currency, set and carry out foreign policy, control affairs between the United States and the American Indians, and settle any disputes between or among states. Congress could not require states to contribute money to the central government, nor to provide recruits for the U.S. armed forces. The Articles of Confederation stated that expenses related to the army and to fighting wars would be paid from the national treasury, but that it would be up to the states to decide how to raise the money.

Each state was to receive one vote in Congress, regardless of the size of the state's population. Delegates to Congress were to be elected annually, and each state would have between two and seven representatives. Congress agreed to admit Canada into the United States if it wished to be admitted, and stipulated that if any other colony wished to join the United States, at least nine of the thirteen states would have to agree.

This chart shows the major provisions of the Articles of Confederation.

The Articles of Confederation

Article I	Establishes "United States of America" as the name of the country.
Article II	Each state is to remain independent. All powers not expressly given to Congress remain with the states.
Article III	The states agree to assist one another if any one of them is attacked.
Article IV	Citizens may travel freely from one state to another. If a criminal flees one state and is found in another, the second state will send him home for trial. Each state shall give full faith and credit to the laws of the rest.
Article V	Voters will elect two to seven representatives to Congress each year. Congress will meet each year on the first Monday of November. Each state shall have one vote in Congress. Freedom of speech and debate in Congress is absolute.
Article VI	Only Congress has the power to set foreign policy, make treaties, conduct war, or maintain a standing army in times of peace. Each state shall maintain a militia and a proper quantity of weapons.
Article VII	State legislatures shall appoint military commanders.
Article VIII	Congress will fund war expenses from a national treasury; each state shall decide how to raise money for its share.
Article IX	Only Congress has the power to determine peace and war. Congress will settle all disputes between or among states. Congress has the sole power to fix weights and measures and to coin money. A majority vote of the delegates is necessary for any congressional action.
Article X	Congress can take no legislative action without the agreement of at least nine delegates.
Article XI	Canada may join the United States if it approves the Articles of Confederation. No other territory can join the United States except by vote of nine states.
Article XII	The United States agrees to pay all debts it contracts.

Article XIII   Every state agrees to be bound by the authority of Congress. The union of the states is to be perpetual.

Executive and Judicial Powers

The Articles of Confederation did not provide for a president or any other chief executive of the new government. Nor did they provide for any national court. The reasons for this were twofold. First, past experience of British rule made the Americans believe that no monarch, or any other head of state, would understand the individual needs of the states or of the people. Second, the states did not entirely trust or agree with one another; they preferred to rule over themselves, rather than answering to elected officials from other states. For example, no Georgian would want to be ruled by someone from Massachusetts; each state was too different from the others in too many ways. Those that were geographically farther apart, of course, had less in common than did neighboring states like North and South Carolina.

Ratification

Congress agreed that ratification of the Articles of Confederation must be unanimous. The major obstacle in the way of ratification was the disputed land between the settled coastal areas of the states and the Mississippi River. In fact, this land was claimed by Britain, and could not belong to any of the states unless they won the Revolutionary War, but the states proceeded on the assumption of a victory. Various states laid rival claims to some parcels of land; those that claimed no land were concerned about the expansion of the rest. The Maryland legislature flatly refused to ratify the Articles of Confederation unless some of the other states gave up their rights to the disputed land.

Virginia and New York, the states that held the most land, set an example by giving up their claims. By 1781, other states had followed suit, and in March of that year, Maryland became the final state to ratify the Articles of Confederation.

Effects of the Articles of Confederation

The Northwest Ordinance

Congress immediately took steps to resolve the problem of the disputed land in the west. The Land Ordinance of 1785 marked off all the land east of the Mississippi into townships and put up 640-acre lots in the townships for sale, at the minimum price of $1 per acre. One section of each township was reserved for a public schoolhouse. The Land Ordinance of 1787, commonly called the Northwest Ordinance, established the rules for governing the Northwest Territory.

The United States in 1787

This map shows the borders of the states as of 1787, including the western lands each state claimed. The Northwest Territory includes the present-day states of Wisconsin, Michigan, Illinois, Indiana, and Ohio.

Congress believed that the Northwest Territory would eventually be settled and that the settlers would want to join the United States. Therefore, it established a process by which this would happen. First, the territory should be divided into three to five smaller parcels of land. Second, Congress would appoint a governor, a secretary, and three judges for each territory. Third, when the population of a territory reached 5,000, voters would elect a legislature and send a nonvoting delegate to Congress. Fourth, a territory would become eligible for statehood when the population reached 60,000. The territory would draft a state constitution; upon congressional approval of the constitution by a Yea vote of nine or more states, the territory would become a state.

The Northwest Ordinance also guaranteed civil rights in the territories and banned slavery. Opposition to slavery had been growing among the northern delegates, who were uncomfortably aware of the irony of declaring their own independence while denying it to the African-American population. However, the southerners refused to give up the system of free labor that had brought them so much prosperity, and the Articles of Confederation gave Congress no power to do anything about it. The Northwest Ordinance stated that escaped slaves seeking sanctuary in the territories must be returned to their owners.

The Economy

It quickly became apparent that the Articles of Confederation were not a sufficiently strong basis for a national government. Because Congress had no power over the states, it could accomplish very little. Any new legislation it wanted to pass required the support of nine states, and delegates within a state often could not agree on how to cast their vote, let alone agreeing with delegates from other states.

Because Congress had given itself no power to tax the states or the people, it had great difficulty conducting the Revolutionary War. The troops often went without food, necessary supplies, and new boots and uniforms because there was no way for Congress to purchase these items. States frequently put off paying their share of these expenses into the national treasury, and Congress had no leverage to make them pay more or pay more promptly. George Washington and the other military commanders were probably more acutely aware than anyone of the weaknesses of the Articles of Confederation, since they saw the evidence of these weaknesses every day in their struggles on the battlefield.

During the war, the United States accumulated a substantial debt. After the war ended, Congress had no means of raising taxes to pay the debt. Congress printed and began to circulate paper money, but merchants refused to accept it, claiming that it had no value. Unemployment rose and business activity fell off, causing an economic depression in 1784. Britain had closed some of its markets to American imports, then flooded the United States with inexpensive goods.

American merchants could not compete with British prices and quickly began to lose money. The desperate economic situation led to Shays's Rebellion.

Daniel Shays was a farmer and a Revolutionary War captain. When Massachusetts began raising taxes on land to help the economy recover, and seized land for nonpayment of taxes, Shays and others rebelled. They shut down debtor courts and marched on Springfield, intending to seize an arsenal of weapons stored there. The governor of Massachusetts called out the militia to stop them. When the fighting began in late January 1787, four of Shays's men were killed. By the end of February, the rebellion had been put down, and political leaders realized that the United States needed a stronger central government.

Foreign Policy

The Articles of Confederation made no provision for a foreign office, making it impossible to force Britain to fulfill its obligations as described in the Treaty of Paris. Congress could also do nothing to prevent the continuing impressment of American sailors into service on British warships.

James Madison of Virginia published his opinions in "Vices of the Political System of the United States" in April 1787. First, Madison argued that the states had failed to comply with reasonable constitutional demands for taxes. Second, some states had trespassed on one another's rights. Third, individual states had entered into agreements with Indians in defiance of the Articles of Confederation. Fourth, the national economic depression made it clear that the states would not voluntarily work together in defense of their common interests. Madison's clear, declarative statements and specific examples impressed many readers. George Washington, who had had every opportunity to observe the concrete results of Congress's impotence during the war, agreed with Madison, writing, "I predict the worst consequences from a half-starved, limping government, always moving upon crutches and tottering at every step."

Madison's arguments, and those of his supporters, convinced the leaders that they would have to try again. In May 1787, delegates from all the colonies except Rhode Island met in Philadelphia to write the U.S. Constitution.

CHAPTER 7 QUIZ

1. _____ headed the committee that wrote the Articles of Confederation.
   A. James Madison
   B. John Dickinson
   C. George Washington
   D. Daniel Shays

2. The Articles of Confederation empowered Congress to do all these things except _____
   A. hold sessions once a year.
   B. levy war and conclude peace.
   C. tax the states and the people.
   D. admit new states to the United States by a vote of nine states.

3. Under the Articles of Confederation, _____ had the most power.
   A. the executive
   B. the legislature
   C. the courts
   D. the states

4. What argument did James Madison make about taxes in his criticism of the Articles of Confederation?
   A. The national government should have the right to tax the states.
   B. The states could not be taxed without their own consent.
   C. Congress had the right to seize land for nonpayment of taxes.
   D. The amount of tax should be determined by the states, not the Congress.

5. Which of these helped lead directly to the economic depression of 1784?
   A. Britain flooded the colonies with low-priced imported goods.
   B. The Articles of Confederation were ratified.
   C. The Northwest Ordinance was passed.
   D. The British forced Americans into service on British warships.

6. Congress established that a new territory would become a state when _____
   A. its population reached 5,000.
   B. its population reached 60,000.
   C. its constitution received at least nine votes in Congress.
   D. it sent a nonvoting delegate to Congress.

7. **Which best describes the governments of the individual states?**
    A. a strong central executive and a weak legislature
    B. a weak central executive and a strong legislature
    C. an even balance of powers between the executive and the legislature
    D. a strong legislature with no executive

8. **Individual states began to write new constitutions or revise royal charters _____**
    A. immediately after the Declaration of Independence was ratified.
    B. immediately after the British surrendered at Yorktown.
    C. immediately after the Articles of Confederation were ratified.
    D. immediately after the Treaty of Paris was signed.

9. **All of these are considered major weaknesses of the Articles of Confederation, except _____**
    A. they did not establish a strong national executive.
    B. they did not give Congress the power to raise taxes.
    C. they did not provide for the addition of new states to the nation.
    D. they did not provide Congress with any means to fund the U.S. army.

10. **Which best describes the purpose of the Articles of Confederation?**
    A. to apportion representation in the legislature according to each state's population
    B. to fix the amount of the debt from the Revolutionary War
    C. to provide a strong central government for the United States
    D. to create a loose association of the individual states

Chapter 8

The Constitution and the Bill of Rights

The Constitution of the United States was ratified in 1788, after months of closed debate among the framers of the document, followed by months of argument in the public sphere once it was printed and circulated. When the U.S. Congress convened in 1789, its members immediately began to debate a series of amendments to the document. These amendments, passed in 1791, are known as the Bill of Rights.

The framers of the Constitution had many interests to try to balance. First, small and large states must to be fairly represented. Second, state and national governments must fairly share their governing powers. Third, individual rights must be protected. Fourth, issues such as slavery, the American-Indian population, and territorial expansion must be addressed. In every area, compromise was the only solution; each state had to give up something it wanted so that the final product would be reasonably fair to all.

Congress designed a federal government with a balance of powers among its three branches. The executive branch would have a president elected for a four-year term. The legislative branch would be a bicameral Congress; one house would represent the states according to population, while the other would represent all equally. The judicial branch would consist of a Supreme Court. Each branch would have certain powers over the other two.

Many Americans were dismayed by the fact that the Constitution ignored the subject of individual rights; however, the required nine states did ratify the document. After the first national elections, Congress drafted a Bill of Rights that set forth many important freedoms and privileges of ordinary citizens. These ten amendments were ratified in the year 1791.

CHAPTER OBJECTIVES

- Describe the makeup of the Constitutional Convention.
- Identify the major historical influences on the U.S. Constitution.
- Analyze the course of debate in the Constitutional Convention.
- Summarize the Constitution and identify the rights set forth in the Bill of Rights.

Chapter 8 Time Line

- 1787 **May 25** Constitutional Convention is convened

  September 17 Constitution is signed

  October *Federalist Papers*

  December 7 Delaware ratifies the Constitution

- 1788 **June 21** Constitution becomes law

- 1789 **April 30** George Washington inaugurated

- 1791 Bill of Rights

The Constitutional Convention

The Constitutional Convention began in Philadelphia on May 25, 1787. Like the Second Continental Congress, the convention met in the State House in Philadelphia (today called Independence Hall because the Declaration of Independence was signed there). Many of the fifty-five delegates had represented their colonies in the First and/or Second Continental Congresses. Benjamin Franklin, George Washington, Alexander Hamilton, and James Madison were among the delegates. Thomas Jefferson and John Adams, both on diplomatic missions in Europe, did not attend the convention. Rhode Island sent no representatives. The delegates unanimously chose George Washington as president of the convention.

The delegates' first decision was to maintain secrecy. They would keep the doors and windows of Independence Hall closed during debate, and they would not discuss the proceedings with any outsiders. The reason for the secrecy was so that each man could speak without fear of outside pressure to change his mind, or fear of reprisal for voting a certain way.

The delegates soon agreed that instead of revising the Articles of Confederation, they would discard them altogether and start fresh. The new document they would prepare would be called the Constitution of the United States.

There were several important historical influences on the Constitution. The first was the influence of the Roman Republic. The second was the British government. The third were the ideas of the Enlightenment. The fourth was their own experience of government within the colonies.

The Roman Republic was an ancient and long-lasting system of government that had a legislative branch (the Senate) and elected officials. Like Americans, Romans did not enjoy universal suffrage; only male property owners could vote, and only men could hold office.

The British government had a long tradition of representation and individual rights. In 1215, the Magna Carta established that the monarch must abide by the laws of the land; it also established certain individual rights and expressed the basic principle that government could succeed only by the consent of the governed. In 1689, the English Bill of Rights specifically listed more individual rights and established that the monarch could not take them away.

A third influence was more recent—the writings of eighteenth-century Enlightenment thinkers such as John Locke and the Baron de Montesquieu. In 1748, Montesquieu's *The Spirit of Laws* described and argued for the separation of powers—a three-branch government (executive, legislative, and judicial) in which each branch had certain checks on the authority of the others. Locke insisted on the rights of the governed to design the government that would rule them.

The final important influence on the framers of the Constitution was their own experience of American government, going back to the Mayflower Compact of 1620. Since the former British colonies were first settled, they had run efficiently and well on a system of representative government.

The Great Compromise

There were two primary causes of disagreement among the delegates. One was the issue of states' rights versus the powers of the central government. The other was the concern for equal representation for small and large states.

The Virginia Plan

With the support of James Madison, Edmund Randolph of Virginia proposed the first detailed plan for a new government. The Virginia Plan called for a bicameral legislature in which each state would be represented in proportion to its population. Randolph's plan also included executive and judicial branches for the national government.

The New Jersey Plan

On June 16, William Patterson of New Jersey presented a second idea for the new government. The New Jersey Plan called for equal representation of all states in both houses of the legislature. The New Jersey Plan did not garner as much support as the Virginia Plan, although many of its ideas appeared in the final Constitution.

Many of the delegates were wary of any notion of direct democracy, but they did believe that since government should represent the people, it must in part be freely elected. Therefore, they agreed on a bicameral legislature with a popularly elected lower house, the House of Representatives, and an appointed upper house, the Senate. The existence of two houses meant that each would provide a check on the power of the other. To settle the question of equal representation of all the states, the delegates agreed that states would be equally represented in the Senate, with two votes for each, but proportionally represented in the House, with larger states having more representatives than smaller ones. Roger Sherman of Connecticut, one of only four men who attended both the Second Continental Congress and the Constitutional Convention, proposed this plan, known as the Great Compromise.

Fierce debate over how to determine a state's population ensued. Southerners wanted their slaves counted toward the total population of their states, because this would mean more representatives in the House. Northern states protested that since slaves were treated as property rather than people, with no civil rights, they should not be counted toward the total population. On

July 11, the Three-Fifths Compromise established that each slave would be counted as three-fifths of a person in determining a state's population.

In August, the debate turned to national control over trade. Over southern protests, the delegates agreed to give Congress the power to pass navigation acts. Over northern protests, they agreed to prevent Congress from passing any laws restricting the slave trade until 1808. As the delegates to the Second Continental Congress had done in 1776, the delegates to the Constitutional Convention passed up a chance to resolve the issue of slavery once and for all. This surrender to compromise would prove to affect the nation more than any other issue over the next two centuries.

By September 8, the debates had drawn to a close and the convention had appointed a committee to write the Constitution in its final form. Gouverneur Morris of New York completed most of this work by September 12, and the Constitution was signed on September 17. On that day, Benjamin Franklin, the oldest of the delegates at age 81, made a speech praising the efforts of the convention and urging the delegates to join in friendship and forget their differences:

> Mr. President, I confess that there are several parts of this constitution which I do not at present approve, but I am not sure I shall never approve them: For having lived long, I have experienced many instances of being obliged by better information, or fuller consideration, to change opinions even on important subjects, which I once thought right, but found to be otherwise. . . .
>
> In these sentiments, Sir, I agree to this Constitution with all its faults, if they are such; because I think a general Government necessary for us, and there is no form of Government but what may be a blessing to the people if well administered, and believe farther that this is likely to be well administered for a course of years, and can only end in Despotism, as other forms have done before it, when the people shall become so corrupted as to need despotic Government, being incapable of any other. . . .
>
> On the whole, Sir, I can not help expressing a wish that every member of the Convention who may still have objections to it, would with me, on this occasion doubt a little of his own infallibility, and to make manifest our unanimity, put his name to this instrument.

An Overview of the Constitution

The Constitution begins with the following Preamble:

> We the People of the United States, in order to form a more perfect Union, establish Justice, insure domestic Tranquility, provide for the common defense, promote the general Welfare, and secure the Blessings of Liberty to ourselves and our Posterity, do ordain and establish this Constitution for the United States of America.

The opening of the Preamble is remarkable for its first three words. "We the People" suggests that symbolically, the government is a democracy, not a republic—that rather than being written by the representatives, the founding document of the nation was actually written and approved by the people themselves. This shows the framers' concern for the Lockian principle of government by the consent of the governed.

The Constitution is divided into seven articles, as follows:

Article I   Describes the legislative branch with two houses, a Senate and a House of Representatives. Senators are chosen by state legislatures; there are two for each state. Representatives are popularly elected; there is one for every 30,000 people in a state (excluding Indians, and counting each slave as three-fifths of one person). Gives the rules by which the legislature will conduct business and pass laws.

Article II   Describes the executive branch, which will be headed by a President. In a system known as the electoral college, voters will choose electors who will in turn cast their votes for president. Sets forth the duties and powers of the President.

Article III   Describes the judicial branch, which will consist of a Supreme Court with nine justices who will serve for life during good behavior.

Article IV	Describes the powers and rights of the states.
Article V	Describes the process by which the Constitution can be amended.
Article VI	States that the Constitution is the supreme law of the land and that no religious test will be administered as a qualification for office.
Article VII	States that the Constitution will become law when nine states have ratified it.

Checks and Balances

The Constitution was specifically designed so that no one branch of the government could establish tyranny over either of the other two branches. Each branch has checks on the power of the others.

- *Executive branch.* The president can veto congressional legislation. The president has the power to nominate Supreme Court justices.

- *Legislative branch.* Congress can override a presidential veto with a two-thirds vote of both houses, and can impeach a president, vice president, or Supreme Court justice for committing "high crimes or misdemeanors. Congress can also refuse to appoint a Supreme Court justice nominated by the president.

- *Judicial branch.* The Supreme Court can overturn congressional legislation that it deems unconstitutional. The chief justice presides over the impeachment of a president. Justices serve for life, under good behavior, and are therefore not subject to outside pressure to keep their seats on the bench.

- *The citizens.* The people have the power of their votes; they can refuse to reelect any president, senator, or representative whom they do not support. Additionally, a free press (guaranteed in 1791 in the First Amendment) is a popular check on the power of all three branches; it reports and comments on their proceedings, keeping the people informed and always reminding elected leaders, candidates for office, and prominent citizens that their actions will be made public.

The Struggle for Ratification

Elbridge Gerry of Massachusetts and Edmund J. Randolph and Thomas Paine of Virginia refused to sign the Constitution, feeling that it gave too much power to the central government. Their refusal foreshadowed the struggle for ratification that would end in the addition of ten amendments to the Constitution. These amendments are collectively known as the Bill of Rights.

Those who supported the Constitution were called Federalists because they had designed a federal government—one in which the national and state governments shared power and authority. Those who opposed the Constitution as originally written were known as the Antifederalists. Both sides took their case directly to the voters in pamphlets, speeches, and newspaper editorials.

The Antifederalists feared a repetition of what had happened between the colonies and Great Britain: that local interests would be ignored in favor of national ones, that a distant central government would ignore the people it had been designed to represent, and that smaller and weaker states would come under the sway of the larger, more powerful states. Above all, the Antifederalists stressed the fact that the Constitution said nothing about the rights of individual citizens.

James Madison had been the best-prepared delegate at the Constitutional Convention. He had shut himself up in his Virginia home for months before the convention, reading historical and political works as he considered what kind of government would best suit the United States. His detailed written notes of the debates in the Constitutional Convention have been a priceless record for historians to study ever since. Now Madison took pen in hand to defend the Constitution. Beginning in October 1787, a series of essays known collectively as the *Federalist Papers* began to appear in print. Signed with the name Publius, these essays presented a variety of reasoned arguments in favor of the Constitution. "Publius" was actually three men: Alexander Hamilton, wrote fifty-one of the essays, Madison, twenty-nine, and John Jay, five. The entire collection was published together in the spring of 1788.

By far the most famous of the *Federalist Papers* is number 10, written by Madison. In this essay, Publius discusses the danger of factions—what we today call "special-interest groups." He argued that the United States included so many factions that only a representative central government, in which all factions had an equal voice, could possibly succeed, as smaller local governments were bound to discriminate in favor of the majority. With so many diverse interests in the national government, Publius argued, there would be no danger of any one faction gaining a majority.

Ratification and Its Aftermath

By May 1788, eight of the nine necessary states had ratified the Constitution: Delaware, Pennsylvania, New Jersey, Georgia, Connecticut, Massachusetts, Maryland, and South Carolina. On June 21st, New Hampshire became the ninth state to ratify the Constitution, making it officially the law of the land.

Virginia was one of the largest and most powerful states; thus, its ratification was especially crucial to the success of the Constitution. After intense debate, Virginia ratified the Constitution with recommendations that it be amended. Led by Antifederalist Patrick Henry, those who opposed the Constitution offered the Congress a bill of rights and twenty suggested changes to the Constitution.

New Hampshire became the ninth state to ratify; Virginia and New York followed. On July 2, Congress announced that the Constitution had been ratified. On September 13, it called for the first national elections. As everyone had expected, George Washington was elected president. John Adams had come in second in the voting and was named vice president. George Washington took the oath of office on the steps of Federal Hall on Wall Street in New York, which was then the national capital. The first Congress of the United States, comprising 59 representatives and 22 senators, convened in New York in March, 1789.

The Bill of Rights

As the First Congress of the United States opened, James Madison immediately moved to begin work on a Bill of Rights. On September 9, Congress submitted twelve amendments to the states; ten of these were ratified and formally became part of the Constitution on December 15, 1791.

The Bill of Rights includes the following important individual rights and freedoms:

The Bill of Rights

First Amendment	Guarantees freedom of religion, freedom of speech, freedom of the press, freedom to peaceably assemble, and the right to petition the government for redress of grievances.
Second Amendment	States that the people have the right to keep and bear arms because a well-regulated militia is necessary to the state.
Third Amendment	Guarantees that private citizens cannot be forced to house soldiers in peacetime, and can be forced to house them in wartime only by the passage of laws to that effect.
Fourth Amendment	Protects the people against unreasonable search and seizure of personal property. Requires probable cause for the issue of a search warrant.
Fifth Amendment	Protects an accused criminal from self-incrimination; outlaws double jeopardy; requires a grand jury indictment for trial; requires due process of law.
Sixth Amendment	Guarantees a speedy and public trial by jury; requires that an accused criminal be told the charges against him and be confronted with the evidence, and guarantees him the right to present his own case and to legal representation.
Seventh Amendment	Requires a trial by jury in any case where the disputed value of property exceeds $20.
Eighth Amendment	Bans excessive bail and cruel or unusual punishment.
Ninth Amendment	States that listing certain rights in the Constitution does not imply that the people do not have other rights as well.
Tenth Amendment	States that any powers not delegated to the national government are reserved to the states, or to the people.

CHAPTER 8 QUIZ

1. **All of these leaders contributed to the** *Federalist Papers* **except** _____
   A. James Madison.
   B. Alexander Hamilton.
   C. Benjamin Franklin.
   D. John Jay.

2. **What power does the president have over the Supreme Court?**
   A. The president can veto legislation.
   B. The president can nominate justices.
   C. The president can appoint justices.
   D. The president can impeach justices if they commit crimes.

3. **In what way is a free press a check on the power of the government?**
   A. It keeps the people informed of the leaders' actions and decisions.
   B. It argues that individual citizens should be allowed to vote.
   C. It establishes the rights and freedoms of the citizens.
   D. It argues for compromise among various factions.

4. **A** *federal* **government is defined as one in which** _____
   A. the state governments have more power than the national government.
   B. the national government has more power than the state governments.
   C. the national and state governments share power equally.
   D. there is a national government but no state or local governments.

5. **The idea for a government with three branches, each with power over the other two, originally came from** _____
   A. ancient Rome.
   B. medieval Britain.
   C. the Enlightenment.
   D. Colonial custom and experience.

6. **How does the Great Compromise differ from earlier ideas for the national legislature?**
   A. It provides for a bicameral legislature.
   B. It requires proportional representation in both houses.
   C. It requires equal representation in both houses.
   D. It provides for proportional representation in one house and equal representation in the other.

7. The Antifederalists' greatest concern about the Constitution was that it did not _____
   A. provide for a balanced government.
   B. address the subject of individual rights.
   C. prevent the danger of factions taking power.
   D. treat the interests of all states impartially.

8. The First Amendment establishes all of the following except _____
   A. freedom of speech.
   B. freedom of the press.
   C. free exercise of religion.
   D. freedom from slavery.

9. All of these except _____ were important in shaping the thinking of the delegates at the Constitutional Convention.
   A. the Magna Carta
   B. *The Spirit of Laws*
   C. the English Bill of Rights
   D. the *Federalist Papers*

10. Proceedings of the Constitutional Convention were kept secret during the period of debate because the delegates _____
    A. did not want to be subjected to outside pressure to vote a certain way.
    B. knew that their work would be unpopular with their constituents.
    C. were afraid of provoking a popular uprising.
    D. knew that foreign spies might report their activities to other governments.

Chapter 9

Establishing a New Nation, 1788–1815

The first 25 years of the new nation were tumultuous. Many obstacles and challenges arose, some of which the framers of the Constitution had foreseen, others of which were unanticipated. During the first four presidential administrations, the nation began to take shape.

George Washington set a precedent for the isolationism that was to characterize American foreign policy for many decades afterward. Washington refused to involve the United States in the French Revolution, and upon leaving office in 1796, he warned his successors to avoid getting involved in foreign wars.

John Adams was the first president to represent a political party. He was the candidate of the Federalists, who believed in strong central government rather than government dominated by the states. Adams struggled successfully to maintain peace with France, at the cost of signing the Alien and Sedition Acts. Many people believed that these acts were unconstitutional because they infringed on individual liberties guaranteed in the Bill of Rights. Kentucky and Virginia passed resolutions declaring that states did not have to obey unconstitutional laws.

Thomas Jefferson became president in 1800; he doubled the size of the United States by purchasing the Louisiana Territory from France. Under Jefferson, the Supreme Court established the principle of judicial review, which gave the Court the right to decide whether a law was unconstitutional and, if so, to strike it down.

Under James Madison, war broke out between the American Indians and the United States. The U.S. troops defeated the Native-American confederation at the Battle of Tippecanoe. Soon after, the United States was plunged into war again, this time with Britain. In late 1814, the Treaty of Ghent ended the war, establishing an alliance with Britain that has continued uninterrupted to the present day.

CHAPTER OBJECTIVES

- Identify the first four presidents of the United States and describe the major events of their administrations.
- Describe the election of 1800 and explain the connection between it and the Twelfth Amendment.
- Describe notable early actions and decisions of the first Supreme Courts.

Chapter 9 Time Line

- **1788**   George Washington elected president
- **1791**   Bank of the United States
- **1794**   Whiskey Rebellion

    Battle of Fallen Timbers

    Jay's Treaty
- **1795**   Pinckney's Treaty
- **1796**   John Adams elected president
- **1798**   XYZ Affair

    Alien and Sedition Acts

    Virginia and Kentucky Resolutions
- **1800**   Thomas Jefferson elected president
- **1803**   *Marbury v. Madison*

    Louisiana Purchase
- **1804–1806**   Lewis and Clark expedition
- **1807**   Embargo Act

- **1808**   James Madison elected president
- **1812**   United States declares war on Britain
- **1815**   Battle of New Orleans

The Washington Administration

George Washington doubted his own ability to lead the new nation he had helped to create. He was not a profound political thinker like Adams, Jefferson, or Madison, and he knew it. However, he had a characteristic unique among all presidents who followed him—he was the universal choice of all the political leaders of the day. Washington commanded profound personal respect and affection from everyone who knew him and had worked with him. His popularity was an important unifying factor in the success of the new nation for its first eight years.

Washington's first action was to decide on the title by which the nation's chief executive should be addressed. His choice, "President of the United States," reassured everyone that the United States would never turn into a monarchy. The title was a simple one and reinforced the notion that the president was no more exalted than any other American citizen.

John Adams served as Washington's vice president. The first Supreme Court had a chief justice, John Jay, and five associate justices. The first presidential cabinet contained only five members, as follows:

- Secretary of State Thomas Jefferson
- Secretary of the Treasury Alexander Hamilton
- Secretary of War Henry Knox
- Attorney General Edmund Randolph
- Postmaster General Samuel Osgood

The Nation's Economy

Alexander Hamilton quickly achieved a prominent position in the administration. Hamilton believed in capitalism—the economic system preached by Scotsman Adam Smith, in which free-market competition determines wages and prices, and ownership of industries and businesses is in private hands. Hamilton's agreement with Smith's philosophy is largely responsible for the way the American economy took shape.

Hamilton's first challenge was to pay off the national debt, which had soared to $77 million because of the war. He felt that it was important to pay the debt rather than allowing it to mount, so that the nation would have good credit with the rest of the world. Hamilton's plan involved selling new bonds to pay off old ones. He also declared that the federal government should be responsible for debts the states currently owed. Since the southern states had already paid their debts, they protested, arguing that the northern states should be forced to pay too. Hamilton compromised with southern leaders by agreeing that the government would move the nation's capital to the South. They would build a new city, the District of Columbia, on a small parcel of land carved from the Maryland-Virginia border. For security reasons, and to prevent jealousy among the states, the capital would be a free city outside state borders. The new capital was renamed Washington, in honor of the first president. George Washington himself never lived in Washington, DC; when the district was marked off for the capital, it was nothing but farms and woodlands. The city, with the required government buildings, had yet to be planned and built.

Congress created the Bank of the United States in 1791. Its charter stated that it was to be jointly owned by the government and private investors, and that it would operate for 20 years. Congress also created a mint, which began to produce the first U.S. coins in 1792. Before this date, each state had printed its own currency.

Hamilton continued to cast about for ways to settle the government's debts. As many political leaders throughout history had done when in debt, he established new taxes. A new tax on whiskey provoked an uprising among farmers in western Pennsylvania; it would take away the handsome profits they had been making by turning their surplus grain crop into whiskey and trading it for supplies. When marshals tried to collect the tax from the Pennsylvania farmers, the farmers resisted. They attacked the officials and planned a march of about 6,000 men on Philadelphia, the nation's temporary capital. Washington called out the militia to put down the Whiskey Rebellion.

Foreign Policy

Meanwhile, the Indians in the Northwest Territory were fighting to defend their lands from the encroaching Americans. Led by Miami chief Michikinikwa ("Little Turtle"), more than 1,000 Indians of various nations banded together and soundly defeated the Americans in a battle along the Wabash River. Washington responded by sending a larger militia west and putting General Anthony

Wayne in charge. In 1794, the Americans defeated the Indians in the Battle of Fallen Timbers. In 1795, the Americans and Indians signed the Treaty of Greenville, which paid the tribes $20,000 for lands in the areas that would become Ohio and Indiana.

In 1789, revolution broke out in France. George Washington, believing that the U.S. army was unprepared to go overseas and fight, stated in 1793 that the United States would remain neutral. This decision was not popular either abroad or at home. The French resented it, since they had come to the Americans' aid during the American Revolution; many Americans opposed it for the same reason.

The British were also causing the new nation plenty of trouble. First, British ships frequently impressed Americans into service in the British navy. Second, Britain had seized a fleet of American ships in the West Indies, falsely claiming that those ships were trading with France. Third, the British were arming the Indians in the Northwest Territory against the Americans. Although the British agreed to abandon their North American forts in Jay's Treaty (1794), the practices of impressment and arming the tribes continued.

When Spain joined France against its longtime enemy Britain, the United States was able to sign Pinckney's Treaty with Spain. This treaty recognized the 31st parallel as the American border with Spanish Florida, and granted the United States navigation rights along the Mississippi River.

Washington was reelected easily in 1792. In 1796, he announced that he would retire at the end of his second term. On leaving office, he urged his successors to "observe good faith and justice toward all nations" but to "steer clear of permanent alliances with any portion of the foreign world."

Political Parties

The nation's first political parties developed during the Washington administration. Washington himself disapproved of political parties; he remains the only president in American history not to represent or belong to one. Factions—the seeds of all political parties—developed quickly around cabinet members Jefferson and Hamilton, who were at odds on most major issues during the administration. Hamilton believed in a strong central government; Jefferson felt that most powers should be left to the states and the people. Hamilton believed in encouraging business and industry; Jefferson felt that agriculture was the most important part of the economy. Hamilton argued that the Constitution had a built-in elastic clause so that laws could be changed or added to suit chang-ing times; Jefferson claimed to be a strict constructionist who believed in the letter of the Constitution. Hamilton wanted an alliance with Britain; Jefferson wanted an alliance with France. Hamilton's supporters called themselves Fed-eralists. Jefferson's adherents called themselves Democratic-Republicans.

The Adams Administration

John Adams, who supported the Federalist view, was elected president in 1796. In a twist of fate, Jefferson, despite being a member of the opposing party, won the second-highest total of votes and thus became vice president. Although Adams and Jefferson had become close friends during the battle for Ameri-can independence, their political differences placed a severe strain on their friendship.

Adams had never been popular among his colleagues. Where Jefferson was silent and reserved, Adams was combative and forthright—an undiplomatic diplomat and a politician who did not know how to play political games. He was known as a warm and loyal friend, his integrity and honesty were agreed to be unimpeachable, and he was intellectually brilliant. However, his blunt outspokenness earned him the dislike of many of the leaders in government.

Foreign Policy

In protest against Jay's Treaty, France had begun seizing American ships in the West Indies. Wanting to avoid war with France if possible, Adams sent diplomats to France to negotiate a settlement. Three French agents asked the American diplomats to pay France's foreign minister a heavy bribe and to lend France $10 million before any negotiations. When Adams informed the Con-gress of this demand, he referred to the French agents as X, Y, and Z, rather than revealing their names. The XYZ Affair turned public opinion even further against France.

Deciding that the best chance to maintain peace lay in a show of strength, Adams ordered a major buildup of the navy. The ploy worked; French foreign minister Talleyrand, alarmed at the prospect of an all-out naval war with the United States, agreed that France would stop seizing American ships. Soon after, American diplomats signed a peace agreement with Napoleon. The issue of relations with France divided the Federalists; many supported Adams's desire to maintain peace, but others had hoped for war and considered that the president had made the United States look weak.

The low point of the Adams administration came with the passage of the Alien and Sedition Acts. These acts, passed by Congress in 1798, allowed the president to deport any foreigner thought to be dangerous to the country, and made it illegal to speak or act against the government. Many people thought that these acts infringed on the liberties they were guaranteed under the Bill of Rights. Jefferson and Madison, who found the acts outrageous, were instrumental in writing the Kentucky and Virginia Resolutions. These state laws, passed in 1798 and 1799, claimed that a state could not be forced to obey a federal law if the law were unconstitutional.

The Alien and Sedition Acts are important because they marked the first time that an American president, balancing the apparently opposing interests of civil liberty and national security, opted for security. The late 1790s were a period of unrest in the United States; war threatened with both France and Britain. In times of unrest or all-out war, leaders have often found it necessary to curtail certain civil liberties in the interest of national security. This would happen time and time again in American history; Adams was only the first of several presidents to take such a step.

The Election of 1800

In the election of 1800, Jefferson and Aaron Burr were the Democratic-Republican candidates, President Adams and Charles Pinckney the Federalists. When the election resulted in a tie between Jefferson and Burr, responsibility for choosing the new president was passed to the House of Representatives. In thirty-five rounds of voting, the House failed to break the tie, at which point Alexander Hamilton took a hand in the proceedings. Hamilton had never agreed with Jefferson's politics, but he disliked and distrusted Burr much more; he therefore persuaded several of the electors to vote for Jefferson, thus swinging the election to him. Later in the session, Congress passed the Twelfth Amendment, which altered the electoral procedure, preventing further crises of this kind. (Personal relations between Burr and Hamilton did not improve; four years after the election, Burr shot and killed Hamilton in a duel.)

Before Adams left office, he took steps to secure the Federalist position in the government. He signed the Judiciary Act of 1801, which created a number of new circuit courts and federal judgeships, then appointed many Federalists to the bench on the night before his term ended. Since Jefferson was of the opposing political party, these "midnight appointments" struck him as a personal insult, and he and Adams would not resume their friendship for several years. Some time after both had retired from politics, Adams wrote a friendly letter to Jefferson, who eagerly responded; the two men continued a lively correspondence for the rest of their lives. In an odd historical coincidence, both men died on July 4, 1826, the fiftieth anniversary of the signing of the Declaration of Independence, whose adoption both had done so much to bring about.

The most significant of Adams's last-minute legal appointments was that of Supreme Court Chief Justice John Marshall, who was to serve more than thirty years and establish many important legal precedents. The most important of these was judicial review, established in a case called *Marbury v. Madison*. Marbury was one of the last-minute judges appointed by Adams; Jefferson ordered Madison, his secretary of state, to forbid Marbury to serve. Marbury sued Madison. The Supreme Court ruled against Marbury on the grounds that the Judiciary Act of 1801 was unconstitutional. This set the precedent for the Court to determine the legality of laws passed by Congress—an important judicial check on the power of the legislative branch.

The Jefferson Administration

The Louisiana Purchase

Jefferson's most important act as president was to double the size of the nation by purchasing the Louisiana Territory from France. With no power base in the West Indies, Napoleon knew that he could never extend the French empire in the Western Hemisphere. He decided to sell his territory and use the funds to expand his power base in Europe. James Monroe, acting as Jefferson's envoy, agreed to purchase the land for Napoleon's price—$15 million, or about four cents per acre.

The Constitution made no provision for a president to spend government money to expand the size of the nation's holdings. This shows that Jefferson acknowledged the justice of Hamilton's position—that the Constitution was an elastic document that was subject to interpretation.

In May 1804, Meriwether Lewis and William Clark set out from St. Louis with a party of guides and explorers, carrying written instructions from President Jefferson. First, they were to seek a water route across the continent to the Pacific Ocean. Second, they were to establish friendly relations with the Ameri-

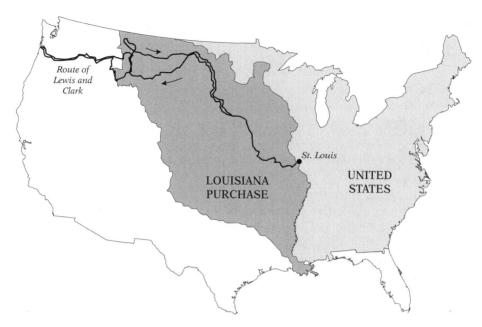

The Louisiana Purchase and the route of Lewis & Clark

can Indians who lived in the territory. Third, they would catalogue examples of unfamiliar plants and animals. Fourth, they would map the territory. Last, they would keep detailed written records of everything they observed and experienced.

The explorers and their guides and companions traveled slowly, following the course of the rivers in a northwesterly direction almost all the way to the Canadian border, where they turned west. On November 7, 1805, the Pacific Ocean came into sight. Lewis and Clark had learned that it was not possible to cross the continent by river without going overland for a part of the way. This issue was highly important for trade, because water was by far the fastest and most efficient way to transport goods. Over land, goods could move only as fast as a team of horses could walk; boats and ships were much faster and less vulnerable to robbery.

While Lewis and Clark and their party followed the rivers westward, Zebulon Pike was exploring and mapping the Mississippi Valley. He traveled west as far as the Rockies, where Pike's Peak was later named in his honor. When Pike ventured along the Rio Grande, the Spaniards who claimed that territory arrested him. They eventually released him, but they kept the written records of his discoveries. However, Pike recalled enough information to write a report that increased the United States' knowledge of the Southwest.

THE MYTH

The Shoshone Indian woman Sacagawea acted as guide and interpreter to the Lewis and Clark expedition.

THE FACTS

Sacagawea was the wife of Toussaint Charbonneau, a French Canadian trapper and guide traveling with the expedition. Because Sacagawea knew only Shoshone languages, she could not understand the speech of most other tribes the expedition encountered, and therefore was of minimal value as an interpreter.

Sacagawea did play two crucial roles on the expedition. First, she facilitated friendly contact between whites and Indians; the presence of a young Shoshone woman in the party appeared to the tribes to guarantee that the white men were trustworthy. Second, she rescued the captains' journals—the invaluable written record of the expedition—when a boat capsized one day on what is now the Sacagawea River.

The Embargo Act

British sailors, claiming to be searching for deserters from their own ship, had tried to board the USS *Chesapeake*; the Americans, wary of any contact with British ships because of their practice of impressment, refused permission. The British crew opened fire on the *Chesapeake*, killing three Americans and impressing four others.

Jefferson's response was to sign the Embargo Act of 1807, halting many American exports. He reasoned that if there were no American ships on the high seas, piracy and British impressment would cease. Jefferson soon realized that his intentions had backfired; the Embargo Act deprived farmers and manufacturers of the market for their goods, and exports fell to one-fifth of previous levels. The Embargo Act was repealed in 1809. The Non-Intercourse Act of 1809 prohibited trade with Britain and France, but allowed it to continue with all other nations. Like the Embargo Act, it was ineffective.

The Madison Administration

In 1808, James Madison became president with a large plurality of electoral votes. A Democratic-Republican and an ally of Jefferson's, Madison had worked harder than anyone to shape the Constitution; he is considered its "father," or most important author. Madison meticulously recorded the debates over the Constitution, providing historians with a valuable record of the framers' original intentions. He also wrote about one-third of the *Federalist Papers*, which did so much to persuade the public to support the Constitution during the ratification period.

Almost immediately, Madison found himself faced with troubles along the western frontier. Tecumseh, a Shawnee chief, had forged an alliance among Indian nations. He believed that if all of the tribes united against the common enemy, the United States, they might prevail and win back their lands.

On November 7, 1811, General William Henry Harrison and his troops fought the tribes at the American camp on the Tippecanoe River in Indiana Territory. The Battle of Tippecanoe ended in defeat for the Indians and the death of their attempt at a national Indian confederation. Senators Henry Clay of Kentucky and John C. Calhoun of South Carolina led an immediate public outcry for war against Britain—the nation that had supported the Indian enemies and supplied them with weapons. In 1812, Madison asked the Congress to declare war.

War on land was not successful, because the Congress had been reluctant to spend money on equipping and paying the army. However, the navy had benefited from a buildup during the Adams administration and was well prepared for war. Sea battles and raids in the Great Lakes, the Caribbean, and around the British isles brought many victories to the Americans.

The British attacked Washington, DC, in August 1814. First Lady Dolley Madison famously escaped from the White House only hours before the British troops burst through the front doors. The British moved south, attacking Baltimore's Fort McHenry. Watching the battle, prisoner of war Francis Scott Key wrote the poem that would later become the lyrics of the American national anthem. The British lost the battle and prepared for a final strike against New Orleans. General Andrew Jackson had prepared a line of earthen embankments, protected by strategically positioned cannons. The British invasion of January 8, 1815, resulted in a decisive American victory. Shortly before the battle, U.S. and British representatives had signed the Treaty of Ghent. Word of the successful treaty negotiations reached the White House at about the same time as the news of the victory at New Orleans.

The War of 1812 had both positive and negative effects on the United States. On the one hand, it strengthened U.S. control over the Northwest Territory. The Treaty of Ghent established friendly relations between Britain and the

United States that have lasted to the present day. On the other hand, the war had divided the nation. New England Federalists opposed the war so strongly that, in a meeting called the Hartford Convention, they discussed seceding from the Union and negotiating a separate peace with Britain. The majority voted instead for a constitutional amendment limiting the powers of Congress and the southern states. When the news of the Treaty of Ghent reached America, Hartford Convention participants were accused of treason. The Federalist Party broke up a few years afterward.

CHAPTER 9 QUIZ

1. _____ is considered the father of the Constitution.
   A. George Washington
   B. John Adams
   C. Alexander Hamilton
   D. James Madison

2. The War of 1812 resulted in a lasting alliance between _____
   A. the United States and the Indians.
   B. Britain and France.
   C. the United States and Britain.
   D. the United States and France.

3. What was the major issue that caused the War of 1812?
   A. the Indian attempt to create a national alliance
   B. the Indian attempt to rebel against the U.S. government
   C. the British alliance with and support of the American Indians
   D. the British practice of impressment

4. The purpose of the Embargo Act was _____
   A. to provoke Britain into a declaration of war.
   B. to curtail exports to Britain or any of its dominions.
   C. to deprive farmers of profits from their surplus crops.
   D. to put a stop to the practice of impressment.

5. **Which best explains the principle of judicial review?**
   A. the power of the courts to decide whether a law is constitutional
   B. the power of the president to appoint judges
   C. the power of Congress to impeach judges
   D. the power of the states to repeal unconstitutional federal laws

6. **Why was the nation's capital city built in the South?**
   A. because the South has a milder climate than the North
   B. because the location chosen was in the center of the United States
   C. to appease Southern resentment over federal payment of northern war debt
   D. to ensure that the capital city would be outside the borders of the states

7. **What was the purpose of the Twelfth Amendment?**
   A. to permit the government to assess certain taxes
   B. to regulate international trade
   C. to change the electoral system
   D. to establish political parties

8. **_____ is the only American president not to belong to or represent a political party.**
   A. George Washington
   B. John Adams
   C. Thomas Jefferson
   D. James Madison

9. **In order to pay off the national debt, Alexander Hamilton _____**
   A. established the Federalist Party.
   B. planned a new national capital city.
   C. threw the election of 1800 to Thomas Jefferson.
   D. assessed new taxes.

10. **Thomas Jefferson believed that _____ was the most important part of the economy.**
    A. agriculture
    B. private enterprise
    C. industry
    D. international trade

PART I EXAM

1. **What do James Madison, Alexander Hamilton, and John Jay all have in common?**
   A. They all signed the Declaration of Independence.
   B. They are all authors of the *Federalist Papers*.
   C. They all served in President Washington's cabinet.
   D. They were all presidents of the United States.

2. **Which was the first nation to establish settled colonies in North America?**
   A. England
   B. France
   C. Germany
   D. Spain

3. **Church officials considered Jonathan Edwards's teachings unorthodox and dangerous because he suggested that _____**
   A. salvation was predetermined before a person's birth.
   B. Christians should confess their sins and repent publicly.
   C. an individual could play an active role in his or her own salvation.
   D. people needed to attend church only when the spirit moved them.

4. **In the months following the Battle of Brooklyn (1776), the American army _____**
   A. steadily retreated north through Connecticut and Massachusetts.
   B. steadily retreated south through New Jersey and Pennsylvania.
   C. drove the British south into Virginia.
   D. drove the British west into the Ohio River Valley.

5. **What was the basic purpose of the Intolerable Acts?**
   A. to establish a standing army in the colonies
   B. to punish Massachusetts for acts of civil disobedience
   C. to establish a state of war between Britain and the colonies
   D. to tax the colonies without their consent

6. **What was the purpose of the Three-Fifths Compromise?**
   A. to determine each state's population
   B. to decide how many states must ratify the Constitution
   C. to determine the number of representatives per state
   D. to decide how many new states could join the United States

7. Thomas Hooker's stance on _____ made him leave New England to found the colony of New Haven.
   A. economic opportunity
   B. slavery
   C. women's rights
   D. the separation of church and state

8. _____ organized the Boston Tea Party.
   A. The First Continental Congress
   B. The Sons of Liberty
   C. The Boston merchants
   D. The royal governor of Massachusetts

9. Which was not a factor in the states' decision to include the right of religious self-determination in their constitutions?
   A. The population of each state already represented several religions and sects.
   B. The lesson of the Salem witch trials had proved the need for the separation of church and state.
   C. Few of the American political leaders were religiously observant.
   D. The desire for independence, including religious independence, was very strong throughout the colonies.

10. The Preamble to the Constitution embodies which principle?
    A. checks and balances
    B. majority rule
    C. taxation without representation
    D. government by the consent of the governed

11. The first human beings to settle the North America emigrated from _____
    A. Africa.
    B. Asia.t
    C. Europe.
    D. the Pacific islands.

12. The Declaration and Resolves of the First Continental Congress demanded all these things except _____
    A. that the British army of occupation return to England.
    B. that Parliament recognize the legitimacy of the local Colonial governments.
    C. that each colony establish its own militia for purposes of self-defense.
    D. that Britain recognize Colonial independence.

13. **Why did the colonists feel free to ignore the Navigation Acts of 1650?**
    A. They did not understand what the acts required.
    B. They had had no say in the wording or passage of the acts.
    C. They denied Britain's authority to regulate Colonial trade.
    D. They could export American goods only to certain nations.

14. **Britain and France went to war in North America over conflicting claims to _____**
    A. the Ohio River Valley area.
    B. the city of New Orleans, Louisiana.
    C. territory west of the Mississippi River.
    D. the colonies along the Atlantic coast.

15. **In *The Spirit of Laws*, _____ was the first person to outline a government of multiple branches with checks and balances.**
    A. John Locke
    B. the Baron de Montesquieu
    C. Thomas Jefferson
    D. James Madison

16. **_____ is an important historical figure because he wrote the influential pamphlet *Common Sense*.**
    A. Thomas Jefferson
    B. Thomas Paine
    C. Benjamin Franklin
    D. John Dickinson

17. **_____ suggested that the colonies establish their own branch of Parliament, whose president would be appointed by the British monarch.**
    A. The Galloway Plan of Union
    B. The Declaration and Resolves
    C. The Articles of Confederation
    D. The Bill of Rights

18. **_____ is a common factor in all American Indian cultures.**
    A. Respect for the natural environment
    B. A migratory lifestyle
    C. Distrust of strangers to the tribe
    D. Active intertribal trade

19. Why did the British government believe that the colonists would purchase British tea imported from India?
    A. It was not covered by the Townshend Acts.
    B. It was brought into the colonies legally.
    C. It was the least expensive tea available in the colonies.
    D. It did not carry any import duty or tax.

20. The Articles of Confederation established which of the following?
    A. a strong central government
    B. a national judiciary
    C. a chief executive officer for the nation
    D. a legislative assembly

21. All these people were prominent religious dissenters in Colonial New England except _____
    A. Anne Hutchinson.
    B. Thomas Hooker.
    C. William Penn.
    D. Roger Williams.

22. The First Continental Congress met in order to _____
    A. discuss declaring American independence from Great Britain.
    B. agree on a united response to the Intolerable Acts.
    C. appoint a commander in chief and raise an army.
    D. choose a delegation to argue the Colonial case before Parliament.

23. The British acquired the colony of New York in 1664, when they _____
    A. purchased it from the Lenape tribe.
    B. invaded it and took it from the Dutch settlers.
    C. signed a treaty with the occupying French settlers.
    D. sailed the *Mayflower* into New York Harbor.

24. The United States is most accurately defined as _____
    A. a democracy.
    B. a republic.
    C. a union of independent republics.
    D. a commonwealth of independent states.

25. **Which best describes the primary European motive for seeking new trade routes by sailing west?**
    A. Europeans were eager to trade in American goods.
    B. Europeans were curious to see the New World.
    C. Existing overland trade routes were slow and dangerous.
    D. Traders were eager to convert Asians to Christianity.

26. **Which document first established the British principle of taxation by general consent of the people?**
    A. the Constitution
    B. the Magna Carta
    C. the Stamp Act
    D. the Articles of Confederation

27. **One reason that the fur trade caused long-term problems for the Indians was that _____**
    A. it changed their style of warfare.
    B. it made them disband the Iroquois Confederacy.
    C. it eroded their lifetime habits of self-sufficiency.
    D. it gave them access to sophisticated tools and weapons.

28. ***Common Sense* was enthusiastically received throughout the colonies because _____**
    A. it suggested that the colonists should dismiss the British army of occupation.
    B. it recommended that the colonies begin an all-out war with Britain.
    C. it petitioned the British monarch for a redress of grievances.
    D. it criticized any system of government based on birth rather than merit.

29. **In the early 1600s, low-church Anglicans left England for Holland primarily because _____**
    A. they were socially ostracized in England.
    B. they wanted to sail for the New World.
    C. they were not permitted to worship as they pleased in England.
    D. they preferred Dutch customs and the Dutch culture to their own.

30. **The Constitution replaced the _____**
    A. Galloway Plan of Union.
    B. Articles of Confederation.
    C. Declaration and Resolves.
    D. Bill of Rights.

31. _____ was the first major event that united people of different colonies against a common enemy.
    A. The Boston Tea Party
    B. The publication of *Common Sense*
    C. The French and Indian War
    D. The Great Awakening

32. The structure of the federal government is based on the principle of _____
    A. universal suffrage.
    B. inalienable rights.
    C. the separation of powers.
    D. hereditary rule.

33. What was the purpose of the *Federalist Papers*?
    A. to persuade readers to support ratification of the Constitution
    B. to persuade delegates to sign the Declaration of Independence
    C. to argue against ratification of the Constitution
    D. to argue that the Articles of Confederation should be replaced

34. The primary threat to the earliest British attempts at establishing permanent settlements in North America was _____
    A. the American Indians.
    B. the French.
    C. the climate.
    D. the government.

35. The Fourth through Eighth amendments to the Constitution all address _____
    A. the rights of suspected or accused criminals.
    B. the basic freedoms of the citizens in everyday life.
    C. the procedure for electing the president of the United States.
    D. the responsibilities of Congress.

36. Delegates to the Constitutional Convention kept their debates secret in order to avoid _____
    A. newspaper coverage.
    B. outside political pressure.
    C. accusations of treason.
    D. foreign spies.

37. Which best describes the purpose of the Mayflower Compact?
    A. to create a governing body for Plymouth Colony
    B. to list the passengers who sailed on the *Mayflower*
    C. to establish peace between the colonists and the American Indians
    D. to declare Plymouth Colony's independence from British rule

38. The French and Indian War worsened relations between Britain and the colonists because _____
    A. the British army made no effort to win the war.
    B. the British army scorned the American soldiers and officers.
    C. the Indians refused to fight on the British side.
    D. the Americans were unable to win a single battle.

39. _____ was a direct appeal to King George III to mediate between Parliament and the colonies.
    A. *Common Sense*
    B. *The Spirit of Laws*
    C. The Olive Branch Petition
    D. The Declaration and Resolves

40. Disagreement over the issue of _____ was the major obstacle to ratification of the Articles of Confederation.
    A. slavery
    B. territorial claims
    C. taxation
    D. proportional representation

41. In the decades before the French and Indian War, control of the Mississippi River was key to _____
    A. the British Colonial merchants.
    B. the British standing army.
    C. the Spanish Catholic missionaries.
    D. the French fur trade.

42. As a check on the power of the legislative branch of the federal government, the judicial branch can _____
    A. impeach the president.
    B. overturn legislation that it deems unconstitutional.
    C. serve for life under good behavior.
    D. remove a justice from the Supreme Court.

43. **As a result of the French and Indian War, Britain gained _____**

    A. the colony of New Orleans.

    B. the Louisiana Territory.

    C. certain Caribbean islands.

    D. Canada.

44. **In 1787, Daniel Shays led an armed rebellion over the issue of _____**

    A. political unification.

    B. taxation.

    C. slavery.

    D. food shortages.

45. **Which best describes the relationship between Pilgrims and Puritans?**

    A. Pilgrims were more extreme than other Puritans.

    B. Puritans were more extreme than other Pilgrims.

    C. Puritans believed in the separation of church and state, but Pilgrims did not.

    D. Pilgrims believed in the separation of church and state, but Puritans did not.

46. **Which of the following was freely elected by the voters, according to the Constitution as originally written?**

    A. the president

    B. members of the Senate

    C. members of the House of Representatives

    D. the chief justice of the Supreme Court

47. **_____ caused the French and Indian War.**

    A. Rival British and French claims to the same territory

    B. Hostility between the British colonists and the Indians

    C. Hostility between the French traders and the Indians

    D. Religious differences between the French and British settlers

48. **The Battle of Concord was immediately followed by _____**

    A. the passage of the Declaration of Independence.

    B. the withdrawal of the American army to Valley Forge.

    C. the siege of the British army in Boston.

    D. the Virginia resolution in Congress.

49. **The primary purpose of the Albany Plan of Union was** _____
    A. to unite the colonies for their mutual defense.
    B. to declare independence from Great Britain.
    C. to set up a national legislative assembly.
    D. to establish a unified national currency.

50. **The colony of** _____ **was specifically founded as an exercise in religious self-determination and equal rights for all.**
    A. New Jersey
    B. Massachusetts
    C. Pennsylvania
    D. Plymouth

PART II

Nineteenth-Century U.S. History

Chapter 10

The Early Nineteenth Century, 1793–1838

The first quarter of the nineteenth century ushered in sweeping changes in the way Americans lived and worked. The Industrial Revolution, westward migration and expansion, the rise to power of Andrew Jackson, and changes in Indian and foreign policy all affected American society.

The Industrial Revolution in America began in 1793, with the invention of the cotton gin. This machine could process as much cotton in one day as 1,000 slaves; southern planters found that it multiplied their profits tenfold. The invention of the steamboat, which could sail upstream against the current, made it possible to move huge boatloads of cotton north; this gave rise to the textile industry in New England. The steamboat and the building of the National Road to Illinois also made it easier for settlers to migrate west in record numbers. With the takeover of Florida from Spain and the admission of several new states, the nation was growing rapidly.

The Monroe Doctrine of 1823, conceived by Secretary of State John Quincy Adams, effectively stopped Europe from taking any further steps to gain power bases in the Western Hemisphere. First, it stated that the United States would regard any further attempt at European colonization in the Western Hemisphere, or any European attempt to retake a colony that had declared itself independent, as a threat against the United States itself. Second, it avoided alienating its European allies by stating that the United States would remain neutral in any conflict between a European nation and such colonies as currently existed.

The election of Andrew Jackson in 1828 marked a new era in politics. Jackson was the first son of recent immigrants and the first "man of the people" elected to the presidency. He was the first to appoint people of similarly humble origins to top posts in his administration. He was the first president to represent the new Democratic Party.

Jackson's most notable action as president was the forced expulsion of American Indians from the United States. He declared publicly that it was for the tribes' protection; the true motive was to push the Indians out to make way for American settlers. The southeastern tribes who were the target of the Indian Removal Act resisted, even fighting the Second Seminole War against U.S. troops, but to no avail. In 1838, the last of them were marched under federal guard to Oklahoma along the "Trail of Tears."

CHAPTER OBJECTIVES

- Identify the major inventions of the Industrial Revolution and their effect on the U.S. economy.
- Describe the major events of the Monroe, John Quincy Adams, and Jackson administrations.
- Explain what happened to American Indians during the Jackson administration.
- Identify the Missouri Compromise and the Monroe Doctrine and analyze their effects.

Chapter 10 Time Line

- 1793   Cotton gin
- 1807   First practical steamboat
- 1815–1819   Great Migration

1816   Election of James Monroe
        Era of Good Feelings

1818   Rush-Bagot Agreement

1819   Adams-Onís Treaty

1820   Missouri Compromise

1823   Monroe Doctrine

1824   Election of John Quincy Adams

1828   Election of Andrew Jackson

1830   Indian Removal Act

1838   Trail of Tears

The Monroe Administration

With the collapse of the Federalist Party and the election of Democratic-Republican James Monroe in 1816, the Era of Good Feelings began. For the first time in American politics, partisan fighting was at a minimum.

Foreign Policy

President Monroe's first concern was to put relations with Britain on a sound footing after the American victory in the War of 1812. Since peace in the Great Lakes region would benefit both Britain and the United States, Monroe's desire for disarmament in that region found a favorable reception in Britain. First, the Rush-Bagot Agreement of 1818 strictly limited the number of warships in the Great Lakes. Second, the U.S.-Canadian border was established at the 49th parallel. Third, Britain and the United States agreed that they would both occupy Oregon Country until 1828, at which time they would set boundaries.

The United States had been watching the series of colonial rebellions in Latin America with interest, as it watched every revolution of a colony against its mother country. Although the United States took no active part in these rebellions, its sympathies were with the rebels. Monroe knew that the European powers would help Spain retake its colonies if they could. In an 1823 speech to Congress, he stated that the United States would remain neutral in any conflict between a Latin American colony and its European mother country. However, the United States would regard any attack on an independent Latin American republic or any further attempts to colonize the Western Hemisphere as an attack on the United States itself:

> With the existing colonies or dependencies of any European power we have not interfered and shall not interfere. . . . It is impossible that the allied powers [of Europe] should extend their political system to any portion of either continent [North or South America] without endangering our peace and happiness. . . . It is equally impossible, therefore, that we should behold such interposition in any form with indifference.

This statement, the terms of which had largely been worked out by Secretary of State John Quincy Adams, became known as the Monroe Doctrine.

Most Americans supported the Monroe Doctrine, although there were those who viewed it with concern, fearing that it would force the United States to become involved in wars outside its borders. The effect of the Monroe Doctrine was what the administration had hoped: European nations made no further efforts to colonize in the Western Hemisphere.

Territorial Expansion

At this time, Spain claimed Florida Territory, which was much larger than the present-day state of Florida; it included parts of present-day Alabama, Mississippi, and Louisiana. Taking advantage of a period when Spain was trying to quell colonial rebellions in South America, the United States annexed West Florida with little difficulty. In the First Seminole War, General Andrew Jackson and his troops put down Seminole Indian uprisings against American claims to West Florida. Jackson exceeded his commission, commanding his troops to seize Spanish forts in East Florida. When he ordered the military execution of two British officials, European leaders condemned the United States. President Monroe did not punish Jackson, but he did return the captured forts to Spain. Monroe and John Quincy Adams argued that if the Spaniards could not control the Seminole population, they must give their rights to Florida to the United States. Unable to match American military force, Spain ceded Florida to the United States in the Adams-Onís Treaty of 1819.

The Great Migration

Between 1805 and 1815, the United States suffered an economic depression. The fall in prices and rise in unemployment came about because the Napoleonic Wars resulted in fewer European buyers for American goods. With no foreign buyers for its cotton, the South was on the point of economic collapse.

With the return of peace in Europe and the northeastern shift from trade to manufacturing, markets opened again and profits soared. The U.S. government offered frontier land grants to veterans to encourage settlement of the West. Between 1815 and 1819, the Great Migration saw record numbers of Americans moving west from New York, Tennessee, Kentucky, and Ohio into Illinois and Indiana. Improved transportation, such as the building of the Cumberland (National) Road, helped make this possible. This paved road, originally a trail blazed by General Edward Braddock in 1755, led westward from Baltimore; by the time it was completed, it stretched all the way to Vandalia, Illinois. The National Road eased the Great Migration, even providing connections with flatboats that allowed settlers to travel down the Ohio River into the Mississippi Valley. It also constituted a trade route on which goods were transported in both directions. Today, the National Road is U.S. Route 40. The Great Migration ended with the Panic of 1819 (see Chapter 12). The former trading posts along the National Road became important manufacturing cities.

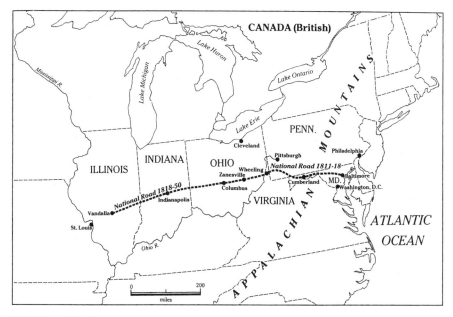

The National Road

The Industrial Revolution

The Industrial Revolution began in Britain around the 1730s, spreading across Europe after the end of the Napoleonic Wars. In the United States, the Industrial Revolution began toward the end of the eighteenth century. This era brought vast changes to a western world that had, in some respects, changed very little over all the preceding centuries. People had always depended largely on the land for survival; both everyday and luxury goods were made one item at a time, by hand; and the key to the economy was the success or failure of the harvest.

With the invention of machines and the beginning of mass production, everything changed. Machines changed the way farmers sowed and harvested their crops. New methods of transportation changed the way crops were taken to market and expanded markets into new territory. Machines made it possible for people to assemble many products simultaneously. Mass production made goods available more cheaply than before.

The invention of the cotton gin in 1793 revolutionized the southern economy. Cotton was a labor-intensive crop because the seeds and fibers had to be separated by hand after the cotton was picked. Eli Whitney of Massachusetts invented a machine ("gin" was short for "engine") that could comb the seeds from cotton fibers automatically. In one day, the cotton gin could process as much cotton as 1,000 slaves could process by hand. By 1800, the cotton yield was 20 times what it had been before the invention of the cotton gin.

The steamboat was another invention that changed the cotton industry. America's many rivers provided an excellent "highway" system for trade by flatboat. The trouble was that flatboats had to be propelled by human power, and it was very difficult to pilot them upstream, against the gravitational flow of the water. In 1807, Robert Fulton of New York unveiled the first practical steam-powered boat, the *Clermont*. Regular steamboat service on the Ohio and Mississippi rivers began in 1811. Steamboats allowed the southern cotton growers to transport their cotton north to the textile mills in a fraction of the time it had taken by flatboat.

For slaves, the combination of the cotton gin and the steamboat spelled disaster. Slavery had begun to decline; it had been outlawed in the North and was proving unprofitable in the South. It cost money to purchase, house, feed, and maintain a large slave population, and no matter how many slaves a plantation had, the work still took time. With the invention of the cotton gin, however, slavery suddenly became profitable again, both for southern plantation owners and for northern textile-mill owners. The rise in profits made some northerners begin to drop their outspoken objections to slavery. However, the issue continued to be a political bone of contention between North and South; the North did not want the South to expand its political power base, and a slowly growing number of northerners continued to object to slavery on ethical grounds.

The Spread of Slavery and the Missouri Compromise

As territories were settled and applied to Congress for statehood, Congress had to debate whether each one would be a slaveholding state or a free state. The issue was representation in Congress, especially in the House of Representatives. Slaveholding states generally voted as one bloc in Congress; naturally, they wanted new states to be slave states so that new senators and representatives would vote with their bloc. For the same reason, free states did not want slavery to spread any farther than it already had. Up to 1819, the balance of power in the Senate had been maintained evenly, with eleven free states and eleven slaveholding states. However, there was an imbalance in the House, where states were represented on the basis of the total population.

Because southern representatives in the House were all white men, and because the most powerful interests in their states were large slaveholders (many of the representatives themselves owned slaves), they all favored slavery. In other words, congressmen from slaveholding states represented the slaves for the purpose of head count only; southern representatives actually voted against the slaves' interests. Northerners opposed the expansion of slavery because of this overrepresentation of white southern interests. (Northern representatives were also all white men, but many of them opposed slavery.)

In 1819, Missouri applied for statehood; its population then included about 10,000 African slaves. Congressman James Tallmage of New York pointed out that Missouri was in violation of the Northwest Ordinance of 1787, which had banned slavery in all U.S. territories. (See Chapter 7.) He proposed admitting Missouri to the Union on condition that it adopt a plan for the gradual phasing out of slavery. Southern representatives, seeing this as a threat to slavery throughout the United States, reacted violently. Henry Clay eventually worked out the Missouri Compromise, which maintained the balance of power in Congress by admitting Missouri as a slave state and Maine as a free state. The

Missouri Compromise also banned slavery in the territory north of Missouri's southern boundary (excluding Missouri itself) at latitude 36°30'. The Missouri Compromise silenced the divide over the issue of slavery for the moment, but it solved nothing; it was only a palliative. The deep division over this issue would continue to haunt American society for many decades.

During this era, voting rights began changing. States began to amend their constitutions, dropping the requirement that voters own property. This nearly doubled the number of eligible voters between 1836 and 1840. At the same time, some southern states revoked the voting rights of free African-American men, turning suffrage into a "whites only" privilege.

John Quincy Adams

With the support of Henry Clay, John Quincy Adams won the presidency in 1824. This son of former President John Adams had literally spent a lifetime in government circles. As a young man, he had served his country as a diplomat, traveling as far away as Russia. As secretary of state under James Monroe, he had negotiated the acquisition of Florida from Spain and conceived the Monroe Doctrine. Like his father, Adams was not personally popular, although for different reasons; the elder Adams had been too outspoken and warmly argumentative, while the younger was aloof, cold, and haughty. Despite his enormous intellectual achievements and the breadth of his vision for the nation, Adams served only one term as president, losing the 1828 election to the wildly popular war hero Andrew Jackson. The people of Massachusetts elected Adams to the U.S. Senate in 1830; he served there with distinction for 18 years, becoming well known throughout the nation as an abolitionist. After leaving the White House, Adams served his country quite literally for the rest of his life; he died in the Senate chamber in 1848.

The Jackson Administration

Andrew Jackson won the presidential election of 1828, partly as the result of what is known today as "negative campaigning." After the 1824 election, Jackson started a rumor that Henry Clay and John Quincy Adams had made "a corrupt bargain" to win the presidency for Adams; he argued that Clay had thrown his support to Adams in exchange for being chosen secretary of state.

This rumor tarnished both Adams and Clay's reputations in spite of their denials, and Jackson was easily swept to victory in 1828.

Jackson was neither a New England intellectual like the Adamses nor a Virginia planter like Jefferson, Madison, and Washington. The son of recent Scottish immigrants, Jackson was born in a log cabin in Tennessee; he was the first "man of the people" to be elected to high office. He was the first president to appoint people from backgrounds like his own to administrative posts, rather than believing that governments should be run by the wealthy or by the educated. Jackson believed that personal merit, not social rank, was the only necessary requirement for holding political office. Popular among voters both for his "common touch" and his military record, Jackson was the symbol around which the new Democratic Party organized itself.

During Jackson's presidency, American politicians began to come to a consensus on the question of Indian policy. American citizens had consistently broken treaties and agreements made with Indians, encroaching on lands they had agreed the tribes could keep. Many government officials began to discuss moving the Indians to lands outside the borders of the United States. Jackson agreed with this point of view. He wrote that such a policy provided the Indians with necessary protection against the evils that the white men would commit against them if they remained within the United States. In 1830, Jackson signed the Indian Removal Act, which forced all American Indians living east of the Mississippi to move to Indian Territory (present-day Oklahoma). The act promised that this land would belong to the tribes perpetually.

The decision, of course, was completely unfair. First, the Indians were not consulted. Second, they were not permitted to go where they liked, but were forced to go to Indian Territory. Third, much of Indian Territory was dry and barren; it would challenge the tribes' ingenuity to get a living on such harsh land. Last, the decision was hypocritical. The American motive was not to protect the Indians, but to take their land away from them.

The tribes did not willingly leave their ancestral lands. The Seminole nation, led by Osceola, fought the Second Seminole War from 1835 to 1842. The United States declared the war over in 1842, having forcibly ejected thousands of Seminoles from their land and killed hundreds more. In Georgia, the Cherokee people took the state to court. Chief Justice John Marshall ruled that Georgia had no right to take away Indian lands, but despite this legal victory, the Cherokee received no federal protection against settlers who stole their property. In 1835, the Cherokee signed a treaty accepting money and land in Indian Territory in exchange for their southeastern lands. They agreed to vacate Georgia by 1838. When that date arrived, federal troops were sent to the Southeast to eject all Indians who had not yet moved west. This forced 800-mile march is known as the Trail of Tears because so many Indians died of hunger, disease, or exhaustion along the way.

CHAPTER 10 QUIZ

1. The Indian Removal Act of 1830 forced the southeastern Indian nations to move to the present-day state of _____
   A. Florida.
   B. Tennessee.
   C. Oklahoma.
   D. Mississippi.

2. Andrew Jackson was the presidential candidate of the newly created _____ Party.
   A. Antifederalist
   B. Democratic
   C. Federalist
   D. Republican

3. In what respect was Missouri Territory in violation of the Northwest Ordinance?
   A. It permitted the ownership of slaves.
   B. It did not have a representative government.
   C. It had no written constitution.
   D. It denied women the right to vote.

4. What was the effect of the Missouri Compromise?
   A. It set aside permanent territory for the Indians in the West.
   B. It helped business and industry to reorganize during the Industrial Revolution.
   C. It set the United States on a path toward the gradual phasing out of slavery.
   D. It maintained an equal number of slaveholding and free states in the United States.

5. **What effect did the Industrial Revolution have on the institution of slavery?**
    A. It made it possible to replace slave labor with mechanical labor.
    B. It made slavery more profitable, thus setting back the cause of abolition.
    C. It made northerners turn even more strongly against slavery.
    D. It made southerners decide to begin phasing out slavery altogether.

6. **The Monroe Doctrine sets forth American objections to** _____
    A. further European colonization in the Western Hemisphere.
    B. further European colonization in North America.
    C. forming alliances with any European nation.
    D. forming alliances with any North or South American nation.

7. **The National Road stretched from** _____
    A. Maine to Florida.
    B. Boston to Washington.
    C. Maryland to Illinois.
    D. Florida to Indian Territory.

8. **John Quincy Adams is a notable figure in history for all these achievements except** _____
    A. serving in the U.S. Senate for 18 years.
    B. conceiving the Monroe Doctrine.
    C. speaking out on the issue of abolition.
    D. leading American troops to victory in battle.

9. **The United States signed the Rush-Bagot Agreement of 1818 as a means of cementing an American alliance with** _____
    A. France.
    B. Britain.
    C. the Seminole nation.
    D. the Cherokee nation.

10. **What is the purpose of the cotton gin?**
    A. to pick cotton
    B. to separate cotton seeds from cotton fibers
    C. to spin cotton fibers into thread
    D. to weave cotton thread into fabric

Chapter 11

Religion and Reform, 1790–1848

The early nineteenth century was a time of great change in American society. With American independence firmly established, and the realization that the new government was proving workable, people turned their attention to two major issues that had been swept aside in the need for unanimity on the question of independence. These two issues were the rights and freedoms of women and slaves.

Throughout the nineteenth century and well into the twentieth, both groups fought for equal rights and equal treatment. The women's rights movement and the abolitionist movement shared many goals and leaders. They had strong arguments on their side: principally, that the founding documents of the United States granted liberty and equality to all the people in theory, but in fact, the leaders denied equality to the entire female population, and denied both liberty and equality to the slaves.

A wave of religious fervor swept the nation from the 1790s to about the 1830s. This Second Great Awakening helped fuel the struggle for full civil rights for all; many preachers pointed out that it was a sin to hold human beings in slavery, and that women were equal to men in the eyes of God. The evangelical revival also gave rise to the temperance movement, in which women literally stormed saloons and destroyed their stock of alcoholic beverages.

In Washington, a new political party had risen to combat Jacksonian Democracy. The Whigs elected their first president, William Henry Harrison, in 1840. They would continue to be a force in politics for the next twenty years.

CHAPTER OBJECTIVES

- Describe presidential politics in the early nineteenth century.
- Describe the Second Great Awakening.
- Explain how the Second Great Awakening affected the temperance and abolitionist movements.
- Describe the fight for women's rights in the early nineteenth century.

Chapter 11 Time Line

- **1790s–1830s**   Second Great Awakening
- **1820s**   American Temperance Society
- **1822**   Establishment of Monrovia (now Liberia), Africa
- **1831**   First issue of *The Liberator*

    Nat Turner's rebellion
- **1834**   Whig Party founded
- **1836**   Election of Martin Van Buren
- **1839**   Publication of *American Slavery as It Is*
- **1840**   Election of William Henry Harrison
- **1848**   Seneca Falls Women's Rights Convention

    Married Women's Property Act

Political Developments

Although Andrew Jackson was very well liked among the general population, there were many in office who disliked and distrusted his policies. A new political party, the Whigs, came into existence in 1834. It was born in opposition to the Democratic Party, which had grown up around Jackson's candidacy for president.

Some Whigs opposed Jackson on personal grounds. Others felt that he was abusing his power, shifting the presidency toward something that was perilously close to a monarchy. The leaders of the Whigs were senators Daniel Webster and Henry Clay. They took their party name from Revolutionary days, when the British Whigs had advocated a relaxation of parliamentary authority over the colonies.

The Whigs ran their first candidates for president in 1836: William Henry Harrison, the hero of the War of 1812; Hugh White; and Daniel Webster. None of the three garnered nearly as many votes as Martin Van Buren, who had been Andrew Jackson's vice president. Van Buren was a New York City politician who had proved a valuable political ally for Jackson, but who lacked Jackson's personal popularity.

In 1840, the Whigs tried again. This time they succeeded in capturing the White House. During a spirited and hard-fought campaign, they painted Van Buren as a remote aristocrat and called themselves "the party of the people." Although William Henry Harrison had an aristocratic background of his own—he was from a wealthy family, and his father had signed the Declaration of Independence—the Whigs successfully portrayed him as a common man with a log-cabin past, just like Andrew Jackson. Harrison also capitalized on his military career, reminding the voters of his victory at the Battle of Tippecanoe. "Tippecanoe and Tyler, too!" became the rallying cry of the campaign, and Harrison and his vice president, John Tyler of Virginia, were elected. The popular vote was close, but Harrison won almost four times as many electoral votes as Van Buren. Harrison ended up serving the shortest term of any U.S. president; after standing unprotected in the rain to deliver his lengthy inaugural address, he became seriously ill, dying only one month into his term. Vice President John Tyler became the first president to step into office when a president died before his term was over.

The Second Great Awakening

The Great Awakening of the mid-1700s had caused an increase in the number of Protestant congregations in America. The new philosophy of salvation by faith in God and by the public confession of sincere repentance for sins, had flown in the face of the Puritan concept of salvation by predestination alone. Large numbers of Americans embraced the idea that they could play a role in their own salvation.

The Second Great Awakening began in upstate New York around the 1790s and continued through the 1830s. Religious revival meetings conducted by fiery evangelical preachers sometimes drew as many as 20,000 people. Like the first Great Awakening, the Second Great Awakening caused a surge in church membership among Protestants, especially Methodists and Baptists. The movement appealed strongly to women and to African Americans, even giving rise to a black Methodist denomination known as the African Methodist Episcopal (AME) Church.

Utopian communities based on religion and philosophy sprang up throughout the United States between 1800 and 1850. People came together with a vision of an ideal society in which everyone would contribute to the good of the whole group. Work, ownership of property, and family life would all be shared.

The religious revival of the early nineteenth century fueled two social and political movements that were to have enormous consequences in American history. The first was the temperance movement, which opposed the consumption of alcohol. The second was the abolitionist movement, which opposed slavery.

The Temperance Movement

Protestant women established the American Temperance Society in the 1820s. Their goal was to discourage people from spending their wages on alcohol and their spare time in saloons. The movement generally targeted men, because they were the worst offenders. In the early nineteenth century, social custom confined women to their homes in their leisure hours; they did not go outside the home for relaxation as men did. No respectable American woman would ever be seen in a saloon or a bar until the twentieth century.

The women who led the temperance movement were no more subtle than the patriots who had dumped chests of tea into Boston Harbor in 1774. They became famous for their aggressive approach to their work—striding into saloons, smashing the glass windows, and taking hatchets to kegs of whiskey, rum, and other spirits until the liquor ran in streams along the board floors. The movement was effective; by the mid-1800s, the national consumption of alcohol had dropped. Temperance advocates continued their crusade against alcohol throughout the nineteenth century. In 1917, they would reach their pinnacle of success with the passage of the Eighteenth Amendment, popularly called "Prohibition" because it prohibited the sale of alcoholic beverages. (Prohibition would be repealed in 1933, having proven a resounding failure. See Chapter 23.)

The Abolitionist Movement

Abolition had been a matter for discussion as long as there had been any slaves in the British colonies. The Pennsylvania Quakers had always spoken out against slavery; prominent Pennsylvanian Benjamin Franklin had founded the first antislavery society in North America. Ministers of the Great Awakening had preached that each individual must live without sin and urge others to do likewise; holding another human being in slavery was naturally regarded as a sin. Even a slave owner like Thomas Jefferson had acknowledged the hypocrisy of founding a slaveholding nation in a document stating that all men were created equal.

Most northern states had outlawed slavery by the early 1800s. The next step was to try to end it in the South. One idea that took shape was to send African Americans to Africa to establish a republic of their own. The colony of Monrovia, named for President James Monroe, was duly established on the west coast of Africa in 1822. Several hundred African Americans had settled the new nation by 1830. By 1847, the original settlement of Monrovia had become the capital city of the Republic of Liberia (*liber* means "free" in Latin) and had its own written constitution modeled on that of the United States.

Most African Americans did not want to emigrate to Africa; they had been born and raised in the United States and regarded it as their home, while Liberia was a foreign nation across an ocean. Their goal was freedom from and equality with white people; they wanted to be treated as free citizens of the United States, with the same rights and privileges as white people. By 1826, there were more than 143 antislavery societies throughout the country, many of them organized and run by free blacks. The fight for abolition and equality would continue, led by both white and black activists.

Many people did not want to wait for gradual change in the laws. They wanted immediate action. Nat Turner, a slave born in 1800, led an armed uprising in August of 1831. The area around Southampton, Virginia, quickly became a scene of terror as Turner and his followers killed any white people they came across; eventually, fifty or sixty people fell victim to the enraged slave and his army. The rebellion did not last long, because Turner's army was far too small to sustain a war; in the end, he and his followers (along with a number of innocent African-American bystanders) were captured and hanged. Southern states were quick to pass harsh new laws that curtailed the few rights and freedoms slaves enjoyed. William Lloyd Garrison, a white journalist, started his famous abolitionist newspaper *The Liberator* in response to the Turner rebellion. Like Turner, Garrison did not believe in waiting for freedom:

...urge me not to use moderation in a cause like the present. I am in earnest—I will not equivocate—I will not excuse—I will not retreat a single inch—AND I WILL BE HEARD.

Women's Rights

When the nineteenth century began, an American woman was not permitted to vote or hold office. By law, she had few rights to her own property or her own earnings. She could not take custody of her children in the event of divorce. There were few colleges or professions open to her. At best, she was a second-class citizen in a republic founded on the principles of liberty and equality. Women could and did point to language in the nation's founding documents that supported their views: for example, the Constitution treats men and women equally, using the word *person*, not *man*, in its description of the qualifications for the nation's highest political offices.

During the Revolutionary War, Abigail Adams had urged her husband to "remember the ladies"—to give women a voice in the new government. John Adams returned a laughing answer by letter, and did not bring Abigail's idea up in congressional debate. However, many women—and even some men—agreed with Abigail. They argued that women were educated and literate, as capable of forming opinions as their husbands; since they had to obey the laws of the land, it was only right that they should be allowed to vote. Otherwise, they were in the same position as the colonists before the Revolution: they were unrepresented in their own government. In effect, they were slaves.

During the 1830s, Sarah and Angelina Grimké, Quakers from South Carolina, began speaking and writing against slavery and for women's rights. In 1839, Angelina Grimké and her husband Theodore Weld published *American Slavery as It Is*, a document that was to convert many readers to the cause of abolition. When male ministers sneered publicly at the Grimkés for daring to speak to mixed audiences of men and women, claiming that such work was appropriate only for men, the Grimkés retorted that men and women were created equal; therefore, if it was moral and right for a man to preach against slavery, it was equally moral and right for a woman to do so. The Grimkés also pointed out that since the U.S. government claimed to derive its power from the consent of the governed, women had just as much right as men to vote.

In 1840, American reformers Elizabeth Cady Stanton and Lucretia Mott attended a World's Anti-Slavery Convention in London. They were outraged to learn that women were not welcome; convention leaders finally agreed to allow them into the hall, but only if they would sit behind a curtain that screened them from the male participants in the convention. The two women vowed to fight such prejudices. In 1848, they organized the Seneca Falls Convention, the first national meeting on women's rights ever held in the United States. More than 300 people came to the small town of Seneca Falls, New York, to hear the speeches. The convention resulted in the Declaration of Sentiments, which called for legal and social reform. Its language deliberately quoted the Declaration of Independence—with the ironic twist of showing how the men who wrote and approved that document had ignored half the population of the United States:

The Declaration of Sentiments

We hold these truths to be self-evident: that all men and women are created equal; that they are endowed by their Creator with certain inalienable rights; that among these are life, liberty, and the pursuit of happiness. . . .

The history of mankind is a history of repeated injuries and usurpations on the part of man toward woman, having as a direct object the establishment of an absolute tyranny over her. To prove this, let facts be submitted to a candid world.

He has never permitted her to exercise her inalienable right to the elective franchise.

He has taken from her all right in property, even to the wages she earns.

He has denied her the facilities for obtaining a thorough education, all colleges being closed against her.

He has endeavored, in every way that he could, to destroy her confidence in her own powers, to lessen her self-respect, and to make her willing to lead a dependent and abject life.

Resolved, that woman is man's equal, was intended to be so by the Creator, and the highest good of the race demands that she should be recognized as such.

In 1833, Oberlin College in northeastern Ohio became the first American college to admit women on an equal basis with men. (It became fully integrated when it opened its doors to African-American students in 1835.) Lucy Stone, one of the first women to graduate from Oberlin, became a famous advocate of abolition and women's rights. Stone kept her maiden name when she married; for some years after, any woman who did the same was called a "Lucy Stoner." Susan B. Anthony, who became close friends with Elizabeth Cady Stanton, focused her efforts on fighting for political rights for women. Anthony argued that until women had political rights, they would have no others. When Anthony boldly went to the polls and cast a vote, she was arrested. In a famous speech defending her action, she quoted the phrase "We, the people" from the Preamble to the Constitution (see Chapter 8), continuing:

> It was we, the people; not we, the white male citizens; nor yet we, the male citizens; but we, the whole people, who formed the Union. And we formed it, not to give the blessings of liberty, but to secure them; not to the half of ourselves and the half of our posterity, but to the whole people—women as well as men. And it is a downright mockery to talk to women of their enjoyment of the blessings of liberty while they are denied the use of the only means of securing them provided by this democratic-republican government—the ballot.

It would take some time for women to earn the right to vote; however, they succeeded in their fight for property rights in 1848 with the passage of the Married Women's Property Act of New York, which entitled married women in that state to own property. In 1860, the act was amended to state that women owned any wages they earned. Other states passed similar laws.

The fight for women's rights—the right to vote, to attend college, to keep one's maiden name, and to speak in public on an equal footing with men—was primarily conducted by middle-class and upper-class women. Working-class women had very different concerns: unsafe working conditions, low wages, and miserable and often unsanitary living conditions, especially in America's growing cities. If they had had time, these were the causes they would have taken up. However, they were too busy with the struggle for survival. The working class would have to wait until the next century for society as a whole to address its concerns.

Literature

Ever since the early Colonial days, the United States had been a literate society. Because Puritans had wanted everyone to be able to read the Bible, all children were taught to read. This did not mean that all Americans could understand complex texts or write sophisticated prose, but the majority could read and write for everyday purposes. In southern states, it was illegal to teach slaves to read or write, but many managed to learn in spite of the ban.

Newspapers, magazines, journals, and books proliferated in this literate society. Before about 1800, most American literature had discussed political issues or provided religious edification; in the early 1800s, American authors began producing imaginative literature intended for entertainment. Most American literature of note from this period came from the Northeast, because this region had been settled the longest and had a more cosmopolitan culture than the rural South. An entire literary community developed around Concord, Massachusetts, where Herman Melville, Nathaniel Hawthorne, Henry David Thoreau, Ralph Waldo Emerson, and Louisa May Alcott were all near neighbors to one another. Henry Wadsworth Longfellow became the first American to earn a living by writing poetry, Edgar Allan Poe was a pioneer in the field of detective and horror fiction, and Walt Whitman of New Jersey and Emily Dickinson of Massachusetts broke literary ground with their poems.

Literary Figures	Major Works	Genre
Louisa May Alcott	*Little Women*	Young-adult novels
	An Old-Fashioned Girl	Novels
	Work	Short stories
Ralph Waldo Emerson	"On Friendship"	Essays
	"Self-Reliance"	
Henry David Thoreau	*Walden*	Memoirs
	Civil Disobedience	Essays
		Travel and nature writing
Nathaniel Hawthorne	*The Scarlet Letter*	Novels
	Tanglewood Tales	Short stories
	"The Minister's Black Veil"	Children's stories
Edgar Allan Poe	"The Fall of the House of Usher"	Short stories
	"The Tell-Tale Heart"	Detective stories
	"The Cask of Amontillado"	Poems
	"The Purloined Letter"	
	"The Raven"	
Walt Whitman	*Leaves of Grass*	Free-verse poems
Emily Dickinson	Poems	Lyric poems
Herman Melville	*Moby-Dick*	Novels
	White-Jacket	Short stories
	"Bartleby the Scrivener"	Poems
Henry Wadsworth Longfellow	"The Midnight Ride of Paul Revere"	Poems
	The Song of Hiawatha	
	Evangeline	

CHAPTER 11 QUIZ

1. **The leaders of the temperance movement opposed** _____
   A. the consumption of alcohol.
   B. the slave trade.
   C. the Whig Party.
   D. women's rights.

2. **The main focus of the Whig Party was its opposition to** _____
   being the strongest branch of the central government.
   A. the president
   B. the House of Representatives
   C. the Senate
   D. the Supreme Court

3. **What effect did the Second Great Awakening have on the abolitionist movement?**
   A. It opposed it by preaching the doctrine of noninterference.
   B. It opposed it by pointing out that slaveholders converted their slaves to Christianity.
   C. It encouraged it by preaching that owning slaves was a sin.
   D. It supported it by boycotting trade with slaveholding states.

4. **What was the effect of Nat Turner's rebellion?**
   A. Southern states began to consider abolishing slavery.
   B. Southern states passed harsher legal slave codes.
   C. Northern states abandoned the cause of abolition.
   D. Northern states began secretly arming the slaves for a future rebellion.

5. **State governments justified denying women the right to vote on the grounds** _____
   A. that women were considered slaves.
   B. that government must be based on the consent of the governed.
   C. of centuries of tradition of male authority.
   D. of the wording of the Constitution.

6. _____ is a notable historical figure for exercising her right to vote and claiming that her action was legal.
   A. Louisa May Alcott
   B. Susan B. Anthony
   C. Angelina Grimké
   D. Elizabeth Cady Stanton

7. The Seneca Falls Convention of 1848 focused on the issue of _____
   A. territorial expansion.
   B. party politics.
   C. women's rights.
   D. abolition.

8. Which best describes the goal of most African Americans in the 1820s and 1830s?
   A. to emigrate to Africa
   B. to migrate to the northern states
   C. to be granted full civil rights
   D. to overthrow the U.S. government

9. On what basis did Andrew Jackson's opponents object to his presidential style?
   A. He was not popular among the citizens.
   B. He wielded too much authority, threatening the balance of powers.
   C. He believed that only well-born, educated men should serve in the government.
   D. He had never served the country in the military.

10. William Lloyd Garrison founded *The Liberator* to convert his readers to the cause of _____
    A. religious conversion.
    B. abolition.
    C. women's rights.
    D. emigration to Liberia.

12

American Economic Development, 1812–1845

As the nineteenth century began, the United States began developing into two distinct cultures, one in the South and one in the North. Advances in technology and improvements in transportation led the South to expand its agriculture, while the North developed a mercantile economy centered on business, industry, and trade. As the century continued, the two societies had less and less in common.

Both southern and northern cultures were divided into social and economic classes. In the North, there were the very wealthy, the middle class, and the urban poor. Many of the urban poor were newly-arrived immigrants; in the 1830s and 1840s, most of these immigrants came from Ireland. Lacking the money to buy land and farm it, they became a laboring class. They worked in mines and factories, built roads and canals, and turned their hand to any other job of work that paid wages.

The struggle between the federal government and the states continued, with the states insisting on their right to disregard federal laws with which they disagreed. Southern states in particular insisted that they were under no compulsion to obey any laws they found unconstitutional, such as tariff acts that drove up the prices of foreign goods. Two financial panics, in 1819 and 1837, suggested that a strong national bank was a necessity, but many people remained unconvinced of this.

CHAPTER OBJECTIVES

- Analyze the financial crises of the early 1800s.
- Compare and contrast northern and southern social classes.
- Explain the doctrine of nullification.
- Describe the American System and its effects.

Chapter 12 Time Line

- 1816   Second Bank of the United States
- 1816   Tariff Act
- 1817–1825   Erie Canal
- 1818   Second Bank calls in all state loans
- 1819   Panic of 1819
- 1829   Doctrine of nullification
- 1830   Railway construction begins
- 1836   Second Bank closes
- 1837   Panic of 1837

The American System

The U.S. economy really began to take shape in the first quarter of the nineteenth century. Congress had refused to renew the charter of the Bank of the United States in 1811, which meant that the government had to look to state banks for funds to repay the debt of the War of 1812. Since state banks did not always have sufficient gold or silver to back up their paper currency, other banks would often refuse to honor that currency. Speaker of the House Henry Clay of Kentucky offered a solution to this emerging economic crisis. His proposal, called the American System, found substantial support in Congress. It consisted of three parts: a national bank, protective tariffs on imports, and a national transportation system.

The National Bank

In 1816, Congress sent a bill to President Madison, asking for a charter for the Second Bank of the United States. Its purposes would be twofold: to establish a standard national currency and to fund federal government services such as the armed forces. Madison promptly signed the bill into law.

In 1818, the Second Bank called in all outstanding loans from state banks. These banks had borrowed more money than they could pay back, and the result was the Panic of 1819. In a frantic attempt to get enough money to pay their debt to the government, banks foreclosed on mortgages and called in loans to customers. In their turn, individual borrowers could not pay back the loans on such short notice, and many had to sell their homes or businesses. With no one to buy the businesses, they closed down, and their workers were suddenly unemployed. The resulting economic depression lasted for several years.

President Andrew Jackson looked with disfavor on the Second Bank, believing that it catered to the interests of the wealthy at the expense of the common working people. The voters apparently agreed with Jackson; when the fate of the bank became a major campaign issue in 1836, Jackson easily defeated his opponent, Henry Clay, who supported renewing the bank's charter. Once reelected, Jackson took steps to close down the Second Bank. He transferred funds to various state banks rather than putting them into the federal bank. Bank President Nicholas Biddle attempted to save the bank by triggering a financial crisis, hoping to show Jackson and the public that they should support an institution that stabilized the national economy. Neither Jackson nor the public was converted to this view; instead, they felt that Biddle was demonstrating conclusively that the bank was a tool to be used against the public.

The bank closed down in 1836, triggering the Panic of 1837. State banks loaned money readily, which meant that speculators were able to buy land. They resold the land at inflated prices, clearing a fast profit. As land prices soared, so did all other prices. President Jackson tried to stem the tide of inflation by stating that the federal government would accept only gold or silver as payment for public land—no paper currency would be accepted. Land sales dropped precipitously, because few people had gold or silver. They tried to trade paper money for gold and silver at the banks, and the banks quickly ran out and then failed. The Panic of 1837 resulted in an economic depression from which the nation did not begin to recover until 1843.

The Tariff Acts

A tariff is a tax or duty on imported goods. The idea behind a protective tariff is to drive up the prices of imports so that people will purchase goods made in their own country. Buying locally, of course, benefits the local economy.

The Tariff Act of 1816 established a 25% tax on imported manufactured goods. This drove up the price of imports to such a degree that southern planters protested, afraid that European nations would retaliate by taxing American cotton. However, northerners were happy to avoid the tariff by purchasing goods from their own factories, thus increasing their own profits.

In 1828, a new Tariff Act doubled the rates set in the Tariff Act of 1816. Southerners had not supported the first act, and thus were furious over the new one. They began muttering about the infringement of the federal government on states' rights. John C. Calhoun, who had originally supported the use of the import taxes to pay for the roads and canals, wrote an essay arguing that no state should be forced to obey any act of Congress that it believed to be unconstitutional. Since the states had created the federal government, the states should have greater power. The position Calhoun took in his essay became known as the doctrine of nullification.

Many voters agreed with Calhoun. Henry Clay, ever the compromiser, successfully urged Congress to pass a reduction in the new tariff. For southerners, this was not enough. South Carolina took the lead, passing resolutions declaring the Tariff Acts null and void and refusing to pay any tariffs to the federal government. If the government tried to collect tariffs, South Carolina would secede from the United States. Clay urged a further compromise one that lowered the tariff rates gradually over the course of ten years. Satisfied for the moment, South Carolina dropped its threats. The tension during this period is known as the Nullification Crisis.

Transportation

The national transportation system had three elements: paved interstate roads, canals, and the railroad. The idea behind the system was to link the agricultural and industrial regions, so that both would benefit economically.

Congress decided to use Tariff Act income to fund new roads and canals. The National Road (see Chapter 10) was begun in 1815 and the Erie Canal in 1817. Within eight years, this 363-mile canal provided a direct and efficient trade route from the Hudson River to Lake Erie.

Railway locomotives came into use in the United States around 1830. The first steam-powered "iron horses" were slow and ponderous; one even lost a race to a flesh-and-blood horse. However, mechanical knowledge advanced quickly, and the train could soon move much faster than any animal. By 1850, American trains were running over thousands of miles of track; by 1869, the railroad reached from New York all the way to California.

The transportation boom created new markets for goods. Before the development of steamboats that could take goods upstream and canals that could carry goods inland from the ocean, most trade had been in local markets. Now sellers could expand into new territories and sell to thousands of new customers. This created a market revolution. As profits grew, so did the sizes of towns and the movement of settlers. Skilled artisans who manufactured items one at a time began to give way to mass production and factories.

The Northern Economy: Social Classes

During the early nineteenth century, the urban economy in the North quickly developed three distinct social classes: the wealthy, the middle class, and the urban poor. All three classes grew rapidly, and it was relatively easy for anyone who acquired enough money to move into a higher class socially.

The Upper Class

Wealthy society lived in an atmosphere far removed from that of the poor or the middle class. The people in this small group, who owned a disproportionate amount of the community's wealth, spent their time together. Wealthy men were involved in politics and had inherited incomes to manage. Wealthy women organized entertainment events for themselves and their friends. The children of the upper class were educated to follow in the footsteps of their parents. Sometimes the wealthy interested themselves in patronizing the performing arts or in charitable work. Most of their time, however, was spent in idleness and the pursuit of pleasure.

The Middle Class

The urban middle class lived very differently. This class was primarily made up of people who owned their own small businesses, who belonged to a profession, or who had good positions in larger businesses. Lawyers, teachers, professors, clergymen, artisans, and shopkeepers were all members of the middle class. These people generally lived comfortable though not luxurious lives.

Because the middle class wanted to appear as distinct as possible from the poorer class, middle-class women did not work—at least, not for wages. While in Colonial times it had been a matter of pride that everyone in a family worked, the middle class made it a matter of pride that their women could afford not to work. Respectable middle-class women were supposed to stay at home, managing the house and raising the children, while the men went out to work at a profession. Middle-class families could usually afford servants; robbed of her traditional housekeeping chores and banned by social custom from working outside the home, a prosperous middle-class housewife lived a life of enforced idleness.

Being confined to such a narrow sphere of activity created deep discontent among many women who had enough intelligence and education to imagine and desire wider horizons than those provided by home and hearth. "The Yellow Wallpaper," an 1892 short story by Charlotte Perkins Gillman, sums up the plight of nineteenth-century middle-class women in its chilling portrait of a young married woman literally driven mad by a husband who refuses to let her write or take part in any other intellectual or physical activity because it might be too much for her nerves. The boredom of respectability helped give rise to the women's rights movement, in which women began to demand college educations, to fight for the right to train for professions, and to have honorable goals other than marriage and motherhood. The women who led the national fight for social, education, and political reform were almost all from the middle class. (See Chapter 11.)

The Working Class

The nineteenth century was a lean time for the urban poor. There were no regulations to protect them, either in the workplace or at home. The factory owner's only goal was profit; therefore, he set wages as low as he could and demanded as many working hours as he dared. The modern concept of the weekend did not exist at the time; Sunday was the only day of rest, and a normal workday lasted from ten to fourteen hours. There were no labor unions or minimum-wage laws to protect the workers' interests. If one worker found the wages too low, another would gladly take his place. Women and children were hired in large numbers for two reasons. First, children were physically small enough for the jobs that involved squeezing into tight spaces. Second, women and children earned much less than men. Factory owners argued that this was justified on two counts: first, men were physically bigger and stronger and got through more work, and second, men had families to support. Of course, this ignored the fact that women were also responsible for supporting themselves and their families.

America's high rate of immigration meant that workers were easily replaced; therefore employers saw no need to spend any of their profits on making the factory safer. Workers were constantly exposed to dangerous levels of industrial pollution, inhaling smoke, chemicals, and lint. Fires and other serious accidents were common; machinery was dangerous to operate at the best of times, and the long, exhausting hours made workers less alert and thus more likely to stumble or to move too slowly for safety. The workers had no rights in the event of severe injury; they were entirely dependent on the generosity of the owner. It became clear that since owners would not treat workers fairly of their own accord, the workers would have to band together to fight for their rights. Eventually, the government would step in and pass laws to ensure humane, reasonable working conditions. (See Chapter 20.)

Conditions at home were no better than those at the factory. Poor people were crowded into apartment buildings without heat or running water. Cities had no sewer systems. There were no laws to regulate the conditions in which landlords maintained their buildings. In this situation, disease spread rapidly. There were few public facilities such as baths, swimming pools, or even green parks where children could play.

The Northern Economy: Immigration

Northern cities grew like weeds for one simple reason—immigration. Thousands of Europeans crossed the Atlantic every year, searching for financial opportunities, an escape from wretched conditions at home, and ownership of property. Most of them crossed on ships that docked in the major northern port city of New York. The North was not only the point of arrival; it was also the center of economic opportunity. Trade, business, and industry were all centered in the North; therefore, immigrants tended to settle in this region. The rural South provided few economic opportunities for any immigrant who did not have the money to purchase a substantial farm.

During the mid-1800s, most immigrants came from Ireland. The potato famine of the 1840s had destroyed the nation's staple crop, causing widespread starvation. Hundreds of thousands of Irish, having nowhere else to go, sailed west. Once they arrived in the United States, they were too poor to buy and farm land, as they had done in Ireland. They remained in the cities, snatching at any opportunity for factory work. Those who moved westward from the Atlantic coast provided most of the labor that built the roads, laid the railroad tracks, and dug the Erie Canal. Irishmen also turned their hand to mining coal in Pennsylvania and unloading freight in Ohio. Irishwomen worked as laundresses, seamstresses, servants, and factory hands.

The Irish immigrants' Catholic religious faith, the distinctive lilt of their speech, their abject poverty, and a long history of conflict between Ireland and England made Anglo-Saxon Protestant Americans despise them. Anglo-Saxon Protestants controlled most of the money and power in the United States. Of course, all members of this group, or their parents or grandparents, had emigrated to America for the same reasons as the Irish—but now that they were in a position of power, they considered themselves superior to the more recent immigrants. This belief—that certain rights and privileges should be reserved for native-born Americans—is known as nativism.

In concrete terms, nativism meant that landlords might refuse to rent to the Irish, or might ask unreasonably high rates. Factory owners might refuse to hire Irish immigrants, or might offer them lower wages. They would probably reserve the most difficult and dangerous jobs for the Irish. Nativists vandalized Irish Catholic churches, attacked immigrants in the streets, and tried to change laws to restrict immigrants' rights. The nativists eventually formed their own political party, called the Know-Nothings in honor of any party member's response when asked about nativist activities: "I know nothing of that."

However, the Irish proved tough enough to survive, to assimilate, and to triumph. By the 1880s, many Irish Americans had gained enormous political power in major cities such as Boston and New York.

German immigrants also flooded into the United States during this era. Most of them settled in the major cities or the rural areas around the Great Lakes. Germans tended to become small farmers or skilled artisans. Because German immigrants generally came to the United States with enough money to be self-sufficient once they arrived, they had a high rate of success. Any German immigrant knew that he or she could rely for help on relatives or friends who had already settled in the United States.

The Southern Economy

The agricultural South and the industrial North had so little in common that the United States was in many ways two separate countries. Their climates and topography were different, their sources of income were different, the businesses in which people worked were different, and their ideas on the subject of slave labor and their notions of how the federal government should be run were poles apart.

The primary difference between the South and North was that the North maintained a mercantile economy and the South did not. In the North, people bought and sold goods; in the South, people generally produced everything they needed. If they could not produce it, they did without it. Wealthy southerners did purchase luxury goods, but these were almost always purchased in the North or imported from Europe because there was very little manufacturing in the South. Instead, the economy was based on growing, harvesting, and exporting crops. There were four social and economic classes in the South: the wealthy planters, the small farmers, the poor whites, and the slaves.

The Planters

Rich planters who owned fifty or more slaves were relatively few in number. They might own hundreds or thousands of acres of land on which they grew cotton, and sometimes rice or sugar cane as well. With a vast number of slaves and also with paid employees, a plantation owner was like a medieval lord. He and his wife, and often their grown sons and daughters, worked together to oversee the day-to-day operations of their land. The planter ran his estate like any other business; he had accounts to keep, correspondence to write, and trades to broker. The planter's lady was responsible for the general welfare of everyone who lived on the plantation; she ran the household, looked after and treated the sick, and managed the staff of house slaves. A typical southern estate was almost entirely self-sufficient; owners and slaves between them either grew or made everything they needed.

The Small Farmers

Small farmers might or might not own a few slaves. They were largely self-sufficient, growing what they needed for themselves and trading their surplus crops for cash and for goods they could not grow or make, such as spices, tea, or tools.

The "Poor Whites"

The "poor white" class was poor because its members lived on barren soil. When a farmer could not coax a good crop from his land, his or her family was bound to suffer. The poorest southern whites owned no slaves. They lived in log cabins and subsisted on what crops they could grow. They had no leisure for education and nowhere to go to get it. Many of them were illiterate. They had very little hope of improving their lot in life.

The Slaves

Slaves were paid nothing for their work, although they were on call every hour of every day. The civil contract required that the plantation owner feed and house them and provide care for them when they fell ill. Since the plantation owner wanted to make the greatest possible profit, he provided no luxuries and very few comforts to his slaves. They were housed in shacks, given the poorest-quality food and not much of it, and clothed either in castoffs from the owner's family or in clothing that they made themselves from the poorest and roughest fabrics. They knew better than to appeal for medical care unless they were seriously ill; no slave wanted to be branded as a troublemaker or a complainer. Plantation owners knew that they had to maintain a healthy and strong workforce in order to turn a profit, but they convinced themselves that African slaves could thrive on a starvation diet and a seven-day workweek.

Somehow, despite the nightmare conditions under which they were forced to live, slaves maintained a rich and picturesque culture of their own. It was a patchwork quilt of memories of a variety of cultures from their home continent of Africa, blended with European-derived elements they had acquired in the New World. Spirituals, for instance, combine African musical elements with biblical lyrics. Slaves told stories, sang, and danced to entertain themselves and one another. Many slave women became skilled in the art of using herbs to heal the sick. Although it was a crime to teach a slave to read or write, many slaves managed to learn anyway; during the mid-1800s, the slave narrative became a popular and widely read genre of autobiography. Escaped slaves, most famously Frederick Douglass, wrote of their experiences in the South: starvation, brutal physical punishment, unceasing hard labor, and constant restraints on their liberty. Slave narratives shocked many readers and converted them to the cause of abolition.

CHAPTER 12 QUIZ

1. European immigrants to the United States almost always settled in the North because of _____
   A. the climate.
   B. the economic opportunities.
   C. their opposition to slavery.
   D. their ignorance of farming.

2. _____ was the primary reason that so many Irish emigrated to the United States in the 1840s.
   A. Famine and starvation
   B. Political conflict between Ireland and England
   C. The desire for religious self-determination
   D. The high cost of living in Ireland

3. Which best defines the term *nativism*?
   A. belief in the civil rights of American Indians
   B. support for the cause of abolition
   C. the belief that people born in the United States should have more rights than immigrants
   D. support for the American System of Henry Clay

4. Henry Clay's economic program contained support for all these except _____
   A. a national bank.
   B. government-controlled industry.
   C. protective tariffs on imports.
   D. construction of roads, canals, and railways.

5. What primarily motivated middle-class American women to begin fighting for equality?
   A. concern over the plight of urban workers
   B. disapproval of slavery in the South
   C. boredom with their enforced idleness
   D. the desire to become wealthy

6. Southerners opposed the Tariff Acts because _____
   A. they did not want to ship cotton north to the textile mills.
   B. they were afraid that Europeans would raise the tariff on American cotton.
   C. they did not want to abolish slavery.
   D. they did not support the creation of a national transportation network.

7. The doctrine of nullification states that _____
   A. any free American man over 21 has the right to vote.
   B. no state has to obey a federal law that it believes to be unconstitutional.
   C. only the Supreme Court can judge whether a law is constitutional.
   D. no state can charge a tariff on goods manufactured in another state.

8. What caused the Panic of 1819?
   A. congressional refusal to renew the charter of the Bank of the United States
   B. the government's creation of the Second Bank of the United States
   C. the sudden rise in immigration from northern Europe
   D. the inability of state banks to repay federal loans

9. A national bank exists for all these purposes except _____
   A. to maintain a standard national currency.
   B. to fund the services provided by the federal government.
   C. to stabilize the national economy.
   D. to tax imported goods.

10. During the wave of mid-nineteenth-century immigration, the Germans had an easier time than the Irish because _____
   A. they arrived with more money.
   B. most of them were Lutherans.
   C. they had been farmers in Europe.
   D. they spoke better English.

Chapter 13

Westward Expansion and Sectional Division, 1830–1850

Between 1830 and 1850, the United States continued to expand its territory. It fought a successful war against Mexico, gaining vast amounts of western and southwestern land in exchange for a cash payment. It admitted two of its largest states, Texas and California, into the Union. It reached a settlement with Great Britain that gave it control of Oregon Country south of the present Canadian border. People flowed westward in a steady stream to settle the new territory; after 1848, migrants chased dreams of finding gold in California.

The trail westward led through the Great Plains, which, as the U.S. expanded, had been set aside for the Indians and was known as Indian Territory. Indians had prospered on this land, hunting wild buffalo and migrating with the herds. The thousands of pioneers traveling west disrupted their lifestyle and also decimated the buffalo population; travelers on the Oregon Trail killed the buffalo for food to sustain them on the journey. At an 1851 conference, the United States and the American Indians reached an agreement highly favorable to the United States. Plains Indians would confine themselves to certain areas rather than ranging freely across the plains, and the United States would compensate them in food and trade goods.

As new states applied to enter the Union, Congress continued to quarrel over the issue of slavery. Southern states threatened to leave the Union if any measures favorable to abolition were passed. In the end, they allowed California to enter the Union as a free state only at the price of the Fugitive Slave Act of 1850—a law that established such harsh measures against escaped slaves that it turned many in the North into antislavery activists.

CHAPTER OBJECTIVES

- Describe the causes and effects of the Mexican War.
- Discuss the westward migration of the pioneers.
- Explain the causes and effects of the Compromise of 1850.

Chapter 13 Time Line

•	1830	Mexico bans American immigration to Texas and bans slavery in Texas
•	1836	Siege of Alamo
		Texas wins independence from Mexico
•	1844	James K. Polk elected president
•	1845	John O'Sullivan coins phrase "manifest destiny"
		Texas admitted to United States; Mexico breaks off diplomatic relations with United States
•	1846	Mexican War begins
		Wilmot Proviso defeated in the Senate
•	1848	Treaty of Guadalupe-Hidalgo
•	1848	Zachary Taylor elected president
	1848–1854	Free-Soil Party
•	1849	California Gold Rush
•	1850	Compromise of 1850
		Fugitive Slave Act of 1850
		Zachary Taylor dies in office; Millard Fillmore becomes president
•	1853	Gadsden Purchase

Westward Migration

In 1776, the United States had occupied a broad strip of land along the Atlantic coast; by 1840, the nation had expanded halfway across the continent. In 1845, magazine editor John O'Sullivan put into words what many Americans had been thinking: it was obvious that the United States should expand to fill the borders of North America between Canada and Mexico, all the way to the Pacific Ocean. He referred to this concept as "manifest destiny":

> The American claim is by the right of our manifest destiny to overspread and to possess the whole continent which Providence has given us for the development of the great experiment of liberty. . . .

In 1846, President James K. Polk signed an agreement with Britain, dividing Oregon Country along the present U.S.-Canadian border. The British moved north of the line and the United States took control of the southern portion, renaming it Oregon Territory; it would eventually become the states of Oregon, Washington, and Idaho. The rights of the Indians in that area were, as always, irrelevant as far as the U.S. government was concerned.

When Americans began moving west to Oregon, they were able to follow trails blazed by the Indians and the fur traders. African American explorer James Beckwourth, attempting to find his way across the Sierra Nevadas, discovered a route to California that was later traveled by thousands of pioneers heading west. Marcus and Narcissa Whitman, missionaries who planned to build a school for the Cayuse Indians who lived in the territory, became the first white family to settle permanently in Oregon in 1836.

Seven years later, the first wagon trains undertook the trek along the Oregon Trail. Families traveling west would wait in Independence, Missouri, until a large group of families had gathered. The wagons would then set off together. This ensured that no pioneer family would be without help if people fell ill or a pregnant woman went into labor. A large group of wagons was also less vulnerable to attack by thieves or American Indian raiders.

The map on the following page shows the route the pioneers traveled. There were so many of them that the ruts their wagon wheels dug into the Great Plains are still visible today.

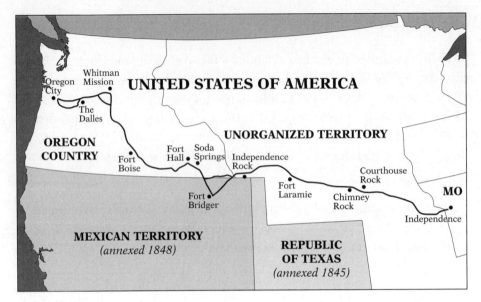

The Oregon Trail

Travelers left Independence in May so that they would be sure to get across the mountains by October, before the annual heavy snowfall made travel impossible. This meant traveling twelve hours a day. The pioneers faced many obstacles. The weather was capricious: sometimes stiflingly hot, sometimes pouring with rain for days on end. Covered wagons provided little shelter. Illness, when it frequently came, spread quickly from one family to another in the close conditions of the camps. Women who were pregnant when the journey began had to give birth out in the open along the trail; since there were no hospitals or doctors, many of them died of complications from the birth. The Whitmans were only one of many families to adopt children who had been orphaned on the Oregon Trail. Apart from replenishing the stock of fresh water and shooting game to cook and eat, it was not possible to restock any supplies during the journey. If people had not brought along what they needed, they had to find ways to manage without it.

However, the pioneers were on the whole a tough and enduring group of people. Thousands of them reached Oregon safely between 1840 and 1860.

The Republic of Texas

When Mexico won its independence from Spain in 1821, the Mexican government began actively enticing Americans to move to Texas, offering them land at low prices. The Mexicans wanted Americans to settle Texas for two reasons. First, the Americans would draw the fire of the Apache and Comanche raiders to whom northeast Texas was home. Second, settlers of Texas would presumably side with Mexico against any attempted U.S. invasion and takeover of Texas.

The plan was so successful that it backfired on the Mexican government. By 1830, American Texans outnumbered Mexican Texans by two to one. Worried that the American settlers would after all be loyal to U.S. interests, Mexico banned further immigration from the United States and prohibited slavery in Texas. However, both bans proved unenforceable.

In 1833, General Antonio López de Santa Anna was elected president of Mexico. When he developed into a military dictator, residents of Texas led an armed rebellion against the government. In 1835, Texans captured the town of San Antonio. In early 1836, Santa Anna arrived at the head of an army to subdue the revolt. The Mexicans laid siege to the Alamo, a fort near San Antonio where the Texans were holding their position. On March 6, Santa Anna's army battled for control of the fort. All the defenders of the Alamo were killed. In April, Sam Houston led the Texans against the Mexicans near the San Jacinto River. They took Santa Anna prisoner and forced him to sign a treaty granting Texas its independence. Sam Houston was elected the first president of the Republic of Texas in 1836. Mexico, pointing out that Santa Anna had signed the treaty under duress, refused to recognize Texan independence.

In 1837, Texas applied to the U.S. Congress for statehood. Since northerners in Congress did not want to admit another slaveholding state to the Union, and even some southern congressmen were hesitant to take a step that would infuriate the Mexican government, Texas remained an independent republic until 1845.

The Mexican War

In 1844, Democrat James K. Polk, former governor of Tennessee, was elected president on the basis of his campaign promise to annex Texas. Henry Clay and James Birney, Polk's opponents, ignored the issue of Texas in their campaigns. Polk won by a narrow margin of popular votes.

The admission of Texas as a state in 1845 proved that Congress had been right to fear a Mexican reprisal; Mexico, which still insisted that Texas was a Mexican state, received the annexation as a declaration of war. There was also a disagreement over the location of Texas' southwestern border, with Mexico drawing the line at the Rio Nueces and the Texas government drawing it much further west at the Rio Grande. The U.S. government inherited this border dispute when it granted Texas statehood.

Hoping to avoid an all-out war with Mexico, Polk offered the Mexican government $30 million for both Texas and California, assuming that the border would be drawn at the Rio Grande. Mexico underwent a change of regime in December 1845, and U.S. envoy John Slidell soon discovered that the new president, Mariano Paredes, would not agree to the sale.

On April 24, 1846, Mexican troops crossed the Rio Grande and attacked General Zachary Taylor's troops. By May 9, the Americans had driven the Mexicans back across the river. When the news arrived in Washington, Congress officially declared war on Mexico.

Fighting continued until 1847. General Winfield Scott and his troops eventually ended the war by laying siege to Mexico City. The Mexicans were forced to surrender on September 14. The following February, the two sides signed the Treaty of Guadalupe-Hidalgo, which was highly favorable to the United States—much better, in fact, than Polk's original offer of $30 million for Texas and California.

TREATY OF GUADALUPE-HIDALGO, 1848

U.S. Concessions to Mexico	Mexican Concessions to the United States
• $15 million cash • United States will pay any damage claims made by U.S. citizens against the Mexican government • United States will grant citizenship to all Mexicans living within the borders of the Mexican Cession	• Territory [including present-day states of California, Nevada, and Utah, and parts of Arizona, New Mexico, Colorado, and Wyoming] collectively known as the "Mexican Cession" • Mexico recognizes Texas as a U.S. state • Mexico recognizes the Rio Grande as the U.S.-Mexican border

The Gadsden Purchase

Secretary of War Jefferson Davis suggested to Mexican ambassador James Gadsden that Gadsden offer Mexico $10 million for a long, narrow piece of land between Texas and California, south of the Gila River. In need of cash after losing the war, Mexico snatched at the offer. On December 30, 1853, the Gadsden Purchase added one more piece to the giant jigsaw puzzle of the United States. Today this land is part of the states of New Mexico and Arizona.

The Election of 1848

When Texas applied for admission to the United States as a slaveholding state, Congress once again had to debate the disturbance of the balance of power. The legislators compromised once again, admitting Texas as a slave state but also extending westward the line of the Missouri Compromise, north of which there was to be no slavery permitted. In 1846, Representative David Wilmot of Pennsylvania suggested the Wilmot Proviso, which stipulated that slavery would not be allowed in any territory acquired in the Mexican War. Southerners threatened to secede from the Union over the Wilmot Proviso, and after heated debate, it was defeated in the Senate.

This dispute over the slaveholding or free status of the formerly Mexican territory became the key issue in the 1848 presidential election. Opponents of slavery formed the Free-Soil Party, represented by Martin Van Buren and Charles Francis Adams. The Whigs chose Zachary Taylor and Millard Fillmore for their candidates, while Lewis Cass and William Butler represented the Democrats. Mexican War hero Taylor was himself a slaveholder, but he did not comment on the issue of slavery during the campaign. The Democrats, who supported slavery, narrowly lost the election to the Whigs, who did not. The Free-Soil Party won several seats in the House of Representatives, ensuring that abolitionist forces would continue to have a voice in the government.

California Gold

At first, the western territories acquired from Mexico had no organized governments. Congress was too busy debating the issue of slavery in these territories to turn its attention to other issues of government. This changed abruptly when the following statement appeared in a newspaper:

> GOLD MINE FOUND—In the newly made raceway of the Saw Mill recently erected by Captain Sutter, on the American Fork, gold has been found in considerable quantities.

The discovery of gold at Sutter's Mill touched off the Gold Rush of 1849—a dash to California in which the entire world participated. Prospectors, called "forty-niners," represented all ethnic groups; they were European Americans, African Americans, Chinese, and Mexicans. Most were young men, unmarried and without family ties, who could easily drop whatever work they had been doing to rush to California in search of the treasure. Because there were no stable governments and no settled society there, the West was a wild, lawless place during the Gold Rush years. Crime and racial and ethnic hostility were rife. Miners and prospectors forced Indians off land that held the promise of rich gold strikes.

Entrepreneurs traveled west in the wake of the forty-niners. They sought a different kind of treasure—not a lucky find of gold nuggets, but the kind of treasure made by running a successful business. There was clearly money to be made by opening the first western saloons, restaurants, boarding houses, laundries, and stores for the miners and prospectors. And that is how the Gold Rush gave rise to one of the classic elements of American culture—blue jeans. Levi Strauss, an immigrant tailor from Germany, made a fortune on his sturdy blue denim work trousers, which featured a diagonal twill weave—in essence, an extra layer of threads in the fabric—that made them hold up well under the tough working conditions in the gold mines. Blue jeans eventually became the most commonly worn garment in the United States.

The Compromise of 1850

California's application for statehood in 1850 threw Congress into turmoil. Southern leaders refused to consider admitting another free state into the United States. They did not want the balance of power disturbed unless it was going to be in their favor, and California's leaders had made it clear that they would not permit slavery.

Once again, it was up to Henry Clay to find a way to get the two sides to meet one another halfway. Clay offered Congress the Compromise of 1850—California would enter the Union as a free state, but Congress would agree to sign a new Fugitive Slave Act into law.

The Fugitive Slave Act of 1850 had several provisions. First, it stated that a slave's status was permanent; even if the slave escaped into a free state, he or she was still a slave. This was a change to the existing law, in which a slave automatically gained his or her freedom by traveling to a free state. Second, the

Act made the permanency of slave status retroactive, robbing all former slaves throughout the United States of their freedom; their former owners now had a right to claim them as property. Third, the Act called for special commissions to hear cases of disputed ownership. In these trials, African Americans had no right to testify in their own defense, and the judges would earn more money if the slave owner won the case. Obviously, such a system was heavily slanted against the chance of a slave winning his or her case; in addition, it placed free African Americans in grave danger of being forced into slavery, because they could not speak for themselves if they were claimed. Fourth, it was now a crime for any American citizen to aid an escaping slave.

The passage of the Fugitive Slave Act had several effects. Hundreds of thousands of free African Americans, afraid of being returned to slavery, crossed the northern border into Canada to escape the reach of American laws. The Underground Railroad, a secret network of people who helped slaves escape from the Deep South into freedom, became more active than ever before. And thousands of whites living in free states, who already opposed slavery, were roused into becoming fiercely active abolitionists.

The Indian Frontier

During this period, Indian Territory comprised most of the vast region known aas the Great Plains. The U.S. government had guaranteed that the Indians had title to this land in perpetuity. However, U.S. expansion westward soon made the "permanent Indian frontier" a fiction.

First, the pioneers migrating westward along the Oregon and California trails had to travel through Indian Territory. The Indians had no objection as long as the settlers were only passing through, rather than claiming any of the land for themselves. Indians and settlers even traded with one another along the journey, and few migrating pioneers were killed by Native Americans in raids or killed any Indians.

Horses enabled the Plains Indians to remain independent and prosperous. Spanish explorers had brought the first horses to North America. Once the tribes learned to breed and ride horses, they had a much easier time chasing and killing buffalo, and following the buffalo herds when they moved. This migratory lifestyle suited the people of the Plains very well.

Once the United States acquired clear title to Oregon Territory and to California and Texas, Indian Territory lay between two sections of settled country.

Migrating pioneers replenished their food supplies by killing buffalo that they encountered on the journey west. Seeking safety, the buffalo herds changed their patterns of migration and grazing, leaving the Indians no choice but to follow the herds. This led tribes to violate one another's hunting grounds in the interests of survival, and intertribal warfare was the result.

The stream of westward migration only grew with time. Between 1849 and 1850, more than 50,000 people traveled across the plains to California, many in search of gold. Such heavy traffic decimated the buffalo herds and put the continued existence of the Sioux tribes in peril. At the urging of concerned Indian agents of the federal government, the White House agreed to hold a conference with the Plains tribes, in which both sides would come to an agreement about compensation to the tribes for their damages, and a right-of-way across the plains for the pioneers.

The conference was held in 1851 near Fort Laramie in present-day Wyoming. More than 10,000 Plains Indians from various tribes attended. Colonel David Mitchell, speaking for the United States, outlined the terms of the proposal. The Indians would agree to cease intertribal warfare; each tribe would promise to remain within its own agreed-upon borders. The tribes would agree that all westbound migrants could cross the Plains in safety. They would also agree to allow the U.S. government to build forts and roads on the Plains. In return, the United States would pay each tribe $50,000 in food and trade goods for the next 50 years. The U.S. government was proceeding on the theory that by the end of that period, the Plains Indians would have become successful farmers.

The treaty had numerous effects. It deprived the Indians of their customary ability to range freely over the Plains, making it more difficult for them to hunt and making them more dependent on the charity of the U.S. government. It moved most tribes out of what would become Kansas and Nebraska into the Dakotas, Montana, Wyoming, the foothills of the Rocky Mountains, and Oklahoma. It deprived the tribes of their sovereignty over the Great Plains, which had been promised to them and their heirs in perpetuity. It hastened the end of the hunting culture of the Plains; with continued westward migration and the prospect of the construction of roads and forts, it was clear that the buffalo herds would continue to be diminished.

CHAPTER 13 QUIZ

1. **The Mexican War was fought over the issue of** _____
   A. territorial control.
   B. slavery.
   C. Indians' rights.
   D. religion.

2. **What happened at the Alamo in 1836?**
   A. The Mexican army defeated the Texan rebels.
   B. The Texan rebels gained independence for Texas.
   C. The U.S. army defeated the Mexican army.
   D. The Mexican army defeated the U.S. army.

3. **The United States bought territory in** _____ **in the Gadsden Purchase of 1853.**
   A. the Great Plains
   B. the Northwest
   C. the Southwest
   D. the Caribbean

4. **Northerners agreed to pass the Fugitive Slave Act of 1850 in exchange for** _____
   A. the purchase of the Mexican Cession.
   B. the establishment of the Underground Railroad.
   C. the Fort Laramie conference on the status of the Plains Indians.
   D. the admission of California as a free U.S. state.

5. **As a result of the Fort Laramie conference, Indians vacated the area that later became the states of** _____
   A. North and South Dakota.
   B. New Mexico and Arizona.
   C. Kansas and Nebraska.
   D. Texas and Oklahoma.

6. **As a result of the Mexican War, the United States gained all the following future states except** _____
   A. California.
   B. Nevada.
   C. Oregon.

D. Utah.

7. **Americans were eager to settle Texas in the 1820s primarily because** _____
   A. Texas was a slaveholding state.
   B. Texas was an independent republic.
   C. they wanted Mexican citizenship.
   D. the land was inexpensive to buy.

8. **The Fugitive Slave Act of 1850 made it legal to** _____
   A. work on the Underground Railroad.
   B. help any slave escape to a free state.
   C. gain freedom by crossing the border into a free state.
   D. deny an accused slave the right to testify in his or her own defense.

9. **What was the purpose of the Underground Railroad?**
   A. to ease overcrowding on city streets
   B. to help slaves escape to freedom
   C. to encourage westward migration
   D. to make transport of goods more efficient

10. **After the Compromise of 1850, many African Americans fled to** _____
    A. California.
    B. Canada.
    C. Mexico.
    D. Texas.

Chapter 14

A House Divided, 1820–1860

The issue of slavery continued to divide the nation. None of Henry Clay's famous compromises had altered the basic situation—that in the South, there was a system of enforced labor, based on racial discrimination, in which the workers were paid no wages and had no rights. The northerners were determined to end slavery throughout the nation; the southerners were equally determined to expand slavery into the West.

West coast states banned slavery absolutely; both California and Oregon insisted on entering the Union as free states. When Senator Stephen Douglas of Illinois proposed that the Kansas and Nebraska Territories be allowed to decide for themselves whether they wanted to be slaveholding or free, he provoked outraged reactions on all sides. Northerners were furious because the Kansas-Nebraska Act overturned the Missouri Compromise, which had outlawed slavery in the territories. Southerners were angry because they thought Douglas should have fought to make Kansas a slave territory.

In 1857, the Supreme Court declared that a slave was a slave no matter where he traveled, even into free territory. The Court also stated that since slaves were property and the Fifth Amendment protected property rights, any law prohibiting slavery anywhere was unconstitutional.

Americans on both sides of the issue took action. Missouri "Border Ruffians" stormed into Kansas Territory before an election and illegally voted a proslavery legislature into office. John Brown and his supporters tried unsuccessfully to start an armed slave uprising in Harpers Ferry, Virginia. Harriet Beecher Stowe published *Uncle Tom's Cabin*, a dramatic story that opened northern eyes to the corrupting influence of slavery on everyone it touched. And in Illinois, a self-educated lawyer named Abraham Lincoln decided to run for national office.

To southerners, Lincoln's election to the White House in 1860 was the final straw. Seven southern states rapidly seceded from the Union, declaring themselves the Confederate States of America.

CHAPTER OBJECTIVES

- Explain the causes and effects of the Kansas–Nebraska Act.
- Discuss the *Dred Scott* case, including the Court's decision and its effects.
- Identify the key figures of the era and explain their roles in the escalating tension between North and South.

Chapter 14 Time Line

- **1845** *Narrative of the Life of Frederick Douglass*
- **1850** Fugitive Slave Act of 1850
- **1852** *Uncle Tom's Cabin*
  Franklin Pierce elected president
- **1854** Kansas-Nebraska Act
  Republican Party formed
- **1855** Kansas elections
- **1856** Pottawatomie Massacre
  James Buchanan elected president
- **1857** *Dred Scott v. Sanford*
- **1858** Lincoln-Douglas debates
- **1859** Raid on Harpers Ferry
- **1860** Abraham Lincoln elected president
  South Carolina secedes from the United States

Sectional Division

As time went on, it became more and more clear that Americans felt more loyalty to their state and region than they did to the nation as a whole. They thought of themselves as Virginians or New Yorkers, northerners or southerners. This marked a change in the spirit of national unity that had existed during the Revolutionary War days.

Sectionalism—loyalty to one's own section of the country—thrived because of opposing attitudes toward slavery. The northern states had outlawed it by the turn of the nineteenth century; the southern states insisted on maintaining it. Each region was determined to force the other to give way. More than once, the South had threatened to secede from the United States if certain antislavery measures were passed.

Southern slaveholders justified slavery on two grounds: economics and racism. They argued that the southern cotton crop was highly important to the national economy, and that it would not be cost-effective to work the plantations with a wage-earning labor force. They also had convinced themselves, and continued to teach every generation of their children, that Africans were an inferior race, fit only for slavery. Southerners argued that black people were not smart or capable enough to take care of themselves; therefore, white slaveholders were actually playing a good and necessary role in taking care of them.

Abolitionists argued that such ideas were nonsense. They pointed out that slaveholders forced slaves to live in conditions of poverty and ignorance and then blamed them for being poor and ignorant—slaveholders, not slaves, were to blame. They could also accurately point out that a large number of slaves were at least half European—free southern white men fathered thousands of children by slave women. It was absurd to argue that slaves were racially inferior to people of European descent, when so many slaves had a large proportion of European genes. For many abolitionists, the wrong of treating people as property overrode all other considerations.

Racism certainly existed in the North, but African Americans in the North had the same basic human and civil rights as all other Americans—to be paid for their labor, to marry, to vote (if male), and to get an education. Northerners to whom economics were more important than racism probably considered that if the South were less prosperous, the North would benefit.

Southerners threatened to secede from the Union when California asked to be admitted to the Union as a free state. Congressional debate became so violent that Senator Henry Foote of Mississippi even threatened to shoot Senator Thomas Hart Benton of Missouri from across the Senate chamber. "Stand out of the way and let the assassin fire!" Benton thundered as other senators hurried to intervene.

By now Henry Clay, veteran of so many congressional debates and author of so many compromises, was a tired old man of 73. Clay urged his colleagues to try to come to an agreement for the sake of the nation as a whole. South Carolina Senator John C. Calhoun, who had been Andrew Jackson's vice president and who was even more frail and ill than Clay, scorned Clay's suggestion. "Let the states agree to part in peace," he wrote. "If you are unwilling that we should part in peace, tell us so, and we shall know what to do."

Daniel Webster of Massachusetts was the next to speak. He supported Clay, urging the senators to preserve the Union in order to avoid war between the North and South. "There can be no such thing as peaceable secession," Webster warned the Senate. "Peaceable secession is an utter impossibility."

Both John Calhoun and President Zachary Taylor died in 1850. New President Millard Fillmore agreed with Webster and Clay that it was more important to preserve the Union than to abolish or even check the spread of slavery. Under the Compromise of 1850, California entered the Union as a free state, but a new, harsh Fugitive Slave Act was passed (see Chapter 13).

Abolitionist Literature

Greatly to the chagrin of the southerners, the passage of the Fugitive Slave Act energized the abolitionist movement in the North. Most northerners opposed the institution of slavery, but many had taken no active steps against it. Two of the most famous works in American literature appeared at this time; they too addressed the question of slavery and fueled the spirit of abolition. The first was the *Narrative of the Life of Frederick Douglass*, appearing in 1845. The second was *Uncle Tom's Cabin*, appearing in 1852.

Narrative of the Life of Frederick Douglass was a slave narrative—an autobiography describing the brutal repressions from which slaves like Douglass had been skillful and lucky enough to escape. In the years following the publication of the *Narrative*, Douglass became famous as a public speaker, most frequently on the issue of abolition. Those who read his book or saw his imposing presence on a speaker's platform were deeply impressed.

Harriet Beecher Stowe's epic novel *Uncle Tom's Cabin* shocked the reading public with its portrayal of an entire society corrupted by slavery—male and female, free and enslaved, enlightened and bigoted, young and old, educated and ignorant, northern and southern, black and white. The novel reveals the evil effects of the slave system on everyone it touches: it corrupts people who are good and noble in other respects into the belief that slaves are not fully

THE MYTH

Uncle Tom, the hero of Harriet Beecher Stowe's abolitionist novel *Uncle Tom's Cabin*, later became an American idiom. To call someone "an Uncle Tom" is to insult him—to suggest that he collaborates with white people to oppress and condescend to African Americans. People who know this idiom assume that it accurately describes Stowe's protagonist.

THE FACTS

Stowe's Uncle Tom is a deeply religious man who works hard without complaining and, when dying, expresses forgiveness for his oppressors. However, he is no "Uncle Tom"—his own conscience, not the orders of his masters, is his ultimate guide.

When the novel begins, Tom is a highly regarded and well-treated house slave to a wealthy planter. When the planter dies and his property and slaves are sold, Tom ends up under a new master, the brutal Simon Legree. When Legree orders Tom to whip another slave to punish her for some infraction, Tom refuses:

> *"I'm willin' to work, night and day, and work while there's life and breath in me; but this yer thing I can't feel it right to do;—and Mas'r, I never shall do it,—never!"*

When Legree beats Tom for his refusal, and later orders Tom to beg his pardon for insubordination, Tom continues to resist:

> *"I did only what I thought was right. . . . I'll be a true and faithful servant to ye. I'll give ye all the work of my hands, all my time, all my strength; but my soul I won't give up to mortal man."*

Later in the novel, Tom urges two miserable female slaves to run away; during a beating so severe that he dies of his injuries, he still refuses to give Legree any information about the escape. In Tom, Stowe created a character of great moral courage.

human. Stowe's novel outsold every book in the United States except the Bible in the years leading up to the Civil War. It was translated into several languages and made her an international celebrity. It opened the eyes of many northerners to the realities of slavery as portrayed in its pages, and it reinforced the abolitionist beliefs of many more. The novel was banned in the South; southerners who read it dismissed it as the ravings of a crazy woman.

New Political Parties

As the battle between the proslavery and antislavery factions continued, northerners formed new political parties in their attempt to combat the spread of slavery and maintain their power base in Washington. The Free-Soil Party, formed in 1848, did not win any electoral votes in the presidential election. However, a number of its candidates were elected to Congress. (See Chapter 13.)

In 1852, the Free-Soilers tried for the White House once again. Their candidate was John Hale of New Hampshire, running against Democrat Franklin Pierce and Whig Winfield Scott, who had served with distinction in the Mexican War. Pierce won in a landslide of electoral votes, and the Free-Soilers gave up the struggle. The Whigs also accepted this defeat as final; they were never again to play a significant role in American politics.

In 1854, the remnants of the Whig Party and the Free-Soil Party joined antislavery members of the Know-Nothing and Democratic parties. This group formed a strong coalition of men determined to end the expansion of slavery in the United States. They called their new party the Republican Party. In 1856, they supported John C. Frémont for president. Frémont, a career army officer and a topographical engineer in peacetime, made a strong showing, but Democratic candidate James Buchanan carried the South and thus won the presidency.

Kansas-Nebraska Act

In 1854, Senator Stephen Douglas of Illinois, soon to go down in history as Abraham Lincoln's most famous political opponent, introduced the Kansas-Nebraska Act into Congress. The act proposed the following:

- That the unorganized territory north of the 37th parallel and west of the Missouri River be divided into two sections, one called Nebraska, the other called Kansas

- That the territories set up their own governments on the basis of popular sovereignty
- That once the territories are organized, Congress proceed with plans for a transcontinental railroad

"Popular sovereignty" meant that the people who settled Kansas and Nebraska could decide for themselves how their governments would work. As everyone in Congress knew, the real meaning of this proposal was that the territories would decide for themselves whether they would be slaveholding or free states. This provision of the act violated the Missouri Compromise of 1820, which had banned slavery in the territory north of Missouri's southern border (excluding Missouri itself). (See Chapter 10.)

Nicknamed the "Little Giant" for his combination of short physical stature and forceful personality, Douglas was a native of Vermont who had settled in Illinois and been elected to Congress in 1842. He championed the issues of westward expansion and states' rights. In Douglas's view, the federal govern-

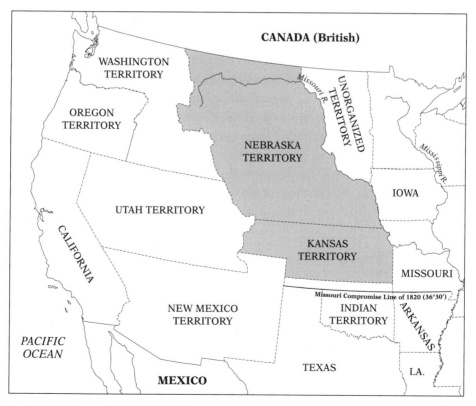

The United States and Territories in 1854

ment had no right to interfere in the issue of whether a territory or state should be slaveholding or free; the people of that state or territory should decide for themselves.

The Kansas-Nebraska Act became law in 1854. Douglas had hoped it would be received as a compromise, since he knew that the new territory would likely end up half slaveholding (Kansas) and half free (Nebraska). He was dismayed to discover that it only divided Congress and the nation further. People argued against the repeal of the Missouri Compromise on various grounds. Some were abolitionists on principle and wanted to stop the spread of slavery. Some argued that if slavery were allowed in the territories, white people would no longer migrate westward in search of jobs; businesses would never pay wages when they could force slaves to work for nothing. For the same reason, white workers who had already settled in the West would be forced out.

Both abolitionist and proslavery groups urged people to move into the territories. Both sides knew that if they could gain a majority in the population of Kansas and Nebraska, the votes on the slavery issue would be decided in their favor. The issue was moot in Nebraska Territory; it was far enough north that it was settled, as Douglas had foreseen, by northerners who had no desire to own slaves. Southerners did not travel far enough north to create a powerful voice in Nebraska politics, and an antislavery legislature was elected without fuss.

Kansas, however, proved to be a battleground. Although few southerners seriously intended to extend slavery into a territory whose climate would not support cotton or rice cultivation, southern politicians were determined to enlarge their political base and to acquire more senators and representatives who would vote their way in Congress.

The election that would choose the Kansas legislature was to be held in March, 1855. Just before the election, 5,000 proslavery Missouri voters marched into Kansas. These "Border Ruffians" had no right to vote there, since they were not residents of the territory, but they were armed and violent, ready to kill anyone at the polling places who tried to prevent them from voting. With these illegal Missouri votes, a proslavery legislature was elected. This legislature immediately passed laws making it a crime to criticize slavery, banning newspapers that wrote antislavery editorials, and even forbidding preachers to speak against slavery from the pulpit. These flagrant violations of their constitutional rights to free speech and a free press infuriated the people of Kansas, who immediately elected their own antislavery legislature, representing the Free State Party. Kansas now had two governments. It was only a matter of time before the two sides would have to confront one another and settle which was to run the territory.

John Brown and "Bleeding Kansas"

The Free State Party had made the town of Lawrence its headquarters. In May of 1856, hundreds of Border Ruffians marched on Lawrence and sacked the town. When this news reached the ears of the fiery abolitionist John Brown, he decided he had waited more than long enough to take action against the slavers.

John Brown was born in Connecticut and had lived in Ohio and upstate New York before becoming a prominent abolitionist in Pennsylvania. He had worked with the Underground Railroad, and all his life had treated blacks as equals. When the Kansas-Nebraska Act was passed, Brown foresaw that Kansas might become a battleground. He had always believed that only an armed uprising of abolitionists and slaves would bring about emancipation.

On May 23, 1856, Brown led a small group of abolitionists to Pottawatomie Creek, a center of proslavery advocates. Brown and his small army kidnapped five of them and hacked their bodies to pieces. The Pottawatomie Massacre outraged southerners and gave the territory the nickname "Bleeding Kansas." In the Senate, Charles Sumner of Massachusetts delivered a scathing speech blaming the violence on the slavers who had insisted on overturning the Missouri Compromise. Two days later, Congressman Preston Brooks of South Carolina retaliated, accosting Sumner in the Senate chamber and attempting to beat him to death with a cane. This murderous attack polarized Americans still further; many who had been neutral were converted to fervent abolitionists, while voters in Brooks's home district sent him gifts to show their approval.

In Kansas, the Free State Legislature broke up in July 1856, convinced that since the majority of the people were antislavery, the principle of popular sovereignty would eventually make Kansas a free territory and then a free state. This indeed happened. The voters elected abolitionists to the legislature, and Kansas drafted a free-state constitution in 1859.

Dred Scott Decision

In 1857, the Supreme Court took a stand on the issue of slave status. A Missouri slave named Dred Scott sued for his freedom on the grounds that he had lived in Illinois and Minnesota—free territories—for four years. The Court ruled against him, stating that slave status traveled with the person, and that Scott did not carry free status back to Missouri with him when he returned there. Chief Justice Roger Taney added that he believed the framers of the Constitution had perceived Africans as "an inferior order, and unfit associates for the white race" and had never intended the Constitution to apply to them. Taney went on to argue that since slaves were property, and the Fifth Amendment prevented anyone from being deprived of property without due process of law, any law against slavery was unconstitutional. The Missouri Compromise had been unconstitutional because it robbed slave owners of their property by conferring freedom on any slaves who were taken into free territory. In practice, this decision meant that Congress had no right to ban slavery anywhere; it had no power to contain the spread of slavery westward or even into the North.

Dred Scott v. Sanford had several immediate effects. First, the newly elected President James Buchanan refused to recognize the free-state government in Kansas. Second, westerners and northerners alike reacted with dismay to the ruling that slavery could expand throughout the country. The West became increasingly closely connected with the North, both economically and politically; thus, the South grew more isolated from the rest of the nation.

Frederick Douglass summed up the antislavery reaction to the *Dred Scott* decision:

> I ask, then, any man to read the Constitution, and tell me where, if he can, in what particular that instrument affords the slightest sanction of slavery? . . .
>
> This very attempt to blot out forever the hopes of an enslaved people may be one necessary link in the chain of events preparatory to the downfall and complete overthrow of the whole slave system.

The Lincoln-Douglas Debates

In 1858, one of the most important figures in American history appeared on the national political scene. Abraham Lincoln, a self-educated Illinois lawyer, had served one term in the House of Representatives, but had not achieved national renown. He returned to politics over the question of slavery, which he opposed, stating plainly that "no man is good enough to govern another without that other's consent." At the Republican convention of 1858, Lincoln gave one of the most famous speeches of his career. He quoted the Bible in the speech's most famous paragraph:

> "A house divided against itself cannot stand." I believe this government cannot endure, permanently, half slave and half free. I do not expect the Union to be dissolved; I do not expect the house to fall; but I do expect it will cease to be divided. It will become all one thing, or all the other.

Republican candidate Lincoln ran against Democratic candidate Stephen Douglas. The two held a series of seven debates between August and October 1858. They argued the important issue of the day—slavery—at length in each appearance. Both men defended their positions on the *Dred Scott* decision, on the theory of popular sovereignty, on the Compromise of 1850, and on the expansion of slavery. Huge crowds turned out to hear the two men speak. In the end, Douglas defeated Lincoln by a slim margin of votes. However, he would soon lose to Lincoln in a much more important race.

Harpers Ferry

On October 16, 1859, John Brown struck what many people referred to afterward as the first blow of the Civil War. Brown had left Kansas and gone east to raise an African American army. His belief in the power of arms to end slavery speedily was unaltered. He captured the interest and excitement of many men, but during the months of preparation for action, many of them grew uneasy or lost faith in Brown and abandoned his cause.

During the night of October 16, Brown and his small remaining band of followers seized the federal arsenal at Harpers Ferry, Virginia, and took sixty hostages. Brown was devastated when no slaves came to the aid of his army. Within 36 hours, Colonel Robert E. Lee and the Virginia militia had surrounded the arsenal, killed many of Brown's men, and compelled the rest to surrender. On December 2, 1859, John Brown was hanged as a traitor. Henry David Thoreau spoke for all enslaved Africans and abolitionists when he wrote that Brown had been "a brave and humane man." Southerners, of course, had the opposite reaction. To them, Brown was a terrorist whose act amounted to a declaration of war on them and on their way of life.

The Election of 1860

In 1860, the Republicans nominated Abraham Lincoln for president. The Democrats, for the first time in many years, were not agreed on a favorite candidate. The Democratic convention nominated Stephen Douglas, but the southerners found him too moderate. They nominated John Breckinridge to run against Douglas and Lincoln.

People cast their ballots along strictly geographical lines. The Deep South voted for Breckinridge, while the Pacific coastal states, the Midwest, and the Northeast voted for Lincoln. Constitutional Party candidate John Bell of Tennessee won in Virginia, Tennessee, and Kentucky, but this accounted for less than six thousand votes. Stephen Douglas carried only the state of Missouri,

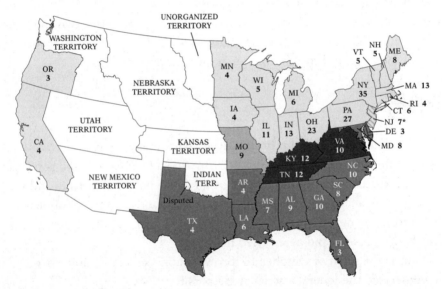

Candidate	Party	Electoral Vote	Popular Vote	Percentage of Popular Vote
Lincoln	Republican	180	1,865,593	39.8
Douglas	Northern Democrat	12	1,382,713	29.5
Breckinridge	Southern Democrat	72	848,356	18.1
Bell	Constitutional Union	39	592,906	12.6

*New Jersey cast four electoral votes for Lincoln and three for Douglas.

Electoral map for election of 1860

although his total popular vote was only five hundred thousand fewer than Lincoln received. See the electoral map.

Lincoln became president because the proslavery faction had divided its votes between two candidates. Although Lincoln had stated publicly and repeatedly that he had neither the constitutional authority nor the desire to abolish slavery in the states where it already existed, southerners hated him. Days after his election, South Carolina seceded from the Union. Alabama, Florida, Georgia, Louisiana, Mississippi, and Texas followed in rapid succession. These states banded together as the Confederate States of America, drawing up a constitution and electing Jefferson Davis of Mississippi as their president. (Arkansas, North Carolina, Tennessee, and Virginia would join the Confederacy in the spring of 1861.) James Buchanan, who would remain president until Lincoln's inauguration, took no action regarding the Confederacy; it would be up to President Lincoln to resolve the situation.

CHAPTER 14 QUIZ

1. **All of these states seceded and joined the Confederacy except** _____
    A. Texas.
    B. Maryland.
    C. Virginia.
    D. Tennessee.

2. **Antislavery candidate Abraham Lincoln was elected president because** _____
    A. support for slavery was not as strong as opposition to it.
    B. he received an overwhelming majority of popular votes.
    C. proslavery voters split their support between two candidates.
    D. he was the personal choice of President James Buchanan.

3. **In *Dred Scott v. Sanford*, the Supreme Court decided that** _____
    A. slave status was permanent and any ban on slavery was unconstitutional.
    B. a person was a slave only in a slaveholding state; he or she gained freedom by entering a free state.
    C. slave status could not be retroactively assigned to any person who had previously been declared free under the law.
    D. freeing any living slaves was unconstitutional, but slavery after the current generation would be permanently banned.

4. **What effect did the novel *Uncle Tom's Cabin* have on the abolitionist movement?**
   A. It gained many supporters for the movement.
   B. It persuaded people to abandon the movement as hopeless.
   C. It demonstrated that the movement was hypocritical.
   D. It brought the movement into national prominence for the first time.

5. **Various antislavery factions banded together to form the _____ Party in 1854.**
   A. Free-Soil
   B. Democratic
   C. Whig
   D. Republican

6. **In what respect did the Kansas-Nebraska Act violate the Missouri Compromise?**
   A. It established slavery throughout the new territory.
   B. It suggested that the territory be divided into two states.
   C. It made slavery possible beyond an agreed-upon border.
   D. It established possible new states west of the Missouri River.

7. **The Border Ruffians are famous for _____**
   A. championing the cause of Dred Scott.
   B. taking the arsenal at Harpers Ferry in Virginia.
   C. supporting John Brown in his antislavery rebellion.
   D. illegally electing a proslavery legislature in Kansas.

8. **John Brown was executed for _____**
   A. taking up arms against the Virginia militia.
   B. speaking out passionately against slavery.
   C. kidnapping and killing proslavers in Kansas.
   D. brutally attacking Senator Charles Sumner in the Capitol.

9. **On what grounds did Dred Scott sue for his freedom?**
   A. that he had lived for years in free territory
   B. that slavery was unconstitutional
   C. that his owner had promised to free him at a certain time
   D. that he was an educated man

10. **Which best describes the political atmosphere in the West during the period before the Civil War?**
    A. allied with the North in support of abolition
    B. allied with the South in support of slavery
    C. not ready to support either the North or the South
    D. ready to support either the North or the South if war broke out

Chapter 15

The Civil War, 1861–1865

Few were surprised when the bitter sectional violence that had divided the nation escalated into an all-out war. The election of Republican Abraham Lincoln had convinced many in the South that they would never succeed in their ambition to spread slavery throughout the nation. A total of eleven states seceded from the Union, forming the Confederate States of America.

The southern motive for war was clear: the southerners were not willing to change their economic and social system, particularly when they felt that the changes were being forced on them by outsiders. Southerners were convinced that northerners had no right to interfere with a system in which they themselves did not participate. The Union motives for the war were more ambiguous. Lincoln's primary goal was to restore the United States of America; he opposed slavery and intended to end it, but freeing the slaves was only a secondary motive for war.

When the fighting began, the Confederacy faced many disadvantages. It was much smaller than the Union and thus had a much smaller population of boys and young men who could serve in the military. The South had few factories, little heavy industry, and much less money than the North. On the other hand, it did have greatly superior generals. This fact alone made the Civil War last probably three years longer than it otherwise would have.

The war began with a string of important victories for the South. When Confederate troops failed to take Gettysburg, however, they lost all hope of winning the war. They would never again penetrate into the northern states. The Battle of Gettysburg was lost on the same day that Vicksburg fell. The war dragged on for another year and a half, but in April 1865, the Confederacy surrendered to the Union.

The cost to both sides was heavy. An entire generation died on the battlefield or from wounds, disease, or starvation—more than 600,000 boys and young men. (This was roughly 20 times the number of soldiers who had died in all previous American wars combined.) There had been little fighting in the North, but many southern towns and cities had been battle sites, and were largely or entirely in ruins. Railroad lines had to be rebuilt and mail service reestablished. Slaves who had been freed by the Emancipation Proclamation suddenly found themselves unemployed and homeless. The defeated South cherished a bitter hatred toward the northerners—a destructive emotion that would fester for many decades to come, and that found immediate expression in the tragic assassination of President Lincoln by an emotionally unstable southern sympathizer. Perhaps most daunting of all, the South would now have to rebuild its entire society to function and prosper without slave labor.

CHAPTER OBJECTIVES

- Identify the advantages and disadvantages of the Union and Confederate armies in 1861.
- Identify the major battles and describe the course of the war.
- Discuss the importance and meaning of the Emancipation Proclamation and the Gettysburg Address.
- Identify the people who played major roles in the Civil War.

Chapter 15 Time Line

1861   **January–February**   Six more states secede from the Union

February   Seceding states form Confederacy and choose Jefferson Davis as President

April   Fall of Fort Sumter, South Carolina

Four more states secede from Union; West Virginia secedes from Virginia

July   First Battle of Bull Run, Virginia (Battle of Manassas)

1862 **February** Fall of Forts Lee and Donaldson, Tennessee

      April Battle of Shiloh, Tennessee

            Fall of New Orleans and Memphis

      September Battle of Antietam, Maryland

            Preliminary Emancipation Proclamation

      November Burnside replaces McClellan as commander of U.S. Army

      December Battle of Fredericksburg, Maryland

1863 **January 1** Emancipation Proclamation

      May Battle of Chancellorsville, Virginia

      June Siege of Vicksburg, Mississippi, begins

      July Attack on Fort Wagner, South Carolina

            Battle of Gettysburg, Pennsylvania

            Battle of Vicksburg

      November Gettysburg Address

1864 Battles of Wilderness, Spotsylvania, and Cold Harbor

      August Siege of Richmond, Virginia, begins

      September Fall of Atlanta, Georgia

      October Union victories in Shenandoah Valley

      November Lincoln reelected

            Burning of Atlanta

1865 Battle of Petersburg, Virginia

      Fall of Richmond

      Confederates surrender at Appomattox, Virginia

      Lincoln assassinated; Andrew Johnson becomes president

President Abraham Lincoln

When Abraham Lincoln took office, all sides pressured him to compromise: either to give in to the spread of slavery or to let the South go its own way. The fact that Lincoln was married to southern belle Mary Todd, whose brothers were in the Confederate Army, made many people doubt his loyalty to the Union and his fitness to lead a war against the South. Lincoln withstood all pressure, never wavering in his conviction that slavery must not spread beyond the current slaveholding states, nor in his determination to bring the southern states back into the Union.

Lincoln was born in poverty in a Kentucky log cabin. He worked hard on his father's farm by day and read every book he could borrow by lamplight at night. At six feet four inches, he towered over most of the men of his day. Lincoln practiced law for some time before serving one term in Congress, then running for the Senate, and finally winning the presidency. In his series of debates with Stephen Douglas, he proved that he was a powerful and eloquent public speaker. Like future presidents Kennedy and Clinton, Lincoln also had a shrewd sense of humor that created a genuine bond between him and the voters. Lincoln was one of the greatest political thinkers and writers and American history.

Strengths and Weaknesses of North and South

The strengths of the Union were obvious from the beginning. In terms of population, the Union was more than twice the size of the Confederacy—and one-third of the Confederate population was enslaved. With a larger population, the North would have a larger fighting force, a greater pool from which to draw replacements for casualties, and more workers who could take over essential noncombat jobs in industry. The North also had greater resources, controlling well over 80 percent of the nation's factories and industry. This meant that it could produce the necessary uniforms, supplies, and weapons itself, without relying on foreign allies or going into debt. The North had about four times as much cash on deposit in banks as the South did. It commanded the loyalty of the U.S. Navy, which was to prove a key weapon in the war; the South would literally have to build its own navy.

Perhaps most important, the South was fighting for a cause that was bound to lose. By outlawing slavery during the late 1700s and early 1800s, the North had moved with the times, while the South refused to recognize that slavery had become an anachronism. For example, the czar of Russia had long since begun the process of emancipating the serfs.

The South had a few advantages. One was the possibility of foreign alliances; Britain and France, two major buyers of southern cotton, might step in to aid the South. The South also had the skilled military leaders. Robert E. Lee was so highly regarded that Lincoln asked him to take command of the Union army. Torn between his loyalty to the United States and his opposition to secession on one side, and his love for his native Virginia on the other, Lee refused. He resigned from the U.S. Army and soon found himself in command of the Confederate Army.

The Start of the War

In April 1861, the Confederates fired on Fort Sumter in Charleston harbor, South Carolina. In the months since secession, the Confederates had taken over federal arsenals, forts, and other property throughout the South. Federal troops inside Fort Sumter refused to surrender, appealing to the White House for help when supplies began running low. Lincoln notified the Confederacy that he was sending supplies for the fort, but no troops or weapons. The Confederates called on the fort's commander to surrender. When he refused, the Confederates shelled the fort.

On April 15, the Union formally declared war. Lincoln called for 75,000 volunteer troops to put down the rebellion. Virginia, North Carolina, Arkansas, and Tennessee swiftly seceded from the Union rather than take up arms against the Confederacy. The mountainous region of western Virginia, where there was little support for slavery, soon seceded from Virginia and was granted statehood as West Virginia in 1863.

On July 21, 1861, in the first full-scale battle of the war, Confederate and Union troops faced one another at Bull Run Creek near Manassas, Virginia. The Union Army was winning the battle when southern reinforcements arrived; seeing the fresh troops advancing on them, the Union soldiers began a disorganized, chaotic retreat toward Washington.

The First Battle of Bull Run had opposite effects on the two sides; it made the South complacent, while it humbled and sobered the North. Many Confederate soldiers were so confident of a quick and easy southern victory that they deserted after the battle, going home to look after their crops. In addition,

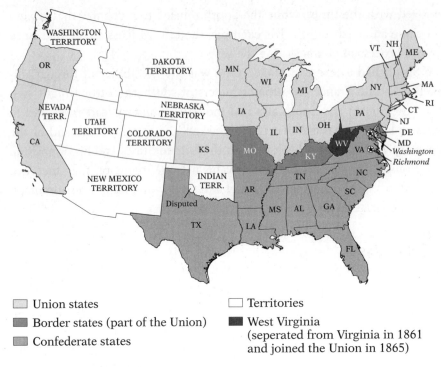

Union states
Border states (part of the Union)
Confederate states
Territories
West Virginia
(seperated from Virginia in 1861
and joined the Union in 1865)

The United States and the Confederacy in 1861

the South failed to take advantage of the victory by immediately marching on Washington, DC; many historians believe that if this had happened, the war might have ended quickly in a southern victory. The North, on the other hand, realized that the Confederate Army would not be easily defeated and began military training in earnest.

STRATEGY AND GOALS

	Union	**Confederacy**
Goals	Restore the Union	Defend the Confederacy
Strategies	• Capture Richmond, Virginia • Gain control of the Mississippi River • Use the U.S. Navy to blockade the South • Divide the South geographically along the Mississippi, fighting a two-front war	• Outlast the North • Invade the North through the Shenandoah Valley

The Union Takes the Mississippi River

In February of 1862, Union troops captured Forts Henry and Donelson and the city of Nashville, Tennessee. These successes accomplished three things. First, the North gained control of Kentucky and western Tennessee, a power base from which it could invade the western half of the South. Second, it gave the Union troops confidence in their ultimate victory. Third, it brought a fierce, determined, and courageous officer named Ulysses S. Grant into prominence.

In the spring of 1862, General Grant marched his troops toward the Mississippi. They broke camp near a little church called Shiloh to wait for reinforcements. The Confederates took them by surprise with a fierce attack. Grant's troops were pushed back to the Tennessee River, but he refused to surrender. When Union reinforcements arrived during the night, the battle began again. After two days of terrible fighting, the Union won. Victory at Shiloh gave the North the advantage in the fight for control of the Mississippi River and the river valley. Both sides had lost thousands of men. The capture of New Orleans by the U.S. Navy, which steadily shelled the two forts that guarded the approach to the city until the Confederates surrendered, completed the Union plan to take control of the Mississippi River and cut the South in two.

The Army of the Potomac

While Grant led successful campaigns in the West and South, General George McClellan led the Army of the Potomac against Johnston and Lee's Confederate forces near the capital cities of Washington and Richmond. Although McClellan excelled at military discipline and trained his recruits well, he was not a capable or skilled commander; the Army of the Potomac won no decisive victories under his leadership. In September 1862, the Confederate Army won a second battle at Bull Run, once again putting itself in a position to march on Washington and failing to do so.

The Battle of Antietam, fought near Antietam Creek in Maryland, was an important Union victory. Two Union soldiers found a discarded piece of paper that turned out to be a copy of the Confederate battle plans. They immediately passed the information on to General McClellan. By the end of the day-long battle, more than 25,000 men lay dead on the battlefield. Having failed to win a victory on Union soil, the Confederates retreated to Virginia. This loss made Great Britain decide not to enter the war on the side of the Confederacy.

The Emancipation Proclamation

In April 1862, Lincoln issued an executive order that freed all the slaves in Washington, DC. In September, he issued the preliminary Emancipation Proclamation, which had two main provisions. First, it stated that as of January 1, 1863, all slaves in any territory in rebellion against the United States would be "then, thenceforward, and forever free." Second, it invited African Americans to enlist in the Union Army.

The proclamation did not extend freedom to any slaves currently in the Union (four slaveholding states had not seceded with the rest). Confederate states that rejoined the Union could thus keep their slaves; those that remained in rebellion would lose them. The entire Confederacy spurned the offer; thus, by U.S. law, slavery officially ended in the old South on the first day of 1863.

Lincoln's purpose in issuing the Emancipation Proclamation was three-fold. His primary goal was to reunite the Union and the Confederacy; if even one Confederate state accepted the bargain and rejoined the Union, it would weaken the Confederacy and thus bring about a Union victory that much sooner. Lincoln also knew that slaves throughout the South would hear of the proclamation; he hoped to win their loyalty and support for the Union cause, and also hoped that many would enlist in the Union Army. Again, if the South lost a significant number of viable soldiers to the North, a southern defeat would come more quickly. (In the end, more than 180,000 former slaves would fight for the Union, many with distinction.)

Lincoln's second goal was to end the era of compromise over slavery once and for all; the issue had divided the nation too violently for too many decades at far too high a cost. If the Confederate states had surrendered in order to keep their slaves, Lincoln would no doubt have advocated gradual emancipation—a plan he had been discussing with the representatives of slaveholding Union states such as Maryland. The alternative was, of course, immediate emancipation—enforcing the Emancipation Proclamation on schedule in states which continued to fight. (As it turned out, the Thirteenth Amendment would abolish slavery throughout the United States on December 6, 1865.) Third, Lincoln believed that slavery was indefensible, on both logical and moral grounds. The Emancipation Proclamation made it clear to all that the days of slavery were numbered.

The Confederates won a great victory at Fredericksburg, Virginia, just before the Emancipation Proclamation was due to take effect. Lee established his troops on high ground overlooking an open plain, in the perfect position to fire on the Union troops when they crossed the plain. Four months later, the South scored another victory at Chancellorsville, where Generals Lee and Stonewall Jackson organized an ingenious double-pronged attack against the Union army. The South suffered a severe blow during the battle, however, when Confederate troops mistook Jackson for an enemy soldier and shot him. Jackson, who had been one of the ablest generals in the Confederate Army, died of his wounds a week later.

THE MYTH

Most people believe that the Emancipation Proclamation freed all American slaves.

THE FACTS

The Emancipation Proclamation freed slaves in the Confederacy only. Its language is very specific. It did not apply to slaves in slaveholding states that had remained within the Union: Maryland, Delaware, Missouri, and Kentucky. Although the document did not say so in so many words, the implication was clear; any rebel—i.e. Confederate—state that rejoined the Union could keep its slaves.

Southern leaders believed, with justification, that the Emancipation Proclamation was something of a political bluff. They were convinced—correctly—that Lincoln intended to end slavery in the United States once and for all, either gradually or immediately. Therefore, they unanimously refused to rejoin the Union under the terms of the Emancipation Proclamation.

Gettysburg: The Turning Point

Lee decided to take his troops north, following his original plan to win the war on Union territory. He gathered 75,000 troops at the sleepy town of Gettysburg in eastern Pennsylvania. This location became the major battle and the turning point of the entire war. Union and Confederate troops fought from July 1 through July 3, 1863, in the hills and farmland around the town. The Union troops were able to maintain the high ground and thus to win the battle. The Confederate Army would never again penetrate into Union territory.

The cost was high on both sides; in three days of fighting, more than 50,000 men and boys were killed or wounded. At a dedication ceremony for a cemetery for the war dead, Abraham Lincoln gave the most famous speech in American history—the Gettysburg Address. The entire speech is only ten sentences long and took less than five minutes to deliver:

The Gettysburg Address

Fourscore and seven years ago our fathers brought forth on this continent a new nation, conceived in liberty, and dedicated to the proposition that "all men are created equal."

Now we are engaged in a great civil war, testing whether that nation or any nation so conceived and so dedicated can long endure. We are met on a great battlefield of that war. We have come to dedicate a portion of that field as a final resting-place for those who here gave their lives that that nation might live. It is altogether fitting and proper that we should do this. But, in a larger sense, we cannot dedicate—we cannot consecrate—we cannot hallow this ground. The brave men, living and dead, who struggled here, have consecrated it far above our poor power to add or detract. The world will little note nor long remember what we say here, but it can never forget what they did here.

It is for us the living, rather, to be dedicated here to the unfinished work which they who fought here have thus far so nobly advanced. It is rather for us to be here dedicated to the great task remaining before us—that from these honored dead we take increased devotion to that cause for which they gave the last full measure of devotion—that we here highly resolve that these dead shall not have died in vain, that this nation under God shall have a new birth of freedom, and that government of the people, by the people, for the people shall not perish from the earth.

Lincoln begins by quoting the Declaration of Independence—"all men are created equal." He speaks movingly of the cause of liberty for which the soldiers gave their lives. He urges listeners to remember why the nation was founded in the first place—to be a society in which all were free, in which the government and the governed were one.

The War of Attrition

Grant laid siege to Vicksburg, Mississippi, organizing the Union troops in commanding strategic position on the bluffs overlooking the river. The siege was successful. On July 3, 1863, the last day of the Battle of Gettysburg, the Union troops gained control of the Mississippi River and effectively cut the western Confederacy off from coming to Lee's aid. In 1864, Lincoln named General Grant supreme commander of the Union Army.

Because he knew that the Union had the advantage of numbers, Grant's strategy was to fight a war of attrition. No matter how many men the Union lost, they could be replaced, while the South had no pool from which it could draw reinforcements. Therefore, every casualty was far more costly to the South than to the North. People described Grant as a butcher because so many of his men were lost—60,000 in one month of 1864—but they agreed that he would never back down. The Union was winning the war of attrition.

As Grant marched toward Richmond, General William Tecumseh Sherman marched toward Atlanta, destroying important railroads and factories that lay in his path. Sherman's men burned the city of Atlanta after they captured it. This Union victory helped to ensure President Lincoln's reelection. Sherman's men then continued east, taking the port city of Savannah in December. Because Sherman attacked important economic assets and resources—warehouses, stores of food, railroads—civilians throughout the South suffered. Sherman's strategy was effective, but it strengthened the deep hatred southerners felt toward "Yankees."

In April 1865, Richmond fell. Unable to get his troops through Union lines to regroup, General Lee surrendered to General Grant. The terms of surrender were signed at the courthouse in the little village of Appomattox, Virginia. To look at the two generals on that day, no one would have imagined that Grant was the victor: he wore a creased, stained, common soldier's uniform that had seen much hard wear in battle, while Lee was resplendent in full-dress Confederate grays, a ceremonial sword at his side.

Grant was generous in victory. He ordered his troops to share their rations with the Confederate soldiers, many of whom were starving. He also insisted that southern soldiers be allowed to keep their guns, horses, and mules so that they would be able to hunt for food and to rebuild their farms as they returned to civilian life.

The Assassination of Lincoln

Across the South, people received news of the defeat with profound bitterness that would take many decades to heal. One excitable young man, the dashing stage actor John Wilkes Booth, was utterly crushed by the news of the Union victory. Booth blamed Lincoln, whom he viewed as the colonists had once viewed King George III: as a tyrant.

President and Mrs. Lincoln decided to attend a performance at Ford's Theater in Washington on April 14. Seeing the announcement in the newspaper, Booth determined to kill the president during the performance. Booth had performed at Ford's Theater and knew its layout well; the employees of the theater knew him and no one questioned his entrance into the building that night.

During the play, when the audience's attention was focused on the stage, Booth crept up the stairs to the presidential box, overpowered the one guard at the door, and pushed the curtain aside. He pulled out a pistol, shot the president in the head at close range, then vaulted over the railing of the box and leaped to the stage below, shouting *Sic semper tyrannis!* (meaning "Thus always to tyrants!") and pushing past the horrified actors to escape through the theater's back door. Lincoln was immediately carried across the street to the nearest house and doctors were brought to him, but they could do nothing; the bullet had caused severe brain damage. Lincoln died early in the morning without regaining consciousness. This marked the first time an American president had been assassinated. On Lincoln's death, Vice President Andrew Johnson automatically succeeded him.

Booth had expected to be hailed as a hero, striking a blow for individual liberty; instead, he was vilified as a murderer, the target of a federal manhunt. Having broken his ankle in his leap to the stage, Booth had not been able to escape very far. He took refuge in a Maryland barn. When troops found him, several days after the assassination, they ordered him to surrender. When he refused to come out, they set fire to the barn and dragged him out, but not before a fatal shot rang out. One of the federal officers claimed to have fired the shot; some historians believe that Booth shot himself rather than be hanged as a traitor. He died of the gunshot wound within a few hours.

Lincoln had been beloved throughout the North. His funeral procession, which took his body home to Illinois by slow stages, was watched in silence by millions of mourners along the route—including future president Theodore

Roosevelt, then a six-year-old child. Roosevelt never forgot the view of the solemn procession from the upstairs windows of his family home in New York City. President Andrew Johnson now faced the daunting task of helping the South rebuild itself.

CHAPTER 15 QUIZ

1. _____ was the last Civil War battle fought in Union territory.
   A. Antietam
   B. Manassas/Bull Run
   C. Gettysburg
   D. Vicksburg

2. In 1861, the Union had all the following advantages over the Confederacy except _____
   A. better military commanders.
   B. a larger population from which to draw troops.
   C. control of most of the nation's heavy industry.
   D. more money in the treasury.

3. Which new state was created from territory that seceded from the Confederacy?
   A. Kentucky
   B. Tennessee
   C. Maryland
   D. West Virginia

4. The Confederate Army might have won the war quickly if it had _____ in 1861.
   A. marched on Washington, DC
   B. captured Richmond, Virginia
   C. defeated the Army of the Potomac
   D. assassinated President Lincoln

5. **The Emancipation Proclamation** _____
   A. freed all slaves in the Union.
   B. freed all slaves in the Confederacy.
   C. freed all slaves serving in the Union Army.
   D. freed all slaves serving in the Confederate Army.

6. _____ **enabled the Union troops to win the Battle of Gettysburg.**
   A. Lincoln's delivery of the Gettysburg Address
   B. Outnumbering the Confederate troops
   C. Maintaining control of the high ground
   D. Having greater skill than the Confederate troops

7. **The taking of** _____ **in 1864 helped to ensure Lincoln's reelection that fall.**
   A. Richmond
   B. Atlanta
   C. Charleston
   D. Vicksburg

8. **The Confederacy hoped for aid from France and Britain because they** _____
   A. were slave-owning nations.
   B. depended on the American cotton crop.
   C. earned profits in the slave trade.
   D. supported the breakup of the United States into two smaller and weaker nations.

9. _____ **provoked the Union into a formal declaration of war on the Confederacy.**
   A. The secession of South Carolina
   B. The march on Washington, DC
   C. The invasion of Pennsylvania
   D. The attack on Fort Sumter

10. _____ **made Britain decide not to form an alliance with the Confederacy.**
    A. The defeat at Antietam
    B. The delivery of the Gettysburg Address
    C. The issuing of the Emancipation Proclamation
    D. The assassination of Lincoln

Chapter 16

Reconstruction, 1865–1877

The Civil War ended in 1865, but the war over African-American civil and political rights was only beginning. The first battle of this long war was called Reconstruction. A Republican Congress was eager to reform the old Confederacy along the lines of the North, where all men had the right to vote and no one owned another person as property. However, two obstacles stood in the way. The first was President Andrew Johnson. The second was the old guard of the Confederacy.

Johnson had supported the Union during the war, but he despised African Americans and did his best to block congressional attempts to extend their rights. For their part, southern whites were determined to restore society to exactly what it had been before the war; they were forced to accept the Thirteenth Amendment, which made slavery illegal, but they passed many laws curtailing the rights and privileges of African-American citizens.

Republicans were able to do something about the first obstacle. Over President Johnson's veto, Congress passed a series of laws that made it possible for African Americans to vote, to hold political office, and to enjoy other important civil rights. However, no Congress ever convened would be able to legislate away deep-seated prejudice, bitterness in defeat, and racism. Using terrorist tactics of violence and intimidation, the South managed to defeat Reconstruction reforms and push African Americans back down to the lowest rung on the social and economic ladder. It would take a century to enforce the three Civil Rights amendments that were passed between 1865 and 1870.

CHAPTER OBJECTIVES

- Identify the Civil Rights amendments and the rights they provided to the people.
- Describe the measures Congress took to support Reconstruction in the South.
- Describe the measures southern states took to fight Reconstruction.
- Analyze the relationship between President Johnson and Congress.

Chapter 16 Time Line

- **1863** Proclamation of Amnesty and Reconstruction
- **1864** Freedmen's Bureau established
- **1865** President Lincoln assassinated

    Vice President Andrew Johnson becomes president

    Black Codes
- **1866** Civil Rights Act of 1866

    Thirteenth Amendment ratified
- **1867** Reconstruction Acts of 1867

    Andrew Johnson impeached; acquitted on all charges
- **1868** Fourteenth Amendment ratified

    Ulysses S. Grant elected president
- **1870** Fifteenth Amendment ratified

Reconstruction Plans under Lincoln

Never doubting a Union victory, President Abraham Lincoln began planning for the post-Civil War era long before the war ended. Lincoln knew that a Union victory would mean sweeping changes in the South—the old Confederacy would have to give way to a new society in which blacks and whites were equals under the law, and a new economy that was not supported by slave labor. In 1863, he issued the Proclamation of Amnesty and Reconstruction. It offered a full pardon to all southerners who swore a loyalty oath stating that they would henceforth obey the U.S. Constitution and accept new federal laws that would end slavery. It stated that any Confederate state would be entitled to rejoin the Union and form a new state government as soon as ten percent of its population had taken this oath.

Many members of Congress, especially Republicans, did not like this "Ten Percent Plan"; they thought it took too much on trust. In 1864, they passed a rival Reconstruction plan called the Wade-Davis Bill after its two sponsors, Benjamin Franklin Wade and Henry Winter Davis. This bill required fifty per-cent of each state's population to take a loyalty oath, and forbade any recon-struction of the government until slavery was abolished. Lincoln would not sign the bill, claiming that it was too inflexible.

However, Congress and Lincoln did agree on the creation of the Freedmen's Bureau, which distributed food and clothing to the many black southerners who had been set adrift by the abrupt end to the plantation system. The Freed-men's Bureau also set up schools and hospitals and helped people find jobs.

President Lincoln was assassinated in April 1865, just days after the Confed-eracy surrendered at Appomattox. John Wilkes Booth killed Lincoln in a mis-guided attempt to avenge the South—misguided because Lincoln was widely known for compassion and had shown every indication that he would treat the southerners with mercy and justice.

Reconstruction under Andrew Johnson

Vice President Andrew Johnson was as different from Lincoln as could be. Although a self-made man who had never identified himself with the slave-owning class, Johnson was a southerner and a profound racist. He supported the Union, but had no sympathy with or liking for African Americans. Johnson believed that whites should control any Reconstruction government in the South.

A few weeks after taking office, President Johnson pardoned all former Con-federate rebels. He also issued a plan for the southern states' readmission to the union, with only three requirements:

- Abolition of slavery
- Nullification of the 1861 Acts of Secession
- Forgiveness of any Confederate government debts to individuals

Former Confederate leaders retained a great deal of power under Johnson's plan. They took over the new state legislatures, where they could pass any laws they liked. Not surprisingly, they passed a variety of laws that constituted a blatant attempt to reestablish slavery in fact if not in name.

Black Codes, as these new laws were called, varied by state, but they all had the same goal: to deprive freedmen of their civil rights. Black Codes banned African Americans from voting, serving on juries, owning guns, or traveling without permits. They segregated the school systems. They passed local laws limiting freedmen's eligibility for jobs other than field labor. Mississippi even refused to ratify the Thirteenth Amendment, which abolished slavery throughout the nation when it was ratified in 1866.

Congress Takes Action

Radical Republicans declared that if the South were allowed to rebuild itself along the lines of the Black Codes, the Civil War had been fought for nothing. They introduced a variety of legislation to counter the Black Codes. First, they extended the authority of the Freedmen's Bureau. It had been intended to operate for only one year, but Congress decided to keep it running. President Johnson vetoed the bill, declaring that the freedmen were not entitled to perpetual charity from the U.S. government. Congress overrode the president's veto, and the bureau continued to function.

Second, Congress passed the Civil Rights Act of 1866, which stated that everyone born in the United States was a citizen and as such was entitled to full civil rights. President Johnson vetoed the Civil Rights Act on the grounds that the federal government had no right to make such a law. Again, Congress overrode the president's veto.

In 1868, the Fourteenth Amendment was ratified. This amendment declared that anyone born or naturalized in the United States was a citizen and could not be deprived of life, liberty, or property without due process of law. It also promised all citizens the equal protection of the law. It did not specifically give former slaves voting rights, but it did tie the number of congressmen per state to its total population of voters. This offered southern states an inducement to allow freedmen to vote; now that they would each be counted as one person rather than three-fifths of a person, southern states would legally have larger populations and thus more representatives in the House.

Radical Reconstruction

1868 was a congressional election year, with one-third of the Senate and the full House of Representatives at stake. White violence against freedmen in the South had become common, and a number of people had been killed. Northerners overwhelmingly supported Republican candidates in the election, since it appeared to them that Johnson's policies were likely to overturn everything they had fought for in the Civil War.

Congress passed the Reconstruction Acts of 1867 in response to a recent outbreak of race riots, including an especially violent confrontation in New Orleans. Republicans argued that the riots proved that the South would never conform to the laws of the United States unless forced to do so; therefore they would apply force. The Reconstruction Acts divided the old Confederacy (except Tennessee, which had already been reconstructed) into five military districts, to be occupied by U.S. troops until two things had happened. First, each district must comply with the Fourteenth Amendment. Second, each state

THE MYTH

Most Americans believe that African Americans throughout the United States were denied the right to vote until the passage of the Fifteenth Amendment.

THE FACTS

When the colonies declared their independence in 1776, each new state legislature sat down to write its new state constitution. These constitutions use language such as "free man" or "freeholder" to describe potential voters—none of them specified that the voters had to be white. Any free black man who met the requirements of age and property ownership (these differed slightly from state to state) was entitled to vote.

This began to change with the rise of racism and the sectional division over the issue of slavery. In 1809, Maryland became the first state to revoke the voting rights of free blacks by making voting a "whites only" privilege. Other southern states followed suit. Northern states, however, generally did not alter their constitutions to prohibit free blacks from voting.

Thus, the Fifteenth Amendment restored suffrage to free African Americans who had enjoyed it in the past. It also granted that right to former slaves for the first time.

must write a new state constitution giving freedmen the vote and the right to hold office.

The Impeachment of Andrew Johnson

Certain that President Johnson would not support the Reconstruction Acts, which had been passed over his veto, Congress passed a law called the Tenure of Office Act. It required Senate approval for the president to fire any government official who had been confirmed by the Senate.

Johnson believed that the law was unconstitutional, and promptly tested it by firing Secretary of War Edwin Stanton, who supported radical Reconstruction. Congress immediately impeached Johnson, citing three reasons: he had violated the Tenure of Office Act, made "scandalous speeches," and "brought Congress into disgrace."

The truth of the matter was that Congress had deliberately passed the Tenure of Office Act in order to provoke Johnson. Republicans believed that he was incompetent to lead the nation; they did not like his leniency toward the leaders of the old Confederacy or his refusal to sign any laws that granted rights to freedmen. Unfortunately for the Republicans, political disagreement with Congress was not grounds for removing a president from office. After an eight-week trial in which it became clear that Johnson had not committed high crimes or misdemeanors—the only legal grounds for impeachment—the president was acquitted by a margin of one vote.

The Election of 1868

The Radical Republicans had overreached themselves in their attempt to impeach the president on trumped-up grounds. The Republican Party was now afraid of losing power in Washington. Republican leaders decided that the best thing to do would be to support the candidate who seemed most assured of an easy victory at the polls. This man was none other than Ulysses S. Grant—who had no experience in politics. Like George Washington and Andrew Jackson before him, Grant was popular with the public purely because of his military success. In the end, thanks to the support of African-American voters in the South, Grant won a narrow victory over New York governor Horatio Seymour.

Acknowledging the importance to their party of the new group of voters, Republican congressional representatives proposed the Fifteenth Amendment, which read:

> The right of citizens of the United States to vote shall not be denied or abridged by the United States or by any State on account of race, color, or previous condition of servitude.

The Fifteenth Amendment was ratified in 1870. It caused an unintended schism in the women's suffrage movement; since it ignored the question of women's rights, many suffragist leaders refused to support it. This in turn caused anger and resentment among African-American women, who felt that the women's movement should support the Fifteenth Amendment and then use it as a lever to fight for their own rights.

African Americans took full advantage of what was, for most of them, their first chance to participate in the political process. All former Confederate states were required to write new state constitutions; African-American delegates took part in all these constitutional conventions. Southern African Americans were elected to state legislatures, to the U.S. Congress, and to a variety of state and local offices.

Thwarted in their attempts to restore the prewar status quo, the former Confederate loyalists reacted by forming a terrorist organization called the Ku Klux Klan. Wearing hoods and robes to hide their identities, white men formed mobs throughout the old Confederacy. They attacked and murdered Republican legislators, both white and black. They attacked and killed any African American who crossed their paths, especially those who had won any economic or political success. They burned homes, businesses, churches, and schools belonging to African Americans.

African Americans responded in a variety of ways. They destroyed property that belonged to Klan members. They protected anyone whom they knew was likely to be attacked. They appealed to the federal government for help. Congress passed the Enforcement Acts of 1870 and 1871, allowing the federal government to use military force against terrorist groups and to prosecute the terrorists. Klan membership declined after these acts were passed.

1876: Election and Compromise

Active Republican support for Reconstruction faded as time passed. Republican efforts had been so successful that the politicians felt that their work was completed, and they began turning their attention to the national economy. The Panic of 1873 threw many people out of work. Democrats found new supporters among thousands of small businessmen and small farmers, many of whom blamed Reconstruction projects for the economic depression. In the 1874 elections, Democrats regained the majority of seats in the House of Representatives. Congress did pass the Civil Rights Act of 1875, prohibiting segregation and discrimination in public places such as restaurants, but this was to be the last active federal effort toward Reconstruction.

Seizing their moment of strength and support among the voting public, the Democrats used terrorist tactics, including murder, to prevent African Americans from voting for Republican candidates in state elections. In 1876, the Democrats used similar tactics in support of presidential candidate Samuel Tilden. Tilden won the popular vote, but the electoral votes in four states were disputed, and in the Compromise of 1877, Congress agreed to name Republican Rutherford B. Hayes president in exchange for the withdrawal of federal troops from the South. Without the support of these troops, the last of the Reconstruction governments quickly collapsed. It would take nearly 100 years for African Americans to have their full civil rights recognized again in the South.

The Rise of Jim Crow Laws

The southern economy still depended on the production and sale of cotton, rice, and tobacco. The large plantations still existed. The crops still had to be harvested. A large labor force was still necessary. However, southerners had to find a way to make their economy function with a paid labor force.

A system known as sharecropping developed. A poor farmer would work a piece of land in exchange for a house or cabin on the farm, tools, a mule, and a share of the crop he or she cultivated. The owner did not have to pay wages until harvest time. Meanwhile, the farmers had to buy food, tools, and supplies on credit, charging them against the money they would earn when they sold their share of the crop. This meant, of course, that when the farmer was paid, he immediately had to turn over most of the money to pay his debts. This crop-lien system ensured that sharecroppers would remain poor. Although the South had begun to rebuild its railroads and to industrialize, factory workers were forced to buy high-priced goods on credit at company stores and to live at high rents in company housing. They were no better off than sharecroppers.

Along with this economic subjugation, those in power in the South installed a system of political and social discrimination. The Civil War had only reinforced the racist attitudes of the old guard of the Confederacy. When African Americans resisted unconstitutional segregationist laws, whites reacted with violence. As the century wore on, lynching became common. A white mob would kidnap a black person who had offended them in some way—perhaps only by failing to stand back to allow a white woman to pass him on the street, perhaps only by operating a successful small business. The mob would then kill the victim, usually by hanging him or her from a tree. They would usually leave the body where it was, as a symbol that they hoped would terrorize and further subjugate the local African-American population. There were thousands of lynchings throughout the South in the last decades of the nineteenth century.

Local and state legislatures passed unconstitutional laws requiring payment of poll taxes and passage of literacy tests before a person could vote. Although there were many poor and illiterate whites in the South, only African Americans—probable Republican voters—were required to take these tests and pay these taxes. When they failed, they were barred from voting. Many of the discriminatory laws that had been enacted in the Black Codes were reinstated. They were popularly known as "Jim Crow" laws, after a song lyric. During the 1830s, white actor Thomas Rice performed a vaudeville act in which he blacked his face, danced a jig, and sang a song containing the phrase "jump Jim Crow." The character became popular, and many other actors performed similar minstrel acts. Many of the ugly racist stereotypes of African Americans in popular culture, which would persist until the time of World War II—rolling eyes, huge lips, a shuffling walk, and a personality compounded of stupidity and hysteria—were based on the comic exaggerations that white minstrel-show actors had invented to make audiences laugh.

African Americans protested that the Jim Crow laws were unconstitutional, but their protests were in vain. In 1883, the Supreme Court declared that the federal government could not apply the Fourteenth Amendment to privately owned businesses. Later, when African American Homer Plessy insisted that as the purchaser of a full-fare railroad ticket, he had the right to ride in any car of the train he wanted, the case went all the way to the Supreme Court.

In an 1896 decision known as *Plessy v. Ferguson*, the Court ruled that as long as a business provided "separate but equal" facilities for customers, it was not in violation of the Fourteenth Amendment. Justice John Harlan famously dissented, standing up strongly for the full civil rights of African Americans under the Constitution. Ironically, he based part of his argument on racist grounds, pointing out that although the Chinese were a different and in his eyes clearly inferior race, Chinese Americans had the right to ride in first-class railroad cars—how, then could the Court deny the same right to an African American? Harlan went on to write "Our Constitution is color-blind and neither knows nor tolerates classes among citizens."

Many African Americans resisted Jim Crow laws, and many achieved a success that was truly remarkable, given the obstacles put in their path. One example was Ida B. Wells, who began as a reporter and eventually owned her own newspaper. She became nationally known as a fighter for African-American and women's rights and the leader of an anti-lynching campaign.

CHAPTER 16 QUIZ

1. Congress impeached President Andrew Johnson because _____
   A. he opposed legislation favorable to African Americans.
   B. he committed high crimes and misdemeanors.
   C. he succeeded Abraham Lincoln as president.
   D. he had fought on the Confederate side during the Civil War.

2. The Reconstruction Acts of 1867 called for _____
   A. separate but equal institutions and public facilities for African Americans.
   B. freeing of all slaves throughout the United States.
   C. setting aside seats in the U.S. Congress specifically for African Americans.
   D. military occupation of the former Confederate states.

3. What was the purpose of the Freedmen's Bureau?
   A. to abolish slavery
   B. to offer aid to former slaves
   C. to retaliate against white mob violence
   D. to reorganize plantations with paid laborers

4. **Many leaders of the women's suffrage movement did not support the Fifteenth Amendment because** _____
    A. it explicitly denied women the right to vote.
    B. it gave black women, but not white women, the right to vote.
    C. it did not give women the right to vote.
    D. it denied former slaves the right to vote.

5. _____ **helped to counter the Ku Klux Klan's terrorist tactics.**
    A. The Reconstruction Acts
    B. The Enforcement Acts
    C. The Fourteenth Amendment
    D. The Fifteenth Amendment

6. **As a result of the Compromise of 1877, Congress agreed** _____
    A. to accept the passage of Black Codes throughout the old Confederacy.
    B. to select a Democratic candidate as president in a disputed election.
    C. to prohibit segregation and discrimination in public places.
    D. to withdraw federal troops from the former Confederate states.

7. **The Supreme Court case *Plessy v. Ferguson* established the principle of** _____
    A. poll taxes and literacy tests.
    B. the crop-lien system.
    C. separate but equal facilities for African Americans.
    D. full civil rights for African Americans.

8. **Jim Crow laws were designed to** _____
    A. balance representation in local and state legislatures in the South.
    B. deprive African Americans of their basic civil rights.
    C. encourage African Americans to vote.
    D. force southern states to comply with the civil rights amendments.

9. _____ **caused the Republican Party to lose support among the voters.**
    A. The Panic of 1873
    B. The passage of the civil rights amendments
    C. The election of Samuel Tilden
    D. The funding of the Freedmen's Bureau

10. **Rutherford B. Hayes became president as a result of** _____
    A. the Panic of 1873.
    B. the Compromise of 1877.
    C. the impeachment of Andrew Johnson.
    D. the Civil Rights Act of 1875.

Chapter **17**

Westward Movement, 1860–1898

The mid-nineteenth century was a period of great change and development west of the Mississippi River. For the American Indians, these years brought disaster. For most other Americans, the West offered opportunity and freedom.

The United States continued to push the tribes farther and farther from their ancestral lands. The American Indians had always been willing to negotiate, but the U.S. government did not honor the treaties it made with them. When negotiation failed, the tribes resisted with force of arms, but they lacked the strength and the numbers of the federal troops. By the end of the nineteenth century, they were settled on reservations and facing the end of their former dominance over the North American continent.

The U.S. government and big business between them worked hard to settle the West. The government offered free land to any homesteader who would claim it and farm it for five years. It also offered tremendous land grants to companies that were willing to build railroads. Companies jumped at the offer, and the railroads became the largest employers of the day, hiring millions of people to work on every aspect of developing and building the national transportation system. Big companies also purchased tracts of land where gold and silver had been discovered, and hired miners to get the precious metals from the ground. The government made prairie land free for ranchers' cattle to range on, making ranching an attractive and profitable venture for many entrepreneurs, large and small.

In the last half of the nineteenth century, the West provided every opportunity for prosperity—land for the taking, a variety of well-paid jobs, and, for most groups, relative freedom from the oppression and discrimination that prevailed against blacks in the Reconstruction South and recent immigrants in northeastern port cities.

CHAPTER OBJECTIVES

- Describe the conflicts between American Indians and the United States in the nineteenth century.
- List the factors that led many Americans to migrate to the West.
- Describe everyday life in the West for ranchers and railroad workers.

Chapter 17 Time Line

- 1849   California Gold Rush
- 1851   Fort Laramie Treaty
- 1859   Comstock Lode discovered
- 1862   Santee Sioux uprising

    Government Land Acts

    U.S. Department of Agriculture (USDA)
- 1864   Sand Creek Massacre
- 1867   Treaty of Medicine Lodge

    Purchase of Alaska from Russia
- 1868   Second Fort Laramie Treaty
- 1869   Transcontinental railroad is completed
- 1870–1890   Cattle boom in Southwest
- 1876   Battle of the Little Bighorn
- 1890   Ghost Dance movement

    Wounded Knee Massacre

Conflicts with Indians in the Great Plains

As Americans continued to migrate westward in search of California gold, farmland, and other economic opportunities, they continued to grab space that the government had set aside for Indians. Again and again, the U.S. government had broken its word to the tribes. Since Europeans first arrived in North America, they had steadily pushed the American Indians farther and farther west, driving them from their ancestral lands.

In 1851, in the First Fort Laramie Treaty, the American government had guaranteed the Plains Indians that they would be left alone in their defined territories, or reservations. In exchange for ceasing to wander the Great Plains as migratory hunters, the Plains Indians accepted money and a guarantee of a yearly delivery of supplies worth thousands of dollars. (See Chapter 13.)

Reality did not turn out according to the treaty. The United States continued to take land, shrinking the size of the reservations. Supplies were not delivered as promised. Since the treaties had limited the tribes' opportunity to provide for themselves by hunting, they depended on those supplies for survival. Without them, some tribes were in grave danger of starvation.

A deep cultural divide existed between the Americans of European descent and the American Indians. The American-Indians' experience of dealing with other tribes had been limited, and had not taught them that treaties were easily broken. Europeans, on the other hand, had warred with neighboring nations for hundreds of years (France against England, Spain against France, Poland against Russia), making treaties on the best terms possible and then breaking them as soon as it was to their advantage. To the Americans, broken promises were a natural element of foreign policy—and to the U.S. government, the American Indians were a foreign population. To the tribes, broken promises were bewildering and ended by causing deep resentment and fury toward the U.S. government and its people.

Naturally, the broken promises ended up leading to armed conflict. In 1862, when the nondelivery of the promised supplies caused grave danger of starvation, the Santee Sioux attacked the local Bureau of Indian Affairs and raided local farms for food. U.S. troops, who were better organized and had more and better weapons, quickly quashed the raids. They executed several of the Sioux and forced the tribe to move to Dakota Territory and later to Nebraska.

Over time, the tribes came to realize that there was no reason to honor any treaty that the American government and military had repeatedly violated. The Plains Indians were migratory, not stationary; they wanted to roam, not to live on settled reservations. They frequently strayed away to hunt buffalo or simply to feel that they were free to go where they pleased. U.S. troops were ordered to try to contain them on their reservations. Sometimes the two groups clashed and people on both sides were wounded or killed.

Sand Creek, Colorado Territory, was the site of an especially shameful episode. Colonel John Chivington ordered his troops to open fire on a large group of Cheyenne Indians, almost all women and children, none of whom had attacked the U.S. troops or done anything to provoke an attack. Chivington's troops massacred 200 Cheyennes that day. When national newspapers printed the story of the Sand Creek Massacre, Americans were horrified. A congressional committee investigated and condemned the massacre, calling for reform in Indian affairs.

Meanwhile, the tribes took direct, violent action against farmers and troops on the Great Plains. The U.S. government called for peace in the Treaty of Medicine Lodge. The southern Plains Indians were moved to reservations in Oklahoma Territory. In the Second Fort Laramie Treaty of 1868, the Sioux agreed to move to South Dakota, to an area they named the Black Hills. For once, the United States had moved a tribe of Indians to rich, fertile lands.

In 1874, American troops invaded the Black Hills. When the troops discovered gold, the government naturally wanted the Sioux to move again. The Sioux took up arms and proceeded to win major battles at the Rosebud Battlefield and the Little Bighorn. At Little Bighorn, General George Armstrong Custer and all his troops were killed. The U.S. Army redoubled its efforts to police the Sioux, and in the end forced them to surrender and move to new reservations.

In these times of great trouble, the American Indians turned to religion for solace and hope. A Paiute named Wovoka assured the Plains Indians that a ritual dance called the Ghost Dance would bring their ancestors back and would ward off further American attempts to destroy their Indian culture. The U.S. military, afraid that the Ghost Dance movement would spread and give rise to further armed conflict, decided to arrest Sioux chief Sitting Bull. A fight broke out when they approached Sitting Bull's cabin, and the troops killed several Indians, including Sitting Bull.

The assassination of their leader disheartened some Sioux and enraged others. Many of them traveled west toward the Pine Ridge reservation with their leader Big Foot. One night in December 1890, the Sioux camped along Wounded Knee Creek on the South Dakota–Nebraska border. In the morning, 500 troops surrounded them and demanded their guns. The Sioux surrendered, but the troops began shooting anyway. At the end of the Wounded Knee Massacre, 150 Sioux and about thirty U.S. soldiers lay dead. The Sioux gave up all further attempts at resistance after this incident. Further West, the U.S. Army also succeeded in relocating the Nez Percé and the Apache.

Settling the Plains and the West

The federal government was eager to settle the West as quickly as possible. The acquisition of territory in the Treaty of Guadalupe-Hidalgo and the discovery of gold in California (see Chapter 13) provided easterners with great incentives to move to the West. Even during the dark days of the Civil War, the federal government continued its efforts to move people westward. This table shows three of the most important laws the government passed.

GOVERNMENT LAND ACTS OF 1862	
Homestead Act	Anyone who staked a claim to up to 160 acres of land could keep it if he or she farmed the land and lived on it for five years.
Pacific Railway Act	Railroad companies could apply for land grants on which to develop and build a transcontinental railroad system.
Morrill Act	Granted 17 million acres of federal land to the states, with the requirement that they sell this land and use the money to found agricultural and engineering colleges.

The Pacific Railway Act had many effects beyond facilitating the development of a transportation system. The railroads became the biggest employers of the day, hiring thousands of people to survey the land, to level the grade over which the trains would pass, to lay the ties and the track, to manufacture the cars and seats, to build and staff the depots and stations, and to drive the trains. The railroads also sold off surplus land to homesteaders, further encouraging western settlement. Chinese immigrants proved to be experts at this kind of work, particularly because of their knowledge of explosives; the promise of jobs on the Central Pacific Railroad brought thousands of Chinese to the United States during the 1860s.

The Central Pacific Railroad Company began laying track at San Francisco and built toward the east, across the Sierra Nevada. The Union Pacific began at Omaha and built westward. The Union Pacific met the Central Pacific at Promontory Point, Utah, in May 1869, near the north shore of the Great Salt Lake. The railroad was largely built with immigrant labor: Chinese laid the track for the Central Pacific, and the Union Pacific workers were overwhelmingly Irish, supplemented by young Civil War veterans and freedmen.

The Transcontinental Railroad

Families in search of farmland had gone westward with the first wagon trains. Then, in the years before the Civil War, a flood of young single men had traveled westward in search of gold, opportunity, freedom, and adventure. In 1865, the end of the war changed the pattern of westward migration once again. Most migrants of this era fell into one of three groups: immigrants, freedmen (and women), and middle-class whites.

Immigrants

So many immigrants had flooded into northeastern port cities that conditions had become overcrowded, unsanitary, and in many cases desperate. Many immigrants had been farmers in their native countries, and they knew that they would have to travel westward beyond the cities to find land. In the cities, many were little better than industrial slave labor; on the Great Plains, they might prosper as independent property owners. The Homestead Act made it possible for millions of poor immigrants to start fresh in the American West. Immigrants from Scandinavian countries and central and eastern European nations like Poland, Austria, and Sweden settled on the Great Plains in large numbers.

Freedmen

The Emancipation Proclamation had freed African Americans in the South, but it had also thrown them out to fend for themselves. As slaves, they had been guaranteed jobs, shelter, and regular meals, however unpaid and inadequate;

now that they were homeless in an area devastated by war, they would be lucky to find work and survive. Reconstruction programs had given African Americans high hopes for the future, but all too soon the southern Democrats prevailed over the Reconstructionists and reinstated much of the old system of segregation and oppression. African Americans traveled west to find good jobs on the railroad, to mine gold and silver, to claim homesteads, to work on the cattle ranches, and to escape the subjugation under which the old guard was determined to make them live. In 1879 alone, more than 20,000 African Americans left the South.

Farming

So many farmers moving to the same geographical area in such a short time brought its own problems. The Great Plains had abundant grassy land, perfect for cattle to graze on or for the cultivation of grain, but lacking in water and timber. Without a reliable water supply, farmers could not irrigate their crops; without timber, they could not build houses or barns. In 1862, the government created the U.S. Department of Agriculture to help settlers address these problems.

Two notable American writers captured the westward migration and farming on the Great Plains in great detail: Willa Cather and Laura Ingalls Wilder. Cather traveled from Virginia to Nebraska with her family in 1873. She wrote several classic novels of immigrant pioneers on the Great Plains. Her best-known novel, *My Ántonia* (1927), tells the story of a Bohemian (Czech) family adjusting to life on the Great Plains. Wilder was born in Wisconsin. As a child, she traveled in a covered wagon to Indian Territory in Oklahoma, to Minnesota, and finally to the Dakota Territory, where her family settled for good. She recounted the story of her childhood and girlhood in a famous series of books called the "Little House" stories. *By the Shores of Silver Lake, Little Town on the Prairie*, and the rest of the series constitute a valuable history of the migrant pioneer experience in the 1870s and 1880s.

Ranching

The cowboy is a popular figure of American myth, but he is not fictional: he really existed. His most important job was to herd ranch cattle to the railroads.

The first Spaniards who came to the New World saw immediately that the Southwest was an ideal place to raise the cattle that they had brought with them. Three hundred years later, Texans were still raising cattle. The industry spread across the Great Plains as the buffalo population dwindled and died out. Ranchers also raised sheep, but this brought on fierce clashes between sheep ranchers and cattle ranchers; each believed that the other's livestock was taking more than its fair share of the available grass. As ranching spread westward and northward, the government determined that ranchers could allow their cattle to graze freely on the open range. Water was scarce in the Southwest, and every successful rancher owned property near a water source.

During the years of the great cattle boom after the Civil War, cowboys were a mixed group of freedmen, Mexicans, Mexican Americans, and Civil War veterans—black as well as white. These men led harsh outdoor lives and earned little money. The first step in herding the cattle to the railroad was the roundup; the cattle had to be gathered from the open range and identified as a particular rancher's property by the brand (an initial or symbol burned into the animal's flesh). The cowboys then drove thousands of cattle over hundreds of miles, usually to railroad depots in Kansas. Besides being outdoors in all types of weather throughout the long drive, cowboys had to watch for stampedes and prevent the animals from straying from the herd. They had to cope with obstacles like unexpected storms and flooded rivers. Once they got the cattle to the depot, the cowboys would be paid for their hard work—and would usually spend their wages immediately, drinking and gambling in the towns.

All cowboys were male, but women worked as hard on the ranch as men did. They had to take care of their own families and also all hands on the ranch. Women made and mended all the clothing, cooked the food, raised the children, and doctored the sick. A woman rancher could also fire a gun, fix anything that got broken, use a branding iron, and herd cattle or sheep to pasture.

A combination of factors ended the cattle boom around 1890. First, ranchers had been so successful that the supply of cattle was starting to exceed the demand, which meant that prices for beef were falling. Second, the invention of barbed wire allowed ranchers to fence off their lands so that others could not have access to the water or grass on their property. This drove many small ranchers and farmers out of business. Third, seven straight months of extremely severe blizzards in 1886–1887 (described by Laura Ingalls Wilder in *The Long Winter*) killed up to 90 percent of the herds. Many ranchers survived by expanding their sheep herds. The era of the cowboy was effectively over.

Mining

The California Gold Rush of 1849 ushered in an era of mining in the West. After the discovery of gold at Sutter's Mill, the next strike was at Pike's Peak in 1858. In 1859, a rich silver vein was tapped in the Carson River Valley in present-day Nevada. The Comstock Lode turned out to be worth more than $500 million. Miners also found gold in the Klondike district on the border of Alaska Territory, which had been acquired by Secretary of State William Seward in 1867. Seward had been roundly criticized for the purchase—people called Alaska "Seward's Folly" or "Johnson's Polar-Bear Garden." The critics were effectively silenced when the miners struck gold. The United States paid Russia $7.2 million for Alaska; by 1900, Americans had mined hundreds of millions of dollars' worth of gold from the new territory.

Mining communities were largely male, and only the strongest could survive in one. Immigrant miners from all nations found themselves forced out by those who had been born in the United States or the territories. Violence abounded, partly because there was no law enforcement authority. Miners had to settle their own differences, and vigilante "justice" was swift and merciless.

CHAPTER 17 QUIZ

1. **Alaska Territory proved a profitable purchase because it was rich in** _____
   A. timber.
   B. coal.
   C. gold.
   D. fur-bearing animals.

2. **The *roundup* refers to the process of** _____
   A. branding cattle as proof of ownership.
   B. gathering cattle together and sorting them by their brands.
   C. herding cattle across the plains to Kansas.
   D. allowing cattle to graze freely on the open range.

3. **Which two immigrant groups laid most of the track for the transcontinental railroad?**
   A. Chinese and Irish
   B. Irish and Italian
   C. German and Czech
   D. African and Chinese

4. _____ stated that a person could keep up to 160 acres of land if he or she farmed it for five years.
   A. The Morrill Act
   B. The Pacific Railway Act
   C. The Homestead Act
   D. The Government Land Act

5. **The** _____ were killed in large numbers at the Wounded Knee **Massacre.**
   A. Apache
   B. Dakota
   C. Cheyenne
   D. Sioux

6. **The United States took back Sioux lands in the Black Hills because** _____
   A. they had found a better place for a Plains Indian reservation.
   B. it was too difficult to ship supplies to the Black Hills.
   C. the land turned out to have deposits of gold.
   D. the Sioux refused to stay in the Black Hills.

7. **What happened at the Battle of the Little Bighorn?**
   A. All the Sioux were killed.
   B. All the American troops were killed.
   C. Sioux chief Sitting Bull was shot.
   D. The Sioux made peace with the U.S. troops.

8. **The transcontinental railroad was completed** _____
   A. before the Civil War.
   B. during the first year of the Civil War.
   C. near the end of the Civil War.
   D. after the Civil War.

9. **Former southern slaves traveled west for all these reasons except** _____

   A. to escape Jim Crow laws passed during Reconstruction.

   B. to find well-paid jobs on the railroad.

   C. to claim homesteads.

   D. to work in factories.

10. **Why did the government establish the Department of Agriculture?**

    A. to address the lack of timber and water in the Great Plains

    B. to settle disputes between cattle ranchers and sheep ranchers

    C. to oversee homesteaders' claims to land

    D. to resolve conflicts between ranchers and farmers

Chapter **18**

The Rise of Big Business and the Gilded Age, 1870–1896

While the issues of Reconstruction were dividing the nation, a tremendous economic boom was going on. The Second Industrial Revolution was a period of enormous change in American society. New inventions that would have seemed miraculous to a previous generation—instant long-distance written communication (the telegraph), the ability to speak to someone in another city (the telephone), a machine that could produce a perfectly printed letter (the typewriter)—became everyday and commonplace in the new world of the postwar nineteenth century.

The technological breakthroughs caused a boom in heavy industry. Since it was suddenly much easier and cheaper to convert iron ore to steel, there was a surplus of steel—which could be put to a variety of uses, such as building and bridge construction. Men at the heads of large corporations made fortunes. The workers to whose labor they owed those fortunes, on the other hand, eked out a miserable existence in poverty. Toward the end of the century, workers finally began to organize into unions and to strike for reasonable living wages and an eight-hour workday.

Hundreds of thousands of immigrants came to the United States in the last half of the century, principally from China and southern Europe. They created a lively and colorful presence in cities, where they gathered in small replicas of their old neighborhoods at home. The new industry also gave rise to a thriving middle class of professionals, highly trained workers, managers, and of course buyers of the mass-produced consumer goods that were becoming so common. The upper classes acquired three-quarters of all the wealth in the nation, thus giving rise to the era's nickname—the "Gilded Age."

CHAPTER OBJECTIVES

- Describe the American economic system (capitalism).
- Describe the rise of labor unions in the nineteenth century.
- Identify the major innovations and inventions of the Second Industrial Revolution.
- Compare and contrast the social classes in late-nineteenth-century America.

Chapter 18 Time Line

- **1835–1838**   Morse invents the telegraph and Morse code
- **c. 1850–1900**   Second Industrial Revolution
- **1850s**   Bessemer process of converting iron ore to steel
- **1853**   Otis invents the passenger elevator
- **1876**   Alexander Graham Bell invents the telephone
- **1879–1882**   Thomas Edison and Lewis Latimer invent and perfect the lightbulb
- **1882**   Chinese Exclusion Act
- **1886**   Great Upheaval

    Haymarket riot

    American Federation of Labor
- **1890**   Sherman Antitrust Act
- **1899**   Thorstein Veblen publishes *Theory of the Leisure Class*

Technological Revolutions

During the Industrial Revolution of the early 1800s, the development of steam power and the cotton gin had drastically changed American society and had caused the economy to explode. At midcentury, the Second Industrial Revolution shook up society and the economy once again. Innovations, new technological processes, and new machines appeared throughout the last half of the nineteenth century.

The development of the Bessemer process was the most important factor in the success of the Second Industrial Revolution. Henry Bessemer of Great Britain and William Kelly of the U.S. both discovered a new, efficient way to convert iron ore into steel. This method, called the Bessemer process, led to a rise in steel production, which in turn made many things possible. Steel was needed for railroad rails tracks, train parts, machines and engines of all types, and the girders of buildings.

Steel gave the United States a completely different appearance. The continent that had been pastoral and relatively undisturbed by anything man-made during the days was now heavily populated with cities full of skyscrapers, railroads crossing from one ocean to the other, and heavy machinery everywhere.

This table shows some of the key inventions and technological breakthroughs of the Second Industrial Revolution.

Date	Inventor	Process or Machine
1830s	Samuel F. B. Morse	Telegraph (1835)
		Morse code (1838)
1850s	Henry Bessemer	Bessemer process
	William Kelly	
1853	Elisha Otis	Mechanized passenger elevator
1867	Christopher Sholes	Typewriter
1876	Alexander Graham Bell	Telephone
1877	Thomas Alva Edison	Phonograph
1879	Edison and Lewis Latimer	Lightbulb
1869	George Westinghouse	Compressed-air brake
1886	Westinghouse and Nikola Tesla	High-voltage alternating electric current (AC)
1893	Charles and Frank Duryea	First practical motorcar in the United States
1903	Wilbur and Orville Wright	First powered piloted plane flight

The Growth of Big Business

An economy has two aspects. The first is the ownership of the business and industry; the second is the determination of wages and prices. Broadly speaking, there are two major economic systems in place in the world. In a capitalist economy, private owners control business and industry, and the laws of supply and demand control prices and wages. In a socialist economy, the government controls business and industry and also wages and prices. The United States has a capitalist economy, founded on the constitutional right to own private property and a distrust of government control that has existed since before the American Revolution.

Until the Civil War, most American businesses had been small, usually owned and operated by one or two people and a small staff. However, a business owner with greater ambitions could not run multiple factories on this plan—the costs and expenses were so high that no individual would have enough cash available to keep the business running. Instead, an ambitious businessman (or woman) would acquire partners; together, they would set up a corporation. In a corporation, owners sell shares of stock in the company. Ordinary people purchase these shares as an investment. In exchange for the money they put in, they regularly receive sums of money based on the company's profits (if any). The more stock a person owns, the larger his share of the profits will be. Soon there were so many big corporations in the United States that a stock market was needed. In a stock market, people buy, sell, and trade their shares, usually acting on the advice of a paid stockbroker.

In the same way that individuals united to form corporations, corporations united to form trusts. A board of trustees runs all the trust's corporations as a single enterprise. When a trust gains control of all the corporations within one industry, it becomes a monopoly. Owners prefer a monopoly system because it eliminates competition and allows them to set prices as high as they please. Consumers oppose a monopoly system because they welcome competition; when corporations cannot monopolize, each one must try to attract customers by lowering prices or producing higher-quality goods.

Public criticism of trusts grew during the last quarter of the nineteenth century. Congress reluctantly acted on the issue by passing the Sherman Antitrust Act. The act banned trusts and monopolies, but failed to state exactly what a monopoly or a trust was. Without strong leadership in Washington that was determined to fight the abuses of big business, the Sherman Antitrust Act was impossible to enforce.

This table shows some of the key figures in American big business during the Second Industrial Revolution.

Industrialists	Business or Industry Name
Andrew Carnegie	Carnegie Steel Company
John D. Rockefeller	Standard Oil
Cornelius Vanderbilt	New York Central Railroad; many other railroads
George Westinghouse	Westinghouse Air Brake Company
George Pullman	Pullman passenger-railroad-car manufacturing company
John Wanamaker	Department stores
R. H. Macy	
Marshall Field	
Frank Woolworth	Five-and-ten-cent stores

Successful industries gave rise to new industries. One was the stock market; another was advertising. Corporations used advertising to persuade people to buy their products or services. They spent a great deal of money on posters, newspaper advertisements, and other promotions. They hired artists to design logos that the public would recognize and remember. Department stores provided fancy bags, packages, and wrappings for people to take their purchases home in. Many companies made their products available by mail order to those who lived in rural areas; the appearance of the latest Sears, Roebuck or Montgomery Ward catalogue in a rural mailbox was an event.

As big businesses grew, middle-class and wealthy Americans enjoyed an era of unprecedented choices of consumer goods on which to spend their money. New stores were opening everywhere. Clothing and other items that had once been expensive were being mass-produced in great quantities. Fancy toys, books, furniture, and other goods of all kinds, both useful and frivolous, were for sale on every block of every major city or large town.

Industrialization and Workers

For the laboring class, the era was one of great hardship. The government preferred to leave business to regulate itself; when it did reluctantly step in, it normally ruled in favor of the owners, not the workers. For example, Congress might establish protective tariffs on foreign goods, so that Americans would buy American goods in preference to the more expensive imports. However, Congress ignored the concerns of the people who made the economy so prosperous—the welders, miners, dyers, tailors, porters, teamsters, and other workers. The reason for this is very simple: people who have wealth and power also have political influence. A business owner might well have a congressman in his immediate family, or see him regularly on social occasions. Workers, of course, had no way of making direct contact with a congressman, and would have had no time to spare from the struggle for survival even if they did.

A business exists for only one reason—to make money. Every action the owner takes, every decision he or she reaches, is focused on profit. Throughout history, business owners have all come to the same conclusion—one of the easiest ways to increase profits is to pay lower wages. Conditions for workers had been terrible in the early nineteenth century (see Chapter 12). Instead of improving during the era of big business, they grew much worse.

Wages were as low as owners could set them. If one worker refused a low wage, a hungrier and poorer person could easily be found to accept it. Laborers worked six days a week, often twelve to fourteen hours per day. Children went to work as soon as they were old enough; management valued these juvenile workers because their wages were lower and they were too young to fight the dreadful working conditions that prevailed. Factories did not provide natural daylight or fresh air unless it was necessary to get the work done more efficiently. There were no guaranteed lunch or dinner breaks, and no place except the bare yards or pavements just outside the building to sit down for a few moments of respite. If a worker fell ill, he or she would usually try to conceal it; staying home because of illness generally meant the permanent loss of the job.

Business and industry can be seen as a system of checks and balances. In the nineteenth century, the owners had all the power. Society eventually devised two powerful checks on the owners. The first was government regulation. The second was the labor union—the organization of workers into a group with the power to negotiate. In the late nineteenth century, government made only one weak attempt, the Sherman Antitrust Act, to regulate business. However, labor unions began to rise and gain power.

Workers came to realize that they had two important checks on the power of an owner. First, they outnumbered the owner; five hundred workers had more power than one owner. Second, their labor was essential to keep the business running. If one worker quit in protest, the owner could replace him. If five hundred workers quit in protest, the business would have to shut down and the owner would be forced to address the workers' concerns.

The first attempts to organize labor into unions began soon after the Civil War. One of the first unions to form was the Knights of Labor, a national union begun by Philadelphia garment workers under the leadership of Uriah Stephens. It began as a union for white, male workers, but in the 1880s it expanded to include women and African Americans (although it still excluded Chinese-American workers). Membership was open to both skilled and unskilled workers of all types. Important leaders of the Knights of Labor included Terence V. Powderly and Mary Harris "Mother" Jones.

By 1886, the Knights of Labor had more than 700,000 members and was growing. The union fought for an eight-hour workday, equal pay for equal work (at that time, women were paid less than men, and black workers less than white), and the passage of laws against child labor.

The Great Strikes

The strike was, and continues to be, a union's most effective weapon against management. The strike is the protest of last resort. Workers walk off the job in protest when management ignores their demands or when labor and management fail to negotiate an agreement. A strike is effective because a business cannot operate without workers. For every day that a factory is closed, or that a railroad does not operate, owners lose enormous amounts of money—and consumers transfer their patronage to rival businesses. Therefore, it is in management's interest to settle a strike as quickly as possible.

In the early days of unions, strikes were quite risky for workers. In the first place, there were so many immigrants coming to the United States that an owner could replace his entire labor force very quickly. Second, workers went without pay during a strike, and it was harder on a worker to lose a day's pay than it was on an owner to lose a day's profits. However, workers struck in spite of the risks. One of the reasons that labor unions traditionally ask their members for dues is to provide a fund of money that will tide workers over during a strike.

Successful labor strikes helped union membership rise. In 1877, railroad workers in fourteen states went on strike, despite an attempt by federal troops to force them to return to work.

The early 1880s brought economic depression to the nation. During a depression, businesses cut expenses by firing workers and lowering the wages of those who remain on the job. Nationwide wage cuts led to a successful railroad strike in 1884 and a violent year of labor–management clashes known as the Great Upheaval of 1886.

In May 1886, a labor strike in Chicago led to a clash between strikers and the police. When two strikers were killed, a rally was called for the next day at Haymarket Square. The protest was peaceful. Suddenly 200 policemen arrived and a bomb exploded; sixty policemen were killed and seven wounded. The police arrested eight prominent anarchists (only one of whom had actually been present), and the courts tried them for incitement to murder, convicting all eight and executing four.

Worker activism slowed after the Haymarket riot, and union membership dwindled. Employers began fighting labor unions by blacklisting any worker who tried to organize his or her colleagues. They forced newly hired workers to sign agreements never to join a union. They brought in strikebreakers to force laborers to return to work, and they also hired replacement workers.

Skilled workers decided to form their own union. In 1886, Samuel Gompers formed the American Federation of Labor (usually called the AF of L, or just AFL) for skilled workers. The AFL was founded, like all labor unions, to fight for the rights of workers, but all too often it colluded with management to the detriment of its own members. The American Railway Union, which struck against the Pullman Company in 1894, was permanently defeated when the strike failed.

Owners opposed unions, claiming that they were "un-American" because they were opposed to the notion of private property. The owner argued that his company was his own private property and therefore he could run it as he saw fit. This view ignored the fact that workers also had the right to do as they pleased; they had the right to walk off the job, to protest, and to fight for better working conditions and higher wages.

Social Classes

High Society

American "high society" was made up of families who had been in America for several generations. Their position in the topmost social rank was not dependent on wealth so much as on ancestry—on the fact that their money was inherited rather than earned in trade. Men in this social class might sit in a law office for a few hours a day, or serve on a board of trustees, but for the most part, high society was idle. Members of this American aristocracy married within their own social set, spent months of every year traveling in Europe, and paid servants to look after all their needs. It was this class and the newly rich that gave rise to the phrase "Gilded Age," a nickname for the decade of the 1890s.

The Newly Rich

The giant industrialists and financiers who had made their money in big business were not considered "upper class." They were self-made men who had earned their money in trade rather than inheriting it from illustrious ancestors. Their greatest ambition was to become part of high society, but high society was not welcoming. American aristocrats considered the newly rich to be a class of social climbers, snubbed them when they met them socially, and excluded them from parties and balls. However, the newly rich eventually used their fabulous wealth to surmount the barricade of class. They often had far more money to spend than the members of the old guard of society; in fact, they were so wealthy that in 1899, socialist Thorstein Veblen described their lifestyle as one of "conspicuous consumption." They lived in enormous mansions and might spend thousands of dollars to host a single evening party.

Edith Wharton and Henry James were the most important novelists to record the lives of these two social classes. In novels such as *The House of Mirth*, *The Age of Innocence*, *The Wings of the Dove*, and *The Golden Bowl*, they depicted the old families of society and the newly rich who schemed and plotted to enter their social circle by marriage or other means.

The Middle Class

The middle class expanded greatly during this era. The rise of industry had meant the creation of millions of jobs for educated, trained workers, such as engineers, architects, lawyers, stockbrokers, and doctors. Young middle-class women had more limited opportunities than their fathers and brothers, but many urban businesses welcomed them into the workforce. Female salesclerks and secretaries earned less than their male counterparts but worked just as efficiently, which made them desirable employees. Most young women left the workforce when they got married; after that, they remained at home to raise children and run a household. Many also found time for volunteer work, such as involvement in the ongoing struggle for women's suffrage or settlement-house work in the cities.

The Immigrants

The lowest social class was largely composed of recent immigrants. At this time in American history, most immigrants who came through New York's Ellis Island—hundreds of thousands each year—came from southern and eastern Europe. At the same time, a flood of Chinese crossed the Pacific, landing at Angel Island off the California coast.

Because these new immigrants did not usually speak English, they were initially isolated from mainstream American life and from immigrants of other nationalities. They generally formed their own small communities within New York or other cities, which provided some continuity with home. Neighbors who spoke their language helped them find work and make friends. The new immigrants also contributed some of their small incomes toward the building of neighborhood churches; these churches played an important role as community centers.

Much of the vitality of American cities, from that day to this, is due to the immigrant presence. Immigrant populations continued to cook familiar dishes, to publish newspapers in their own languages, and to observe religious and cultural festivals as they had done at home.

Immigrants faced both social and professional discrimination. Socially, they were regarded with suspicion by the previous generation of immigrants, now that the latter had been in the country long enough to feel that they were "real Americans." As immigration continued to rise, a new nativist movement grew up in protest against it. Despite the fact that the United States was an entire nation of immigrants and still continued to be the United States, nativists feared that immigrants from so many different cultures would drastically alter American society. They did not want immigrants bringing in new ideas, lowering the working wage, or taking jobs away from people who had been born in the U.S. All nativists ignored the fact that their own families had once been immigrants.

Professionally, immigrants took the lowest-paid jobs in business and industry. Many had been skilled workers at home, but had no money with which to establish a business in the United States. They had to take any work that was available in order not to starve. Because they were newcomers and frequently did not understand much English at first, they often did not know their own rights, and owners found it easy to bully and intimidate them.

Up to this time, almost all immigrants to the United States had been either European or African—and Africans had little power or influence socially, except among themselves. This changed with a wave of Chinese immigrants who crossed the Pacific Ocean in search of jobs. Nativist Americans of European descent treated the Chinese as an unwelcome foreign population for three reasons. First, they could not comprehend Chinese languages. Second, they had never seen anything like the traditional Chinese dress. Third, the Chinese had distinctly non-European physical characteristics that nativist Americans immediately labeled "inferior" to Caucasian features. Anti-Chinese prejudice culminated in the Chinese Exclusion Act of 1882, which denied U.S. citizenship to anyone born in China. This meant that no Chinese immigrant could ever become a citizen, although his or her children born in the United States were automatically citizens. The Chinese Exclusion Act also banned further Chinese immigration to the United States.

CHAPTER 18 QUIZ

1. A *monopoly* is defined as _____
   A. a business owned by a group of partners.
   B. a group of corporations run by a board.
   C. a trust that controls all the corporations within a single industry.
   D. a company that sells stock to investors.

2. Government largely failed to regulate big business because _____
   A. workers were reluctant to form labor unions.
   B. owners had too much political power and influence.
   C. workers wanted to change the American system of government.
   D. owners refused to establish reasonable safety measures in the factories.

3. The Chinese Exclusion Act stated that _____
   A. no Chinese immigrant could ever become a U.S. citizen.
   B. no child of Chinese immigrants could ever become a U.S. citizen.
   C. Chinese immigrants could not be legally employed in the United States.
   D. Chinese immigrants must be processed into the United States through Angel Island.

4. Why were self-made businessmen generally unwelcome in high society?
   A. because they were not sufficiently wealthy
   B. because they earned their money in trade
   C. because they were recent immigrants
   D. because they spent too much time traveling in Europe

5. Socialist Thorstein Veblen used the phrase "conspicuous consumption" to describe the lifestyle of _____
   A. the aristocracy.
   B. the newly rich.
   C. the middle class.
   D. the immigrants.

6. The purpose of a labor union is _____
   A. to run a business without the owner.
   B. to take owners to court over unsafe working conditions.
   C. to overturn the system of capitalism.
   D. to give the workers power to negotiate with the owner.

7. The Haymarket riot was a clash between police and _____
   A. political protestors.
   B. anarchists.
   C. supporters of strikers.
   D. Chinese immigrants.

8. Samuel Gompers is an important figure in history because he _____
   A. perfected the Bessemer process.
   B. invented the elevator.
   C. founded the American Federation of Labor.
   D. supported the Sherman Antitrust Act.

9. A strike is a powerful weapon in worker–owner negotiations because _____
   A. it halts production in the factory.
   B. it gets the U.S. government involved.
   C. it leads to major riots and protests.
   D. it brings the dispute to the courts for arbitration.

10. The telegraph was a means of _____
    A. speaking to someone a long distance away.
    B. communicating instantly over a long distance.
    C. converting iron ore into steel.
    D. traveling quickly from one place to another.

Politics and the Call for Reform, 1865–1900

The last half of the nineteenth century brought prosperity to many and poverty to many more. Immigrants continued to flood into the United States by the millions, usually taking the lowest-paid jobs and living in the poorest housing. Their acceptance of the situation meant that business owners, managers, and landlords had little incentive to improve wages or living and working conditions. However, many people tried to do something on an individual basis. The settlement-house movement brought help into the neighborhoods where it was most needed. Political machines also provided essential improvements such as sewer systems to cities, albeit at a price.

As manufacturing and service workers began to unionize and demand better working conditions, farmers began to try to do the same. National and regional Farmers' Alliance movements formed, bringing farmers together to address their most important financial and political concerns. By the end of the century, the Alliance movements had won major concessions for farmers.

People who were financially well off saw no need for reform, and those who profited from the widespread corruption in politics and business did not seek reform either. On the other side, millions of people clamored for a more democratic society, feeling that the United States had become a nation ruled by the wealthy for the wealthy. Most presidential elections during this era turned on the question of reform. Some progress was made, but major reforms would have to wait until the turn of the century and the rise to the presidency of the pugnacious, determined, fearless Theodore Roosevelt.

CHAPTER OBJECTIVES

- Describe the social and political atmosphere in the big cities in the last half of the nineteenth century.
- Describe the progress made in agricultural reform.
- Analyze national politics between the elections of Presidents Grant and McKinley.

Chapter 19 Time Line

- **1867**   National Grange movement founded
- **1870s** Farmers' Alliance movement begins
- **1872**   Ulysses S. Grant reelected president
- **1876**   Rutherford B. Hayes elected president
- **1880**   James A. Garfield elected president
- **1881**   Garfield shot; Chester A. Arthur becomes president
- **1883**   Congress passes Pendleton Civil Service Act
- **1884**   Grover Cleveland elected president
- **1888**   First mass-transit system in the United States (Richmond, Virginia)

    Benjamin Harrison elected president
- **1889**   Hull House opens
- **1896**   William McKinley elected president

The Rise of the Big Cities

The enormous influx of immigration made cities like New York grow. Between 1860 and 1900, fourteen million immigrants came to the United States. A great many of them settled in the port of entry. This skyrocketing population led to many changes in America's largest cities. New buildings were constructed to house the growing population. New schools and hospitals opened. Mass-transit systems were put into operation. Settlement houses came into existence in the poorest neighborhoods.

Many immigrants could afford nothing better than tenement housing. Typical tenement buildings in New York were five or six stories high, with no heating systems or indoor plumbing. A typical family apartment was one sizable room, whose windows usually overlooked dark airshafts or alleys, with the wall of the neighboring building almost close enough to touch. There were no rent regulations, so a landlord could demand whatever rent he wanted, and tenants had only two choices: pay it or go somewhere else. A landlord was under no legal obligation to maintain the property in good condition. Conditions outside the buildings were no better; there was no public garbage collection, so trash was everywhere, which of course added to the smells, discomfort, and disease. Jacob Riis documented tenement life in an important work of photojournalism called *How the Other Half Lives* (1890). Many prosperous people were sincerely horrified when Riis's work opened their eyes to the miserable conditions in which their neighbors were living. People began calling for reform.

The American settlement-house movement began in the 1880s with the goal of helping urban working families and immigrants. Jane Addams and Ellen Gates Starr established one of the first settlement houses, Hull House, in Chicago in 1889. Addams's goals were

- To offer classes to laborers and immigrants
- To bring culture and the arts to the poor neighborhoods
- To provide safe day care for the young children of working parents
- To train young middle-class women for useful careers in education or social work
- To provide the neighborhood with a social gathering place

Hull House accomplished all this and more. People from the neighborhood could go to Hull House to hear a concert, view an art show, take English lessons, learn to read, and send their children to classes. Hull House provided a place for social gatherings and political meetings. Settlement-house workers could help recent immigrants with many questions, such as finding a doctor or a job.

Settlement houses like Hull House and New York City's Greenwich House succeeded because they were located in the heart of the neighborhoods. Settlement-house volunteers often lived in the house; they were part of the neighborhood and its activities. To the working poor, this made the house a community center rather than a charitable handout.

After 1860, more and more states began passing laws that required all children to go to school. By 1900, more than 70 percent of all American children were attending school. More and more colleges also opened as the population continued to grow. However, reform was needed. Many schools, especially those in poor urban neighborhoods, did not have adequate space or facilities for the students. In addition, college tuition was usually too expensive for any but the wealthy. And the wages paid to immigrants and laborers were so low that they continued to send their children out to work.

As the cities grew larger, mass-transit systems came into existence, enabling people who lived far from the center to travel to and from the cities easily and cheaply. In 1888, Richmond, Virginia became the first city to have a trolley system. In the early 1900s, New York City began operating its first city-owned subway lines. The subway tunnels were largely dug by Italian immigrant labor. Italians were also hired to pave the walls of each subway station with decorative tile mosaics, because they were skilled at this kind of tile work.

Big-City Politics

Immigrants were generally active in politics, eager to vote, and attentive to the issues they faced as big-city dwellers. Immigrants were largely responsible for the success of the political machines of the late 1800s. A political boss would set a party position, then identify the men he felt were best fitted to support his position in public office. The boss was in charge of a staff of district leaders called "precinct captains"—men who maintained close relationships with the voters in their own neighborhoods. A precinct captain would get his hair cut by the neighborhood barber, eat his lunch at the corner chop house, and drink his beer at the neighborhood saloon. He knew the voters by name, and he knew what services they needed. He promised them that his party would provide these services if its candidates were elected. The captain then reported back to the boss, who pressured local businesses and contractors to provide the people with what they wanted.

Under the rule of the political bosses, streets were paved, water and sewer systems were installed and maintained, sidewalks were constructed, and fences were put up around dangerous construction sites. The bosses backed major urban improvement projects that employed thousands of immigrants. Many of the bosses came from recent immigrant—often Irish—stock themselves; they understood the problems of their constituents and helped them.

The boss expected and accepted graft, but argued that it was honest graft, because he kept his promises to the voters. The boss himself did not hold office, but in order to maintain his power, he had to be sure that his candidates were elected. When it appeared that the voters would not support a candidate, the boss would usually resort to violence or fraud. William Marcy Tweed, the boss of New York City throughout the 1860s, was eventually discredited by the political cartoons of Thomas Nast. Another political boss, John "Honey Fitz" Fitzgerald, eventually became mayor of Boston; his grandson John Fitzgerald Kennedy ended up in the White House.

Politics in Washington

During the heyday of the political bosses' authority in the cities, Ulysses S. Grant was president of the United States. Republicans, fearing for the future of Reconstruction, felt that Grant's popularity as a war hero would ensure his election. He won a narrow victory, thanks to the votes of African Americans in the South (see Chapter 16).

The Grant administration proved to be an era of political scandals. Two wealthy financiers named Jay Gould and James Fisk wanted a monopoly over the gold market. To drive up the price of gold, they wanted to keep as much of it out of circulation as they could. This meant convincing President Grant not to sell gold from the U.S. Treasury. When Grant refused to be a party to the scheme, Gould defied him, spreading rumors that the government would sell no more gold. Speculators took fright and began buying and selling gold. Determined to defeat Gould and his cronies, Grant immediately ordered the sale of $4 million worth of the government's gold. This scotched Gould's scheme, but it also drove the price of gold down so suddenly that many investors and speculators lost everything they had risked in the market.

In 1872, the public became aware of a dirty scheme hatched a few years previously by Schuyler Colfax, Grant's vice president. This plot had involved a group of congressmen who had pocketed money that came from Colfax's construction company. This company, Crédit Mobilier, had overcharged the Union Pacific Railroad by millions, and these undeclared profits had gone straight into the pockets of Colfax and his cronies. Grant had had nothing to do with this scandal, but it surfaced during his presidency and tarnished his reputation by association.

In this climate of scandal, reformer and newspaper editor Horace Greeley ran for president. He was backed by a liberal faction of the Republican Party and also by many Democrats who wanted Grant out of office. However, Grant's popularity with the voters was high, and he easily won the election. Greeley died less than a month later.

When Republican candidate Rutherford B. Hayes became president in 1877 (see Chapter 16), he caused a split in his own party by suggesting a program of civil-service reform, so that government employment would be based on merit rather than influence. The Stalwarts opposed civil-service reform; the Half-Breeds supported it. Conflict between these two factions made Hayes decide not to run for reelection. The Republicans agreed to compromise, nominating Half-Breed James A. Garfield for president and Stalwart Chester A. Arthur as his running mate. With Reconstruction over, most voters saw little difference between Republicans and Democrats; Garfield narrowly won the election of 1880 over General Winfield Scott. His presidency ended abruptly in early July of 1881, when Stalwart supporter Charles Guiteau shot him in a train station. Garfield received a relatively minor wound; however, medical science at the time was primitive, and he died a couple of months later of complications from the wound.

President Arthur vowed to make Garfield's reform program a reality. In 1883, he signed the Pendleton Civil Service Act, which required competitive examinations for about 10 percent of all jobs in the federal bureaucracy. Naturally, Arthur lost the support of the Stalwarts, and they nominated Half-Breed James Blaine for president in 1884. Mugwumps—a nickname given to reform-minded Republicans—deserted their party to support Democrat Grover Cleveland, acknowledged on all sides to be an honest man. Cleveland won a narrow victory in a campaign in which he took no part in the vicious mudslinging that supporters on both sides indulged in.

President Cleveland immediately extended the Pendleton Act to cover many more government positions. His reforming zeal made him unpopular among many career politicians, but he nevertheless won the nomination in 1888. He won the popular vote, but lost the electoral vote to Republican Benjamin Harrison. Harrison and the Republicans abandoned Cleveland's reform program, spending so much money to reward their supporters that they were nicknamed "the Billion Dollar Congress."

Populism

Although major reforms in big business and labor would have to wait until after the turn of the century, reform did take place in agriculture. The first step toward improving conditions for farmers had been the creation of the U.S. Department of Agriculture (see Chapter 17). The next step occurred when farmers realized that, like laborers in the manufacturing and service sectors of the economy, they could organize. Individually they were powerless; together they were strong.

During the late 1800s, farmers faced many challenges. Some of them were in desperate economic straits. Their profits had gone down while their expenses had gone up. Ironically, success had led to failure; after years of bountiful harvests, the supply of fresh produce and grain was exceeding demand. This imbalance caused prices to fall. Meanwhile, the railroads continued to raise prices for shipping, and manufacturers who sold equipment such as plows were also charging more. Farmers had little choice but to go into debt.

Oliver Kelley founded the National Grange in 1867 as a social organization for farmers, but as their troubles increased, it became a voice for farmers' mutual concerns. The Grange began to address political and economic issues. Grange members formed cooperatives to buy equipment and necessary supplies in bulk, thereby saving money. They put their crops together and pooled the costs of shipping and hauling. They also pressured state legislatures to regulate railroad freight and grain storage costs. Their insistence began paying off during the 1870s, when many farming states passed laws to standardize such rates. In 1887, the Grange farmers had their first taste of national success when Congress passed the Interstate Commerce Act. This act stated that railroads had to charge reasonable rates, could not refund large shippers secretly, and could not charge more for a short haul than for a long-distance haul. It created an Interstate Commerce Commission to regulate the railroads, but it gave the commission so little means to enforce its authority that it was useless.

The Farmers' Alliance began in Texas during the 1870s. It organized cooperatives, offered farmers low-cost insurance, and constituted a powerful political lobby for tougher bank regulations and government ownership of the transportation system.

In the South, the Alliance movement was racially segregated, like every other aspect of southern life. By 1900, the Colored Farmers' Alliance had largely disappeared from view; it did not have the power to fight both the southern Alliance and the interests of big business.

Farmers urged the printing of more paper money and a return to the coining of silver, which Congress had ended in 1873 in a return to the gold standard. This standard limited the amount of money in circulation to the amount of gold owned by the U.S. government. In 1878 and 1890, Congress passed acts legalizing the coining of silver in the hope that it would help a poor economy. This did not happen fast enough for the farmers, who successfully backed numerous candidates for office in the 1890 congressional elections. Pro-silver candidates won more than 40 seats in Congress as well as several governorships.

The Alliance movement gave rise to a new political party: the Populist Party. The key planks in the Populist platform were

- A graduated income tax
- Regulation of banks
- Government ownership of the railroads and the telegraph lines
- Unlimited coinage of silver
- Restrictions on immigration
- A shorter workday
- Voting reforms

The Populist candidate for president in 1892 was James Weaver, running against Republican Benjamin Harrison and Democrat Grover Cleveland. Although Weaver won 22 electoral votes, Cleveland had the support of labor, and he became the only president in American history to serve nonconsecutive terms in office.

In response to a severe financial panic in 1893, triggered when one of the major railroad companies failed, President Cleveland decided to return the nation to the gold standard. Many disagreed with his decision, and once again silver became the major issue of a presidential campaign. In 1896, William

Jennings Bryan ran for the Democrats against Republican William McKinley. The Populists decided to support Bryan rather than running a candidate of their own, because Bryan was an outspoken proponent of abandoning the gold standard and coining more silver.

Bryan was a colorful character, a lawyer, and a charismatic public speaker. Some time later, he and Clarence Darrow would oppose one another in the controversial Scopes trial, which would decide the fate of a Tennessee school-teacher who taught the theory of evolution in the classroom. (See Chapter 23.) At the 1896 Democratic convention, Bryan gave the famous "Cross of Gold" speech, arguing passionately for the coinage of silver:

> We have petitioned, and our petitions have been scorned; we have entreated, and our entreaties have been disregarded; we have begged, and they have mocked when our calamity came. We beg no longer; we entreat no more; we petition no more. We defy them. . . . we will answer their demand for a gold standard by saying to them: You shall not press down upon the brow of labor this crown of thorns, you shall not crucify mankind upon a cross of gold.

The quiet Republican candidate William McKinley won a narrow victory over Bryan. Voting split along economic lines; rich people voted for McKinley, because they had nothing to gain from an increase in the amount of money in circulation. Everyone else voted for Bryan. Popular demands for reform would be addressed in the near future by a man who was as charismatic as Bryan— William McKinley's vice president, Theodore Roosevelt.

CHAPTER 19 QUIZ

1. The Republican Party split in the late 1870s over the issue of _____
   A. immigration restrictions.
   B. a return to the gold standard.
   C. civil-service reform.
   D. reform in farming policies.

2. The precinct captains of a big-city political machine were responsible for _____
   A. drumming up support among individual voters.
   B. paying graft to the political boss.
   C. running for offices such as mayor or city councilman.
   D. providing necessary public services to the people.

3. Jacob Riis is an important figure in U.S. history for _____
   A. founding successful settlement houses in big-city neighborhoods.
   B. documenting tenement living conditions in *How the Other Half Lives*.
   C. serving as the political boss of New York City.
   D. fatally shooting President James A. Garfield.

4. All these U.S. presidents supported political reform except _____
   A. James A. Garfield.
   B. Chester A. Arthur.
   C. Grover Cleveland.
   D. Benjamin Harrison.

5. What was the purpose of the Grange movement?
   A. to unite farmers for their mutual benefit
   B. to support Democratic candidates for high office
   C. to wipe out the system of political bosses in the big cities
   D. to return the United States to the gold standard

6. The Populist Party supported all of the following except _____
   A. government regulation of institutions such as the telegraph system.
   B. a return to the gold standard.
   C. restrictions on immigration.
   D. reasonable hours for laborers.

7. The _____ brought about reform in the federal bureaucracy.
   A. Billion Dollar Congress
   B. Interstate Commerce Commission
   C. Stalwart Party
   D. Pendleton Act

8. Jane Addams is an important historical figure for her work in _____
   A. national politics.
   B. social reform.
   C. public education.
   D. journalism.

9. The federal government passed the _____ in response to pressure from the Grange movement.
   A. Interstate Commerce Act
   B. Pendleton Act
   C. Populist platform
   D. Chinese Exclusion Act

10. What was the basic purpose of the settlement houses?
    A. to help immigrants and the urban working class
    B. to recruit support for the political bosses
    C. to register voters throughout the big cities
    D. to ensure that all children attended school

PART II EXAM

1. **The Chinese were highly valued as railroad workers because** _____
   A. they were among the most recent immigrants to the United States.
   B. they were experienced at handling explosives.
   C. they had built railroads in China.
   D. they usually spoke English very well.

2. **The term *impressment* refers to the practice of** _____
   A. destroying kegs of whiskey and other alcoholic beverages.
   B. confessing one's sins and repenting at a public revival meeting.
   C. kidnapping men and forcing them into service on board ship.
   D. returning runaway slaves to their owners.

3. **In the Gettysburg Address, Lincoln quotes from** _____ **in the phrase "dedicated to the proposition that all men are created equal."**
   A. the Constitution of the United States
   B. the Emancipation Proclamation
   C. the Declaration of Independence
   D. the presidential oath of office

4. **A big-city political boss believed that it was his responsibility to** _____
   A. see that necessary public services were provided for the residents.
   B. mediate between the voters and the mayor.
   C. ensure that the city newspapers remained free to print what they wanted.
   D. support owners in disputes between workers and management.

5. **As a result of the Mexican War, the Texas–Mexico border was established at** _____
   A. the Rio Nueces.
   B. the Rio Grande.
   C. the Gila River.
   D. the Wabash River.

6. **Which best describes the Alliance movement?**
   A. a movement to settle the Great Plains and the West
   B. a movement to unite industrial workers
   C. a movement to fight for women's rights
   D. a movement to unite farmers for their mutual benefit

7. _____ gave rise to the founding of the African Methodist Episcopal (AME) Church.
   A. The temperance movement
   B. The Second Great Awakening
   C. The Seneca Falls Convention
   D. The Emancipation Proclamation

8. **The Homestead Act stated that** _____
   A. the states would receive land on which they were required to build colleges.
   B. any immigrant who worked on the building of the transcontinental railroad would automatically earn U.S. citizenship.
   C. anyone who claimed up to 160 acres of land and farmed it for five years could keep it for free.
   D. anyone who established a successful business out west did not have to pay income tax.

9. **The Confederates had the advantage of** _____ **over the U.S. Army as the Civil War began.**
   A. a larger population from which to draw troops
   B. better military commanders
   C. more money in the treasury
   D. more factories and heavy industry

10. **The Monroe Doctrine states that the United States** _____
    A. will never take part in a war between European nations.
    B. will remain neutral if a Western nation rebels against an attempted European takeover.
    C. will fight any further European attempts at colonization in the Western Hemisphere.
    D. will colonize all of North America between the Mexican and Canadian borders.

11. **All of these states were part of Oregon Territory except** _____
    A. Idaho.
    B. Montana.
    C. Oregon.
    D. Washington.

12. The Bessemer process made it possible to _____
    A. form labor unions.
    B. establish a national highway system.
    C. communicate instantly over a long distance in writing.
    D. convert iron ore into steel efficiently.

13. A settlement house served its neighborhood residents as all of the following
    except _____
    A. a social gathering place.
    B. a meeting area.
    C. a day-care center.
    D. a public school.

14. The primary job of a cowboy was to _____
    A. round up the cattle and herd them to the railroad depots.
    B. keep an eye on the cattle while they were freely grazing on the prairies.
    C. clash with the sheep ranchers.
    D. patrol the boundaries of the ranch to prevent cattle theft.

15. Nat Turner is a historically significant figure because he _____
    A. gave the famous "Cross of Gold" speech to the Democratic convention.
    B. proposed the Kansas-Nebraska Act to Congress.
    C. published the abolitionist newspaper The Liberator.
    D. led an armed slave rebellion in Virginia.

16. Once _____ was over, voters saw much less difference between
    the Republican and Democratic parties.
    A. the Civil War
    B. Reconstruction
    C. the Grange movement
    D. westward expansion

17. The forced march known as the Trail of Tears moved the _____
    Indians to Indian Territory.
    A. Delaware and Lenape
    B. Seminole and Cherokee
    C. Sioux and Apache
    D. Zuñi and Pueblo

18. **During the Civil War, President Lincoln's primary objective was** _____
    A. to free the slaves.
    B. to preserve the United States.
    C. to form foreign alliances.
    D. to compromise with the rebels.

19. **Abolitionists in Congress agreed to pass the Fugitive Slave Act of 1850 in exchange for** _____
    A. the admission of Texas to the United States as a slaveholding state.
    B. the admission of California to the United States as a free state.
    C. a ban on slavery in all U.S. territory acquired in the Mexican War.
    D. a ban on slavery north of Missouri.

20. **Charles Guiteau is famous in history for** _____
    A. organizing a major labor union.
    B. fatally shooting President James A. Garfield.
    C. running for president on the Populist Party ticket.
    D. inventing the telegraph.

21. **The Alien and Sedition Acts curtailed which constitutional right?**
    A. the right of free speech
    B. the right to own property
    C. protection against cruel and unusual punishments
    D. the right to trial by jury

22. **Which American author is famous for her detailed descriptions of everyday life on the western frontier?**
    A. Edith Wharton
    B. Louisa May Alcott
    C. Laura Ingalls Wilder
    D. Emily Dickinson

23. **The term _nativism_ refers to a prejudice against** _____
    A. slaves and former slaves.
    B. recent immigrants.
    C. Democrats.
    D. American Indians.

24. President _____ was impeached on trumped-up grounds because the majority pary in Congress disagreed with him politically.
    A. Grover Cleveland
    B. Andrew Johnson
    C. Ulysses S. Grant
    D. Benjamin Harrison

25. Owners used all these methods to fight labor unions except _____
    A. blacklisting workers who tried to form unions.
    B. hiring strikebreakers to force workers back to their jobs.
    C. bringing in new workers to replace those who went on strike.
    D. closing down their businesses permanently.

26. Andrew Jackson is described as the first _____ to serve as president of the United States.
    A. military hero
    B. member of the Federalist Party
    C. member of the southern planter class
    D. man of the people

27. The Battle of Gettysburg is considered the turning point in the Civil War because it was the last time that _____
    A. the Confederacy penetrated into the North.
    B. the Confederate Army won a major battle.
    C. African American soldiers played a significant role.
    D. the Union Army suffered heavy casualties.

28. Which U.S. president did not support reform in the federal bureaucracy?
    A. Grover Cleveland
    B. Benjamin Harrison
    C. Chester Arthur
    D. James Garfield

29. The term *Black Codes* refers to _____
    A. constitutional amendments that granted civil rights to former slaves.
    B. state laws passed in the former Confederacy that robbed former slaves of their civil rights.
    C. measures taken by the federal government to ensure southern compliance with the Emancipation Proclamation.
    D. land grants made to former slaves who wanted to resettle in the West.

30. **The temperance movement opposed** _____
    A. the abolition of slavery.
    B. westward expansion into American-Indian territories.
    C. the passage of the Civil Rights amendments.
    D. the consumption of alcoholic beverages.

31. _____ **is most famous in history as being the U.S. Army's most successful general during the Civil War.**
    A. Ulysses S. Grant
    B. Robert E. Lee
    C. Stonewall Jackson
    D. George McClellan

32. **During the early nineteenth century,** _____ **caused most immigrants to settle in the North.**
    A. economic opportunity
    B. racial prejudice
    C. inability to speak English
    D. preference for factory work

33. **In the 1870s, the Democratic Party gained the support of farmers who blamed** _____ **for the economic depression.**
    A. the influx of immigrants
    B. westward migration
    C. the Union victory in the war
    D. Reconstruction programs

34. **What was the purpose of Henry Clay's American System?**
    A. to effect a compromise between northern and southern political interests
    B. to create a long-term solution to economic problems
    C. to expand voting rights to all adult men, regardless of property ownership
    D. to establish a new political party

35. **Americans criticized William Seward for purchasing Alaska until** _____ **was discovered there.**
    A. oil
    B. gold
    C. timber
    D. coal

36. Pennsylvanians initiated the Whiskey Rebellion over the issue
    of _____
    A. territorial rights.
    B. taxation.
    C. temperance.
    D. voting rights.

37. American "aristocrats" closed ranks against the newly rich because the
    latter _____
    A. were from fine old families.
    B. had made their fortunes in business and industry.
    C. were descended from immigrants to the United States.
    D. did not believe in an ostentatious lifestyle.

38. What crime did the "Border Ruffians" commit in 1855?
    A. They took up arms against the U.S. government.
    B. They voted in a territory in which they were not resident.
    C. They seceded from the United States.
    D. They kidnapped and slaughtered a group of pro-slavers.

39. The American Federation of Labor is significant because it was _____
    A. the first union of skilled workers.
    B. the first union of unskilled workers.
    C. the first union to include black workers.
    D. the first union to lead a successful strike.

40. During the Nullification Crisis, South Carolina threatened to secede from the
    United States over the issue of _____
    A. abolition.
    B. women's rights.
    C. protective tariffs.
    D. industrialization.

41. The term *trust* refers to _____
    A. a group of corporations run by the same board.
    B. a group of stockholders in the same corporation.
    C. all the corporations that offer the same goods or services.
    D. a business that offers shares of stock for sale to investors.

42. **Britain and the United States have been allies since the end of** _____
    A. the War of 1812.
    B. the Revolutionary War.
    C. the Mexican War.
    D. the French and Indian War.

43. **The Plains Indians agreed to settle on reservations in exchange for promises of** _____
    A. respect for their rights as migratory hunters.
    B. opportunity to assimilate into American society.
    C. cash payments and supplies.
    D. the granting of U.S. citizenship.

44. **The town of Harpers Ferry is significant in U.S. history as the site of** _____
    A. John Brown's rebellion against the United States.
    B. the first battle of the Civil War.
    C. Abraham Lincoln's delivery of the Gettysburg Address.
    D. the capital city of the Confederate States of America.

45. **The Kansas-Nebraska Act stated that** _____
    A. one of the two would enter the United States as a free state, the other as a slaveholding state.
    B. Kansas and Nebraska would both enter the United States as free states.
    C. Kansas and Nebraska would both enter the Union as slaveholding states.
    D. Kansas and Nebraska would decide for themselves whether they wanted to permit slavery.

46. **Under a capitalist economic system,** _____
    A. businesses are privately owned.
    B. the government establishes wages and prices.
    C. the government owns and operates heavy industry.
    D. the workers own the means of production.

47. **Which best describes the relationship between Plains Indians and U.S. citizens during the era of westward migration?**
    A. They held aloof from one another.
    B. They fought a brief all-out war.
    C. They occasionally traded with one another.
    D. They were mutually friendly and helpful.

48. The invention of the _____ made skyscrapers practical.
    A. telegraph
    B. lightbulb
    C. passenger elevator
    D. typewriter

49. Alexander Hamilton is famous for all of the following except _____
    A. choosing the location of the nation's permanent capital.
    B. serving as the first secretary of the Treasury.
    C. serving as president of the United States.
    D. fighting a duel with Aaron Burr.

50. Voters in the Deep South did not support Stephen Douglas for president in
    1860 because _____
    A. he was in favor of abolishing slavery.
    B. he supported states' rights over the rights of the federal government.
    C. he was a candidate of the Republican Party.
    D. he held views that they considered too moderate.

Part III

Twentieth-Century U.S. History

Chapter **20**

The Progressive Era, 1900–1920

The turn of the new century brought relief to the laboring classes who had had such a severe struggle during the last half of the 1800s. Finally, a president came to the White House who would fight on behalf of the people.

Theodore Roosevelt believed that as president, it was his responsibility to look after the welfare of all the people, not only the wealthy. Roosevelt believed that a democratic republic like the United States should have no social class barriers, that all should prosper according to ability and talent, and that the government must regulate big business, since business had demonstrated that it would not treat either its workers or its customers fairly on its own.

Under Roosevelt and his successor, William Howard Taft, the federal government passed important legislation to regulate business and sued numerous trusts and monopolies. Roosevelt was concerned with reform on all levels: social, political, and economic. Meanwhile, Progressives across the nation pushed for local and state political reforms. They succeeded in making many changes in the electoral process, giving the people a greater direct voice in their own government.

Investigative journalists and novelists also concerned themselves with present-day social ills. Magazine articles exposed the shady and dishonest business dealings of men like John D. Rockefeller of Standard Oil. Full-length books informed readers about the living and working conditions of immigrants in city slums and big factories. When comfortable, middle-class Americans realized that these issues affected them directly, they were horrified and pushed for change.

When Woodrow Wilson became president in 1912, he continued to fight for reform. Wilson signed a great deal of important legislation that protected workers and regulated business practices. He reformed the national financial system, creating the powerful Federal Reserve. The ratification of the Nineteenth Amendment under Wilson marked the greatest triumph of the era of reform, finally enfranchising the female half of the adult population.

CHAPTER OBJECTIVES

- Describe economic, political, and social reforms during the Progressive Era.

- Identify and analyze the constitutional amendments passed under the Progressives.

- Identify the significant figures of the era and describe their contributions to politics, journalism, and/or reform.

Chapter 20 Time Line

- 1890   National American Woman Suffrage Association

- 1901   William McKinley assassinated; Theodore Roosevelt becomes president

- 1902   Newlands Reclamation Act

    United Mine Workers strike

- 1903   Elkins Act

- 1904   Roosevelt reelected

- 1906   *The Jungle*

    Hepburn Act

    Pure Food and Drug Act

- 1908   William Howard Taft elected president

- 1909   Payne-Aldrich Tariff

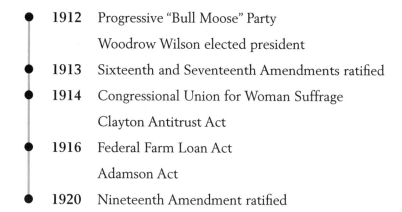

1912   Progressive "Bull Moose" Party

Woodrow Wilson elected president

1913   Sixteenth and Seventeenth Amendments ratified

1914   Congressional Union for Woman Suffrage

Clayton Antitrust Act

1916   Federal Farm Loan Act

Adamson Act

1920   Nineteenth Amendment ratified

The Progressive Era

While the Populist Party had been born in response to farmers' concerns, the Progressives were filled with reforming zeal by the ills of urban life. Their mission was to wipe out political corruption; to improve living conditions, especially in poor neighborhoods; and to support workplace legislation. Progressives did not believe that the upper class should enjoy a luxurious lifestyle while oppressing and starving the lower classes. They believed that all social classes should be able to live decently and in reasonable comfort, to earn fair living wages that would support their families, and to get an education. The United States was a prosperous nation; it was only fair that all levels of society should reap the benefits of prosperity, which all played a role in creating.

Progressivism attracted the prosperous middle class, which had grown by several millions since 1870. Both men and women played active roles in the movement. Although it was becoming much more common for middle-class women to earn college degrees, it was still difficult for them to find acceptance in many professions. The Progressive movement gave them a chance to put their knowledge and skills to use.

One of the most important concerns of the Progressives was abuse in big business. Progressives were well aware that the laborers, not the owners, did all the hard work and were therefore responsible for the profits of which they received so meager a share.

Most industrial laborers worked 10 to 14 hours a day, six days a week. The modern concept of the weekend did not exist, nor were workers paid extra for working overtime. There was no guaranteed minimum wage. Businesses were unregulated, so they did not have to put any safety precautions in place. Long working hours led to exhaustion, and exhaustion led to clumsiness; workers were often severely maimed or killed in industrial accidents, either because unsafe practices were in use or because workers were half-asleep on the job. Progressives called for an 8-hour workday, a minimum wage across all industries, safer working conditions, and an end to child labor. They believed that working parents should be paid enough to allow their children to go to school.

The Muckrakers

Naturally, business owners opposed the Progressives; safety regulations, shorter working hours, and a guaranteed minimum wage would eat into their profits. The Progressives retaliated against this opposition by exposing the worst practices of big business in the daily press. Theodore Roosevelt was the first to apply the term *muckrakers* to the investigative journalists of the day. He compared a reporter to a groom working in a stable: both dug under the surface and raked up the muck and corruption beneath. One issue of *McClure's Magazine* advertised the following articles on its front cover:

PITTSBURG: A CITY ASHAMED
LINCOLN STEFFENS'S exposure of another type of municipal grafting; how Pittsburg differs from St. Louis and Minneapolis.
IDA M. TARBELL on the Standard [Oil] tactics which brought on the famous oil crisis of 1878.

Trusts and monopolies were unpopular with most Americans because they drove up prices by eliminating free-market competition for customers. Readers snapped up copies of *McClure's* and other similar magazines and newspapers, gleeful at seeing the hated business tycoons exposed. Many muckrakers even wrote full-length books, such as *Following the Color Line* by Ray Stannard Baker and *The Shame of the Cities* by Lincoln Steffens. Novelists picked up on many of the same themes. In 1906, Upton Sinclair's *The Jungle* exposed the shocking practices in the meatpacking industry. Horrified meat-eating readers of *The Jungle*, knowing that they could count on support from the White House, pushed for reform in the industry. Government inspectors' reports soon showed that Sinclair had not exaggerated. One report read in part as follows:

> We saw meat shoveled from filthy wooden floors, piled on tables rarely washed, pushed from room to room in rotten box carts. In all of which processes it was in the way of gathering dirt, splinters, floor filth, and the expectoration of tuberculous and other diseased workers.

Reform under Roosevelt

Vice president Theodore Roosevelt, a Spanish-American War hero (see Chapter 21) and former governor of New York, became the nation's youngest president when William McKinley was assassinated in 1901. Roosevelt was fearless, outspoken, charismatic, and determined to govern as he saw fit, rather than answering to any special interests. Roosevelt opposed the class distinctions and the economic situation that kept the lower classes down; he believed that such distinctions had no place in a democratic society. He referred to his domestic goals as "a square deal, no less and no more" for all citizens. Roosevelt believed that big business had a role to play in society, but he also knew that business owners would put their profits above all other considerations. Therefore, he was determined to pass laws that would force compliance with certain standards, ensuring fair hours, wages, and working conditions.

Economic Reforms

Roosevelt had a chance to put his Square Deal program into action in 1902, when the United Mine Workers went on strike demanding recognition of their union and higher wages. Roosevelt offered to appoint a commission of arbitrators who would hear both sides and settle the dispute. Neither the workers nor the owners liked the sound of this. Owners were afraid of Roosevelt because he had clearly stated that he believed in regulating big business. Workers distrusted him because no previous president had ever supported them in a dispute. However, after the strike had dragged on for several months, both sides agreed to the president's proposal. The commission ruled that the owners must raise wages and shorten working hours, but that they did not have to recognize or bargain with the union. This was the first time that any president had ever achieved a result that protected workers and the public, at least to some extent. For the moment, both sides expressed satisfaction with the commission's ruling.

The U.S. government sued the Northern Securities Company, a railroad monopoly that controlled shipping between Chicago and the Northwest. The courts sided with the government, claiming that the Northern Securities Company had violated the Sherman Antitrust Act. So many more lawsuits followed that Roosevelt was nicknamed a "trustbuster." Roosevelt also sought to strengthen the government's power to regulate the railroads. The 1903 Elkins Act and the 1906 Hepburn Act gave the Interstate Commerce Commission its first real authority to enforce rules. These new ICC powers were later extended by Roosevelt's successor William Howard Taft.

Roosevelt acknowledged the growing public concern about the food and drug industry. Like all others, this industry was unregulated at the time Roosevelt took office. There were no ingredient labels on packaged foods or medicines. Con artists could call themselves doctors, mix up any concoction they wanted, and sell it as a cure-all for aches and pains. Dangerous drugs such as opium were available over the counter. And no one but the workers knew what went on in plants where foods were processed and packaged. *The Jungle* and the press opened readers' eyes to the unsanitary conditions that prevailed in such plants, and proved that regulation of the industry was necessary for the sake of public health and welfare.

In 1906, Roosevelt signed the Pure Food and Drug Act into law. It required that all food and beverage containers, including those for medicines, be clearly labeled with the ingredients of their contents. It banned the manufacture, sale, or transportation across state lines of harmful or poisonous substances.

The following table shows the key elements in Roosevelt's program of reform.

1902	**Newlands Reclamation Act**	Stated that money from the sale of federal land was to be used to irrigate and reclaim land
1903	**Elkins Act**	Outlawed rebates to shipping companies
1906	**Hepburn Act**	Authorized the ICC to set railroad rates and to regulate all companies engaged in interstate commerce
1906	**Meat Inspection Act**	Required federal inspection of meat that was shipped across state lines
1906	**Pure Food and Drug Act**	Outlawed the manufacture or sale of harmful substances; required ingredient labels on food and drug containers

Conservation

Roosevelt was the first president to involve the federal government in protecting and preserving the environment. As a boy, "Teddy" had planned to grow up to be a biologist or zoologist; animals and birds fascinated him. As an adult, he had owned and operated a ranch and had hunted big game in Africa. Roosevelt loved the outdoors and the natural wilderness, and was determined to use his authority as president to protect it.

Roosevelt's friend Gifford Pinchot first coined the word *conservation* to describe the protection of the natural environment. Roosevelt set aside millions of acres of federally owned land, including the Grand Canyon and the Petrified Forest, as forest reserves and national parks. Conservatives supported Roosevelt's actions, noting that Pinchot was right: the natural resources that fed big business must be preserved so that they would continue to give of their abundance.

Political Reform

The Progressives also involved themselves in political reform. They were determined to give the voters a greater voice in their own government, and to wipe out the big-city political machines. Voters also complained about national politics, feeling that their senators and congressmen were nothing more than the slaves and puppets of the big business owners who had paid so much money to get them elected.

The first step the Progressives took was to fight for reform on the local level, where voters selected delegates who nominated candidates for office. Progressives supported the direct primary, in which voters cast their votes directly for the candidates. Between 1902 and 1916, most states switched to a direct-primary system.

The Constitution granted the citizens the right to elect their representatives in Congress directly—but only those in the House of Representatives. Those in the Senate were chosen by the state legislatures. In 1913, thanks to Progressive efforts, the Seventeenth Amendment established direct popular election of senators.

The Progressives also fought for a secret, uniform ballot. At that time, political parties printed their own ballots in different colors, so that anyone could see how anyone else was voting. This made it easy for the precinct captains and any representative of a powerful vested interest to identify anyone not voting the way they wanted him to. This open voting system made intimidation easy; few voters wanted to risk retaliation by displeasing any strong-arm interests. With a uniform ballot, voting would be private and secret. By 1910, most states had bowed to Progressive pressure and converted to a secret ballot.

Progressives also believed that the people needed a mechanism by which they could propose or reject legislation on the state level. The following table shows three measures, all supported by the Progressives, that would make this possible. By 1916, most states had adopted all three.

Initiative	If 5 to 15 percent of all voters sign a petition proposing a new law, that law must appear on the ballot to be approved or rejected by direct popular vote.
Recall	Voters have the power to vote an elected official out of office before his or her term ends.
Referendum	If 5 to 15 percent of all voters sign a petition requesting it, a recently passed law must be placed on the ballot so that voters can either approve or veto it.

Many Progressives ran for local political office. Some became mayors and were able to play key roles in reforming big-city politics. Samuel M. "Golden Rule" Jones of Toledo and Tom Johnson of Cleveland were two Progressive mayors in big Ohio cities. They accomplished such goals as reforming the police force, establishing fair tax systems, opening schools for young children, and improving city living conditions. Other Progressives, like Robert La Follette of Wisconsin, became state governors. Their influence on reform at the state level was profound and effective. Many of their fellow governors followed their example.

Some middle-class Americans began backing away from the Progressive movement because they felt it was almost too successful. Its goal had been to help the working class, but some middle-class Americans did not want working-class lives improved too much. They did not want the lower classes to gain too much political or economic power, because they felt this would threaten their own position. This is a major theme throughout all human history—a class with power always feels threatened when the classes below it begin to acquire power of their own.

Reform under Taft

William Howard Taft, who had served in Roosevelt's cabinet, was elected president in 1908 with Roosevelt's support. Taft continued many of the programs that Roosevelt had initiated. His administration filed nearly a hundred lawsuits against trusts. He set aside more public lands as reserves. He supported the elimination of child labor. He signed the Department of Labor into law. Under Taft, Congress passed laws mandating safer working conditions in mines and an 8-hour workday for the laborers in any company that did business with the federal government. Under Taft, the Sixteenth Amendment, providing for a federal income tax proportional to the amount a person earned, was proposed; it was ratified shortly after he left office.

Taft lost the support of Roosevelt and the progressive wing of the Republican Party when he signed the Payne–Aldrich Tariff into law. This tariff raised the prices of consumer goods and led people to accuse Taft of breaking faith with the voters. Taft also had a falling-out with Gifford Pinchot over the sale of a vast tract of land in Alaska to the timber industry. In fact, Taft had an extremely positive record on environmental and reform legislation, but the perception on the part of Roosevelt and the public was that he had failed. During the congressional elections of 1910, Roosevelt actively supported candidates who opposed Taft. His program, which he called New Nationalism, called for laws that would protect the people. The goals of New Nationalism were better and safer working conditions, improved public health, and the regulation of big business. "The citizens of the United States must effectively control the mighty commercial forces which they have themselves called into being," stated Roosevelt.

Roosevelt decided to run for president again in 1912. When Taft won the Republican nomination in spite of the popularity of his opponent, Roosevelt's supporters created the Progressive or "Bull Moose" Party and nominated Roosevelt as a third-party candidate. With the Republican voters divided between Roosevelt and Taft, the Democratic candidate—quiet, scholarly Governor Woodrow Wilson of New Jersey—won in a landslide of electoral votes to become president in 1912. Like both Taft and Roosevelt, Wilson was a Progressive by inclination. He described his domestic agenda as the "New Freedom."

Reform under Wilson

Wilson was determined to lower tariffs. In 1913, he signed the Underwood Tariff Act, which reduced tariffs to their lowest levels in fifty years. Next, he addressed banking reform. Democrats and Progressives favored a banking system run by the government; Conservatives argued that private banks should have more control. Wilson compromised by signing the Federal Reserve Act of 1913. This created a national board to run the banking system and twelve Federal Reserve banks under combined federal and private control. It did not alter the status of all the private banks, which could borrow money from the Federal Reserve banks when necessary.

Like Roosevelt and Taft, Wilson believed in regulating big business. In 1914, he signed the Clayton Antitrust Act, which clarified the nebulous Sherman Antitrust Act by stating specifically what corporations could and could not do. It protected small businesses from being swallowed up by larger ones.

Under Wilson, Congress passed the Federal Farm Loan Act of 1916. This law, which was greeted with jubilation by farmers across the country, set up a special banking system for farmers only. Any farmers could borrow from one of the federal farm loan banks at a low rate of interest.

Like Roosevelt, Wilson believed in the arbitration of labor strikes. A national railroad strike in 1916 led to the passage of the Adamson Act, which reduced the workday for railroaders from 10 to 8 hours, but maintained wages at their existing levels. The strike was averted, with the workers gaining an important victory. Wilson also supported congressional legislation that, for the first time, offered financial compensation to workers injured on the job.

The Nineteenth Amendment

The most important reform of all—because it affected more than 50 percent of the adult population—gained enough ground during Wilson's presidency to become law in 1920. The Nineteenth Amendment finally granted adult women the right to vote.

In 1890, Elizabeth Cady Stanton and Susan B. Anthony had helped to found the National American Woman Suffrage Association. The association pushed for voting rights for women on the state level, and by 1901 it had succeeded in four western states. In 1914, Alice Paul formed the Congressional Union for Woman Suffrage, which became the National Woman's Party in 1916. The party's goal was simple: to pass an amendment giving women the vote.

Paul and her followers picketed the White House daily, pointing out the inconsistency of Wilson's position: he supported workers but denied women their rights. They chained themselves to fences when policemen tried to arrest them. Many went on hunger strikes. All these tactics kept the struggle for suffrage in the newspapers and before the public eye.

In 1916, Carrie Chapman Catt devised what was later called "Catt's Winning Plan." Adopting her ideas, the association won victories in several states, getting legislation passed that gave women the vote. When the United States entered World War I, women proved their importance to the nation by playing a major role in the war effort. President Wilson, recognizing the justice of women's claim to full rights, spoke out in favor of universal suffrage in 1918. The Nineteenth Amendment was ratified in 1920. At long last, Abigail Adams's desire that the men running the government should "remember the ladies" had been gratified.

CHAPTER 20 QUIZ

1. **The Progressive Era was characterized by** _____
   A. expansion of U.S. territory.
   B. financial panics.
   C. economic, social, and political reform.
   D. a cultural and artistic renaissance.

2. _____ **were actively opposed to the Progressive agenda.**
   A. Women
   B. Industrial workers
   C. Farmers
   D. Business owners

3. **Public response to Upton Sinclair's *The Jungle* was largely responsible for the passage of** _____
   A. the Newlands Reclamation Act.
   B. the Meat Inspection Act.
   C. the Payne-Aldrich Tariff.
   D. the Clayton Antitrust Act.

4. **The Progressives believed that reform of big business was necessary because** _____
   A. conditions were unsafe and workers were not fairly paid.
   B. businesses were not sufficiently profitable.
   C. industry was a drain on the American economy.
   D. industry was harmful to the natural environment.

5. The Seventeenth Amendment altered the electoral process for _____
   A. the presidency.
   B. the Senate.
   C. the House of Representatives.
   D. the Supreme Court.

6. The term *referendum* refers to _____
   A. the regulation of industrial practices.
   B. the conservation of the natural environment.
   C. the citizens' right to vote on recent local legislation.
   D. the creation of a secret ballot.

7. Which president oversaw major reforms in the banking system?
   A. Theodore Roosevelt
   B. William Howard Taft
   C. Woodrow Wilson
   D. William McKinley

8. President Woodrow Wilson described his program for the nation
   as _____
   A. the Square Deal.
   B. the Golden Rule.
   C. the New Nationalism.
   D. the New Freedom.

9. The direct primary system, in place throughout the United States by 1916,
   allowed voters to _____
   A. vote directly for the candidate of their choice.
   B. vote for delegates who would then vote for the candidate for office.
   C. vote by secret ballot.
   D. vote on recently passed local legislation.

10. Alice Paul is historically significant for _____
    A. investigative journalism.
    B. leading the battle for women's suffrage.
    C. speaking out on the issue of conservation.
    D. leadership in labor unions.

Chapter 21

The United States Becomes a World Power

Although the United States had acquired an empire, it was one continuous tract of land (plus the Alaska territory). Unlike the great European powers, the United States had not traveled the world, acquiring faraway colonies. This changed as the nineteenth century gave way to the twentieth. The United States had several motives for acquiring colonies. The first was to gain trade partners on favorable terms. The second was to establish naval bases. The third was simply to prove to the world that it was a great power.

The United States produced all the wheat and manufactured goods its people needed, but it did not have the right climate to produce other necessities, such as coffee, sugar, and rubber. Colonies could provide these raw materials; they would also serve as a market for surplus wheat and manufactured goods. When a nation controls a colony, that nation can dictate the terms of trade—it can purchase colonial raw materials at low prices and sell its own goods to the colonists at high prices.

The United States acquired a highly desirable colony in the central Pacific Ocean—the sugar-producing Hawaiian Islands. Hawaii became a U.S. territory and served as both a trading partner and a strategically important naval base. As a result of the Spanish-American War, the United States acquired the territories of Guam, Puerto Rico, and the Philippines. It also made Cuba a protectorate.

In 1903, the United States took control of a narrow slice of the Isthmus of Panama, where a canal that connected the Pacific and Atlantic oceans was under construction. The United States hired Caribbean workers to complete the job, and the Panama Canal opened with great fanfare in 1914. This period also saw the beginning of the tendency of the United States to be "the policeman of the world" with its continual uninvited interference in the affairs of Latin American nations.

CHAPTER OBJECTIVES

- Identify the colonies and territories that came under U.S. control before World War I.
- Describe the course of the Spanish-American War.
- Identify the key figures of the era and describe their contributions in foreign affairs and journalism.

Chapter 21 Time Line

- **1875** Hawaiian sugar exempted from U.S. tariffs
- **1880s** French begin to dig Panama Canal
- **1890** McKinley Tariff
- **1893** Queen Liliuokalani abdicates
- **1898** United States annexes Hawaii

  Battleship *Maine* explodes off Cuba

  Spanish-American War
- **1899** Open Door Policy

  United States acquires control over Samoa
- **1900** Boxer Rebellion
- **1902** Philippine Government Act

  Platt Amendment
- **1903** Hay–Bunau-Varilla Treaty
- **1905** Roosevelt brokers peace treaty between Russia and Japan

- 1914 Panama Canal completed
- 1916 Jones Act of 1916
- 1917 Jones Act of 1917

Pressure to Expand

While domestic reforms were under way at home, the United States developed a new agenda outside its borders. The United States had always been inclined to expand its influence, taking over any available land and subjugating the people who already lived there, but until the late 1800s, this tendency had been confined to North America. From the late 1800s until World War I, the United States began flexing its muscles and testing its powers overseas.

The American desire for expansion had the same motives as the European colonization drive during the Age of Exploration (see Chapter 1). The United States wanted to establish new markets for its exports, to acquire lands that could supply raw materials the United States lacked, and to gain a reputation as a major military and political force in world affairs. Some Americans also argued that the United States had a moral duty to spread democracy through the world; others felt that invading and taking control of a foreign nation was hardly moral or justifiable.

The United States already had long-established trade relationships with European nations. It looked to Africa, Asia, and the Caribbean and Pacific islands as new markets for its abundance of grain and manufactured goods. Since European powers had already colonized most of Africa, the United States turned its attention to the Pacific. Because of their climate, the Pacific islands were or could be made major producers of sugar, rubber, coffee, and other raw materials that the United States could not supply for itself.

Trade with China and Japan

China

The United States had begun trading with China in the late 1700s. In 1843, China expanded trade options for the West by opening five ports for trade. After losing an 1895 war with Japan, China was weakened, and four European nations were quick to take advantage and seize exclusive trade rights over various parts of China. Afraid of being left out in the cold, the United States created an Open Door Policy that contained three principles:

- Any nation that had a trade agreement with China would extend that agreement to other nations
- Only Chinese officials could collect tariffs and duties on imports and exports
- Harbor, trade, and tariff rates would be equal for all nations trading with China

European nations that received official notice of the Open Door Policy ignored it; the United States took their silence for consent. After the Boxer Rebellion of 1900, Secretary of State John Hay reinforced the Open Door Policy.

Japan

Trade between the United States and the tiny island nation of Japan had begun in 1854, when the United States forced Japan to end its centuries of isolation. Japan had had no contact at all with the outside world in hundreds of years, but it proved eminently adaptable to modern life and soon became a world power. In 1904, Japan attacked Russia. The United States brokered a peace treaty between the two nations in 1905, for which President Roosevelt was awarded the Nobel Peace Prize.

The United States Annexes Hawaii

In 1875, the United States signed a treaty with King Kalakaua of the Hawaiian Islands, a chain of eight large and many tiny islands 2,000 miles off the coast of California. U.S. officials decided that Hawaii would make a splendid naval base and fueling station for merchant ships. In the treaty, Hawaii gained exemption from tariffs on the sugar it exported to the United States. In exchange, Kalakaua agreed not to cede any territory to any foreign power.

In 1886, the United States demanded full control over Pearl Harbor, which it wanted for a naval base. When Kalakaua refused, a group of vested American interests secretly formed the Hawaiian League. These traders, planters, and merchants decided that, for their economic profit, they must overthrow the king and influence the United States to annex Hawaii. Their first step was to force Kalakaua to sign the "Bayonet Constitution" (so called because the king was forced to sign it at gunpoint). The Bayonet Constitution limited the monarch's power and the right of Hawaiians to hold political office. In 1890, the McKinley Tariff granted all nations the right to ship sugar to the United States duty-free. The price of sugar fell, and the Hawaiian economy felt the impact.

In 1891, Liliuokalani became queen of Hawaii. Supporters of the Hawaiian League staged a major protest when she announced that she intended to overturn the illegal Bayonet Constitution. With support from armed American marines, the Hawaiian League installed Sanford Dole as president of a new government. Rather than see Hawaiian lives lost in battle, Liliuokalani abdicated.

When the Dole government petitioned the United States for annexation, President Grover Cleveland ordered an investigation. Disgusted by the flagrant illegality of the Hawaiian "revolution," which had in fact been stage-managed by rogue Americans acting independently of the U.S. government, Cleveland ordered the Dole government disbanded. Sanford Dole defied the president, refusing to step down. Cleveland was not willing to go to war to restore Liliuokalani to her throne, but he did refuse to annex Hawaii. However, President William McKinley annexed Hawaii in 1898, ignoring the protests of the vast majority of Hawaiians. Hawaii became a U.S. territory in 1900.

The Spanish-American War

> You take the Spanish-American War. . . . That was Mr. Kane's war. We didn't really have anything to fight about. But do you think if it hadn't been for that war of Mr. Kane's we'd have the Panama Canal?

In 1941, a muckraking biography of William Randolph Hearst opened on American movie screens. Titled *Citizen Kane*, this splendid film gives newspaper editor and owner Charles Foster Kane (a thinly disguised stand-in for Hearst) credit for having deliberately provoked the Spanish-American War with the inflammatory headlines in his newspapers. This was no exaggeration on the part of the filmmakers.

Born in 1863 to millionaire parents, Hearst owned major newspapers across the United States. Hearst thought like a businessman rather than like a journalist; his goal was to sell as many papers as possible, not necessarily to give the public accurate information. He had no objection to exaggerating or inventing facts in order to create sensational stories. This "yellow journalism" became the

New York Journal's trademark. With what one historian later referred to as the "acme of ruthless, truthless newspaper jingoism," Hearst used the *Journal* to push the United States into a war with Spain.

In 1896, Cuba was trying to win its independence from Spain. Knowing that the dramatic events of the rebellion would interest his readers, Hearst encouraged his reporters to exaggerate the facts and stir up American resentment against Spain. Many Americans sympathized with the Cuban revolutionaries, who were fighting a tyrant just as the Americans themselves had once fought Great Britain. *Journal* stories deliberately played on this sympathy, actively pressuring the U.S. government to declare war on Spain. President McKinley resisted the pressure.

The spark that set off the war was the sudden explosion of the American battleship *Maine*, anchored off the Cuban coast in case its crew should be needed to protect American property or lives. What caused the ship to blow up is still unknown; independent investigations at the time suggested that it might have been either accident or an underwater mine. Few people seriously believed that it was an act of war on Spain's part, since Spanish diplomats had been working hard to avoid an all-out war with the United States. Ignoring the facts, Hearst put the story of the *Maine* on the front page for several days, with headlines such as:

- THE WARSHIP *MAINE* WAS SPLIT IN TWO BY AN ENEMY'S SECRET INFERNAL MACHINE.
- THE WHOLE COUNTRY THRILLS WITH THE WAR FEVER
- HOW THE *MAINE* ACTUALLY LOOKS AS IT LIES, WRECKED BY SPANISH TREACHERY, IN HAVANA BAY

With the people clamoring for action, McKinley felt that he had no choice but to reject Spain's request for a peace agreement. On April 25, 1898, Congress declared war. It would be fought on three fronts: in Cuba, in Puerto Rico, and in the Philippines, which served at the time as a Spanish naval base.

Commodore George Dewey led a fleet of American warships from the coast of Hong Kong to the Philippines a few days after Congress declared war. The American ships easily overpowered the Spanish fleet guarding the Manila harbor. The Filipinos had been rebelling against Spanish rule for two years and were easily enlisted to help the Americans conquer Manila. The war in the Philippines ended in August 1898.

Unlike the navy, which had covered itself with glory in the Philippines, the army was not adequately prepared for a land war in Cuba. The United States did not maintain a large standing army in peacetime, and the only uniforms the soldiers were supplied with were made of heavy wool—highly unsuitable for the tropical climate of Cuba.

Theodore Roosevelt had joined the army, which placed him in command of a cavalry unit nicknamed the Rough Riders, whose goal was to capture the high ground above the city of Santiago. The Rough Riders charged up San Juan Hill under a hail of Spanish bullets, and had control of the high ground by nightfall. The U.S. Navy sank the entire Spanish fleet off the coast of Cuba, and the war ended two weeks later when Spain surrendered. Fighting in Puerto Rico had already ended. The United States agreed to pay Spain $20 million for the Philippines, Cuba gained its independence from Spain, and Spain ceded Guam to the United States.

After the War

The Philippines

After the defeat of the Spanish fleet, Filipino patriot Emiliano Aguinaldo had taken the lead in setting up a provisional government. Aguinaldo became the island nation's first president. The Filipinos had been given no say in the matter of their annexation by the United States, and they were furious that the United States expected to control the islands in return for having driven the Spanish out. The United States had plans for the Philippines. It would serve as a naval base. It would be a handy central location for trade in Asian and U.S. goods, saving thousands of miles of transport. It would provide a new market for American goods. It would be a cheap source of raw materials that the United States needed.

From the Filipino point of view, U.S. annexation amounted to a betrayal. Armed conflict between a U.S. army of occupation and Filipino patriots raged for three years. In 1902, the United States finally put down the rebellion. The U.S. Congress then passed the Philippine Government Act, which established a bicameral legislature and a governor. Filipinos would elect their own representatives to the lower house; the United States would appoint the governor and the members of the upper house. In 1916, the United States passed the Jones Act of 1916, giving Filipinos the right to elect members of the upper house.

Cuba and Puerto Rico

Although he had allowed Hearst's tactics to push him into a war he did not support, President McKinley acted decisively once the war was over. He installed temporary governments in Cuba and Puerto Rico, claiming that Americans must be in charge until order was restored. McKinley appointed Leonard Wood governor of Cuba. Wood immediately took two practical steps to improve everyday life in Cuba. First, he provided money for the construction of schools. Second, he funded a sanitation system that drained pools of standing water throughout the island, thus removing the mosquitoes' breeding ground and the constant threat of deadly yellow fever and malaria.

Despite these points in his favor, Wood was an autocrat. He supported a constitutional amendment making Cuba a U.S. protectorate and requiring it to provide an American naval base. If Cuba accepted the Platt Amendment, U.S. troops would cease to occupy the island. The Cuban legislature reluctantly voted for the amendment in 1902. The following year, Cuba and the United States signed a trade agreement that profited both countries.

At first, Puerto Rico was ruled just as the Philippines had been, with a U. S.-appointed governor and Senate and a Puerto Rican-elected House of Representatives. The Jones Act of 1917 restored to Puerto Ricans the right to elect their own Senate.

The Panama Canal

As early as the mid-1500s, people had conceived of the idea of a canal across the Isthmus of Panama that would link the Atlantic and Pacific oceans. Such a canal would eliminate the need for westbound ships to sail all the way around South America to reach the Pacific Ocean. In the 1800s, Frenchman Ferdinand de Lesseps began to make this vision a reality. Lesseps had designed and overseen the construction of the Suez Canal, which linked the Mediterranean and Red Seas across a narrow neck of Egyptian land; he was confident of success in Panama. However, the effort was a failure. Workers died of yellow fever and dysentery in such great numbers that France abandoned the project.

The United States had watched the progress of the canal project with interest, and stepped in as soon as the French gave up the attempt. In 1903, John Hay proposed a bargain to the government of Colombia, which controlled Panama at that time. Colombia would give the United States a 99-year lease on the Canal Zone, a strip of land 6 miles wide and 50 miles long, across Panama.

In exchange, the United States would pay Colombia $10 million outright and $250,000 a year thereafter. The Colombians rejected the offer.

However, Colombia had reckoned without Panamanian leaders who wanted independence and believed that U.S. control of the canal would help them achieve it. In 1903, Philippe Bunau-Varilla, chief engineer of the canal project, brokered a deal between President Roosevelt and leaders of the Panamanian resistance. The United States agreed to support the Panamanian revolution in exchange for permanent sovereignty over a 10-mile-wide canal zone. The revolution ended swiftly, with victory for the Panamanians and the United States. Construction of the Panama Canal was completed in 1914. Most of the workers had been recruited from the Caribbean islands. They faced many dangers, including sudden avalanches of earth and disease; 6,000 of them died before the project was completed.

Control of the Panama Canal meant control of an important shipping lane. The United States would administer the canal and earn fees from every nation that sent ships through it. The United States could use the canal at no charge.

The Panama Canal

Promoting Economic Growth

In order to gain economic control over various Latin American nations, the United States frequently intervened in their affairs. In 1905, President Theodore Roosevelt issued the Roosevelt Corollary to the Monroe Doctrine, outlining U.S. policy toward Latin America:

> **The Roosevelt Corollary**
> . . . under no circumstances will the United States use the Monroe Doctrine as a cloak for territorial aggression. We desire peace with all the world, but . . . There are, of course, limits to the wrongs which any self-respecting nation can endure. It is always possible that wrong actions toward this Nation, or toward citizens of this Nation . . . may result in our having to take action to protect our rights; but such action will not be taken with a view to territorial aggression, and it will be taken at all only with extreme reluctance and when it has become evident that every other resource has been exhausted.

Latin American nations frequently failed to repay bank loans to Europe. This gave the United States the excuse to send in troops to "protect" the Latin American nations against potential European military retaliation for nonpayment. These American armies of occupation, which were sent south without invitations or permission from the nations concerned, usually stayed in place for some years.

When Taft succeeded Roosevelt, U.S. policy shifted. Taft believed in so-called dollar diplomacy—in investing U.S. money in Latin American nations. This way, these nations would owe money to the United States, not to Europe. They would have trade relations with the United States. The United States would build businesses in these nations, and would hire workers there. Taft acted in the hope that such a policy would create greater trust and friendship between the Western nations.

Woodrow Wilson, who succeeded Taft, felt that politics, not economics, was the way to gain influence over Latin America. He used military force to aid rebellions and establish constitutional governments throughout Latin America.

CHAPTER 20 QUIZ

1. **The Roosevelt Corollary clarifies** _____
   A. the Constitution.
   B. the Declaration of Independence.
   C. the Platt Amendment.
   D. the Monroe Doctrine.

2. **The Jones Act of 1916 established voting rights in** _____
   A. Cuba.
   B. Puerto Rico.
   C. Hawaii.
   D. the Philippines.

3. **Hearst newspapers published lies and exaggerations about the explosion of the *Maine* in order to** _____
   A. push the United States into declaring war on Spain.
   B. help Spain defeat the Cuban attempt to gain independence.
   C. reduce public support for the Spanish-American War.
   D. support the Dole government in Hawaii.

4. **Queen Liliuokalani of Hawaii abdicated in order to** _____
   A. persuade the United States to annex Hawaii.
   B. protest the signing of the Bayonet Constitution.
   C. prevent an all-out war between Hawaii and the United States.
   D. become president of a representative Hawaiian government.

5. **The Open Door Policy established rules governing international trade with** _____
   A. Japan.
   B. China.
   C. Cuba.
   D. Hawaii.

6. **The United States made no attempt to colonize Africa because** _____
   A. it was not rich in natural resources or raw materials.
   B. European nations had already colonized most of the continent.
   C. the Africans put up fierce armed resistance against any attempt at colonization.
   D. Africa was too far from the United States to be a useful trade partner.

7. The United States wanted to acquire control over Hawaii primarily because it was an abundant source of _____

   A. pineapples.
   B. gold.
   C. sugar.
   D. wheat.

8. _____ is important in military history as a successful naval commander during the Spanish-American War.

   A. Theodore Roosevelt
   B. George Dewey
   C. Emiliano Agualdino
   D. John Hay

9. Which best describes Spain's position at the time of the explosion of the *Maine*?

   A. eager for war against the United States
   B. deliberately provoking the United States into declaring war
   C. hoping to avoid all-out war with the United States
   D. unconcerned about the possibility of war with the United States

10. The United States wanted to acquire foreign colonies for all these reasons except _____

    A. to demonstrate that it was a great power.
    B. to acquire trade partners on favorable terms.
    C. to gain sources of raw materials necessary for American industry.
    D. to recruit young men to serve in the American military.

Chapter 22

World War I and Its Aftermath, 1914–1920

The United States had entered the twentieth century an isolated nation, both geographically and politically. It had played no role in conflicts between other nations, but simply pursued its own territorial conquests and fought wars involving its own direct concerns.

The Spanish-American War marked the beginning of the end of this splendid isolation. For the first time, the United States fought in a war that was no concern of its own—a rebellion of a colony against the dominant nation that controlled it. Even in this case, however, the United States had territorial aims of its own to pursue.

World War I—called at the time "the Great War"—marked the United States' first major entry into world affairs. The war began in 1914, but the United States did not become directly involved in it until three years of fighting had gone by. The United States supplied money and arms to the Allied or Entente powers (Britain, France, and Russia) as early as 1915, but did not declare war on the Central powers until 1917. The first American troops did not enter the trenches until 1918.

The United States came out of the war in a strong position. The traditional European powers—Britain, France, Germany, and Russia—were severely weakened. Millions of their young men had been slaughtered, their armies and navies were destroyed, their economies were devastated, and much French land and many villages lay in ruins. By contrast, the United States had lost relatively few soldiers and ships, and its home front was far away from the fighting. The war effort had had a positive effect on the American economy.

The fact that the war might easily have been avoided led President Woodrow Wilson to insist on the creation of a League of Nations—an international organization in which representatives of member nations would discuss conflicts over a table, attempting to resolve them peacefully. In Wilson's vision, armed conflict should be only a last resort. If one nation behaved aggressively, all other nations should unite against it, thus effectively putting a stop to its attacks or encroachments. This vision became a reality in 1920, but without U.S. participation. A full-scale United Nations, which all the great powers of the world would join, had to wait until after World War II—a war that might have been prevented had Wilson's dream of a modern Round Table come true.

CHAPTER 22 OBJECTIVES

- Identify the causes of World War I.
- Explain how the United States became involved in World War I.
- Describe the course of the fighting.
- Describe conditions on the home front during the war.
- List and explain the major provisions of the Fourteen Points and the Treaty of Versailles.

Chapter 22 Time Line

- 1908   Austria-Hungary annexes Bosnia-Herzegovina

- 1914   **June 28**   Gavrilo Princip assassinates Archduke Franz Ferdinand of Austria-Hungary

  August   World War I begins in Europe

- 1915   **May 7**   German U-boats sink *Lusitania*

  Trench warfare begins

  United States begins giving financial support to Allies

  Great Migration (1915–1930)

- 1916   National Defense Act
- 1917   Selective Service Act

    February 3   United States severs diplomatic relations with Germany

    March 1   Publication of Zimmermann Telegram

    April 6   United States declares war on Germany

    June 9   Espionage Act

    October 21   U.S. troops arrive on Western Front

    November 7   Russian Revolution

- 1918   **January 8**   "Fourteen Points" speech

    September–October   Massive influenza epidemic

    November 11   Germany surrenders; armistice signed

- 1919   **June 28**   Peace conference and signing of Treaty of Versailles

    September   Wilson suffers severe stroke

War Breaks Out

World War I—called simply "the Great War" at the time, since no one knew that there would later be a World War II—was a conflict over territory. Both Serbia and Austria-Hungary claimed the right to control the tiny kingdom of Bosnia-Herzegovina. Austria annexed the territory in 1908, provoking Serbian anger and vows of revenge.

In June of 1914, as Archduke Franz Ferdinand and Archduchess Sophie of Austria-Hungary rode through the streets of Bosnia's capital, Sarajevo, in an open car, a Serbian nationalist named Gavrilo Princip shot and killed them both. Many historians believe that if Austria had invaded Serbia immediately, the war would have been between these two nations only and would have been concluded quickly. However, while Austria hesitated, Russia began to mobilize its army in preparation for the defense of its fellow Slav nation Serbia. Germany considered this mobilization a serious threat of war and promptly came to Austria's defense by declaring war on Serbia.

The German military had long assumed that it would one day have to fight a war against France and Russia and had worked out a war plan, known as the

Schlieffen Plan after the officer who designed it. The Schlieffen Plan called for an immediate march on France through Belgium, which stood between their borders. The German army would then march south, capture the capital city of Paris, and thus sew up a quick victory on the Western Front before the Russians had time to muster an attack on Germany from the east.

However, the army did not proceed according to the Schlieffen Plan. Due to disagreements among the commanding officers, the army turned aside before reaching Paris and met the French army on the Marne River. When the French unexpectedly won the Battle of the Marne, the Germans changed their plans; the Western Front would now become a setting for trench warfare. By this time, Britain had declared war on Germany.

Trench Warfare on the Western Front

Both sides dug hundreds of miles of trenches stretching roughly along the north-south axis of Europe, from the North Sea to the border of Switzerland. The trenches served the infantry on both sides as both home and fort throughout four years of fighting. The trenches were dreadful places, especially on the British-French side. Assuming that the war would be over quickly, the Allies had dug their trenches hastily. They were always muddy, often knee-deep in rainwater, crawling with lice and rats, sweltering in summer and freezing in winter. Soldiers had no way to keep themselves, their sleeping places, their rations, or their precious personal possessions clean or dry. The German trenches were somewhat more bearable; the German army had taken a much more methodical approach to trench building, laying down board floors and installing electricity.

German and French trenches were only a few miles apart, with the zone between them labeled "no-man's-land." When the order to attack came, soldiers would leap out of their own trenches and rush at the enemy trenches with their guns firing.

No-man's-land had no cover; it was open and barren ground. For centuries, European soldiers had been fighting battles in which the armies clashed on open ground, with the stronger side usually winning a decisive victory in short order. The types of weapons used meant that most combat was up-close and hand-to-hand; eighteenth- and nineteenth-century muskets and rifles had little accuracy over a long distance, and swords and sabers were meant only for hand-to-hand combat.

Modern weapons were entirely different. Machine guns, grenades, and other new weapons developed during the Industrial Revolution were most effective from a distance. They were best suited to an ambush-style combat, with soldiers firing on the enemy from the protection of trees, buildings, or, in this case, trenches. Since the attacking soldiers were charging forward across open ground, the defenders in the trenches could fire on them from a position of relative safety. Through four years of trench warfare, neither the Germans nor the French seemed to grasp this lesson; the generals continued to send their men forth from the trenches to be slaughtered by enemy fire. Millions of soldiers on both sides died, and neither side ever advanced its lines more than a few miles into enemy territory. The Western Front was a stalemate throughout most of the war.

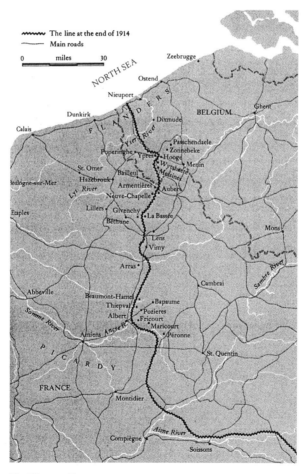

The Western Front

The United States Enters the War

Although the United States maintained an official policy of strict neutrality, few individual Americans felt neutral about the war. Millions of them were recent European immigrants, or children or grandchildren of European immigrants. They still had emotional ties to those nations; many of them still had family in Europe. The majority of Americans who had an opinion supported the Allied or Entente side. In spite of partisan feelings, however, the vast majority of Americans believed that the United States should not send troops to Europe.

It clearly would not be possible for the United States to remain detached for long; international alliances demanded that it would have to commit itself to one side or the other. Both Britain and Germany violated American neutrality on the seas.

The British navy blockaded Germany and set mines in the North Sea. The British insisted on searching all ships entering the North Sea and intercepting any goods that appeared to be bound for Germany. This included American ships. Wilson registered official protests with the British government, but the practice continued.

Germany had built an impressive fleet of U-boats (*Unterseeboots*, or submarines). U-boats were a highly effective weapon because they could not be detected. They could sail quietly underwater and then suddenly blow up a ship on the surface that had had no warning of their approach. Part of the Germans' war plan from the beginning had been to use the U-boats to cripple the British navy. The Germans had openly announced that any ship entering the naval war zone around Britain might be subject to attack—that Germany did not recognize any nation's neutrality in the war zone. The German embassy published this notice in American newspapers:

> Travelers intending to embark on the Atlantic voyage are reminded that a state of war exists between Germany and her allies and Great Britain and her allies. . . . travelers sailing in the war zone on ships of Great Britain or her allies do so at their own risk.

Warnings like this did not stop Americans from traveling. Wilson stated that any injury to Americans or American property would be considered a violation of neutrality, and that the United States would not let it pass.

On May 7, 1915, German U-boats sank the *Lusitania*, a British passenger liner. The ship had been carrying more than a hundred American passengers, as well as a shipment of American arms destined for Britain. Americans were furious. Wilson demanded that Germany halt submarine warfare on civilian merchant ships. By 1916, the United States could no longer claim neutrality; it had provided millions of dollars in cash and weapons to the Entente powers.

In 1916, Wilson took several steps to prepare the United States for war, although he still hoped to avoid it. He signed the National Defense Act, which doubled the size of the armed forces. He built up the size of the National Guard. He signed a bill that gave millions of dollars to the navy. Most Americans shared Wilson's earnest hope that these preparations would prove unnecessary. In the presidential election of 1916, Wilson campaigned as the candidate who would keep the United States out of the war. Theodore Roosevelt publicly stated that he considered it America's duty to send troops to Europe without delay; he failed to win his party's nomination for president. Wilson won the election over Charles Evans Hughes, whom Roosevelt reluctantly supported. Voters associated Hughes with Roosevelt's eagerness for war and backed away from supporting him. A political advertisement that appeared in the papers on Election Day accurately captured voters' sentiments:

> You Are Working—*Not Fighting!*
> Alive and Happy;—*Not cannon Fodder!*
> Wilson and Peace with Honor?
> or
> Hughes with Roosevelt and War?

Europeans interpreted Wilson's victory as a clear indication that the United States would stay out of the war. However, Germany provoked the United States again and again by resuming its U-boat attacks on all ships, including merchant ships. In March of 1917, U.S. newspapers published the Zimmermann Telegram, sent by German foreign secretary Arthur Zimmermann to the German minister in Mexico, suggesting an alliance between Germany and Mexico against the United States. The telegram stated that in the event of a German victory, Mexico would be given back a large portion of the southwestern United States. Americans regarded this telegram as a clear threat, and Wilson decided that he had no choice left but to ask Congress to declare war. It did so on April 6, 1917.

The American Army

The United States had always maintained an all-volunteer army, but World War I changed this. So few men volunteered for service that Congress passed the Selective Service Act, requiring all men and boys between the ages of 21 and 30 (the age range was later extended to 18 to 45) to register with their local draft boards. Troops were racially segregated, with many of the worst duties being assigned to Latinos, American Indians, foreign-born men, and African Americans. All these diverse groups served bravely, often with distinction. The contributions of the ten thousand American Indian troops even convinced Congress to pass a law in 1924 granting all American Indians U.S. citizenship. Thousands of women eagerly grasped the opportunity to go overseas; they were banned from combat positions, but the Medical Corps welcomed them as nurses, doctors, and ambulance drivers. The Red Cross and other charitable agencies also sent women overseas to work in hospitals and aid European refugees.

The first American troops reached France in June 1917. When they arrived in Paris on July 4, one officer saluted the tomb of Lafayette and called aloud: "Lafayette, we are here!" acknowledging that the Americans were now repaying the debt they owed to the French for coming to their aid during the Revolutionary War.

U.S. warships escorted merchant ships that carried American troops, volunteers, and urgently needed supplies for the relief of their British and French allies. This effectively checkmated the German U-boat offensive. The Americans also laid mines in the North Sea, through which the U-boats had to travel on their way home to Germany.

The Home Front

The federal government took several steps to fund the war and conserve resources. First, Congress raised taxes, bringing in added revenue of about $10 billion. Second, the government sold war bonds and persuaded Americans, through advertising, that it was their patriotic duty to buy them. A war bond is, in effect, a loan from a citizen to the government. The citizen gives the government, say, $10 in exchange for a bond—a slip of paper with a $10 face value. The purchaser can redeem the bond later for the face value plus whatever interest has accumulated. The longer the purchaser holds the bond, the more money it will be worth when redeemed.

The newly created Food and Fuel Administrations regulated the production and supply of crops and coal. Americans began growing their own vegetables in what were called "victory gardens." People went without meat on certain days of the week, without bread on others. The Fuel Administration promoted "heatless Mondays" so that people would conserve fuel on at least one day of the week.

The War Industries Board began regulating steel and other major industries, setting their prices and production levels. Many business owners loudly objected to this interference with free enterprise. However, they grew quiet when their profits soared.

The National War Labor Board arbitrated disputes between workers and management. In keeping with the reforming spirit of the Progressive Era, the board usually decided in favor of the workers. Union membership rose to unprecedented levels. Since so many men had left their jobs to join the army or navy, thousands of women took their place in a variety of jobs from bricklayer to teamster.

African Americans also took advantage of the new opportunities. Between about 1915 and 1930, hundreds of thousands of them moved from the segregated South to the North, where they hoped to find well-paid jobs and a respite from racial discrimination. This movement is known to history as the Great Migration. They soon found that there was no lack of racism in the North; still, they were able to earn more money in a less oppressive atmosphere.

Many people felt that the United States was manipulating the poor and the workers to fight a war that would benefit no one. The Socialist Party, led by Eugene Debs, was especially active against the war. So were the Industrial Workers of the World, the Quakers, and other organizations. Labor strikes organized specifically to protest the war drove Congress to pass the Espionage and Sedition Acts, which made it illegal to "utter, print, write, or publish any disloyal or abusive language" about the government, the American flag, or the military. Although these acts clearly violated the First Amendment, hundreds of people were convicted and sent to prison for speaking out.

Victory and Armistice

In the fall of 1917, French troops began to mutiny. They had been fighting in the trenches for what seemed like forever, making no advance, seeing their comrades blown to pieces beside them, and knowing that all the while the generals were safe, well behind the lines of fire. They refused to go on fighting. New heart was brought to the French and the other allied troops by the arrival of the Americans.

Events took an unexpected turn when Russia decided to abandon the war. A socialist revolution had been stirring in Russia for some time, and it finally boiled over in the streets in 1917. The czar abdicated. The radical Bolsheviks won a power struggle with the Socialists; Bolshevik leader Vladimir Ilyich Lenin became the new head of the Russian government. Wanting to get out of the war in Europe as quickly as possible to settle its own domestic affairs, Russia signed an armistice with Germany in early 1918.

The Germans now launched a final, massive attack on the Western Front. With the aid of fresh U.S. troops, the Allies were able to beat them back. Then the Allies launched a counterattack. Fighting raged into the autumn of 1918. Finally, in the Battle of the Argonne Forest, it became clear that Germany would have to surrender. One African-American regiment fought so bravely at the Argonne Forest that France later awarded it the nation's highest military honor, the Croix de Guerre (Cross of War).

On November 9, Germany announced the abdication of Kaiser Wilhelm II. Early in the morning of November 11, the leaders on both sides signed the armistice. At 11 A.M., the guns stopped firing for the last time.

Determining the Peace

The Fourteen Points

Before the war had ended, Woodrow Wilson and his advisers had laid out an impressive plan for maintaining world peace. Wilson's plan, called the Fourteen Points, was first disclosed to Congress in a speech in January. Here is an excerpt:

> What we demand in this war, therefore, is . . . that the world be made fit and safe to live in; and particularly that it be made safe for every peace-loving nation which, like our own, wishes to live its own life, determine its own institutions, be assured of justice and fair dealing by the other peoples of the world as against force and selfish aggression.

Wilson then laid out the "Fourteen Points" of his program for peace. The first five points were general; they described how international relations should be conducted in the future. These points included an argument for free trade and free access to the seas for all nations. The next eight points dealt specifically with how the map of Europe should appear at the end of the war, the insistence that all armies of occupation must return home, that national frontiers should be drawn along appropriate ethnic borders, and that no nation would maintain dominion over another that wished to be independent.

The League of Nations

The final point stated that an international organization must be formed, one that would protect the interests of large and small nations on an equal basis. Representatives of member nations would work together to maintain world peace and to attempt to settle international disputes across a table before resorting to the battlefield. The American people responded positively to Wilson's idea for a League of Nations, and Wilson insisted that a clause agreeing to the creation of the league be included in the Treaty of Versailles.

The Treaty of Versailles

The peace conference convened in January 1919 at Versailles, the palace that King Louis XIV's architects had built for him in the countryside near Paris. The selection of this impressive symbol of French power as the place to sign the treaty was a deliberate attempt to intimidate the Germans. The conference itself had also been carefully arranged to humiliate the German representatives. They were forced to travel to Versailles by a local train through many of the major battlefields, and to view the destruction for which the treaty would demand that they take sole blame.

For the first time in history, a non-European nation would play a major role in the peace settlements. U.S. troops had been a decisive factor in the last year of the fighting, and the United States had a level of industrial and economic might that dwarfed those of the European nations; additionally, the United States had lost comparatively few troops during the war.

The leaders of the great powers were divided in their goals. U.S. President Woodrow Wilson wanted to establish a lasting peace in Europe. Premier Georges Clemenceau of France wanted to humiliate Germany. Prime Minister David Lloyd George of Britain wanted to achieve a new balance of power, rather than weakening Germany so much that France would take its place as the sole great power on the European continent. Italian Prime Minister Vittorio Orlando wanted to recover certain Italian territory from Austria.

Despite having fought on the winning side, Russia—soon to become the Soviet Union—took no part in the negotiations at Versailles. Far too much mutual distrust existed between Russia and the Western Europeans on both political and economic grounds. The Russians resented the lack of European support for their new government, while the Europeans considered that the Russians had sold them out by withdrawing from the war and making a separate peace with Germany. Economically, the forces of communism and capitalism were inherent enemies.

Provisions of the Treaty of Versailles

- Created new nations (Czechoslovakia and Yugoslavia)
- Restored the independence of Poland, Finland, Latvia, Lithuania, and Estonia
- Restored Alsace-Lorraine to France
- Gave France control of Saarland region until 1934
- Designated the Rhineland, a demilitarized zone between Germany and France
- Created the League of Nations, an international peacekeeping force
- Drastically and permanently reduced the German military
- Forced Germany to admit full responsibility for the war
- Charged Germany billions of dollars in reparations

Wilson opposed the final two clauses. He saw no point in heaping so much blame on Germany, which had suffered as much as any other European nation. He also knew, as did all the other leaders, that Germany could not possibly hope to pay reparations on such a massive scale. However, the French and English representatives insisted on putting all the blame on Germany. They felt that to do otherwise would be to dishonor the memories of the millions of their countrymen who had fallen during the war.

Wilson returned to the United States in July 1919 and laid the Treaty of Versailles before Congress. Because of the objections of a faction led by Henry Cabot Lodge, Congress refused to approve the treaty. Lodge and his followers were immovably opposed to the League of Nations. Another group of senators agreed to accept the League of Nations, but opposed a provision that committed the United States to defend any member nation that was attacked by an outsider. Hoping to sway public opinion to his side, Wilson embarked on a speaking tour of the country. During the tour, he suffered a severe stroke; he survived and served out his term, but historians are agreed that he exercised little control over events from then on. The League of Nations became a reality, but without American participation.

The Costs of the War

Casualties of the Great War totaled more than 37 million people—an entire generation of Europeans of all nations (including several thousand Americans), either dead or severely wounded. Millions more died of a severe flu epidemic that struck not only Europe, but the rest of the world as well. Many soldiers would never recover from the horrors of combat; they were left in a condition of mental illness called *shellshock*. Chronic nightmares, hallucinations, severe depression, lethargy, and outbreaks of violent behavior were common symptoms of shellshock. Today, doctors refer to this result of combat experience as post-traumatic stress disorder.

Moreover, "an age was dead and gone," as Woodrow Wilson commented in a 1918 speech. The tank had replaced the cavalry regiment. The machine gun had replaced the bayonet. Elected ministers of state had replaced almost all the hereditary monarchs. Mechanized warfare was a horror that no one had anticipated.

The United States, geographically far removed from the combat, emerged from the war far stronger than the European powers. The war effort had bolstered the American economy; in addition, fighting side by side with the British and French had cemented good relations between the nations and given the United States a level of power and influence over Europe that would persist for a century. This influence showed at Versailles, where the United States was an equal participant in the peace process despite not having participated equally in the fighting. The balance of international power had shifted from the Old World to the New. The United States was on its way to becoming a superpower.

CHAPTER 22 QUIZ

1. _____ was forced to assume total responsibility for World War I.
   A. Austria-Hungary
   B. France
   C. Germany
   D. Russia

2. A major faction in Congress opposed the League of Nations
   because _____
   A. it did not want the United States to become a superpower.
   B. it did not want the United States to have to go to war to defend
      another nation.
   C. it did not support Wilson's bid for reelection.
   D. it had been on the losing side in World War I.

3. Wilson's Fourteen Points is best described as _____
   A. a declaration of war.
   B. a program for international peace.
   C. an economic policy.
   D. a redesign of the American military.

4. What was the purpose of the National War Labor Board?
   A. to recruit African-American workers to travel north for jobs
   B. to increase membership in labor unions
   C. to arbitrate disputes between workers and management
   D. to monitor the civilian use of energy and other rationed resources

5. Trench warfare resulted in a stalemate primarily because _____
   A. weather conditions made it too problematic.
   B. modern weapons were not suited to that style of combat.
   C. the German army had to divide its forces on two fronts.
   D. the French trenches were badly and hastily dug.

6. The _____ proposed an alliance between Mexico and Germany.
   A. Espionage Act
   B. Treaty of Versailles
   C. Zimmermann Telegram
   D. National Defense Act

7. The U.S. government took all these steps to fund the war effort and conserve resources except _____
    A. raising the income tax.
    B. selling war bonds.
    C. regulating industry production levels.
    D. requiring people to grow their own produce.

8. Which of the great powers did not take part in the negotiations at Versailles?
    A. Britain
    B. Germany
    C. Russia
    D. The United States

9. The Americans' main goal at Versailles can best be described as _____
    A. the achievement of a lasting peace in Europe.
    B. the reestablishment of a balance of power.
    C. the humiliation and ruin of Germany.
    D. the redrawing of national borders along ethnic lines.

10. A major "first" in the Great War was _____
    A. the outbreak of battles in the empires outside of Europe.
    B. the impressive military force demonstrated by Germany.
    C. the alliance between France and Russia.
    D. the decisive participation of a non-European nation.

Chapter 23

The Jazz Age, 1919–1929

The Jazz Age, the Roaring Twenties, the era of the flapper: the decade between the 1919 Treaty of Versailles and the 1929 stock market crash has many nicknames. Many people view the Jazz Age as the true beginning of the twentieth century and the modern era. Technology brought great changes to everyday life. People watched moving pictures on screens and bought records with the latest jazz tunes recorded on them. They sold the family piano to make room for a phonograph and a radio. They bought one of Henry Ford's new automobiles.

World War I ushered in a decade of American prosperity—except for the working class, which lost many of the gains it had made during the Progressive Era. The rich grew richer, and there were more expensive items for them to spend their money on. Women made the most of the freedoms they had won during the war, changing everything about their appearance, clothing, and behavior.

An explosion of artistic creation acknowledged the darker side of life. Artists who had come of age as members of the "Lost Generation" wrote about the death of innocence in the trenches of World War I, and about the impossibility of romance surviving in the modern world. Jazz music was cheerful and catchy, but it was built on slave songs and the blues. Segregation existed in nightclubs that African Americans could enter only through the back door—as performers or members of the kitchen staff.

Politically, the 1920s marked a return to conservativism. Three Republican presidents passed tax cuts for the wealthy, but opposed labor-friendly legislation. The party of the Jazz Age ended as suddenly as it had begun: on October 24, 1929, the stock market crashed.

CHAPTER OBJECTIVES

- Describe the social and cultural changes that took place in the United States during the Jazz Age.
- Describe economic conditions under Presidents Harding, Coolidge, and Hoover.
- Identify the major figures of the decade and describe their contributions in the arts, sports, politics, and crime.

Chapter 23 Time Line

- **1919** Chicago White Sox throw World Series

  Eighteenth Amendment (Prohibition) ratified

- **1920** First licensed radio broadcasts

- **1923** Equal Rights Amendment proposed

- **1925** Scopes trial

  F. Scott Fitzgerald publishes *The Great Gatsby*

- **1927** Charles Lindbergh completes first solo flight across the Atlantic

  Babe Ruth hits 60 home runs for the New York Yankees

  Model A Ford

  Warner Brothers releases *The Jazz Singer*

- **1929** St. Valentine's Day Massacre

- **1931** Empire State Building

- **1933** Twenty-First Amendment ratified, repealing Eighteenth Amendment

The Arts

The nickname "the Jazz Age" perfectly sums up the tone of life during the 1920s. To many people, the decade was one long party. The economy was booming, and wealthy and middle-class Americans had plenty of money to spend. A great variety of consumer goods were available, and a flood of advertisements tempted the money out of people's pockets.

The name "Jazz Age" comes, of course, from jazz—the popular music of the era. Jazz is a combination of spirituals, work songs, the blues, and ragtime. It comprises a variety of African musical elements, such as syncopation, call-and-response, and the famous "blue note"— a note that literally does not belong in the key of the song, and thus sounds "blue" or haunting. These elements, blended with European musical elements of harmony and melody, combined to create a new, genuinely American musical idiom.

Jazz bands usually featured trumpets, trombones, saxophones, clarinets, piano, and drums. All members of a jazz band were talented improvisers and soloists. They worked on a basic tune, changing it around in almost every conceivable way. Jazz was upbeat even while recognizing the sorrows that lay beneath the African-American experience. The new sound was more than just popular—it was a craze. The new technologies of recorded music and radio broadcasting helped to spread the popularity of jazz far beyond the big cities where the musicians performed. Jazz became especially popular in France, where it influenced an entire generation of important composers, including Maurice Ravel, Igor Stravinsky, and Erik Satie.

After they recovered from the shock of the "Black Sox" scandal (discussed later in this chapter), people went back to the ballpark to cheer for George Herman "Babe" Ruth. Born in Baltimore, Ruth was a star pitcher, but proved to have such power and accuracy as a hitter that he was soon made an outfielder so that he could play every day. In 1927, Ruth hit 60 home runs—his nearest competitor that year hit only 19. Along with his talent, Ruth had an expansive personality that was perfectly suited to the Jazz Age. He smoked big cigars, wore ankle-length fur coats in winter, dressed snappily, ate heartily, and spent money lavishly.

Architecture began changing the look of American cities during the 1920s. New York City's Chrysler Building, completed in 1930, soared to a height of 77 stories; farther downtown, the Empire State Building topped it a few months later at 102 stories. With their steel-girder construction, their escalators and fast elevators, their sparkling rows of glass windows and chrome trim, and the breathtaking views from their rooftop observatories, buildings like these epitomized modern times.

Two major artistic movements peaked during the 1920s: the Harlem Renaissance and the Lost Generation. The Harlem Renaissance was a direct result of the Great Migration of African Americans to the North. Many African Americans settled in Harlem, a neighborhood in northern New York City. They formed a community of creative artists—musicians, writers, photographers, painters, and poets. Poet Langston Hughes, novelist Nella Larsen, writer James Weldon Johnson, and jazz musicians Duke Ellington and Louis Armstrong were key figures of the Harlem Renaissance.

Ironically, Harlem was a segregated neighborhood. The Cotton Club, perhaps the most famous nightclub of the era, featured the best-known black musicians of the day. However, African Americans could enter the Cotton Club only through the stage door; they were not permitted to be part of the all-white audience. Some African Americans fought such discrimination by their actions. For example, Harold and Fayard Nicholas of the Nicholas Brothers dance act often performed at the Cotton Club and frequently accepted invitations to join audience members at their tables. Young boys at the time, the Nicholas Brothers struck their own quiet blow for integration: polite, well-dressed, and charming, they proved that African Americans were in no way unfit to sit with whites in any audience.

In 1924, Paul Robeson attracted enormous attention when he became the first African-American actor to play the Shakespearean role of Othello (a character Shakespeare clearly describes as a black man) opposite a white actress playing Desdemona. (In previous U.S. productions, the role had always been played by a white actor in blackface.) Robeson was universally acknowledged as a splendid talent, but this did not protect him from being the target of ugly racial slurs in hotel elevators or other public places.

Expatriate American writer Gertrude Stein named her artistic friends of the 1920s "the Lost Generation." Ernest Hemingway, F. Scott and Zelda Fitzgerald, John Dos Passos, Dorothy Parker, John Steinbeck, Dashiell Hammett, and many others had been disillusioned by the failure of world leaders to resolve their differences peacefully or speedily, and by the horrors of trench warfare. Their writing took on a cynical edge that was new to American literature. F. Scott Fitzgerald's *The Great Gatsby* (1925) perfectly captured the Jazz Age—its gaiety, its cynicism, and its essential hollowness. The story of Gatsby showed that there was no place for romanticism anymore. Similarly, Ernest Hemingway's *The Sun Also Rises* (1926) depicted the generation that had survived the war, but at the price of permanent psychological and physical damage.

Politics in the 1920s

In 1920, Republican Party candidate Warren G. Harding ran for president against Democrat James Cox. Harding coined the word *normalcy* to describe what he thought the United States needed after the dramatic and chaotic years of World War I. Cox, on the other hand, seemed to promise continued involvement in foreign affairs, as his campaign focused on the League of Nations. The voters liked the sound of a focus on domestic problems rather than foreign affairs, and Harding was elected in a landslide.

Harding did not share the goals of the Progressives. His administration reduced taxes on wealthy Americans and also reduced government spending. By 1922, the government deficit had turned into a surplus. In 1922, Congress raised tariffs to their highest levels ever, which encouraged people to buy American-made goods. Lowering taxes on the wealthy was intended to encourage them to spend the money they had saved on their taxes; this would supposedly stimulate the economy, and the benefits of that would "trickle down" to the poorer classes. The economy prospered under this trickle-down policy (at least in the short term), but poor and working-class Americans—who far outnumbered the wealthy—grew poorer under it, not richer.

The federal government had ceased to enforce antitrust laws, and businesses grew more prosperous. However, workers did not get their fair share of the profits. While owners' profits increased by 60 percent over the decade, workers' incomes rose by only 10 percent.

The last days of the Harding administration and the beginning of the Coolidge administration were disturbed when corruption in the White House came to light. Several of Harding's close associates who had been given cabinet positions were discovered to have abused their power in order steal millions of dollars. Harding was greatly disturbed by the scandals, but he died suddenly before he could begin to confront those responsible. Coolidge, his vice president, fired the officials who had been implicated in the scandals.

Because the economy was prospering, Coolidge was easily reelected in 1924. Coolidge cut taxes on the wealthy even further than Harding had, and kept government spending at an all-time low. Coolidge opposed laws designed to help the workers, claiming that such programs would not be good for the national economy.

Herbert Hoover, Coolidge's secretary of commerce, was elected president in 1928. His opponent was Governor Alfred Smith of New York. A Catholic, Smith was the first non-Protestant to run for president. Protestants conveniently forgot their own history of refusing to separate church and state in early New England; they claimed that a Catholic president would bow to the authority of the pope in Rome. Ironically, Protestant ministers did the very thing they were objecting to; they used their own religious influence to persuade their congregations to vote against Smith. Smith dismissed these scare tactics as ridiculous, pointing out that he had held high political office for many years without consulting the Catholic Church on political issues. Despite the fact that not he but his opponents were proving themselves religiously intolerant, Smith lost the election; the continued economic prosperity under Republican administrations and Smith's opposition to Prohibition combined with Protestant paranoia to defeat him.

The Rise of the Flapper

One of the most notable changes taking place during the 1920s was in women's behavior, speech, and dress. During World War I, as men went overseas to fight, women had replaced them in such jobs as house-painting, stonemasonry, plastering, and driving trucks and taxis. In 1920, women finally won the right to vote. Having come so far toward full civil rights and freedoms, women would not turn back. One of their first steps was to throw off the restrictions that had dictated fashion for many years. Until the 1920s, skirts had come down to the shoetops. Women had worn corsets, stays, and other confining undergarments. Bodices were boned to make the body conform to the shape of the gown. Women never cut their hair short; they grew it long and thick, pinning it up in braids, knots, twists, or whatever the fashion of the decade called for. Suffragists had begun to set an example against the most extreme of these fashions (for example, they had shortened their skirts to ankle length for ease in walking), but it was left to the flappers to bury them for good.

The flapper, as the liberated young woman of the Twenties was called, cut her hair as short as a boy's. She shortened her skirts to just below the knee, showing her legs in sheer silk stockings and her feet in pretty shoes. Her loose-fitting party dresses were made of sheer fabrics, had no sleeves, and were cut low in back and front. Day dresses were more modest, but still had short skirts and a comfortable, loose-fitting shape. Undergarments were skimpy and comfortable; corsets were a thing of the past. The flapper was determined to flaunt her freedom.

Flappers also behaved very differently from women of earlier decades. They smoked, drove their own automobiles, played sports, earned wages outside their homes, and took part in daring adventures such as flying planes. They supported an Equal Rights Amendment and had the satisfaction of seeing it proposed in Congress in 1923. They laughed at the notion of chaperones. In earlier decades, when a young man called on a girl, the two would not be left alone together; in the 1920s, that changed.

The Rise of the Automobile

One thing that drastically changed the American landscape was the rise in the popularity of the automobile. Henry Ford installed an assembly line that drove down the price of his sturdy, efficient little cars even further. The car under construction would travel slowly through the factory along a conveyor belt. As it reached a worker, he would add the next part. When it reached the end of the line, the automobile would be finished.

This method had several advantages. It doubled production and reduced costs, and made each worker an expert at installing his particular car part. However, it also destroyed the old artisanal satisfaction a worker had once been able to take in making something with his own hands. It reduced workers to the level of machines. It was also physically damaging to workers; since they always performed the same task, they always used the same set of muscles. This led to overworking some body parts while others got no exercise at all.

By the end of the decade, there was one car on the road for every five Americans. This meant a huge change in the way cities looked; they now had lines of cars parked along every street, with lanes of moving cars trying to edge their way through the busy traffic. Old, established cities such as Boston and Philadelphia had not been designed to accommodate cars; houses had no driveways or garages, and many streets were barely one lane wide. Newer cities such as Los Angeles and Chicago, which were still very much under construction in the 1920s, took cars into account in their architecture and city planning; for example, streets were wider. Cars also added to what was rapidly becoming a severe air-pollution problem.

Cars made it possible to travel as quickly as the railroad, but on one's own schedule. People in business no longer had to live within easy walking distance of their jobs; they could now drive. This eventually became a major factor in the development of suburbs and urban sprawl.

Another technological change of the 1920s was the spread of the use of electricity. By 1930, more than two-thirds of all American homes had electricity, which in turn made new entertainment options possible—radios and phonographs. Recorded music was truly revolutionary; until this technology was developed, people had to be in the room with the performer in order to hear music. Now it was available at the turn of a crank. Where a generation earlier there had been a piano in almost every middle-class living room, now there was a radio and a phonograph.

Organized Crime: The "Black Sox" Scandal and Prohibition

For organized crime, the 1920s was an era of publicity and huge profits. Organized crime functioned in much the same way as the political machines of the 1860s and 1870s (see Chapter 19). An organized-crime boss was at the top of the pyramid. Several trusted associates worked directly with him. Under them were a much larger number of criminals who dealt directly with saloon owners, wholesalers, jockeys, ballplayers, and anyone else the boss wanted to twist around his thumb to make himself a profit. Instead of pressuring these people to vote a certain way, gamblers would pressure athletes to lose a race or throw a game. Once a person had given in to the pressure and committed a crime, the boss had a hold over him and could use this hold to blackmail the person into continuing to do what the crooks and gamblers wanted him to do.

The "Black Sox" Scandal

In 1919, gamblers persuaded members of baseball's Chicago White Sox to throw the World Series, which they were heavily favored to win, to the Cincinnati Reds. An upset victory by the Reds would make the gamblers a fortune, because they would be betting against the odds—putting up less money and winning more.

The players were persuadable because major-league baseball functioned as a form of indentured servitude. It was a monopoly, but one that enjoyed an exemption from antitrust laws. At the end of each season, a ball club could either trade a player or retain his services for the coming season; the player was literally an indentured servant who had no right to decide his own fate. The owners controlled salaries, keeping them as low as possible so that their profits would be greater. Frequently they offered bonuses to players, then later refused to pay them. The players had no agents and no union to protect them when promises were broken. Under this system, they had no more reason to feel loyal to the team owners than slaves ever had to their masters.

Gamblers, knowing there was money to be made, often offered players attractive sums of money to throw games. Before the World Series of 1919, this had taken place on only a relatively small scale. The players' motivation was very simple: they were severely underpaid and undervalued, with no leverage to fight for higher wages or better working conditions, and the gamblers offered them good money. In the end, eight White Sox players agreed to throw the World Series.

It was not long before the fix was discovered. Word had spread among the gamblers, and so many of them had bet on the underdog Reds that it became clear to many insiders, such as the sportswriters, that something was going on. However, the public remained in the dark. When the White Sox players eventually confessed in court that the games had been fixed, the nation was shocked. At the time, baseball was the only professional team sport in the U.S., and it was enormously popular. Eliot Asinof summed up the national reaction in his book about the "Black Sox" scandal:

> There is no way to gauge the extent of the damage on the American psyche. It is impossible to add up bitterness like a batting average. How great was the layer of cynicism that settled over the nation? How many kids developed tolerance for a lie, for a betrayal, for corruption itself?

Prohibition

The era of Prohibition began in 1919, when the Eighteenth Amendment made it illegal to consume or sell alcoholic beverages or to transport them across state lines. The Eighteenth Amendment proved to be a resounding failure. Although alcoholism and alcohol-related deaths declined, Prohibition had a number of unfortunate side effects that the temperance advocates had failed to anticipate.

The one thing Prohibition did not do was stop anybody from drinking. The United States was, on the whole, a nation of moderate drinkers. Most Americans would have agreed that excessive drunkenness was bad for society and that perhaps saloons and bars should be closed or regulated, but Prohibition took the law to a level that most people considered unreasonable. The vast majority of adult Americans were affronted at the government's attempt to regulate their private behavior, and they considered that they had a right to defy Prohibition on an everyday basis. The defiance of Prohibition gave rise to new vocabulary words: *speakeasy* (an underground nightclub that served alcoholic beverages), *bootleg* (a term for alcohol that was manufactured or sold illegally), and *bathtub gin* (alcohol distilled at home in the bathtub).

Because consumers continued to provide a market for alcohol, but its production had been made illegal, gangsters were handed a perfect opportunity to make fortunes. Al Capone and his mobsters soon controlled most of the sales of liquor in the Chicago area. Wars between gangs over the control of alcohol production and sales developed. The climax came on February 14, 1929, when Capone's gang mowed down seven members of a rival gang with machine guns. This incident became known as the St. Valentine's Day Massacre.

There was so much violent crime associated with Prohibition that the FBI established a special group of agents to deal only with Prohibition cases. This agency, headed by Detective Eliot Ness, was called "the Untouchables." The huge wave of organized crime convinced Americans to repeal Prohibition in 1933, but by then the damage had been done. The criminal networks were firmly established, and millions of formerly law-abiding Americans had fallen into the habit of breaking laws simply because they personally did not support them.

The Scopes Trial

The two major influences on American life and thought—Enlightenment reason and fundamentalist religion—clashed in a Tennessee courtroom in 1925. The state of Tennessee had passed a law that outlawed the teaching of the theory of evolution in its public schools. Fundamentalist Christians denied the scientific theory that human beings had evolved from more primitive life forms, and that if one went back millions of years, all life forms had a common biological ancestor. They disputed the theory of evolution on emotional and religious grounds, rather than on scientific ones. They argued that the biblical statement that God had created human beings in his own image disproved the theory of evolution. Fundamentalists were so opposed to the theory of evolution that they tried to prevent it from being taught in schools.

Science teacher John Scopes went ahead and taught the theory of evolution anyway, having read that the American Civil Liberties Union (ACLU) was willing to pay the costs of defending any teacher who defied the Tennessee law. The ACLU believed that the law was unconstitutional. The Scopes trial would put their belief to the test.

Clarence Darrow, one of the nation's most famous criminal lawyers, agreed to defend Scopes. William Jennings Bryan appeared for the prosecution. The presence of these two nationally known figures guaranteed widespread press coverage; everyone in the United States followed the trial in the newspapers. The judge refused to allow any professional scientists to testify about the theory of evolution, clearly exposing his own pro-fundamentalist bias. Darrow's response was to put Bryan on the witness stand and ask him questions about the Bible. Since many statements in the Bible contradict one another, and many others are ambiguous, Bryan was made to look like a fool for protesting that every word of the Bible was literally true. The jury found Scopes guilty and fined him $100 (the conviction was later overturned on a technicality), but the absurdity of Bryan's testimony convinced many that the side of the Enlightenment had won an important victory in all but name.

CHAPTER 23 QUIZ

1. **The term *flapper* refers to which of the following?**
    A. a liberated young woman
    B. an organized criminal
    C. a jazz musician
    D. an artist of the Harlem Renaissance

2. **The Lost Generation artists felt "lost" because of** _____
    A. the passage of the Eighteenth Amendment.
    B. the persistence of segregation in the United States.
    C. their faith in the eternal power of romance.
    D. their experiences during World War I.

3. **Warren G. Harding became president because he made** _____ **a priority.**
    A. foreign affairs
    B. social reform
    C. the domestic economy
    D. women's rights

4. **Assembly-line production had all these advantages except** _____
    A. it reduced the costs of manufacture.
    B. it doubled the output of the factory.
    C. it increased worker satisfaction.
    D. it made goods available at lower prices.

5. **Prohibition had all the following effects except** _____
    A. stopping Americans from drinking alcoholic beverages.
    B. increasing the profits in organized crime.
    C. creating a national atmosphere of scoffing at laws.
    D. causing major outbreaks of gang violence.

6. **On what grounds did William Jennings Bryan and his followers oppose the theory of evolution?**
    A. support for rival scientific theories
    B. the testimony of professional scientists
    C. literal belief in certain statements in the Bible
    D. sympathy with the influence of the Enlightenment

7. **Which of the following is a notable figure of the Harlem Renaissance?**
   A. Clarence Darrow
   B. Langston Hughes
   C. F. Scott Fitzgerald
   D. Al Capone

8. **Calvin Coolidge was reelected in 1924 because of _____**
   A. his foreign policy.
   B. his opposition to Prohibition.
   C. the country's economic prosperity.
   D. his support for social programs.

9. **All of these people except _____ were important authors who were members of the Lost Generation.**
   A. Ernest Hemingway
   B. John Dos Passos
   C. Dorothy Parker
   D. Duke Ellington

10. **Which best describes the Republican economic theory during the 1920s?**
   A. If wages rise, workers will spend more money and thus benefit the economy.
   B. If taxes on the wealthy are lowered, their spending will stimulate the economy.
   C. If businesses form trusts, wages and prices will go down.
   D. If tariffs are put into place, businesses will lower production.

Chapter 24

The Great Depression, 1929–1939

In late October 1929, the United States entered the worst economic crisis in its history. The stock market crashed, and the Great Depression began.

The Great Depression was worse than any of the many financial panics the United States had weathered since the 1790s. It was much more widespread, and it lasted much longer. Across the nation, banks failed, businesses closed down, and workers were laid off. Landlords evicted tenants who could not pay their rent. Lenders foreclosed on borrowers who could not meet their payment obligations. To the average American, it appeared that suddenly, no matter where you looked, no one had any money.

Most people blamed the crisis on President Herbert Hoover, for two reasons: first, he had failed to predict it, and second, he seemed both unwilling and unable to do anything about it. In 1932, Hoover lost his bid for reelection to an individual who struck most voters as being both willing and able to help them: Franklin Delano Roosevelt.

Roosevelt established the New Deal, a group of programs that offered immediate relief. Its goals were threefold: to provide jobs for the unemployed, to repair the economy, and to install safeguards to prevent any recurrence of the crisis.

The New Deal did not end the Depression, but it did many positive things. It created millions of jobs. It paid workers to build bridges, highways, and public buildings. It kept hundreds of artists employed entertaining those who badly needed an occasional escape from their daily worries. It restored the nation's banks to a sound financial footing. During Roosevelt's first term, unemployment dropped by about 8 percent. Unsurprisingly, he was reelected in 1936 in the greatest landslide in 100 years.

CHAPTER OBJECTIVES

- Explain what caused the Great Depression.
- Describe the goals of the New Deal and identify its major programs.
- Discuss the Dust Bowl and its impact on small farmers in the Great Plains.

Chapter 24 Time Line

- **1928** Herbert Hoover elected president
- **1929** Stock market crashes
- **1930–1932** Bank failures across the nation
- **1932** Franklin D. Roosevelt elected president
- **1933** Fifteen million Americans unemployed

  New Deal programs put into effect
- **1934** "Second New Deal" programs created
- **1936** Roosevelt reelected president

  Margaret Mitchell publishes *Gone With the Wind*
- **1939** Marian Anderson sings at Lincoln Memorial

  John Steinbeck publishes *The Grapes of Wrath*

The Stock Market Crash

The Jazz Age literally ended with a crash. On October 24, 1929, investors suddenly began selling their shares of stock. Since no one was buying, prices immediately plummeted. October 29 saw another round of frantic selling—sixteen million shares by the end of the day. By the end of December 1929, investors in the stock market had lost more than $30 billion—more than it had cost the U.S. government to contribute money, weapons, and troops to World War I.

The simple cause of the stock market crash was that people all over the country had gotten into the habit of buying things they could not afford. The practice of buying on credit had become common during the 1920s. People did not buy stocks on credit, but they did borrow money to buy stocks—a practice called margin buying. Speculators would borrow money and buy stock, then keep an eye on its value and sell it as soon as its price went up. The large number of speculators meant that share prices were constantly fluctuating, usually upward.

The market was booming, but only on the insubstantial foundation of unpaid debt. When buyers suddenly lost confidence in the market and began selling their shares, the prices dropped, but the debts still fell due. Banks failed because people could not repay their loans. There was no mechanism in place to protect a bank from failing—when this happened, all the bank's depositors lost whatever money they had saved. Many people panicked at the news of the bank failures and tried to withdraw their money from their own banks, only to be told that the money was no longer there.

Like individuals, businesses lost money when the banks closed. Many businesses failed because they could not pay their debts. When a business failed, all of its workers were left without jobs. By 1933, the U.S. gross national product was only about half of what it had been in 1929. More than 50,000 businesses had failed, and 13.5 million people—more than 20 percent of the wage-earning population—had lost their jobs.

The era ushered in by the stock market crash was known as the Great Depression. An economic depression occurs when prices and wages fall and unemployment rises. The Great Depression got its name because it lasted for more than a decade—highly unusual for an economic crisis.

Hoover's Response to the Depression

President Hoover stated publicly that "the Government should not support the people." Himself a self-made man, Hoover believed in rugged individualism—people rescuing themselves by their own efforts. For quite some time, he simply refused to accept that the economic crisis was so widespread and so grave that people could not help themselves, no matter how much they wanted to. Eventually, between the public, the newspaper reports, and his advisers, Hoover was reluctantly convinced to take steps to help the needy. His administration spent hundreds of millions of dollars on public works projects such as the construction of Boulder (later renamed Hoover) Dam in Nevada. The Federal Farm Board, established in 1929, loaned farmers money and bought up tons of their surplus crops that no one else could afford. However, these policies did not go far enough to help those who needed it most, and economic conditions did not improve.

Millions of Americans who had always worked hard and supported themselves and their families were suddenly destitute. Some of those who lost fortunes in the stock market committed suicide. Others found themselves begging for food or money, or standing in long lines outside missions and charities for free bowls of soup or sandwiches. Many young people, especially boys, stowed away aboard railway boxcars and rode the freight trains for free, going long distances across the country in search of whatever work they could find.

Landlords regularly evicted those who could not pay their rent. Often, landlords would wait until a tenant who owed money had left his apartment, then change the locks and either throw the person's belongings out into the street or keep them as partial payment for the unpaid rent. Homeowners were also evicted; many could not make their mortgage payments, and their houses were taken away from them. Newly homeless people formed communities called Hoovervilles, in ironic tribute to the president who had made it all possible. Shelters in these makeshift communities were made of oversize cardboard boxes, giant packing crates, scraps of tin, boards, and any other building material that came to hand. Hoovervilles were usually in vacant lots, under bridges, or on the outskirts of towns.

Hoover's opponent in the 1932 presidential election was Governor Franklin Delano Roosevelt of New York. At the Democratic Convention, Roosevelt stated that the Republican leaders had "failed in national vision, because in disaster they have held out no hope." Roosevelt won the election in a popular and electoral landslide, carrying 42 states and winning seven million more votes than Hoover. Voters extended their blame for current conditions to the entire Republican Party; the Democrats won substantial majorities in both houses of Congress.

Franklin and Eleanor Roosevelt

FDR, as Roosevelt was often called, was a distant cousin of former president Theodore Roosevelt. FDR grew up in a wealthy New York family and married his cousin Eleanor Roosevelt (the former President Roosevelt's niece), who always joked that she accepted him only because it would save her having to have the monograms on her luggage changed.

Both Roosevelts were personalities. FDR quickly became a symbol of hope for the people. He was a natty dresser, with his hat tilted back and his cigarette holder clamped between his teeth at a jaunty angle. He exuded confidence, decisiveness, and good cheer. To see him riding in a car or standing behind a podium, no one would have imagined that this strong, vigorous-looking man could not walk unaided. A severe bout of polio in 1921 had confined FDR permanently to a wheelchair. He never allowed his physical disability to prevent him from taking on any challenge or to defeat his optimism or his courage. The start of his first inaugural address summed up his outlook on life:

> . . . first of all, let me assert my firm belief that the only thing we have to fear is fear itself—nameless, unreasoning, unjustified terror which paralyzes needed efforts to convert retreat into advance.

Partly because her husband's disability made long-distance travel very difficult for him, and partly due to her own convictions concerning her duty as first lady, Eleanor Roosevelt made more of her position in the White House than any of her predecessors had done. She wrote a daily newspaper column and traveled all over the country making speeches and inspecting the living conditions of those left destitute by the Depression. She spoke to all classes of Americans personally, listening to their individual concerns and taking careful notes of her impressions to bring back to the president. Everyone who ever met Mrs. Roosevelt was impressed by her unfailing courtesy and kindness. FDR considered Eleanor one of his most observant and valued advisers.

The Early Phases of the New Deal

"I pledge you, I pledge myself, to a new deal for the American people," FDR told the cheering crowds at the Democratic nominating convention in 1932. The New Deal marked a complete break with the policies of the 1920s. It consisted of a set of fifteen programs designed to bring both immediate and long-term relief to the economy and to the people. Roosevelt considered his New Deal to be a "war against the emergency," and as soon as he took office, he asked Congress to grant him special powers to take action. The New Deal marked a shift in the balance of national power, from the legislative branch to the executive, of a sort that Washington had not seen since the Civil War. In its way, the Great Depression was every bit as much a national crisis, and strong leadership was essential. Congress agreed with the president that emergency measures were called for, and promptly passed all of the New Deal programs.

This table lays out some of the programs of the New Deal and what they accomplished.

1933	
Emergency Banking Act	Closed down all banks, examined their books, and reopened those that were solvent
Farm Credit Administration	Made low-interest, long-term loans to farmers for mortgages, equipment, and taxes
Economy Act	Proposed balancing the federal budget
Civilian Conservation Corps	Paid $30 a month to boys and young men to work in national parks and plant trees throughout the West
Federal Emergency Relief Administration	• Distributed $500 million to states for direct aid to families • Matched every $3 that cities and towns spent on relief projects with $1 in federal aid
Agricultural Adjustment Administration	Paid farmers to grow fewer crops, thus bringing prices up (later declared unconstitutional)
Tennessee Valley Authority	Built dams, provided electricity, and otherwise greatly improved conditions in the Tennessee Valley, one of the nation's poorest regions
Home Owners' Loan Corporation	• Made low-interest, long-term mortgage loans • Protected people from losing their houses
Banking Act of 1933	• Created the FDIC (see next row) • Authorized branch banking
Federal Deposit Insurance Corporation	Insured individual bank deposits of up to $5,000
National Recovery Administration	Regulated businesses by establishing minimum wages and other standards to protect workers
Public Works Administration	Contracted private firms to hire millions of people to build bridges, post offices, highways, and other structures
Civil Works Administration	Created millions of low-skill jobs such as cleaning city streets
1934	
Securities and Exchange Commission	Regulated companies that sold stocks and bonds
Federal Housing Administration	Insured all bank loans made for the construction and repair of houses

FDR had designed the programs of the New Deal with three main goals: to bring immediate relief to those who were suffering, to bring the economy back to prosperity, and to put safeguards in place so that the same situation would not occur again. Programs such as the Civil Works Administration and the Public Works Administration accomplished the first goal. The Agricultural Adjustment Administration and the Tennessee Valley Authority helped to accomplish the second goal. New organizations such as the Securities and Exchange Commission and the FDIC were put into place with an eye to the third goal.

Despite the relief it provided to millions across the country, not everyone supported the New Deal. African Americans regarded it with a wary eye because it did not always give them the same benefits as whites. The National Recovery Administration set lower wages for black workers, while other programs segregated them from white workers. Roosevelt also refused to support a federal antilynching law. Throughout his long tenure in the White House, FDR was a pragmatist, not an idealist. He always believed that the larger picture of a situation was more important than any individual details. In his view, pressing for civil rights legislation was less important than doing the best possible job at leading the nation out of the Depression.

However, FDR showed his support for civil rights in other ways. He signed the Indian Reorganization Act of 1934 into law. This legislation attempted to help American Indians both financially and socially. FDR appointed more than 100 African Americans to a wide variety of government jobs. He also appointed the first female cabinet secretary, Frances Perkins.

Many of the actions FDR took to help African Americans were taken at Eleanor Roosevelt's urging. Mrs. Roosevelt was a champion of civil rights. She made national headlines in 1939 when the Daughters of the American Revolution (DAR) withdrew a concert booking for Marian Anderson, one of the greatest classical singers of the era, on the grounds of racial prejudice. Mrs. Roosevelt was a DAR member. When she learned that the DAR had denied Anderson the chance to perform at Constitution Hall solely because the singer was black, she immediately and publicly resigned from the organization. She then arranged for Anderson to sing the planned DAR concert from the steps of the Lincoln Memorial. Nearly 75,000 people stood quietly on the grounds outside the memorial, shoulder to shoulder, to hear Anderson sing. The concert opened with "My Country, 'Tis of Thee"—an ironic choice, given its reference to the United States as a "sweet land of liberty."

Conservatives were another group that opposed New Deal programs. Republicans hated FDR and the New Deal; they claimed that he was turning the United States into a socialist society and that he was destroying big business and free enterprise. Not all Democrats supported the New Deal either; some thought it did not go far enough, while others thought it should include different programs.

The New Deal did not pull the nation out of the Great Depression. However, it did substantially improve the lives of millions of people in both the short term and the long term. Some of its programs, such as the Federal Deposit Insurance Corporation, continue today to protect people against losing their life's savings in another bank failure. The New Deal brought electricity and indoor plumbing to many regions where they had previously been found in very few homes. This improved public health and sanitation as well as improving the standard of living. During the New Deal, the South finally began to rely more on modern industry and less on cash crops like cotton.

The Second New Deal

The 1934 congressional elections showed that no matter what the critics thought, the public was solidly in favor of the New Deal. Democrats gained even more seats in Congress. This put FDR in a position to initiate more programs that he hoped would help the economy recover over the long term, rather than simply bringing immediate relief to those who needed it.

The "Second New Deal" included two especially important programs: the Works Progress Administration (WPA) and the Social Security Act. Created in 1935, the WPA replaced the Civil Works Administration. Over eight years, it employed more than eight million people in construction work, research projects, and teaching jobs. It set aside $300 million for Federal Project Number One, which employed thousands of writers, actors, painters, designers, and musicians. The purpose of Federal Project Number One was twofold: to provide jobs for unemployed artists and to encourage American arts and culture by supporting them financially.

The Social Security Act of 1935 provided unemployment insurance to those who lost their jobs, guaranteed all American workers a government pension once they turned 65, and made payments to disabled workers and to the widows and children of workers. All workers paid a small percentage of each paycheck into a government-administered fund. Once they reached age 65, they would then receive monthly checks based on the average yearly amount of their earnings. In this way, Social Security would pay for itself.

In 1936, FDR ran for reelection against Republican Governor Alfred M. Landon of Kansas. Union and Socialist Party candidates also appeared on the ballot. FDR found it an easy campaign, since all he had to do was remind farmers, workers, and businessmen that they were better off now than they had been when he took office. FDR won the election in the greatest landslide in a century, carrying every state except Vermont and Maine, and winning 11 million more votes than Landon.

The Dust Bowl

Severe droughts during the mid-1930s turned the Great Plains into the Dust Bowl. The soil of the Great Plains did not retain moisture well to begin with; this made it perfect for growing wheat and corn, but it meant that trouble would occur if there was a significant drop in rainfall. The Great Plains had so few major natural sources of water that it was not easy to irrigate crops; farmers depended on regular rainfall.

During this time, it did not rain for months on end. The loose topsoil blew about in the frequent high winds, creating constant dust storms. Across 50 million acres of land, crops failed or yielded poorly. To counteract the effects of the drought, the Civilian Conservation Corps planted millions of trees throughout the Dust Bowl. These trees created a windbreak that helped reduce the erosion of the soil substantially by 1939.

By that time, many small farmers had lost everything they had. Tenant farmers had been forced off their land; owners, deciding that there was no sense in keeping barren land, mailed eviction notices to tenants and then sent heavy tractors in to tear up the soil. The tractors did not go around the farmhouses, but steamrolled over them as well. Tenants—some of whose families had farmed that land for generations—protested, but in vain. When the tractors came, the farmers loaded their few belongings into their shabby old trucks and drove west along Route 66, hoping to find work in the California fruit orchards. Novelist John Steinbeck made the journey with one family of Oklahoma farmers, or "Okies," as they came to be called, and recorded the experience in his classic novel *The Grapes of Wrath*. Steinbeck described in detail the fierce competition for jobs picking fruit or harvesting cotton. Since so many people were desperate for work, the growers offered lower and lower wages, knowing that no one could afford to turn down their offers. These migrant workers had no unions, and whenever anyone tried to argue for decent housing or to organize the other workers, the growers would bring in the police to arrest the "troublemaker" on trumped-up charges.

Opponents of the New Deal might dismiss *The Grapes of Wrath* as fiction, but they could not do the same with the photojournalism of Dorothea Lange, Walker Evans, Gordon Parks, and Margaret Bourke-White. Their cameras captured the toil and endurance of migrant workers, sharecroppers, and the homeless under horrifying living conditions. *Migrant Mother*, Lange's 1936 photograph of a migrant woman and her two children, is something of a poster image summarizing the misery of the Great Depression. After seeing photographs like *Migrant Mother*, Californians began insisting on decent housing and sanitary conditions for the millions of seasonal migrant workers.

Escape

Whenever they could, Americans escaped the terrible difficulties of everyday life by seeking entertainment. It cost nothing to listen to the radio, which broadcast all the latest jazz, the dance music of the big bands, classical concerts, and comedy programs like *The Jack Benny Show*. One October night in 1938, as people changed radio stations to see what was playing, they were startled to hear what purported to be a news flash that aliens from Mars had invaded the United States. Something of a nationwide panic was halted only when the radio network explained that it was a fictional news flash, part of a science-fiction dramatization of H. G. Wells's *The War of the Worlds*. Those who had been listening to director Orson Welles's Mercury Theater broadcast from the beginning had known this all along and were amused by the panic.

For a few cents per person, a whole family could spend an entire day at the movie house. They would see a newsreel, cartoons, a first feature, live entertainment, and then a second feature. The Hollywood movie-studio system was one of the few industries that paid good salaries throughout the 1930s. Hollywood produced hundreds of films a year throughout the decade. By the late 1930s, some films were being shot in Technicolor, attracting even more moviegoers than before.

The most popular novel of the decade was *Gone With the Wind* (1936), written by Atlanta housewife Margaret Mitchell to entertain herself while she recovered from an ankle injury. This sweeping, romantic story of Civil War heroine Scarlett O'Hara captivated the entire nation; readers cheered for Scarlett as she endured starvation and poverty like their own and came out on top.

In 1939, *Gone With the Wind* was made into an equally popular and acclaimed Technicolor film.

CHAPTER 24 QUIZ

1. **An economic depression occurs when _____**
   A. wages and prices rise and unemployment falls.
   B. wages and prices fall and unemployment rises.
   C. wages, prices, and unemployment all rise together.
   D. wages, prices, and unemployment all fall together.

2. **Why did Congress grant President Roosevelt special powers at the start of his first term?**
   A. because the Great Depression was a serious national crisis
   B. because Roosevelt was elected in a landslide
   C. because Congress and Roosevelt represented opposing political parties
   D. because he was related to former president Theodore Roosevelt

3. **First Lady Eleanor Roosevelt was especially active on the issue of _____**
   A. foreign affairs.
   B. civil rights.
   C. the domestic economy.
   D. women's rights.

4. ***The Grapes of Wrath* describes the experiences of _____**
   A. farmers migrating westward in search of work.
   B. African Americans moving north to find jobs.
   C. people relying on breadlines in major cities.
   D. New Deal workers building bridges and highways.

5. **Which industry continued to pay high salaries and earn profits during the Great Depression?**
   A. the agricultural industry
   B. the banking industry
   C. the livestock industry
   D. the motion-picture industry

6. Dorothea Lange is a notable American in the field of _____
   A. politics.
   B. photojournalism.
   C. big business.
   D. transportation.

7. Conservatives who opposed FDR's New Deal policies claimed that
   he _____
   A. was destroying big business and free enterprise.
   B. was not providing enough new jobs.
   C. had failed to combat the rise of unemployment.
   D. did not pass enough civil rights legislation.

8. Hoover took all these steps to combat the Great Depression
   except _____
   A. funding public works projects.
   B. establishing the Federal Farm Board.
   C. reorganizing the banking system.
   D. buying up surplus farm crops.

9. The New Deal had all of these major goals and objectives
   except _____
   A. to bring immediate relief to the unemployed by providing money, jobs,
      or both.
   B. to help the economy recover.
   C. to provide universal employment throughout the United States.
   D. to restructure the banking and business systems to prevent a future
      economic crash.

10. The term *Hooverville* _____
    A. is a nickname for the White House during Hoover's administration.
    B. refers to a community of homemade shacks housing the unemployed.
    C. is a derogatory reference to Congress in the Hoover administration.
    D. refers to the stock market on the day of the 1929 crash.

Chapter 25

World War II, 1936–1945

Historians agree that the peace treaty signed in 1919 at the Congress of Versailles was one of the major causes of World War II; the second war arose as a natural consequence of the first, and both can fairly be described as wars of German aggression.

Concurrently with the war in Europe, Japan abandoned treaties it had signed with Allied powers and expanded its control over Manchuria and the Pacific islands. When Japan perceived the United States as a threat to its expansion, it launched an attack on the U.S. naval base at Pearl Harbor. This attack brought the United States into the world war.

After 1942, the Allied powers (Britain, France, and the Soviet Union) seized the upper hand on the battlefields for two reasons, both very important and both related to the American entry into the war in 1941. First, they outnumbered the Axis (German and Italian) troops; the United States and the Soviet Union could provide fresh troops in almost unlimited numbers, and the Italians changed sides in 1943, leaving Germany alone. Second, American factories were far from the fighting, out of danger of Axis bombing or capture, and were a source of unlimited supplies: weapons, ammunition, ships, tanks, and so on.

The change to a war economy pulled the United States out of the Depression. People who had feared the onset of war had decided to reelect FDR to an unprecedented third term as president. As he had guided the nation through the worst of the Depression, Roosevelt would continue to guide it through war.

World War II raged on until 1945. From 1942 onward, the Allies won battles steadily, but the Germans and Japanese proved to be stubborn and tough enemies, very difficult to defeat. All the Allied ingenuity was necessary to win the war.

Racial prejudice characterized both sides during the war. In the United States, the federal government rounded up tens of thousands of Japanese Americans and imprisoned them in hastily constructed camps throughout the West. In Germany, the Nazi regime was largely based on racial prejudice. German leader Adolf Hitler had a fixed, obsessive idea that people he termed "Aryan," meaning "purebred" Germans and other Nordic Europeans, were racially superior to Slavs and Jews, whom he described as *Untermenschen*, meaning literally "subhuman." His government revoked the civil and constitutional rights of all Jews throughout Germany and the nations it controlled, then forced them into concentration camps where they were starved, tortured, and finally executed in gas chambers. Millions of other non-Aryans, such as Romany and Slavs, were also dragged to the death camps.

In the spring of 1945, with the Soviets invading Berlin, Hitler committed suicide. Germany surrendered unconditionally within the week. Japan held out somewhat longer, refusing to surrender until two nuclear bombs were dropped on the cities of Hiroshima and Nagasaki.

In terms of lives lost and damage done, World War II was by far the costliest war in history. As it ended, the Allies began to realize that they would have to take extraordinary steps to prevent any such international outbreak of war in the future.

CHAPTER OBJECTIVES

- Explain the causes of World War II in Europe.
- Explain why Japan attacked the United States in 1941.
- Describe the course of the war in Europe and in the Pacific.
- Explain how the United States achieved victory in the war.
- Discuss the consequences of the war for all nations that took part.

Chapter 25 Time Line

- **1921**   Washington Conference

    Four-Power Treaty and Nine-Power Treaty

    Mussolini founds Fascist Party in Italy

- **1924**   Dawes Plan

- **1927**   Kellogg-Briand Pact

- **1933**   Adolf Hitler becomes chancellor of Germany

    Good Neighbor policy

- **1935**   Nuremberg Laws deprive German Jews of citizenship

- **1936**   Germany annexes Rhineland

    Germany and Italy unite as Axis powers

- **1938**   Munich Conference

    Germany annexes Austria

- **1939**   Germany and Soviet Union sign nonaggression pact

    Germany and Soviet Union take over Poland from opposite sides

    Britain and France declare war on Germany

- **1940**   Germany invades Belgium and marches on to France; Allies retreat at Dunkirk

    Germany sets up puppet Vichy regime in southern France

    Winston Churchill becomes prime minister of Great Britain

    Italy declares war on France and Great Britain

- **1941**   United States and Great Britain sign Atlantic Charter

    Germany invades Soviet Union; Soviet Union joins Allies

    Japan bombs Pearl Harbor; United States declares war on Japan

    Germany declares war on United States

- **1943**   Axis forces surrender in North Africa

    Mussolini deposed

    Italy signs armistice with Allies

- **1944** **June 4**   Rome falls to Allies

  June 6   D-Day landing of American forces on Normandy beaches

  August 25   Allies liberate Paris

  October   Battle of Leyte Gulf

  December   Battle of the Bulge

- **1945** **February**   Yalta Conference

  Battle of Iwo Jima

  March   Allies invade Germany

  April   Battle of Okinawa

  Death of FDR; Harry S. Truman becomes president

  May 7   Germans surrender; V-E Day

  July   Potsdam Conference

  August 6   Bombing of Hiroshima

  August 8   Soviet Union declares war on Japan; invades Manchuria

  August 9   Bombing of Nagasaki

  September 2   Japan signs surrender

American Neutrality

Ever since the end of World War I, most Americans had supported a foreign policy of neutrality. Americans hoped to remain on friendly terms with all nations, not to be dragged into conflicts with any. Most Americans saw no point in foreign alliances. Owing to its huge size and its geographical isolation from Europe and Asia, the United States felt invulnerable to attack from them; in its own hemisphere, the United States enjoyed excellent relations with Canada and was much too wealthy and powerful to fear any of the Latin American nations. Congress felt that it spoke for the people when it refused to join either the League of Nations or the World Court.

However, the United States was included in various diplomatic meetings during the 1920s and 1930s. These meetings discussed world disarmament.

The Washington Conference of 1921 resulted in three major treaties, shown in this table:

Five-Power Naval Treaty	United States, Britain, Italy, France, Japan	• British and U.S. navies will be the same size • Japanese navy will be 60 % of that size • French and Italian navies will be 50 % of the size of the Japanese navy
Four-Power Treaty	Britain, United States, France, Japan	All four nations will respect one another's territories in the Pacific
Nine-Power Treaty	Britain, United States, France, Italy, Japan, Belgium, China, Netherlands, Portugal	• China's territorial integrity is guaranteed • Open Door Policy will continue

The United States also pulled back on its imperialist tactics in Latin America. FDR announced the Good Neighbor Policy, which pledged that the United States would respect the rights of its neighbors and would expect the same respect in return. FDR withdrew troops from Latin American nations, agreed to Cuba's request to repeal the Platt Amendment, and improved relations with Mexico.

The United States reduced the rate of World War I debt owed by Allied nations. Because it was clearly impossible for Germany to make reparations on the schedule that had been agreed to at Versailles, the Dawes Plan of 1924 drew up a new schedule for these payments..

German Expansionism and the Outbreak of World War II

Woodrow Wilson had been right to try to dissuade the victors in World War I from demanding an admission of war guilt and impossible reparations from Germany. The combined effects of reparations and the Great Depression (due to international banking and trade, the U.S. economic collapse halted Europe's progress in recovering from the devastation of the war) caused German inflation to reach such epic proportions that at one point, a loaf of bread cost a staggering 400 billion marks. Germany eventually compromised with both France and the United States over the reparations, and the German economy began to recover as the rest of Europe struggled back toward financial health as well.. When Adolf Hitler took power in 1933, he began the process of German rearmament, which had been outlawed by the Treaty of Versailles.

Austrian rather than German by birth, Hitler rose to supreme power from utter obscurity. He had been a failure all his life, often living on charity, unable to settle down to any profession until he joined the German army during the Great War. Hitler served with some distinction in a low rank, and felt great personal bitterness over Germany's defeat. He used his extraordinary ability to stir the emotions of crowds to gain power; his rhetoric about the greatness of the German Empire struck a nerve with people who desperately needed decisive leadership. Hitler won support by using simple slogans and propaganda to appeal to national pride, emotion, and prejudice. He had no experience in government or politics, nor did he have the skill or the desire to present logically thought-out social programs. Therefore, the established German political parties made the great mistake of underestimating him and his mass appeal. By 1932, the Nazi (short for "National Socialist") Party that he had founded was the most powerful party in Germany. Hitler himself was appointed chancellor in 1933; he soon made himself an absolute dictator.

Totalitarian governments had also risen to power in Russia and Italy. In Italy, Benito Mussolini founded the Fascist Party in 1919. In 1922, Mussolini forced the king to make him a dictator. From then on, the Fascists and the Italian army ruled the country. Italy pushed into North Africa, where it soon controlled Libya and Ethiopia.

In the wake of the Bolshevik Revolution of 1917, the Russians had reorganized their government and renamed the nation "Union of Soviet Socialist Republics" (it was also called "Soviet Union" or just "USSR"). In 1924, Joseph Stalin took over the Soviet government. With the power of the Communist Party and the Red Army behind him, he reorganized large and small farms and estates into vast cooperatives on which people were forced to work. Anyone who disagreed with official Soviet policy was sent to a labor camp. Historians have estimated that about 30 million Russians died during his regime—some of starvation or disease, but most either succumbed to the brutal conditions in the labor camps or were executed at the order of the dictator.

Once Germany was rearmed, Hitler ordered an occupation of the Rhineland in 1936. In 1938, his army invaded and annexed Austria, and in 1939 Czechoslovakia. Secretly, Hitler and Stalin signed a pact agreeing that neither would attack the other, and that they would invade Poland from opposite sides and divide it between them. When the invasion of Poland began, both France and England declared war on Germany. Germany soon invaded France through Belgium; it would occupy Paris for the next few years. At this time, Winston Churchill became prime minister of Britain.

Hitler quickly abandoned the nonaggression pact. In 1941, German troops invaded the Soviet Union. The Soviets were taken completely by surprise, but soon rallied a fierce opposition against the invaders. Hitler's attack had the immediate effect of bringing the Soviet Union over to the Allied side of the war. With its enormous army, the Soviet Union would prove crucial to the outcome of the war.

FDR Reelected

In 1940, FDR ran for reelection once again. This marked the first time that any president had run for a third consecutive term in office. Historians agree that if the world had been at peace in 1940, FDR would probably have thrown his support to another prominent Democratic leader rather than seeking reelection himself. However, given the likelihood that the United States would soon be at war again, FDR decided to run. He had the overwhelming support of his party. Republican Wendell Willkie, a former Democrat and New Deal supporter who had no political experience, opposed him.

The economy was beginning to recover from the worst of the Great Depression, and the issue that concerned voters the most was whether the United States would take part in the war in Europe. Both Willkie and Roosevelt pledged to keep the United States neutral—Willkie at all costs, FDR if possible. Roosevelt made it clear that the United States would not seek a battle with any nation, but would immediately defend itself if it were attacked directly.

FDR won the election decisively, winning 449 electoral votes of a possible 531 and nearly 55 percent of the popular vote. "What counted," wrote one historian, "was the feeling that in a dangerous world the United States had better not change horses in midstream." The same feeling would contribute to Roosevelt's election for a fourth term in 1944.

Pearl Harbor: The United States Enters the War

"Yesterday, December 7, 1941—a date which will live in infamy—the United States was suddenly and deliberately attacked by naval and air forces of the Empire of Japan." Everyone listening to the president speak on the radio knew that this meant that the United States would finally join the war.

A large part of the U.S. Pacific Fleet rode at anchor in Pearl Harbor, Hawaii (then a U.S. territory, not yet a state), and hundreds of planes awaited action on the base's airfields. Troops assigned to duty in the Pacific were very happy with their lot; as long as the United States was not at war, they could enjoy the gorgeous climate of the islands. None of them ever imagined that they were in any danger. U.S. officials had intercepted coded messages and knew that a Japanese attack was being planned, but they were unable to find out where or when. The public knew nothing of this.

Japan had repeatedly violated the Washington Conference treaties, invading and conquering Manchuria and attacking U.S. ships near Nanjing in 1937. After increasingly sharp exchanges between Japanese and American diplomats, Japan attacked Pearl Harbor with the intention of wiping out the U.S. Navy and reducing the United States to the status of a second-rate power.

With no warning, Japan began bombing the base at 8:00 A.M. on December 7. The Japanese destroyed twenty warships and 200 airplanes, and killed about 2,400 Americans in the attack. The bombing was highly efficient and very successful, and left the United States no choice but to declare war.

Mobilization in the United States

World War II brought the U.S. economy out of the Depression. After the attack on Pearl Harbor, all thought of neutrality was forgotten. The United States was committed to defeating Japan and also to helping the Allied powers defeat the Germans. American civilians readily accepted rationing of goods that were needed for the troops and the war effort: sugar, coffee, cigarettes, silk (needed for parachutes), tires (needed for rubber), and canned goods. Clothing styles changed in order to conserve fabric: skirts were shorter; dress styles were plainer, without flounces or ruffles; trouser cuffs and jacket lapels were narrowed; and the deep hems common before 1941 were now tiny.

Between 1940 and 1943, more than 450,000 Americans took jobs in the munitions industry. Unemployment dropped to below 1929 levels and wages rose. The military employed hundreds of thousands, including women, who served as nurses and in a variety of noncombat jobs. Many of them ended up serving in Europe and the Pacific.

After the attack on Pearl Harbor, FDR signed legislation that ordered the forced evacuation of all Japanese Americans—about 120,000 immigrants and children of immigrants—living on the West Coast. No specific charges were ever made against any of them, nor was there the slightest reason to suspect any of them of disloyalty to the United States. Despite these facts, both the government and the people gave in to racist fears; the Japanese Americans were relocated to internment camps throughout the western states. Located in barren areas far from the coast, these camps had few comforts, although they were a far cry from the concentration camps of Nazi Germany.

Many Japanese Americans enlisted in the U.S. Army and served with distinction. Those who did not enlist remained in the camps and were not released until 1945. Not until 1988 were the survivors offered an official apology from the federal government. This executive order marked the low point of FDR's legacy.

Military Campaigns in Europe

The Axis powers had the upper hand in European fighting until late 1942. Their armies were the aggressors; they had been preparing for war for years and were well organized for the fight. They also controlled the vast majority of Europe and a sizable chunk of North Africa. However, the fact that they were trying to fight a war on several fronts at once weakened and divided their forces. Allied forces hoped to exploit this weakness.

Allied advantages included both numerical strength and geography. Both the Soviet Union and the United States had huge populations on which they could draw for troops. Germany and Italy, with much smaller populations, had comparatively fewer troops. U.S. industries were also a major asset for the Allies: the United States could produce an unlimited supply of weapons, ammunition, ships, tankers, and planes. The campaign in North Africa was fought throughout the summer and fall of 1942. British forces led by General Bernard Montgomery pursued German forces led by General Erwin Johannes Rommel, who was one of the most skilled commanders on either side. However, Rommel was outnumbered and eventually lost ground in the Battle of El Alamein.

The Germans had invaded the Soviet Union in 1941. They had marched east to Leningrad and laid siege to it. The people of the city underwent slow starvation for many months before the siege was lifted. The hatred for Germany that this siege created would be revealed a few years later when the Soviets marched into Berlin.

The Soviets eventually penned up the invading Germans in the city of Stalingrad, starving them into surrender early in 1943. The combination of the Soviet and North African victories caused the tide of the war to turn in the Allies' favor.

The War in Europe, 1943–1944

When the American forces arrived in Europe, they planned with Allied leaders to begin their attack in the Mediterranean region. Under the command of General Dwight D. Eisenhower, U.S. forces invaded North Africa in November 1942. At this time, France was entirely under German control: the northern half was occupied by Germany, and the southern half was ruled by the puppet Vichy regime. Morocco and Algeria were under Vichy control. In spite of fierce resistance from the Vichy army, the combined British and U.S. forces soon controlled North Africa and blocked supply lines between Germany and Italy. In May 1943, the Allies forced the surrender of Axis troops in Tunisia, the last Axis stronghold in Africa.

With North Africa under their control, the Allies then turned their attention to Italy. They invaded Sicily in July 1943 and soon controlled it. From here, they intended to launch an attack on the Italian mainland. Italy gave way promptly, signing an armistice with the Allies that brought Italian troops over to the Allied side. Allied armies took over Naples in October 1943 and Rome in June 1944. By this time, Italian rebels had located Mussolini and executed him.

Throughout 1943, the Allied air force bombed Germany. Their goals were to destroy railroad lines, munitions factories, weapons arsenals, and other strategic locations. They also hoped to break the spirit of the German people by destroying their civilization, just as the German air attacks on Great Britain had been intended to break the British spirit. Allied bombs killed tens of thousands of German civilians and destroyed about 70 percent of the buildings in virtually every large city in Germany, including some of its oldest and most beautiful cities, such as Dresden.

The Battle of the Atlantic was fought between the navies of the various nations. German U-boats piled up an impressive record of attacks on Allied ships until 1943. By that time, the Allies had improved sonar technology to help them to pinpoint the underwater locations of the submarines . By 1944, the Allies had again taken control of the seas.

The Invasion of Normandy

The U.S Army was not as well trained or well prepared as the German army. However, the United States knew that it was crucial to win the war against the Germans in occupied France; to go in and lose on the Western Front would probably mean losing the entire war. Therefore, U.S. commanders worked out an agreement with Great Britain to launch a surprise offensive in northern France as soon as they felt the army was ready. Operation Overlord—the plan to invade France along the beaches at Normandy, on the southern shore of the English Channel—was placed under the command of General Eisenhower. Working with Allied military staff, Eisenhower established a trail of false and misleading clues that led the Germans to expect that the invasion would take place in a different location.

The Germans had fortified the Normandy beaches with mines and traps, but Hitler was convinced that the invasion would take place at Calais and did not send troops to Normandy. About 150,000 Allied troops crossed the Channel from Britain, either in planes or aboard transports. Many drowned or were killed in parachute drops, but the survivors were able to overrun the beaches and begin marching south and east. Meanwhile, another Allied force was marching north from the Mediterranean, and the Soviet army was fighting the Germans on the eastern front. On August 25, 1944, the Allies marched into Paris and liberated that city from German occupation.

In December 1944, the Germans launched a fierce assault on the Allied troops in the Ardennes region of Belgium and northern France. They pushed Allied troops back so far in one place that they bulged into the line of defense, nearly breaking through and giving the Battle of the Bulge its name. The Allies were outnumbered by more than two to one, but they flatly refused to give in to the Germans' demand that they surrender. When reinforcements came, the Allies pushed the Germans back. By January, the Germans knew that they had lost the Battle of the Bulge. It was clear to everyone but Hitler that Germany would soon have to surrender.

In February 1945, Winston Churchill, FDR, and Joseph Stalin met at Yalta to plan for peace. Stalin promised that the Soviet Union would join the fight against Japan within three months of Germany's surrender. The three leaders then agreed that they, along with France, would occupy Germany after the war. They also discussed plans for a new League of Nations.

Surrender in Europe: V-E Day

In 1945, Soviet troops were marching westward toward Berlin, while Allied troops approached it from the southeast. In April, the Soviets were the first to march into Hitler's capital city, where they took brutal revenge on the people.

Unable to face the loss of his power, or to contemplate the punishment and public humiliation he would undergo as the primary cause and also the loser of the war, Hitler committed suicide on April 30. Germany surrendered a week later, ending the war in Europe.

As the British and American troops marched eastward, liberating Austria and Poland, they discovered the concentration camps where millions of Jews and other "non-Aryans" of Central and Eastern Europe, notably the migratory Sinti and Romany peoples, had been rounded up for slaughter in a deliberate massacre of innocents known to history as the Holocaust.

Since the camps were in their own backyards, and since their own friends and neighbors had been dragged away and imprisoned in them, a fair number of Europeans, especially Germans and Poles who lived nearby, were more or less aware of the camps and their significance. Across Europe, many courageous individuals had helped to hide their Jewish friends or aid them in other ways. However, no nation made any official attempt to put a stop to what was happening. Historians continue to debate the leaders' reasons, with explanations ranging from deep-seated racism to the belief that the survival of Europe as a whole was a more urgent priority than protecting the prisoners in the camps.

The Allied troops, particularly the Americans, were unprepared for the horrors they found when they liberated the camps. The prisoners had been shorn of their hair and starved to two-thirds or one-half their normal body weight; registration numbers were tattooed on their arms; exhaustion and disease had robbed them of all their vitality. There was large-scale cremation equipment at some camps, and massive common graves at all of them. There were huge, neatly sorted piles of human hair, gold dental fillings, eyeglasses, clothing, and shoes. Almost all the camp guards had committed suicide or fled in terror of the approaching Allied armies.

War in the Pacific

Military Campaigns in the Pacific, 1942–1943

Japan followed the attack on Pearl Harbor with similar attacks on U.S. naval bases in the Philippines, Burma, Hong Kong, and other places. After the onslaught on the Philippines, General Douglas MacArthur led a U.S. retreat to Australia. The Japanese took thousands of American and Filipino prisoners at Bataan and forced them on a death march through the jungle on the way to the prison camps. Close to 10,000 of the prisoners died.

By 1942, Japan was planning to invade the Pacific Coast of the United States. In the Battle of the Coral Sea, British and American forces fought back the Japanese advance. In the Battle of Midway, the United States again defeated the Japanese air force and navy. In the Battle of Guadalcanal in the Solomon Islands, the U.S. fleet once again battled the Japanese fleet and won a major victory.

The United States had one major advantage over the Japanese. While U.S. interceptors were able to decode Japanese radio messages, the Japanese had no similar luck with the U.S. codes. The United States had established a special signal corps of Navajo Indians, who broadcast coded messages in their own language. Since the Japanese had no knowledge of Navajo, they were never able to decipher these messages, which would have given them advance warning of American troop movements and other plans.

The U.S. Marines in the Pacific Islands

A long string of islands lay like the beads on a necklace along the Pacific Ocean between Japan and Australia. (See the map on the following page.) The Allied plan was to use the U.S. Marines, who had the reputation of being the toughest branch of the armed forces, to take over certain key islands and use them as power bases as they made their way north toward Japan. This strategy was put into place in November 1943 in the Gilbert Islands. American troops quickly took over Makin Island, but Tarawa was heavily fortified and also protected by a surrounding coral reef. Nearly 3,000 Marines were killed or wounded in the assault on Tarawa, but in the end the United States won the battle.

The Marines moved on to secure the Marshall Islands, then moved north toward the Marianas. Thousands on both sides died in the battles for Saipan and Guam. The Japanese were trained to give no quarter; their commanders had decreed that capture or surrender was the ultimate dishonor, and that it would be better to commit suicide than to allow oneself to be captured. Therefore, the Japanese felt they had nothing to lose by continuing to fight, everything to lose by giving in. American Marines had not been prepared for this attitude or for the brutality it entailed. They soon became equally brutal in response.

By August 1944, the United States had taken control of the Marianas and their valuable airstrips. In October, the troops were ready to take back the Philippine Islands. The Battle of Leyte Gulf became the decisive battle in the war between Japan and the United States. In February 1945, U.S. troops finally invaded the capital city of Manila, and the battle was over.

The United States used the Pacific islands as air bases from which to send out bombing raids on Japan. The planes bombed most of Japan's major cities, causing heavy damage. Still the Japanese refused to surrender. In February 1945, the Marines met the Japanese again on the island of Iwo Jima, only 650 miles from the coast of Japan's main island. In one of the most brutal battles of the war, in which thousands on both sides were killed, the United States finally gained a victory after six weeks of fighting. Loud cheers broke out among the American troops when they saw their flag go up atop Iwo Jima's Mount Surabachi. The flag was taken down within a few minutes, to be preserved as a souvenir for the battalion, and a replacement was put up. Photographer Joe Rosenthal, who had scaled a nearby hill too late to catch the real flag-raising on

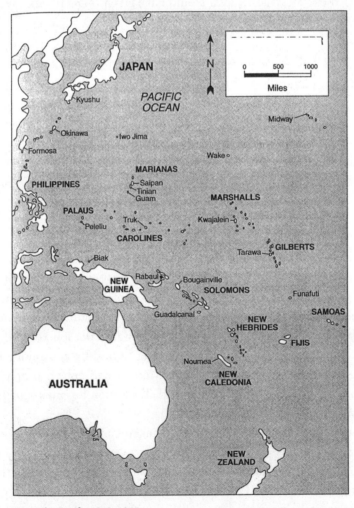

War in the Pacific 1943–1945

film, snapped a photograph of six Marines raising the replacement flag. Ironically, this photograph became one of the most famous images in American military history, although in truth it depicts only a reenactment of the actual event.

One more battle remained in the Pacific, since Iwo Jima had not brought about a surrender. The U.S. forces invaded Okinawa unchallenged. Five days later, the Japanese opened fire on them. About 150,000 soldiers, two-thirds of them Japanese, were killed in the fighting.

Nuclear War against Japan

FDR did not live to see the end of the war in Europe. He died on April 12, 1945, at his favorite retreat in Warm Springs, Georgia. FDR had been president for so many years and had courageously held the nation together through such hard times that his death devastated the nation as Abraham Lincoln's had done many years before. With Roosevelt's death, Vice President Harry S Truman took office.

The news from Europe made it clear that the German surrender was imminent; this allowed Truman to turn all his attention to the war against Japan. Faced with the implacable Japanese attitude of fighting until their last soldier had been killed rather than surrendering, Truman decided to use the deadliest weapon in history: the atomic bomb, the world's first nuclear weapon.

European and American scientists had developed the bomb between 1942 and 1945 in a research project called the Manhattan Project. The first bomb was successfully tested in New Mexico in July 1945. It was clear that the bomb would wreak unimaginable destruction; nevertheless, Truman believed that it would save lives in the long run by ending the fighting immediately. On August 16, the United States dropped the first atomic bomb on the Japanese city of Hiroshima. The blast killed more than 75,000 people and laid every building in the city flat. A second bomb, even more destructive, was dropped on Nagasaki three days later. The bombing achieved Truman's goal of immediate surrender; the Japanese, stunned at the extent of the damage and the number of deaths, signed formal terms of surrender on September 2nd.

Today, all the great powers of the world understand the destructive long-term effects of radiation poisoning. No one knew anything about this in 1945—not the atomic scientists and not the U.S. government. All the United States knew was that the atomic bomb was much more powerful than any previous weapon. It had not planned or anticipated the terrible, long-term suffering of thousands of Japanese civilians affected by the huge blasts of radiation.

Results of the War

The Allied forces had crushed the German attempt to conquer Europe. The Nazi Party was disbanded and discredited; many of its key figures killed themselves or fled to South America. Those captured in Europe were tried as war criminals. Germany lost all the territory it had conquered during the war. Much of Japan was destroyed by nuclear bombs.

Europe's population was devastated by the war. The Soviet Union was the hardest hit of all, with 9 million soldiers and 17 million civilians dead. The total deaths for all other European nations combined were about 6 million soldiers and about 12 million civilians, including the refugees of all nations who died of starvation, disease, or stray bullets. Approximately 6 million Jews, Sinti, and Romany were massacred in the Nazi concentration camps. Thousands more Europeans were lucky enough to emigrate overseas before or during the war; most would never return.

Not only people, but whole cities, were casualties of the war. Much of central Europe lay in ruins. Germany was utterly destroyed by Allied bombs. The beautiful capitals of Berlin and Vienna were unrecognizable, nothing but smoking heaps of loose bricks, chunks of concrete, and wrecked hulks of buildings. Cities and villages across Italy and Poland had been reduced to piles of stones. Transportation systems across the continent were wrecked. Everyday necessities such as fresh water, fuel, electricity, and food were unavailable. Sanitation was impossible in bombed-out cities. Governments were in disarray or had been removed from power.

The war ended a long era of European domination of the globe. For the next 50 years, only two nations dominated world affairs: the United States and the Soviet Union. The tremendous power the Soviet Union would soon wield was not immediately apparent at the end of World War II; the case was quite otherwise with the United States. The United States emerged strong from the war for three reasons. First, the munitions industry had completely reinvigorated the American economy. Second, American casualties had been very low compared to European losses. Third, the war had had only a minimal impact on American civilians, since apart from the one bombing attack on Pearl Harbor, they were far removed from the combat zones.

The leaders meeting in Potsdam for the peace conference had an enormous rebuilding task before them.

Provisions of the Potsdam Conference

- Austria and Germany would each be divided into four zones of occupation: Soviet, British, U.S., and French.
- The capital cities of Vienna and Berlin would be divided into four zones of occupation, as above.
- The Allies would help to rebuild German industry and reestablish local German governments.
- German refugees would be helped to return to their homes.
- Poland would retain the German territory it had taken during the war.
- Germany would pay reparations to all Allied nations, with the Soviet Union taking the largest share as the greatest sufferer.

The leaders at Potsdam were outwardly civil, but inwardly distrustful of one another. Stalin did not want the United States imposing a capitalist economy on Germany. In addition, he deeply resented the fact that the Allies had waited until 1944 to invade Normandy, while Soviet soldiers were fighting desperately in the east. On his side, President Truman did not want the Soviets to gain too much control over Poland and Eastern Europe. These mutual suspicions grew as time went on. Before long, they would lead the world into the Cold War.

The United Nations

The League of Nations had failed to prevent World War II. National leaders agreed that they needed to design a new, stronger peacekeeping organization. Delegates from the United States, China, the Soviet Union, and Britain wrote a proposal for an organization to be called the United Nations. Delegates from fifty nations then met to discuss the proposal and write a U.N. charter. It established a General Assembly, in which all member nations would have an equal voice, and a 15-member Security Council. Of the fifteen seats on the Security Council, ten would rotate among nations; the other five would be permanently held by Britain, China, France, the Soviet Union, and the United States.

CHAPTER 25 QUIZ

1. **The Soviet Union joined the Allied nations in 1941 because** _____
   A. Germany invaded Poland.
   B. Germany reneged on the nonaggression pact.
   C. the United States entered the war.
   D. Italy entered the war.

2. **Why did the Germans fail to prevent the Allied invasion of Normandy in 1944?**
   A. They did not believe the Allies intended to invade France.
   B. They were concentrating on winning the war at sea.
   C. They already knew that they would lose the war.
   D. They expected the Allies to invade at a different location.

3. **Which European nation suffered by far the heaviest losses in the war?**
   A. Austria
   B. Germany
   C. Poland
   D. the Soviet Union

4. **Truman ordered the bombing of Hiroshima and Nagasaki in order to** _____
   A. force an immediate Japanese surrender.
   B. test the capabilities of the atomic bomb.
   C. persuade the Soviets to take part in the war against Japan.
   D. avenge American losses in the Pacific theater of war.

5. _____ **was the catalyst that brought the United States into World War II.**
   A. The German and Soviet invasions of Poland
   B. The German bombing of Britain
   C. The Japanese attack on Pearl Harbor
   D. The forced march from Bataan

6. **When the Americans arrived in Europe, they began a concerted war effort** _____
   A. on the eastern front.
   B. on the Western Front.
   C. in North Africa.
   D. in the Balkans.

7. _____ was the site of a major battle between the U.S. Marines and the Japanese.

   A. Berlin

   B. The Argonne Forest

   C. Okinawa

   D. Hiroshima

8. Why did the United States force Japanese Americans who were Pacific Coast residents into internment camps in 1942?

   A. documentary proof that Japan had been trying to recruit them as spies

   B. as a gesture of revenge for the Japanese attack on Hawaii

   C. race-based fears that they would be more loyal to Japan than to the United States

   D. to protect them from the threat of future attacks

9. As a result of the Potsdam Conference, Germany was _____ after the war.

   A. occupied by Allied armed forces

   B. destroyed by atomic bombs

   C. made a member of the United Nations

   D. ordered to disband its entire military force

10. The United States and _____ were the only two combatants to emerge from the war as major world powers.

    A. Japan

    B. France

    C. Germany

    D. the Soviet Union

Chapter **26**

The United States in the Postwar Era, 1945–1960

World War II was over, but instead of bringing peace to the world, it ushered in a new era of conflict, the Cold War, that was to last for forty-five years. The conflict was known as a "cold" war because the opponents—the United States and the Soviet Union—did not actually fire shots at one another. Instead, they maintained a hostile standoff.

The Soviet Union was the only European nation to emerge from the destruction of World War II as a superpower. By 1949, it had begun to manufacture and stockpile nuclear weapons in order to keep pace with the world's only other superpower, the United States. Given their antithetical political systems and economic policies, the United States and the Soviet Union were natural enemies; throughout the Cold War, each tried to limit the other's sphere of influence. However, the development of nuclear weapons in the 1940s meant that both sides had to move very carefully; neither was willing to risk a nuclear holocaust that might literally destroy the world.

From the Asian point of view, the term *Cold War* is a misnomer. When civil wars erupted in Korea and Vietnam (see Chapter 29), the Soviets backed one side and the United States the other. Hundreds of thousands of civilians and soldiers died during the Korean and Vietnam wars, but neither outcome made much difference to the overall Cold War.

In the United States, fear of the Soviet Union led to an era of anti-Communist hysteria. Congressional investigations pandered to this public fear, ruining lives with questions and accusations that violated the civil rights of hundreds of people.

Americans enjoyed an era of prosperity and plenty after the hard times of the Great Depression. The GI Bill of Rights gave veterans the chance to get a college education, buy a farm, attend training school for a particular profession, or start a business. This enabled many veterans to marry, start families, and move to the newly built suburbs. People bought cars, television sets, and quantities of other consumer goods.

Society was beginning to integrate. The war had proved to many that African Americans were the equal of whites. By the mid-1950s, federal legislation and important Supreme Court decisions had desegregated public schools and public transportation. The Brooklyn Dodgers baseball team set an example of integration in private business by signing Negro League star Jackie Robinson in 1947.

CHAPTER OBJECTIVES

- Define the term *Cold War* and identify the nations on each side of the conflict.
- Compare and contrast Eastern and Western Europe after World War II.
- Discuss the changes in American society during the period 1945–1960.
- Discuss the beginnings of the Civil Rights movement.
- Explain the issues in the Korean War and what the results were.

Chapter 26 Time Line

- **1945**   Potsdam Conference
  1945–1949   United Nations founded
  Nuremberg Trials
- **1945–1951**   United States occupies Japan

- 1946   "Iron Curtain" speech

     Allies divide Korea into two zones

- 1947   Brooklyn Dodgers sign Jackie Robinson
- 1948–1951   Marshall Plan

     Truman reelected President

- 1949   North Atlantic Treaty Organization (NATO) founded
- 1950   Korean War begins
- 1952   *Brown v. Board of Education*

     Dwight D. Eisenhower elected president

- 1953   Korean armistice
- 1955–1956   Montgomery bus boycott
- 1956   Eisenhower reelected

The Beginnings of the Cold War

In 1946, Winston Churchill made an important speech on the current state of world affairs. He spoke the following memorable sentences:

> From Stettin in the Baltic to Trieste in the Adriatic, an iron curtain has descended across the Continent. Behind that line lie all the capitals of the ancient states of Central and Eastern Europe. Warsaw, Berlin, Prague, Vienna, Budapest, Belgrade, Bucharest and Sofia; all these famous cities and the populations around them lie in what I must call the Soviet sphere, and all are subject in one form or another not only to Soviet influence but to a very high and, in many cases, increasing measure of control from Moscow.

Many Americans did not want to acknowledge the truth of Churchill's perceptions; they wanted to believe that the victory over the Nazis had made the world safe. However, most people recognized that Churchill had been correct. The immediate American response was containment. The United States believed that it might be possible to prevent Soviet influence from spreading any further, and that containment was a necessary first step toward pushing the Soviets back inside the borders of their own territory. In what became known as the Truman Doctrine, President Truman stated that the United States would support any nation or region that the Soviets threatened to take over or subjugate.

Between about 1944 and 1947, every Eastern European nation except Greece either established a Communist state (usually called a "people's republic") or was absorbed into the Soviet Union—just as Churchill had predicted. One-party rule under an absolute dictator was the most common form of government behind the Iron Curtain.

Stalin claimed that the USSR needed these allies as a safety zone between itself and the West for its own security. Germany had twice invaded Russia and inflicted tremendous damage and loss of life; Stalin was determined to prevent any further overland attacks. Additionally, from the Communist point of view, capitalist nations were inherently enemies.

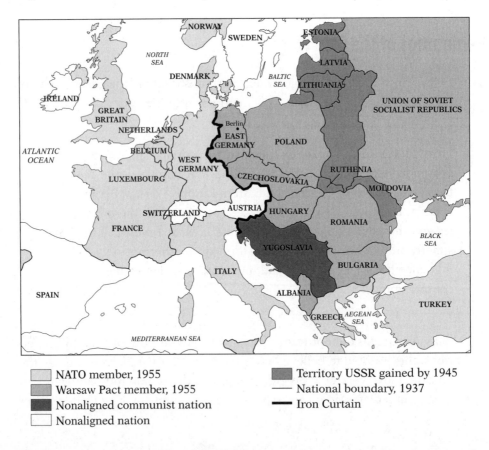

International Organizations

Since the Communist and non-Communist members of the United Nations were mutually hostile and distrustful, many heads of state felt that they would do well to form smaller international unions for their mutual protection. Two such organizations were formed; the members agreed that if any nation in the group were attacked, all the others would come to its defense.

Organization	Date Formed	Members
North Atlantic Treaty Organization (NATO)	1947	Belgium
		Britain
		Canada
		Denmark
		France
		*Greece
		Iceland
		Luxembourg
		Netherlands
		Norway
		Portugal
		*Turkey
		United States
		*West Germany
Warsaw Pact	1955	Albania
		Bulgaria
		Czechoslovakia
		East Germany
		Hungary
		Poland
		Romania
		Soviet Union
		* nation that joined NATO after 1947

Rebuilding Europe

When Communist forces took over Czechoslovakia in 1948, the U.S. Congress realized the seriousness of the Soviet threat to European democracy. They voted for full funding of the European Recovery Program, universally known as the Marshall Plan.

General George C. Marshall, secretary of state and former army chief of staff, created a foreign-aid plan which would provide almost unlimited U.S. funding for the necessary repairs to Europe's cities, highways, and railways. Any European nation that requested such aid would receive it. In the end, the Marshall Plan provided $13 billion to war-torn Europe as an outright gift, not a loan. Although the economies of Europe were already achieving near miracles of recovery through their own efforts, Marshall Plan funds played a crucial role in rebuilding—but only in the West and in Yugoslavia, where Josip Broz Tito refused to permit any Soviet interference. Stalin refused to allow any Soviet-controlled nation to accept what he regarded as a blatant American attempt to buy Eastern European friendship.

Thanks to their own superhuman efforts, plus the boost provided by the Marshall Plan, Western European countries returned to normal much faster than anyone would have expected on seeing the destruction wrought by the war. Infrastructure was rebuilt, theaters reopened, and people went back to work. Many difficulties, including food shortages and rationing, continued to exist for some time after the war, but governments took what steps they could to bring their nations back to prosperity.

Behind the Iron Curtain, however, conditions were quite different. Although one benefit of Communist rule was full employment, jobs were assigned without regard to individual preferences, and wages were low. Housing was overcrowded—an entire family sharing a one-room apartment without a private kitchen or bathroom was typical in all Soviet cities. In addition, there were constant shortages of necessities, and luxury goods were a thing of the past. Behind the Iron Curtain, there was never any guarantee that shops would have anything to sell. When people heard that a market had just received a truckload of, say, fresh eggs, a long line of customers would appear at that market as if by magic, because it might be the last chance for eggs for a month or more. People carried shopping bags called "perhaps bags" everywhere they went, just in case—perhaps—there might be something to buy and carry home. Barter, rather than cash purchases, became common. The state owned and ran all businesses and industries, so no one had any personal pride or vested interest in doing a good job or seeing his or her business succeed.

Anti-Communist Hysteria and McCarthyism

The American desire to contain the spread of communism affected life at home. Any number of Americans belonged to the Comintern—the International Communist Party. The founding philosophy behind communism is simply expressed: each person should contribute what he or she can to society and the economy, and take as much as he or she needs. Americans who joined the party believed that this ideal was compassionate, generous, and fair. They supported the Communist recognition that workers deserved a fair share of a business's profits. Communism was especially appealing under the New Deal and during the war years, because it was the opposite of the Fascist regimes that had risen in Germany, Italy, and Spain. (It was only in the years after World War II that people all over the world realized that in practice, communism and fascism amounted to exactly the same thing: a military dictatorship or police state based on censorship and oppression. In Communist nations, citizens were not free to make their own basic choices.)

Any U.S. citizen is free to belong to any political party; it has never been a crime to be a Communist. During the Cold War, however, many Americans apparently forgot this fact. Their irrational fears created a "Red Scare" (red being the symbolic color of communism) in which it became unsafe to be a Communist or even to have Communist sympathies.

In 1938, the House of Representatives had created the Un-American Activities Committee to investigate Fascist groups in the United States. In 1947, this committee began investigating suspected Communists. Its investigation of many prominent people in the Hollywood film industry made national headlines, since movie stars were celebrities. One group of writers and directors who became known as the Hollywood Ten invoked their constitutional right not to answer the committee's questions. They were jailed briefly, and after this they were blacklisted in Hollywood. Hollywood studios existed to make profits, and did not want their films boycotted by audiences who had given in to anti-Communist hysteria. Therefore, they refused to hire those who were publicly suspected of being Communists. Fearing the same fate, many Hollywood figures gave the committee the names of anyone they thought might be a Communist or a Communist sympathizer. Others, including Humphrey Bogart, Katharine Hepburn, and Lauren Bacall, courageously opposed the committee.

The Hollywood Ten were not the only people whose lives and careers were ruined. The FBI investigated any group or individual who was accused of being a Communist. One of the most famous victims of the illegal investigations was internationally acclaimed concert singer and actor Paul Robeson. Robeson, like many African Americans, had spoken publicly about the unequal treatment of his race in the United States. He had visited the Soviet Union and been favorably impressed by his experiences in a land where he perceived no such racial discrimination. When Robeson refused to answer the committee's questions about his political beliefs, pointing out that such questions were illegal, his passport was taken away. Since no one in the United States would hire a suspected Communist, he was effectively deprived of the means of earning his living.

In 1950, a Wisconsin senator named Joseph McCarthy falsely claimed to have a list of more than 200 Communists currently employed by the U.S. Department of State. This claim, made at a press conference, touched off an era of hysteria that was unparalleled since the Puritan "witch hunts" of the 1600s. McCarthy used his sudden rise to national prominence to ruin the lives of hundreds of people—against none of whom he had any evidence beyond bare accusation. By 1954, McCarthy had been discredited. Ever since this disgraceful era in American history, the word *McCarthyism* has been used to refer to dirty tactics like those that he used—hurling unfounded accusations, slandering opponents, and playing on the fears and prejudices of the public to gain its support.

The Truman Administration

President Harry S Truman faced numerous challenges, including the threat of nuclear war abroad and anti-Communist hysteria at home. However, Truman, a plain-spoken, solidly middle-class Midwesterner, was not the man to back down when faced by a challenge: he was stubborn, determined, and steadfast in his convictions.

Truman supported the GI Bill of Rights, which provided money for veterans to go to college, start businesses, or buy farms or houses. Millions of Americans from the lower classes became the first in their families to get a college education; in the past, most college graduates had been wealthy or upper middle class. In effect, this made American society far more democratic than it had previously been. Truman also ended racial segregation in the armed forces and the federal bureaucracy, and supported repeal of the Chinese Exclusion Act in 1952. White southern Democrats, outraged by Truman's support for African Americans, vowed not to vote for him in 1948. Truman campaigned vigorously and, in a major upset in American political history, defeated Thomas A. Dewey by more than two million votes. Truman was one of the few who thought, the day before election day, that he would win; one Chicago newspaper even printed the next day's early edition with the headline "DEWEY DEFEATS TRUMAN" without waiting for the official results.

During his second term, Truman proposed the "Fair Deal," a series of programs modeled on the New Deal. His programs had limited success in a Congress that was no longer as heavily Democratic as it had been under FDR. However, the minimum wage went up and Social Security was expanded to cover millions more people.

The Eisenhower Administration

Popular World War II hero Dwight D. Eisenhower, whom everyone called "Ike," was elected president in 1952. Eisenhower described himself as fiscally Republican, but socially Democratic. He reduced the size of the federal bureaucracy and cut farm subsidies, but he also expanded Social Security and unemployment benefits, increased the minimum wage, and increased spending on education.

Until 1949, the United States was the only nation that had the technology to make nuclear weapons. However, Soviet scientists, following the same research path as their Western counterparts, had developed their own bomb by 1949. A nuclear arms race ensued; by 1960, the United States had about five times as many nuclear weapons as the Soviets. Nuclear weapons were enormously expensive, and the U.S. economy thrived under Eisenhower.

The possession of nuclear weapons made both superpowers very cautious. The United States had dropped nuclear bombs on Japan in 1945, so the world knew exactly how destructive such weapons were. Neither side in the Cold War wanted to cause a nuclear holocaust. However, both superpowers played key roles in two conventional wars, one in Korea and the other in Vietnam. (See Chapter 29 for a discussion of the Vietnam War.)

The Korean War

Japan had occupied Korea during World War II; during the war, the Soviet Union had fostered a Korean Communist Party within the USSR. In 1945, the victorious Allied leaders agreed to divide Korea geographically. The Soviets occupied the industrial North, which was proclaimed the Korean Democratic People's Republic under Chairman Kim Il Sung in 1948. Despite its name, North Korea was a one-party Communist state. The Americans occupied the agricultural South, which became the Republic of Korea under President Syngman Rhee in 1949.

The United States and the Soviet Union pulled their armies of occupation out of Korea in 1949 without resolving the tension between the two Koreas, which were bound to clash, given their different systems of government. North Korea invaded South Korea on June 25, 1950, with the goal of uniting the nation under Communist rule. United Nations forces, primarily Americans, fought on the side of South Korea, while Communist China sent troops to aid the North Koreans.

Eisenhower campaigned on a pledge to end the Korean War. By July 1953, with Eisenhower threatening to use nuclear weapons against North Korea, both sides agreed to an armistice. The terms restored the status quo that had existed before the war: Korea was divided along the 38th parallel, with the northern half under Communist rule and the southern half under democratic rule.

Social Changes, 1945–1960

The two biggest changes in everyday life in the United States after World War II were the migration to the suburbs and the invention of television. Suburbs were planned communities outside major cities. Developers bought large tracts of land and built entire communities. One of the most famous of these was Levittown, Pennsylvania, just across the Delaware River from the city of Trenton, New Jersey. Levittown was a community of more or less identical houses with garages, driveways, wide streets, and spreading lawns. Other Levittowns sprang up throughout the region. Newly- or recently-married veterans and their spouses thought the suburbs were ideal places to raise children. Because houses and cars were affordable in the postwar era, it was possible to live in the suburbs and work in the city. Racism also played a role in the white flight to the suburbs; thousands of African Americans had settled in northern cities during the Depression and World War II, and many whites refused to accept them as friends and neighbors. By 1960, almost one-third of the U.S. population—including only a very few black people—had moved to the suburbs.

The other major change was the habit of watching television. This "radio with pictures" was universally popular. People could watch a variety of programs on television: news broadcasts, comedies like *I Love Lucy*, sporting events like baseball games, game shows like *The $64,000 Question*, and dramas like *Playhouse 90*. Since anyone who owned a television could turn it on for free at any time, television networks could not charge audiences money. Instead, they paid their expenses by selling airtime to advertisers, who knew that their commercials would be viewed by thousands, perhaps millions, of people in their homes.

Civil Rights

Several important blows for racial integration were struck during the 1940s and 1950s. One was President Truman's integration of the armed forces and the federal bureaucracy. Another was Jackie Robinson's appearance in a Brooklyn Dodgers uniform in 1947. Until that spring, major-league baseball had had an unofficial "whites only" agreement. Black players had the Negro Leagues, with great stars like Satchel Paige, Oscar Charleston, and Cool Papa Bell. Dodgers' general manager Branch Rickey, determined to bring quality players to his team regardless of their race, sought out Robinson and offered him a contract. When players on other teams threatened to go on strike rather than play against an African American, National League president Ford Frick issued this statement:

> I do not care if half the league strikes. . . . I don't care if it wrecks the National League for five years. This is the United States of America, and one citizen has as much right to play as any other. The National League will go down the line with Robinson, whatever the consequences.

Robinson endured a difficult season of taunts, jeers, and death threats from the public, and a measure of hostility from many players. However, his superb skills eventually won his teammates and the fans over to his side. Other teams began hiring black players, and the Negro Leagues soon folded. Since baseball was played almost every day over the course of a six-month season, fans saw integration at work on a daily basis. This had a mitigating effect on many people's prejudices. Baseball is only a game, but it played an important role in the Civil Rights movement by making a highly visible statement about integration.

In Montgomery, Alabama, a tired seamstress named Rosa Parks refused one day give up her bus seat to a white passenger. In the segregated South, the rule was that white bus passengers sat in the front, black passengers in the back; if a white person got on when all the seats were filled, a black person had to give up his or her seat. Parks defied this rule and was arrested. The Montgomery Improvement Association initiated over a year-long citywide bus boycott, while the National Association for the Advancement of Colored People (NAACP) appealed Parks's case. In November 1956, the Supreme Court declared that segregated seating on city buses was unconstitutional. This case brought Martin Luther King, Jr. into prominence for the first time.

The final factor was the integration of schools. In 1952, the Supreme Court first heard a case called *Brown v. Board of Education*. African-American lawyer Thurgood Marshall called into question the "separate but equal" principle from *Plessy v. Ferguson*, arguing that segregation was not only unnecessary, but actively harmful to black students. In 1954, the court decided in favor of desegregation, noting that separate school systems were inherently and inevitably unequal. This decision made the segregation of public schools illegal as of 1954.

Reaction among white southerners was very much what it had been when slavery was outlawed. They were furious. Throughout the South, integration came slowly and painfully. The first black students to attend white schools had to be escorted by armed guards; even this did not stop white people from throwing rotten vegetables at them, jeering at them, and calling them foul names. However, the students continued to attend school in spite of constant harassment and threats. They were among the bravest Americans to play a role in the Civil Rights movement that would shape the following decade.

CHAPTER 26 QUIZ

1. **The Marshall Plan offered aid to** _____
   A. all the nations of Europe.
   B. all nations behind the Iron Curtain.
   C. all nations that had fought for the Allies during the war.
   D. all nations west of the Iron Curtain.

2. _____ **was one advantage of life under Communist rule.**
   A. Freedom of expression
   B. Comfortable housing
   C. High wages
   D. Full employment

3. **Which best describes the result of the Korean War?**
   A. a victory for Communist North Korea
   B. a victory for democratic South Korea
   C. a stalemate
   D. anarchy

4. **All of the following were fully racially integrated in the 1940s and 1950s except** _____
   A. major-league baseball.
   B. the armed forces.
   C. the public schools.
   D. the suburbs.

5. **Paul Robeson spoke admiringly of the Soviet Union because of its** _____
   A. hostility to the United States.
   B. racial equality.
   C. system of labor camps.
   D. courage during World War II.

6. **The term** *McCarthyism* **refers to the political technique of** _____
   A. campaigning for votes in small towns and rural areas.
   B. taking one's case to the people by means of radio and TV broadcasts.
   C. deliberately slandering opponents with false accusations.
   D. debating issues freely and seriously.

7. All these events made American society more democratic during the postwar era except _____
   A. the desegregation of the armed forces.
   B. the passage of the GI Bill of Rights.
   C. the activities of the House Un-American Activities Committee.
   D. the Supreme Court decision in *Brown v. Board of Education*.

8. All these people played major roles in the Civil Rights movement except _____
   A. Dwight D. Eisenhower.
   B. Thurgood Marshall.
   C. Rosa Parks.
   D. Jackie Robinson.

9. _____ was an important national priority during the Truman administration.
   A. The integration of society
   B. The nuclear arms race
   C. Winning the Korean War
   D. Reforming the banking system

10. The purpose of NATO and the Warsaw Pact was _____
   A. to create a stockpile of nuclear weapons that would be available to all member nations.
   B. to establish a common currency among the member nations.
   C. to abolish trade barriers among the member nations.
   D. to unite the member nations for their mutual defense if attacked.

Chapter 27

The New Frontier and the Civil Rights Movement, 1960–1964

The presidential election of 1960 brought the Democratic Party back to the White House. John F. Kennedy took the helm of American politics at a challenging and dangerous time, when the threat of nuclear war was at its height and Cold War tensions were growing.

At home, the Civil Rights movement that had begun in the 1950s continued to make advances. Under the leadership of Martin Luther King, Jr., African Americans organized nonviolent protests throughout the segregated South. The quiet, well-behaved protesters, exercising their First Amendment rights to "peaceably assemble," provided a strong contrast to the brutal armed policemen and the jeering crowds of segregationists. The protesters won public opinion over to their side, and by 1964 the Civil Rights Act had been signed into law, ending segregation in fact about 100 years after the Civil Rights amendments to the Constitution had ended it in law.

In foreign affairs, the United States was brought to the brink of nuclear war at least twice. East German officials under Soviet control, deciding to put a stop to the exodus of East Germans into West Berlin once and for all, built the Berlin Wall. The United States did not want to go to war over this issue, but Kennedy did fly to Berlin and give a strongly worded speech claiming that the rule of Communism had clearly failed when the East Germans had to resort to building a wall to keep people from leaving. Closer to home, the Cuban Missile Crisis developed when the Soviets installed nuclear missiles in Cuba, 90 miles from the U.S. coastline. During a tense two weeks, Kennedy responded with a naval blockade of Cuba. Although both nations were poised for nuclear war, Soviet premier Khrushchev withdrew at the last moment, ushering in a new era of attempting to find common ground between the two superpowers.

The nation and the world went into shock when Kennedy was assassinated on a campaign trip to Dallas, Texas. Lyndon Johnson took over the presidency and was soon to reshape the nation's domestic policies.

CHAPTER OBJECTIVES

- Discuss the election of 1960.
- Discuss Kennedy's foreign policy in Cuba and Berlin.
- Discuss the Civil Rights movement in the 1960s.
- Identify the significant figures of the era and describe their contributions.

Chapter 27 Time Line

●	1960	John F. Kennedy elected president
		Sit-ins in South
		Student Nonviolent Coordinating Committee formed
●	1961	Summit meeting between United States and Soviet Union
		Berlin Wall
●	1962	Cuban Missile Crisis
●	1963	Birmingham protests
		"I Have a Dream" speech
		Limited Nuclear Test Ban Treaty
		Kennedy assassinated; Lyndon B. Johnson becomes president
●	1964	Twenty-Fourth Amendment ratified
		Civil Rights Act of 1964

The Election of 1960

During President Truman's first term in office, Congress passed the Twenty-Second Amendment, which limited a president to two terms in office. The Republican majority in Congress wanted to ensure that no Democratic president would ever again, like FDR, be elected to four terms. Had this amendment not been ratified, the popular Dwight D. Eisenhower might well have served a third term; however, he had to step down in 1960.

The election of 1960 pitted Democratic Senator John F. Kennedy of Massachusetts against Republican Vice President Richard Nixon of California. Both men had been elected to the U.S. Congress in 1946; both had progressed from the House to the Senate, Nixon in 1950 and Kennedy in the following term. Kennedy had served there ever since, while Nixon had been Eisenhower's vice president since 1952, and hoped to profit from Eisenhower's enormous popularity. As a Catholic, Kennedy faced the same prejudice and bigotry that had helped to defeat Al Smith in 1928 (see Chapter 23), but American society had grown more tolerant in the intervening years. Whenever the issue came up, Kennedy handled it with poise and confidence, assuring voters that, he believed in the strict separation of church and state and that as president, he would neither speak for the Catholic Church nor permit it to speak for him. Religion was not a decisive factor in the 1960 election.

Kennedy was a charming and witty man whom audiences found irresistibly attractive. His appearance and personality combined to convey a youthful energy and optimism that people found appealing. Kennedy was also a highly skilled campaigner, good at dealing with people and with the press. Nixon's style was quite different; he had considerable political experience and was highly intelligent, but his stiff manner, his distrust and suspicion of reporters, and his determination to ignore his advisers and make all his own campaign decisions helped to defeat him. He was also handicapped in many people's minds because of his association with the House Un-American Activities Committee and because of the McCarthy-style campaign tactics that he had used throughout his political career.

The contrast between the two candidates was never more apparent than during the first televised presidential debates in history. Kennedy looked pleasant, open, and relaxed on camera; he also had a considerable command of the facts on the issues that came up in questions. The cameras were not nearly so kind to Nixon, and Kennedy's unexpected skills as a debater put Nixon on the defensive.

In November, the popular vote was so close that the outcome took a few days to call, but in the end Kennedy was chosen. Nixon later started a rumor that if he had demanded a recount of the votes in Illinois, the results might have been reversed. Nixon asserted that he had decided, for the good of the nation, that demanding a recount would be wrong. The facts belie the rumor: Kennedy won 303 electoral votes, Nixon 219, and Virginia Senator Harry Byrd 15. If Illinois' 27 electoral votes had been moved to Nixon's column, the totals would have been Kennedy 276, Nixon 246. With 270 electoral votes required to become president, Nixon would still have lost the election.

The Kennedy White House was characterized by style and flair. Many people have described the Kennedys as the closest thing the United States has ever had to a royal family. Much of this was due to First Lady Jacqueline Bouvier Kennedy. Mrs. Kennedy came from an upper-class family, had been educated in Paris, spoke French and Spanish fluently, dressed stylishly, and charmed everyone with her beautiful manners. She undertook the major project of restoring many of the public rooms in the White House, working hard to make it a visual record of presidential history. When the project was completed, the first lady gave a highly popular televised tour of the rooms, giving many Americans their first chance to see the inside of the Executive Mansion. Mrs. Kennedy also invited many of the day's most prominent artists and writers to White House state dinners, creating a cultural atmosphere that the White House had conspicuously lacked under the Trumans and Eisenhowers. The Kennedys were the youngest couple ever to live in the White House, and their two toddlers were popular subjects for photographers.

Foreign Policy

Cuba

The Bay of Pigs

As soon as he took office, Kennedy was plunged into dealing with pressing foreign policy concerns. President Eisenhower had done nothing to resolve the Cold War hostility with the Soviet Union. In 1959, rebel leader Fidel Castro had seized power in Cuba, turning it into a Communist state that he ruled as a military dictator. The presence of a Communist nation and potential Soviet ally only 90 miles from the U.S. coast was of grave concern. Before Eisenhower left office, the Central Intelligence Agency (CIA) had developed a plan to remove Castro from government. Kennedy approved the plan, which called for invading the island at a coral reef known as the Bay of Pigs. The invasion was a disastrous failure, marking the low point of Kennedy's administration. It strengthened the alliance between the Soviet Union and Cuba and increased the hostility that both nations felt toward the United States.

The Cuban Missile Crisis

Soviet leader Nikita Khrushchev met Kennedy for the first time at a European summit, and came away believing that the U.S. president was inexperienced and weak. Khrushchev therefore tested the United States by installing nuclear arms in Cuba. This meant that either Cuba or the Soviets could strike the United States from a very short distance away. It was a clear threat of a nuclear attack.

Kennedy responded by establishing a naval blockade of Cuba. He announced to the American people that the U.S. Navy would turn back all armed Soviet ships headed for the island. Both sides prepared for battle. The Soviet ships approached the blockade, then, to the surprise of the Americans, wheeled around and sailed back toward the USSR. Khrushchev then wrote to Kennedy, offering to dismantle the nuclear base in Cuba if the United States would agree to withdraw its own nuclear missiles from certain sites in Europe.

This was the closest that the two nations ever came to launching a nuclear war. Both Kennedy and Khrushchev acknowledged that they could not allow such a war to happen. From then on, the two nations began to try to find common ground and to achieve what later became known as *détente,* or "peaceful coexistence." In 1963, the two nations, along with Great Britain, signed the Limited Nuclear Test Ban Treaty, which ended the testing of nuclear bombs in the atmosphere and underwater.

Berlin

At Potsdam in 1945, the United States and the Allies had agreed to occupy Germany. (See Chapter 25.) There were several reasons for the occupation. First, the Allies wanted to purge Germany of Nazism and punish any surviving Nazis. Second, they intended to help the Germans set up a new, democratic government. Third, they would work with the Germans to install a new bureaucracy, including a police force. Fourth, they would work to reestablish society and the German economy, including everything from the school systems to the postal service to the transportation network.

The Soviets occupied the eastern half of Berlin; the western half was divided into American-, British-, and French-occupied zones. Before long, the three Western powers united their zones into one for economic purposes; Stalin's refusal to go along with their plan effectively made Berlin into two cities.

The Berlin Airlift

Since Berlin was many miles behind the Iron Curtain, West Berlin was entirely isolated and geographically very vulnerable to threats from the Soviets. In 1948, the USSR blocked all ground access to West Berlin, declaring that they had the right to do as they saw fit with East German roads, bridges, and railways. This was in effect an attempt at a siege; if supplies could not be delivered, the city would be forced to capitulate to Soviet control. The United States immediately organized the Berlin Airlift, which brought in food, fuel, and other supplies by plane. It took a good many flights to supply an entire city; on some days, American planes landed in West Berlin every few minutes. In 1949, the Soviets accepted defeat and ended the blockade. Soon after this, West Germany officially parted from East Germany. At that point, the two nations became known as the Federal Republic of Germany (West), a parliamentary democracy headed by Chancellor Konrad Adenauer, and the German Democratic Republic (East), a one-party Communist state headed by Chancellor Walter Ulbricht.

The Berlin Wall

During the 1950s, hundreds of thousands of East Germans sought economic opportunity, intellectual and artistic freedom, and political asylum by the simple means of walking or taking the subway across the border into West Berlin, then relocating to West Germany or another Western nation. By 1961, nearly 20 percent of the East German population had defected. The East Germans and the Soviets were well aware of this, and knew that it was the worst possible publicity for their system; they were especially concerned because the people most likely to escape to the West were intellectuals, artists, professors, scientists, and other valuable and highly trained professionals. They took drastic measures to stop the flow of emigration. One August morning in 1961, Berliners woke up to discover that during the night, the army had secretly begun construction of a physical barrier that entirely encircled West Berlin—a barbed-wire fence that would soon be replaced by a massive concrete wall, complete with armed guards and dogs.

THE MYTH

Kennedy used the German phrase *Ich bin ein Berliner* in his June 1963 speech at the Berlin Wall; the speech has always been known as the *Ich bin ein Berliner* speech. Ever since, there has been a legend that he made a ridiculous error—that in German, the word *Berliner* refers to a popular German jam-filled pancake or doughnut.

THE FACTS

Like many words, *Berliner* has more than one correct definition. The English word *pitcher*, for example, can refer either to a vessel used to hold beverages or to a baseball player who throws fastballs and curves. In German, as in English, context makes the speaker's meaning clear. In some regions of Germany, *Berliner* does indeed refer to the popular sweet dessert, but in Berlin and throughout the country, it also means "a person from Berlin."

On the day of his speech, Kennedy told his German interpreter that he wished to speak to his audience in their own language. The interpreter, a native German speaker from Berlin, would not have made a mistake in the wording, and would never have embarrassed a head of state from a friendly nation by telling him the wrong phrase. Video footage of the speech clearly shows the huge Berlin crowd roaring their approval when Kennedy attempted to speak their language (albeit with a strong Boston accent!).

Kennedy ended his speech with the words: "All free men, wherever they may live, are citizens of Berlin, and, therefore, as a free man, I take pride in the words *Ich bin ein Berliner.*" Literally, the phrase means "I am a Berliner (a person of Berlin)"; figuratively, Kennedy was saying, "I—and by extension all my countrymen—stand as one with the people of Berlin."

The Berlin Wall stopped the unquestioned westward migration. From that time on, East Germans had to have special permits to cross the border, and could stay in the West only for very limited periods of time. Travel from West to East was still unrestricted, but West Berliners had to carry identification so the guards would allow them to return home. In the Berlin metro system, the border between the two halves of the city became the last stop on all west-bound trains. Many people still found ways to escape. Some hid in the trunks of cars; some clung to the undercarriage of trains; some openly made a run for it. Some escapes were successful; others ended in death. The Berlin Wall soon became the most recognizable symbol of the Cold War era. In June 1963, Kennedy gave a memorable speech on the Western side of the Wall, in which he summed up the basic flaw in the Communist system:

> Freedom has many difficulties and democracy is not perfect, but we have never had to put a wall up to keep our people in, to prevent them from leaving us.

Kennedy had continued Eisenhower's policy of stockpiling nuclear weapons, but he had also created programs of his own to contain Communism in a more peaceful and constructive way. The Peace Corps recruited Americans to serve in a variety of foreign countries for two-year terms as teachers, farmers, engineers, doctors, and so on. When it began, the Peace Corps served 44 nations. This program helped foreign economies to recover, brought new technology to developing nations, and created good relations between them and the United States. It continues to this day.

The Civil Rights Movement

The Civil Rights movement is the name for the post-World War II campaign for the rights that African Americans had been granted on paper during and after the Civil War, but had all too often been denied in reality. Society had already taken some important first steps toward equality (see Chapter 26). President Kennedy supported the Civil Rights movement; his successor, President Johnson, passed substantial federal Civil Rights legislation. Both were frequently obliged to send federal troops to the South to deal with outbreaks of savagery between the police and the protesters.

In 1957, Martin Luther King, Jr. became the leader of the Southern Christian Leadership Conference (SCLC). This association of black churches adopted the philosophy of nonviolent resistance that King had learned from studying the writings of Mohandas Gandhi of India. Young followers of King and the SCLC formed their own organization, the Student Nonviolent Coordinating Committee (SNCC, pronounced "snick"). Jesse Jackson, who would later run for president of the United States, played a major role in SNCC activities.

The SNCC launched a campaign of sit-ins in 1958. Small groups of black students would go to whites-only lunch counters and sit down. When waitresses refused to serve them, they replied that they would not leave until they had been served. They remained until closing, studying their books, and returned the next day. Onlookers taunted them, poured ketchup and sugar over their heads, and threw food at them; the students continued to sit, not responding to the provocation. The sit-ins continued into 1960 and made national headlines. In the end, the students' determination and perseverance paid off; restaurants all across the South began serving black customers.

Participation in the Civil Rights movement was dangerous. Southern police officers and segregationists were frequently guilty of brutal beatings and other acts of violence. In the first years of school desegregation, armed guards had to protect black students from possible harm. NAACP secretary Medgar Evers is an example of a Civil Rights champion who was shot down and killed.

The nonviolent protests advocated by King worked because they provoked segregationists into behaving violently and thus alienating the general public. It was clear to most of the country by this time that the era of segregation had come to an end, and that Jim Crow laws were unconstitutional.

In 1963, the SCLC began concentrating its nonviolent protests on the city of Birmingham, Alabama. One protester described Birmingham as "the hardest and most mean-spirited establishment in the South." Many school-age children took part in the demonstrations, which drew a great deal of newspaper and television coverage. Americans across the country were horrified at the photographs and film of armed policemen setting dogs on crowds of peaceful protesters, or spraying fire hoses at large groups that included small children. Public opinion was quickly won over to the side of the protesters.

In the summer of 1963, the protesters gained one of their most important objectives. President Kennedy asked Congress to pass a bill that would make segregation in public places illegal. To celebrate this success and to keep the movement in the public eye, Civil Rights leaders organized a series of speakers at the Lincoln Memorial in Washington, D.C., where Marian Anderson had sung her historic concert in 1939 (see Chapter 24). In the most famous speech of his career, King described his dream of what the United States might become when it finally lived up to its promise of liberty and equality for all:

> Five score years ago, a great American, in whose symbolic shadow we stand today, signed the Emancipation Proclamation. . . . But one hundred years later, the Negro still is not free.
>
> . . . I have a dream that one day this nation will rise up and live out the true meaning of its creed: "We hold these truths to be self-evident: that all men are created equal."
>
> . . . when we let [freedom] ring from every village and every hamlet, from every state and every city, we will be able to speed up that day when all of God's children, black men and white men, Jews and Gentiles, Protestants and Catholics, will be able to join hands and sing in the words of the old Negro spiritual, "Free at last! free at last! thank God Almighty, we are free at last!"

King alluded to the text of the Gettysburg Address (which begins "Fourscore and seven years ago") and quoted from the Declaration of Independence. He quoted the lyrics of "My Country, 'Tis of Thee," the song Marian Anderson had used to begin her historic concert. He reminded everyone that African Americans had had full civil rights legally for the past 100 years, and that making that law into everyday fact was long overdue.

One year later, as King looked on, President Lyndon Johnson signed the Civil Rights Act of 1964 into law on July 2. The act had the following provisions:

- Banned racial, gender, religious, and ethnic discrimination in employment
- Made segregation illegal in all public places
- Allowed the federal government to sue public school systems that did not obey desegregation laws
- Removed certain voter-registration restrictions

The Space Race

When he became president, Kennedy challenged the scientific community to put a man on the moon by the end of the decade. Both the United States and the Soviet Union had already begun experimenting with space flight. In 1961, Soviet astronaut Yuri Gagarin became the first human being to orbit the Earth.

The United States matched this achievement in 1962, when John Glenn duplicated Gagarin's feat. Throughout the 1960s, the U.S. and Soviet space programs raced to be the first to have an astronaut walk on the surface of the moon. The United States finally accomplished this goal in 1969.

Kennedy's Assassination

On the morning of November 22, 1963, the president and first lady were riding in an open car through the streets of Dallas, campaigning for the 1964 election. Kennedy had brushed aside warnings from some of his close associates that he was taking a serious risk by making this appearance; his pro-Civil Rights stance had made southern segregationists hate him bitterly.

As the motorcade drove slowly through the Dallas streets, a young malcontent named Lee Harvey Oswald shot the president in the back of the head from the window of a schoolbook warehouse. Kennedy was rushed to the nearest hospital, but nothing could be done to save him. Within hours, a white-faced Mrs. Kennedy stood beside Lyndon Johnson as he took the oath of office. Oswald was apprehended promptly, and was shot in his turn by a gunman named Jack Ruby, who later died in prison. An investigation headed by Supreme Court Chief Justice Earl Warren found that both gunmen had acted alone, but this did not prevent a lively industry of conspiracy theorists from springing up.

Some days afterward, Washington, DC, was silent except for military drumbeats, its streets lined with crowds of mourners. In a solemn parade, the president's body was taken to Arlington National Cemetery, high on a hill overlooking the city. At the end of the parade, a thoroughbred black horse, riderless to symbolize the fallen leader, stepped with his head held high.

The president was mourned on every continent. Arthur Schlesinger, Jr., a prize-winning historian and one of Kennedy's close advisers, spoke for millions when he wrote:

> Above all he gave the world for an imperishable moment the vision of a leader who greatly understood the terror and the hope, the diversity and the possibility, of life on this planet and who made people look beyond nation and race to the future of humanity.

CHAPTER 27 QUIZ

1. **What was the purpose of the Berlin Airlift?**
   A. to get supplies to West Berlin in spite of the blockade
   B. to help people escape from East Berlin or East Germany
   C. to return German refugees to their homes after the war
   D. to provide aid to nations behind the Iron Curtain

2. **One important reason for the Allied occupation of Germany was** _____
   A. to help Germany rearm.
   B. to discuss plans for the United Nations.
   C. to obliterate all surviving elements of Nazism.
   D. to divide the country into two independent nations.

3. **The Berlin Wall was built in order to** _____
   A. prevent Westerners from entering East Berlin.
   B. prevent East Germans from entering West Berlin.
   C. block Allied or Western access to West Berlin.
   D. prevent violence from breaking out in Berlin.

4. **The main reason that public opinion outside the South turned against the segregationists was** _____
   A. the segregationists' violent and brutal behavior toward the peaceful protestors.
   B. the protestors' threat to take up arms against the segregationists.
   C. the active participation of white people in the protest movement.
   D. the threat that the United States would once again be torn apart by a civil war.

5. **Which best describes the Southern Christian Leadership Conference (SCLC)?**
   A. an underground paramilitary organization
   B. an organization of black college students
   C. an association of black churches
   D. a national political party

6. **The Civil Rights protest groups modeled their nonviolent philosophy on the teachings of** _____
   A. Jesus.
   B. Confucius.
   C. Muhammad.
   D. Gandhi.

7. **The sit-ins of the late 1950s focused on _____**
    A. desegregation of restaurants.
    B. the elimination of voting restrictions.
    C. integration of the public schools.
    D. integration of the armed forces.

8. **The "I Have a Dream" speech alluded to all these moments in U.S. history except _____**
    A. Marian Anderson's 1939 concert at the Lincoln Memorial.
    B. Abraham Lincoln's delivery of the Gettysburg Address.
    C. the repeal of Prohibition.
    D. the Declaration of Independence.

9. **Which event marked a major turning point toward peace in the Cold War?**
    A. the Berlin Airlift
    B. the building of the Berlin Wall
    C. the Bay of Pigs invasion
    D. the resolution of the Cuban Missile Crisis

10. **All these people played major roles in the Civil Rights movement except _____**
    A. Martin Luther King, Jr.
    B. Jesse Jackson.
    C. Medgar Evers.
    D. Richard Nixon.

Chapter 28

The Great Society, 1964–1968

A career politician from Texas, Lyndon B. Johnson seemed at first glance an unlikely champion of anti-poverty and civil rights legislation. Nonetheless, he became the president most responsible for ending racial segregation, and he pushed important social legislation through Congress that continues to protect the needy.

Johnson became president when Kennedy was assassinated. He carried out Kennedy's goal of making segregation illegal. After winning reelection in 1964, Johnson launched a major anti-poverty program known as the Great Society.

The Great Society is important in American history because it focused on a group that had received little benefit from any previous reform legislation—the rural poor. Urban workers had unionized and had benefited from legislation passed during the Progressive Era (see Chapters 19 and 20). European immigrants had worked hard and had seen to it that their children became educated, assimilated, productive citizens. However, the rural poor in the postwar era, coming from a background of generations of poverty, ignorance, and lack of choices, could not help themselves. The Great Society offered them opportunities that millions of them made the most of. As a result of legislation passed during the Johnson era, twelve million Americans rose above the economic poverty level.

The Civil Rights movement did not end with the signing of the Civil Rights Act of 1964. African Americans continued to fight for their rights, especially at the polls. By 1968, millions of unregistered African Americans had registered to vote, participating in the political process for the first time.

In the same era, women were fighting for their rights. With the sympathy of Presidents Kennedy and Johnson, and with Johnson's active support, women gained legal rights to equal pay. They also formed their own lobbying organization and continued to fight for greater social equality.

CHAPTER OBJECTIVES

- Discuss the career of Lyndon B. Johnson.
- Identify and describe the programs of the Great Society.
- Discuss the split that occurred in the Civil Rights movement in the late 1960s.
- Describe the women's movement in the late 1960s.
- Identify key figures of the era and match each one to his or her contributions to political developments and social reform.

Chapter 28 Time Line

- **1962**   Rachel Carson publishes *Silent Spring*
- **1963**   Lyndon B. Johnson becomes president
- **1964**   War on Poverty

  Great Society

  Johnson reelected

  Twenty-Fourth Amendment ratified
- **1965**   Medicare and Medicaid

  Malcolm X assassinated

  Department of Housing and Urban Development

  Corporation for Public Broadcasting

  Voting Rights Act

- **1966**   Black Panther Party
- **1968**   Poor People's Campaign

Martin Luther King, Jr. assassinated

Robert F. Kennedy assassinated

Lyndon Baines Johnson

Lyndon B. Johnson had run for president in 1960 against John F. Kennedy. At the Democratic convention, when it became clear that Kennedy would be the nominee, he startled his closest advisers by asking Johnson to be his running mate. The two men were very different in style and approach, although they shared many political goals.

Born and raised in Texas, Johnson had been a schoolteacher before running for Congress. He had served as Senate majority leader for a number of years and had compiled an impressive record of getting legislation passed: everyone agreed that Johnson had a knack for persuading his colleagues to vote their consciences, even when it meant crossing party lines. Johnson's presence on the Democratic ticket was responsible for Kennedy's showing as strongly as he did in the South; this was Johnson's own region, and he was well liked.

Although Johnson's experience and political savvy would have been of great value to the Kennedy administration, Kennedy's advisers disliked and distrusted him and largely ignored him. However, when Johnson was suddenly elevated to the presidency in 1963, he asked all of Kennedy's cabinet members to stay on. Johnson intended to see Kennedy's policies through, especially the Civil Rights Act.

In January 1964, Johnson launched the War on Poverty. Kennedy had conceived this program, but had not lived to see it through Congress. Johnson, who described himself as "an old Roosevelt New Dealer," was fully committed to social programs that would give opportunities to those who had been denied them for many decades. Johnson proposed the creation of the Office of Economic Opportunity, which administered anti-poverty programs such as Head Start (preschool education) and the Job Corps (work training for youth). Johnson also created the first Indian aid program that was run by the Indians themselves.

Johnson introduced his vision for the United States, which he called the Great Society, in speeches in the spring of 1964. He described an America that truly provided equal opportunity for all. In effect, this speech was Johnson's declaration of what he would do if elected president that fall. Johnson defeated Republican opponent Barry Goldwater in November in a popular and electoral landslide.

The Great Society

Johnson wasted no time in making his vision of a Great Society a reality. People remembered years later that on the night of his inauguration, he reminded them to get to bed early because there was hard work ahead the next morning. Johnson used his tremendous skills as a negotiator to persuade Congress to pass important social programs. All but about 20 of some 200 bills he presented to Congress between 1964 and 1968 became law.

This table shows the key programs of the Great Society.

Job Corps	Work training program for people aged 16 to 21
Head Start	Preschool education program for children from low-income families
Elementary and Secondary Education Act	Provided federal funding for schools in poor regions
Medicare	Federally funded health insurance for people age 65 and over
Medicaid	Federally funded health insurance for the needy
Corporation for Public Broadcasting	Federally and privately funded television network whose mission was to show educational programming
Omnibus Housing Act	Provided funding for urban renewal, and housing assistance for low-income families

Programs such as public TV and the National Endowment for the Arts improved the lives of all Americans. However, Johnson especially wanted to help the rural poor. He never forgot his young days in the classrooms of Texas, where he had taught the children of migrant workers and other poor people. These were the people he wanted to help the most because he felt they needed it most. Johnson believed that the purpose of government was to serve the people.

The Great Society also addressed environmental legislation. Years before, Roosevelt and Taft had passed important legislation in this area (see Chapter 20), but the post-World War II era threatened the environment with hazards that had not existed during the Progressive Era. Millions of cars on the highways contributed to an enormous air pollution problem. Air conditioners gave off dangerous fumes. In 1962, marine biologist Rachel Carson published *Silent Spring*, a book describing the devastation that chemical pesticides had wrought on the countryside. The spring, once a season of chirping birds, had become silent; hundreds of thousands of birds had died from exposure to DDT and other pesticides, or from eating the insects the DDT had poisoned. These pesticides harmed humans as well by contaminating the water and food supplies. Carson's book and the public response to it were responsible for a permanent ban on DDT, the most harmful of the pesticides. Johnson also urged Congress to pass laws that would control and improve air and water quality, along with other environmental bills.

The Supreme Court also contributed to the Great Society during the Kennedy–Johnson era. Led by Chief Justice Earl Warren, the Court set several important precedents during the 1960s. *Gideon v. Wainwright* stated that courts must provide attorneys for accused criminals who could not afford their own. *Escobedo v. Illinois* stated that an accused person had the right to have an attorney present during questioning by the police. *Miranda v. Arizona* stated that anyone being arrested must be informed of his or her rights to remain silent and to consult an attorney, in words familiar to millions from their repetition in television crime dramas.

The Warren Court decisions were important because they were designed to protect those who lacked education, wealth, power, and influence. Wealthy and middle-class Americans were usually well educated; they already knew their legal rights and could afford their own lawyers. The rest of society—by far the majority of those who got into trouble with police or the law—usually ended up as confused victims of a system whose workings they did not understand. The primary effect of the Warren Court decisions was to make the American justice system much more fair.

The Great Society lifted millions of Americans above the poverty level. It was an era of hope for those who had long ago lost hope. Later in Johnson's term, the Vietnam War (see Chapter 29) diverted funding from domestic social programs to the military. By the time Johnson left office, the Great Society had declined. However, some of its most important programs are still in place, providing essential services to those who need them most.

Civil Rights in the Late 1960s

Martin Luther King Jr.'s belief in nonviolence as an effective weapon against segregation began to lose its influence as the 1960s wore on. Other black leaders emerged in the movement, including many who wanted African Americans to take a more active role in achieving full equality.

One of the most important areas on which the movement concentrated was voter registration. In the segregated South, candidates for office were always white, and Jim Crow laws made it next to impossible for black Americans to vote; many did not bother to register anymore. In 1964, the Council of Federated Organizations coordinated voter registration drives throughout the South. Segregationists fought the voter registration drives by attacking, beating, and even shooting at the organizers. In the summer of 1964, known as "Freedom Summer," the voter registration project began recruiting white volunteers, hoping that segregationists might be more reluctant to attack them. When segregationists murdered two of these white volunteers, Johnson ordered the FBI to investigate.

In early 1965, King and others organized a peaceful Selma-to-Montgomery march to show support for voter registration. Police attacked the marchers with clubs and other weapons. President Johnson immediately called for a voting rights bill, which Congress passed in the summer of 1965. The Voting Rights Act put the voter registration process under federal, not state, control. Throughout the South, federal officials registered voters while segregationists, thwarted, stood by, furious but unable to do anything about it. African-American voter registration soared in the segregated South—in some areas it increased by more than 225 percent between 1965 and 1968.

The Nation of Islam

The original purpose of the Civil Rights movement had been to gain full equality in law and in fact for black Americans. In the mid-1960s, new black leaders began to advocate different goals and ideas. Elijah Muhammad, leader of the Nation of Islam or Black Muslims, urged African Americans not to join whites, but to create their own republic within the United States. Many members of the Nation of Islam changed their names, which had originally come to their families from white slave owners: Cassius Clay became Muhammad Ali, and Malcolm Little began referring to himself as Malcolm X.

Malcolm X criticized King and the other nonviolent leaders. He argued that black people should take what was theirs by right rather than negotiating for it. Rather than fighting for integration, he urged black people to consider separatism. His view attracted many Black Muslims. In 1965, however, a trip to Mecca changed Malcolm's views on separatism. When he began urging the unity of all Americans, three members of the Nation of Islam assassinated him.

The Black Panthers

Stokely Carmichael, a longtime SNCC member with his fair share of experience of segregationist violence, coined the phrase "black power" to describe what he claimed African Americans really wanted: separatism and recognition of their strength. The Black Power movement gave rise to the Black Panther Party, which advocated black separatism rather than integration and assimilation. Many Black Panthers openly carried guns and called for all African Americans to defend themselves if they were attacked or abused by the white establishment. They set the example by having a number of shootouts with police; Black Panther founder Huey Newton was convicted of manslaughter after one of these battles. This insistence on a violent response gave rise to a series of urban riots in major cities across the nation. It also caused many middle-class white Americans to lose sympathy for the Civil Rights movement.

In 1968, a sniper assassinated Martin Luther King Jr. African Americans across the nation were furious; a week of rioting killed 45 and injured thousands.

The Women's Movement

Throughout American history, women as a group had suffered unequal treatment under the law. Men—including free African men—had had the right to vote in 1776; women had to wait until 1920. Women had had to fight society's expectations in order to get an education and to be accepted in most professions. Upon her marriage, society expected a woman to give up her name and her job to run a household and raise children. Although running a household was a full-time job, the housewife was paid nothing; she was as dependent on the generosity of her husband as slaves had been on the generosity of their masters. For women who had been accustomed to earning a paycheck when single, this was galling and humiliating. Housework and motherhood provided little to satisfy the trained intelligence of college-educated women.

By the 1960s, some aspects of women's subordination in law and custom had changed. During the war years, many women had gone out to work in traditionally male jobs and had proved themselves very capable. By the 1960s, more and more middle- and upper-class young women were getting college educations. With college degrees, they were able to compete for skilled, highly-paid jobs. Women such as Congresswoman Jeanette Rankin and First Lady Eleanor Roosevelt were role models for those who wanted to achieve something in the professional world.

However, there were still inequities in the system. Few women were hired for government posts or elected to office. Throughout the workforce, women were generally paid less than men to do the same jobs. In 1963, President Kennedy signed the Equal Pay Act, which required employers to pay male and female workers the same wage for the same job. However, this act covered only about one-third of all working women because it did not apply to major industries such as agriculture and service.

The Civil Rights Act of 1964 included a provision called Title VII that outlawed sexual discrimination in employment. Ironically, this amendment to the act had been attached by a senator who opposed it; he had assumed that Title VII would lead to the entire act being voted down!

In June 1966, writer and activist Betty Friedan and other women formed the National Organization for Women (NOW). Since its inception, NOW has lobbied Washington politicians to ensure social and economic equality for women.

CHAPTER 28 QUIZ

1. The original purpose of the Corporation for Public Broadcasting was to provide _____

    A. news programs that were not funded by big business.

    B. programming on public affairs and current events.

    C. free daytime television.

    D. educational programming.

2. Rachel Carson is historically significant for bringing public attention to a major crisis in _____

    A. women's rights.

    B. African American rights.

    C. the national economy.

    D. the environment.

3. The Black Panther Party supported _____

    A. Great Society legislation.

    B. black integration and assimilation.

    C. black separatism and violence in return for violence.

    D. nonviolent sit-ins and peaceful protest marches.

4. All these programs were part of the Great Society except _____

    A. the Corporation for Public Broadcasting.

    B. the National Organization for Women.

    C. the Job Corps.

    D. the Omnibus Housing Act.

5. The Warren Court handed down decisions that had the effect of _____

    A. making the justice system more fair.

    B. improving the natural environment.

    C. decreasing the number of Americans living in poverty.

    D. negating the progress made under the Great Society programs.

6. The onset of _____ hampered the further development of Great Society programs.

    A. the Black Power movement

    B. the Vietnam War

    C. the women's movement

    D. the decisions of the Warren Court

7. Many Black Muslims changed their names in the 1960s because _____
   A. their religion required them to take Arabic names.
   B. their names were originally those of their ancestors' white masters.
   C. they did not believe in nonviolent protest.
   D. they were determined to win the right to vote.

8. The Head Start program provided _____ for low-income families.
   A. job training
   B. federally funded insurance
   C. preschool education
   D. urban renewal

9. All these people were associated with the cause of black separatism
   except _____
   A. Huey Newton.
   B. Stokely Carmichael.
   C. Malcolm X.
   D. Martin Luther King, Jr.

10. _____ is historically significant for playing a major role in the
    women's movement.
    A. Rachel Carson
    B. Betty Friedan
    C. Jeanette Rankin
    D. Earl Warren

Chapter **29**

The Vietnam War, 1961–1975

The Vietnam War was unlike any other war in which the United States had participated. It lasted for more than ten years, it was never formally declared by Congress, and it ended in an inglorious retreat.

The United States became involved in Vietnam because American leaders wanted to contain communism in Asia. Rather than supporting the Vietnamese declaration of independence under Ho Chi Minh, the United States helped to broker an international agreement that divided Vietnam into two nations, which were to reunite and hold free elections in 1956. Meanwhile, the United States backed the government of Ngo Dinh Diem in South Vietnam and sent troops to help train the South Vietnamese army. Deservedly unpopular, Diem was assassinated in 1963, just three weeks before Kennedy.

Lyndon Johnson stepped up bombing in Vietnam and sent hundreds of thousands more troops. However, the Viet Minh and their southern allies the Viet Cong proved impossible to pin down in conventional battles. They fought the war on their own terms, by jungle ambush. U.S. bombs were destructive, but they were ineffective at accomplishing any strategic objectives.

Richard Nixon became president in 1968 on a promise to end the war, which had stirred up unprecedented public opposition, particularly among young Americans. He lied to Congress, the people, and the military about his intentions and actions, secretly invading and attacking neutral Cambodia. In 1975, the Americans were forced to abandon the fight.

The unveiling of the Vietnam Veterans Memorial on the Mall in Washington, DC, in 1982 helped the nation to heal. This memorial publicly honored the Vietnam veterans for the first time.

CHAPTER OBJECTIVES

- Describe the political situation that arose in Vietnam after World War II.
- Compare and contrast the policies of Ho and Diem.
- Explain how the United States got involved in the Vietnam War.
- Describe the course of the fighting.
- Explain how the Vietnam War ended, and describe its effects on the United States at home.

Chapter 29 Time Line

● 1940   Japanese occupy French Indochina (Vietnam)

● 1941   Ho Chi Minh organizes the Viet Minh

● 1945   Japan withdraws from Indochina

         Viet Minh declare independence

● 1946   U.S. allies with French against Vietnamese

● 1954   Viet Minh defeat French at Dien Bien Phu

         Geneva Conference on Indochina: Vietnam divided along 17th parallel

● 1955   Ngo Dinh Diem becomes president of Republic of Vietnam (South Vietnam)

● 1960   National Liberation Front and Viet Cong begin attacking South Vietnam

● 1960–1963   American troops go to South Vietnam, first as military advisers, then as combatants

● 1963   Diem assassinated

         Tonkin Gulf Resolution

- **1965**   Military draft in United States

  Operation Rolling Thunder

  First national antiwar demonstration in Washington, DC
- **1966**   Congressional hearings on Vietnam
- **1968**   Tet Offensive

  Robert F. Kennedy assassinated

  Richard Nixon elected president
- **1969**   U.S. troop withdrawals begin

  United States bombs Cambodia
- **1970**   Kent State massacre

  Tonkin Gulf Resolution repealed
- **1971**   Twenty-Sixth Amendment ratified

  The *New York Times* publishes the Pentagon Papers
- **1972**   Major North Vietnamese invasion of South Vietnam

  Nixon reelected
- **1973**   Cease-fire agreement between United States and North Vietnam

  War Powers Act
- **1975**   Saigon evacuated; South Vietnam surrenders to North Vietnam
- **1982**   Vietnam Veterans Memorial dedicated

Background: Vietnam

The East Asian peninsula of Vietnam is a long, narrow country, bordered by China, Cambodia, Laos, and the South China Sea. The Chinese wanted control of this fertile rice-growing nation, and occupied it from 200 BC until AD 939, when the Vietnamese won a measure of independence. In 1428, Vietnam finally won complete independence from China.

France seized control of Vietnam, Cambodia, and Laos in 1883, combining the three nations into one colony called French Indochina. Nguyen Tat Thanh, one of the leaders of the Vietnamese resistance to French authority, became known to history as Ho Chi Minh, or "He Who Enlightens." During the 1940s,

Ho organized a resistance movement known as the Viet Minh, or the League for the Independence of Vietnam. In 1945, France refused to accept Ho's declaration of Vietnamese independence; the United States supported France, both because it was a longtime ally and because Ho was a Communist.

After World War II, one Southeast Asian/Pacific Island nation after another turned Communist, seeming to prove Eisenhower's "domino theory" that when one fell, it would knock the next one over. The United States poured money into the French effort to regain control over Indochina, while Communist China aided the Viet Minh. The guerrilla tactics of the Viet Minh were very effective against a French fighting force that was unfamiliar with the Vietnamese jungles. At Dien Bien Phu in northern Vietnam, the Viet Minh outnumbered and trapped the French. American reinforcements never arrived; President Eisenhower did not want to commit American troops to another war in Asia so soon after their return from Korea. The French surrendered on May 7, 1954.

The peace conference in Geneva involved several nations: France, Vietnam, Cambodia, Laos, China, the Soviet Union, Great Britain, and the United States. China had two goals: to limit American influence in Asia, and to prevent Vietnam from becoming a strong, united nation. The United States wanted to limit Communist influence in the region. In the end, the nations agreed to divide Vietnam along the 17th parallel, with the Viet Minh taking control in North Vietnam and the French taking control in the south. With the United States abstaining, the other nations agreed that in 1956, Vietnam would hold general elections and reunify the nation under one government.

With American backing, government official Ngo Dinh Diem became president of the Republic of South Vietnam in 1955; in a so-called election, he received far more votes than there were voters to cast them. Diem was highly unpopular among his subjects for several reasons. First, he was a Catholic in a Buddhist nation. Second, his policies benefited the rich and harmed the working poor. Third, he placed his relatives, regardless of their abilities, in powerful positions in the government. Fourth, he was ruthless to all who disagreed with him politically, often having people tortured or imprisoned.

The Geneva Accords stated that Vietnam should have had free elections in 1956. Diem refused to hold the election, as he was certain that he would lose to Ho Chi Minh in spite of secret U.S. operations to sabotage a likely Communist victory. Underground resistance to Diem's policies continued. The Viet Minh had taken control of North Vietnam, but many of its members had stayed in South Vietnam. Now the Viet Minh in the north began sending weapons to those in the south, who became known as the Viet Cong. In 1960, they formed an organization called the National Liberation Front with the goal of overthrowing Diem's government and reuniting the two halves of Vietnam under Communist rule.

The United States Sends Troops

Eisenhower was the first U.S. president to send troops to Vietnam, although the number was limited to several hundred "military advisers" whose job was to train the official army of South Vietnam (not the Viet Cong). Sharing Eisenhower's apprehension about the spread of communism in Asia, Kennedy committed more troops to the peninsula. By 1963, there were more than 16,000 U.S. troops in Vietnam, and Kennedy had authorized them to respond to the fierce assaults of the Viet Cong. It was this gradual buildup of troops and the escalation into combat by slow stages that was responsible for the lack of an official declaration of war by Congress.

In 1963, Henry Cabot Lodge, the U.S. ambassador to South Vietnam, scheduled meetings with Diem; the United States hoped to persuade Diem to relax a brutal campaign he had launched against the Buddhist population. When Diem refused to discuss his actions with Lodge, the United States gave its support to a group of South Vietnamese who intended to unseat Diem. When the plotters murdered Diem and his brother, the United States was taken aback, not having anticipated an assassination. Three weeks later, Kennedy himself was assassinated. It was then up to Lyndon Johnson to deal with the American involvement in Vietnam.

The Vietnam War Expands

Early in the morning of July 30, 1964, South Vietnamese patrol boats shelled two small North Vietnamese naval bases in the Gulf of Tonkin. In retaliation, North Vietnamese torpedo boats attacked the U.S. destroyer *Maddox*, which was stationed in the waters of the Gulf of Tonkin. The *Maddox* and the nearby *Ticonderoga* fired on the torpedo boats, sinking one and damaging the other two.

At the time, President Johnson was campaigning for reelection and felt that he needed to appear aggressive in the eyes of the voters. On August 4, Johnson received a report from the navy stating that although visibility in the Gulf was not good, the North Vietnamese appeared to have attacked again. During the afternoon, someone leaked the news of this second attack to the press, erroneously saying that it was a certainty rather than a possibility. In the years since, official documents have made it clear that this apparent second attack probably never took place; foggy weather conditions and ambiguous sonar readings misled the naval commanders. The Johnson administration knew that the press announcement was wrong, but was afraid that denying or correcting it would look like either cowardice or a cover-up.

That evening, the United States launched an air attack on North Vietnamese bases and patrol boats. At midnight, Johnson spoke to the American public on television, informing them of the "unprovoked attacks" by the North Vietnamese and stating that he had asked Congress to authorize the use of military force against North Vietnam. Congress agreed to pass the Gulf of Tonkin Resolution, effectively signing away its own constitutional power of declaring war:

Resolved by the Senate and House of Representatives of the United States of America in Congress assembled, That the Congress approves and supports the determination of the President, as Commander in Chief, to take all necessary measures to repel any armed attack against the forces of the United States and to prevent further aggression.

The resolution went on to state two important things: first, that it would expire as soon as the president determined that peace had been securely established, and second, that Congress could repeal it at any time by majority vote.

In November, Johnson was reelected president. Early in 1965, he ordered the Selective Service to begin sending out draft notices. Because of the system of draft deferments and exemptions, young men and boys from poor or working families served in far greater numbers than those from well-off families. For example, college students—most of whom were from upper- or middle-income families—were eligible for deferments. In 1965, almost 25 percent of all U.S. casualties in Vietnam were African Americans, although they made up only about 10 percent of the total American population. Hispanics also served in Vietnam in disproportionate numbers. More than 10,000 women served in Vietnam as field nurses and in other positions where they were in the thick of the fighting, although they did not actually carry guns in combat. More than 40,000 more women served as volunteers with organizations such as the Red Cross.

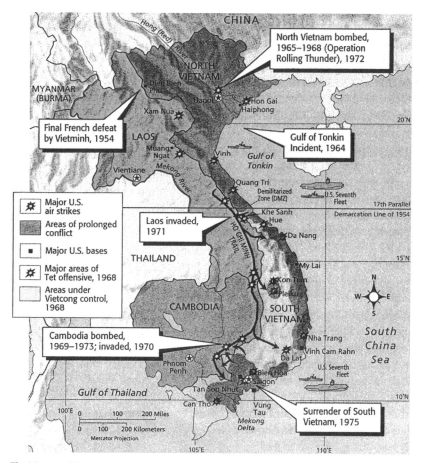

The Vietnam War

Combat in Vietnam, 1965–1968

Hoping for a quick victory, the U.S. armed forces launched an air war called Operation Rolling Thunder against the North Vietnamese and the Viet Cong. It proved completely ineffective. The Vietnamese were adept at guerrilla warfare, hiding in the jungles, traveling through them unerringly, and ambushing U.S. troops, always catching them by surprise. Supplies traveled between the Viet Minh and the Viet Cong along the Ho Chi Minh Trail, a complicated pathway through the jungles. Bombing was of no avail against the efficiency of the jungle route. If an American bomb destroyed a bridge, the Viet Cong either rebuilt it or swam the river it crossed. The Viet Cong also built a series of underground bomb shelters where its fighters could hide themselves, their weapons, and their supplies in safety.

Conventional bombs were not the only American weapons. Firebombs filled with napalm and cluster bombs that showered sharp slivers of metal were popular weapons. Troops sprayed forests with a deadly chemical known as Agent Orange. It killed most vegetation, thus robbing the Viet Minh of their jungle cover.

When the bombing proved ineffective, the United States tried ground war. Between 1965 and 1967, the United States sent another 300,000 troops to Vietnam. Because of the guerrilla style of war and the fact that they were much less familiar with the jungles than the Vietnamese, the Americans had little chance of making any progress. Their attempts to stamp out Viet Cong resistance grew increasingly more desperate; in the end, hundreds of thousands of Vietnamese civilians were killed, caught in the crossfire. Many South Vietnamese joined the Viet Cong.

Protest and Dissent at Home

The Vietnam War was different from World War II in almost every possible respect. The United States entered World War II as a united nation; no one objected to fighting Japan, because Japan had directly attacked the United States. Once the United States was involved, there were no serious objections to sending troops to Europe as well. Americans believed that it was right and proper for the United States to aid its European allies in the fight against Germany. In addition, the United States had come out of World War I strong and victorious; Americans expected the same result in World War II. The moral issues surrounding World War II were simple and clear: to defend Europe against unprovoked German aggression, and to defend the United States against Japan.

The Vietnam War was different in many respects. The moral issues were murky—so much so that a large-scale antiwar movement developed. Americans joined the antiwar movement for a variety of reasons. Some were pacifists who did not believe in any war. Some wanted their tax dollars to go to the social programs of the Great Society rather than to the Defense Department. Some were afraid that the war would escalate into a nuclear conflict. Some did not understand why the United States was interfering in the affairs of a tiny, poverty-stricken Asian nation on the other side of the world. Some knew young men and women who were serving in Vietnam and wanted their loved ones home again. Some were angry that black men were expected to fight and die for a nation that discriminated against them at home; boxing champion Muhammad Ali was only one of many Black Muslims who requested conscientious objector status on the grounds of religion.

Television coverage made a significant contribution to the antiwar movement. The Vietnam War was the first war to receive daily TV coverage in an era when almost every American home had a TV set. People had seen newsreel footage of World War II and the Korean War in movie theaters, but this was not the same as seeing such footage every evening in one's own home. Television coverage was big business; TV news networks joined the major newspapers in sending reporters and photographers to Vietnam to cover the action.

Americans soon became aware that the optimistic statements from the White House did not seem to match the unrelenting combat they saw on television night after night. Journalists in Vietnam who saw the action for themselves also criticized the administration for having lost control of the war.

On April 17, 1965, some 20,000 people came to Washington, DC to hold the nation's first large-scale antiwar protest. The organizing group, Students for a Democratic Society, sent Congress a petition calling for an immediate end to the war. Similar demonstrations would be held often during the next ten years. Many young men burned their draft cards in protest, or fled to Canada to avoid having to serve in a war that they thought was unjustified. Others agitated for more political power. Young men could be drafted into the military at age 18; they argued that if they were old enough at 18 to die for their country, they were old enough to vote for the leaders who sent them to war. There was widespread support for this logic, and the Twenty-Sixth Amendment, which lowered the voting age from 21 to 18, was ratified in 1971.

The antiwar movement divided the generations. The World War II generation felt that the young antiwar protestors were unpatriotic and cowardly. In countless families, parents found themselves at serious political and philosophical odds with their sons and daughters.

The Tet Offensive

On January 30, 1968 (the Vietnamese New Year, or Tet), the North Vietnamese and the Viet Cong launched a major offensive against U.S. troops and their allies, fighting them even in the streets of downtown Saigon. The United States and the South Vietnamese repelled the attackers and lost only about a tenth as many soldiers as the Communists, but the offensive was a tactical success for the North Vietnamese because it proved that they would never give in and that they might launch an attack anywhere at any time.

In March 1968, Johnson announced that he would not run for reelection (he was eligible to do so under the Twenty-Second Amendment because he had served less than two years of Kennedy's term). The leading Democratic candidate was the enormously popular Senator Robert F. Kennedy, who had served in his brother's cabinet as attorney general. Kennedy had spoken out on the issue of Vietnam, calling for a negotiated settlement. When he was shot by an assassin after the California primary election, the Democrats lost their best hope of keeping the White House. Republican Richard Nixon, promising that he had a secret plan to end the war, was elected in a close contest against Johnson's vice president, Hubert Humphrey.

The War under the Nixon Administration

Nixon and his national security advisor Henry Kissinger came up with a plan to turn the war over to the Vietnamese by gradually withdrawing American troops. Nixon hoped that this strategy would result in a stable, democratic South Vietnam. The North Vietnamese agreed to peace talks only on condition that the United States set a date for the withdrawal of troops. As it turned out, withdrawal was a slow process; there were still 24,000 American soldiers in Vietnam at the end of Nixon's first term.

Early in 1969, Nixon personally ordered the bombing of Cambodia, the neutral nation that bordered on Vietnam. Nixon believed that this strategy would force the Vietnamese to abandon the Ho Chi Minh Trail and prove to the North Vietnamese that the United States was militarily forceful. Nixon informed no one—not Congress, not the voters, not even key military leaders—about the bombing of Cambodia. In 1970, when the Cambodians overthrew their government in favor of a pro-U.S. leader, Nixon finally revealed his strategy. He then sent tens of thousands of United States and South Vietnamese troops to Cambodia.

Nixon's attack on Cambodia was an important issue because it directly addressed the balance of power that is built into the Constitution. Article I, Section 8 of the Constitution specifically grants Congress the power to declare war. Article II, Section 2 specifically states that the president is commander in chief of the military. In other words, only Congress can declare war, but only the president can dictate how a war will be fought once it is under way. In this way, the legislative and executive powers balance each other in the area of foreign affairs. When Nixon informed Congress of the U.S. attack on Cambodia, Congress was outraged: the president had taken upon himself the congressional power to declare war.

Nixon argued that the Tonkin Gulf Resolution gave him the power to take any action he saw fit to bring about peace in Vietnam. Congress argued that the Tonkin Gulf Resolution did not permit the president to make war on a neutral nation without congressional consent. Congress repealed the Gulf of Tonkin Resolution in 1970; when Nixon refused to acknowledge the repeal, Congress cut off funding for the war. In 1973, Congress would pass the War Powers Act, which allowed a president to commit troops to a foreign war for only 60 days without congressional approval.

Across the country, Americans began a new wave of antiwar demonstrations. In 1970, after someone set fire to a Kent State University ROTC building, National Guard troops were sent to the university to restore order. They fired at random into a large group of students, none of whom were demonstrating at the time, killing four students and wounding nine more. The Kent State massacre and a similar incident a few days later at Mississippi's Jackson State College shocked the nation and set off a chain of strikes and demonstrations on college campuses across the country.

In 1971, former Defense Department official Daniel Ellsberg gave the *New York Times* copies of secret government documents for publication. Known ever since as the Pentagon Papers, these documents revealed that successive U.S administrations had lied to the public about their policies and actions in Vietnam. Public support for the war, already low, was eroded even further by this concrete evidence that the government had acted in bad faith.

The End of the War

Kissinger and the North Vietnamese leader Le Duc Tho had been meeting secretly since 1969, trying to reach a peace settlement agreeable to both sides. In January 1973, after a final fierce bombing assault by the United States had failed to force a surrender, Le Duc Tho and Kissinger agreed on the following terms:

- A cease-fire
- U.S. help in rebuilding South Vietnam
- An exchange of prisoners of war

In 1975, the military government that had been established in South Vietnam collapsed. North Vietnamese troops invaded Saigon. The last remaining Americans, along with more than 100,000 Vietnamese, were evacuated by helicopter. On April 30, 1975, South Vietnam finally surrendered; the two halves of the nation were officially reunited under Communist rule in 1976.

The war was a dreadful disaster for Vietnam. The land was devastated and hundreds of thousands had been killed. Thousands more had been driven from their homes and lost everything they had. Cambodia was in similar distress. Exposure to the poisonous Agent Orange had disabled thousands of civilians, as well as soldiers on both sides.

CHAPTER 29 QUIZ

1. **Diem refused to hold elections in 1956 because** _____
   A. he did not trust the United States.
   B. he did not believe in the possibility of civil war.
   C. he had not participated in the Geneva Accords.
   D. he believed that he would lose to Ho.

2. **The Tonkin Gulf Resolution gave the president the power to take all necessary measures to** _____
   A. attack any foreign nation.
   B. sign peace treaties with foreign nations.
   C. repel foreign attacks on the U.S. military.
   D. amend the Constitution.

3. _____ **inspired Congress to repeal the Tonkin Gulf Resolution.**
   A. The Kent State massacre
   B. The bombing of Cambodia
   C. The election of Richard Nixon
   D. The release of the Pentagon Papers

4. **The Tet Offensive proved to the United States that** _____
   A. the Vietnamese would eventually gain their independence.
   B. the Viet Minh and the Viet Cong would never surrender.
   C. the war could not be won without bombing Cambodia.
   D. it would have to send more troops to Vietnam.

5. **Which best describes the effect of television coverage of the war on the American public?**
   A. It made the public aware that the White House was not being honest about the situation.
   B. It helped the public to understand the issues over which the war was being fought.
   C. It rallied the public in support of the war.
   D. It discouraged the public from taking any part in the political process.

6. **All these combined to make the United States launch a 1964 air attack on North Vietnam except** _____
   A. misinformation from the navy in the Gulf of Tonkin.
   B. an untrue or exaggerated statement made to the American press.
   C. campaign pressure on Lyndon Johnson to appear bold and decisive.
   D. official requests for U.S. aid from South Vietnam.

7. **The purpose of Operation Rolling Thunder was** _____
   A. to defend the capital city of South Vietnam.
   B. to retaliate for the assassination of Diem.
   C. to win a victory quickly.
   D. to destroy North Vietnam.

8. **All of the following contributed to the antiwar movement except** _____
   A. fear that the war would escalate into a nuclear conflict.
   B. television coverage that showed exactly what combat was like.
   C. the release of the Pentagon Papers.
   D. the passage of the Gulf of Tonkin Resolution.

9. **By secretly bombing Cambodia, Nixon violated the constitutional principle of** _____
   A. separation of powers.
   B. judicial review.
   C. national security.
   D. freedom of information.

10. **Which best describes the official end to the war as far as the U.S. role was concerned?**
    A. The United States surrendered to North Vietnam.
    B. The United States withdrew as part of a cease-fire agreement.
    C. The United States defeated North Vietnam.
    D. U.S. troops continued to occupy South Vietnam until reunification.

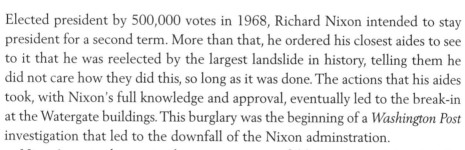

Chapter **30**

The Nixon Era and Watergate, 1968–1974

Elected president by 500,000 votes in 1968, Richard Nixon intended to stay president for a second term. More than that, he ordered his closest aides to see to it that he was reelected by the largest landslide in history, telling them he did not care how they did this, so long as it was done. The actions that his aides took, with Nixon's full knowledge and approval, eventually led to the break-in at the Watergate buildings. This burglary was the beginning of a *Washington Post* investigation that led to the downfall of the Nixon adminstration.

Nixon's major legacy to the nation was twofold. On the positive side, he eased the tense American relationship with the Soviet Union and paved the way for more cordial relations with China. On the negative side, he played the leading role in a major political conspiracy to subvert the electoral process.

The important issue involved in the Nixon scandals is the notion of representative government and the power of the law over all citizens. The Americans' early experience of being ruled without representation had led them to devise a government of checks and balances to ensure that the government could not become tyrannical. The Constitution does not allow the president the same privileges as a dictator or an absolute monarch. Nixon's behavior violated this principle. When asked about his illegal activities, he was quoted as saying "If the president does it, it isn't illegal." Nixon genuinely believed that the president was above the law, with absolute power to make whatever decisions he believed were in the best interest of the nation. He believed that a Nixon presidency was in the nation's best interest; on that basis, he did everything he could to ensure that he got reelected and he clung to his official position even when the nation began to turn against him.

Nixon's position—that the U.S. president is above the law—is simply not tenable. The U.S. Constitution is based on long-standing British principles that state that no one, including the monarch, is above the law; the Magna Carta of 1215 spells this out clearly. By the same token, the U.S. Constitution includes procedures by which the president can be removed from office for "high crimes and misdemeanors." If a president can commit crimes, he is clearly not above the law.

CHAPTER OBJECTIVES

- Describe foreign policy under the Nixon administration.
- Describe Nixon's domestic policies.
- Discuss the Watergate scandal and the fall of the Nixon presidency.

Chapter 30 Time Line

- **1968**   Richard Nixon elected president
- **1969**   Warren Burger appointed to the Supreme Court
- **1970**   Congress creates the Environmental Protection Agency
- **1971**   Nixon aides begin to compile "enemies list"
- **1972**   Nixon visits China

  Nixon visits Soviet Union; signs SALT Treaty

  Break-in at Democratic headquarters in Watergate buildings

  Nixon reelected
- **1973**   Senate begins investigating Watergate scandals

  Vice president Agnew resigns; replaced by Gerald Ford

  Saturday Night Massacre

- **1973–1974**   Energy crisis
- **1974**   Taped Oval Office conversations made public

  Nixon resigns; Ford becomes president

  Ford pardons Nixon

  Carl Bernstein and Bob Woodward publish *All the President's Men*

Richard Nixon

Richard Nixon began his political career in his native state of California, running for Congress during the 1940s. He took advantage of the postwar "Red Scare" to accuse his opponents of sympathizing with communism; the accusations were false, but the mere mention of the word *communism* was enough to alienate voters at that time. Before he joined the Senate, Nixon had been active in the House Un-American Activities Committee. (See Chapter 26 for more on this committee.) Eisenhower only reluctantly agreed to accept Nixon as his running mate in 1952, for lack of a better candidate; many Americans, including many Republicans, were uneasy about Nixon's fitness to hold high office.

Nixon believed that the press was little more than a hostile conspiracy against him; still, the majority of the nation's newspapers endorsed him for president. After losing to Kennedy in 1960, Nixon returned to California and ran for governor in 1962. During this campaign, he deliberately leveled false charges at his Democratic opponents—suggesting, for instance, that they had helped to lead a political riot in San Francisco in 1960. Nixon's campaign also sent out mailings purporting to come from the Democratic Party and released doctored photographs of Governor Pat Brown, the incumbent, that pictured him with people he had never actually met. These unethical tactics failed to win Nixon the election. However, he would use them again in the future.

The 1968 Election

Well aware that no Republican could beat Lyndon Johnson in 1964, Nixon sat out the presidential election. By 1968, however, the situation had changed. Americans desperately wanted some stability in society. John F. Kennedy, Martin Luther King Jr, Medgar Evers, Malcolm X, and Robert F. Kennedy had all been assassinated; Governor George Wallace of Alabama had been paralyzed by an assassin's bullet. The war in Vietnam raged on with no end in sight. War protesters continued to demonstrate. Nixon capitalized on the unrest by depicting himself as a law-and-order candidate who would bring new leadership to the nation and restore peace both at home and abroad.

The Democratic Party was deeply divided over the issue of Vietnam. Antiwar demonstrators clashed violently with police in Chicago during the Democratic Party convention. These riots were a symbol of the generational split that the Vietnam War had created at home. The younger generation had created a counterculture, burning draft cards, smoking marijuana, taking drugs, running away from home, dressing in outlandish styles, and defying all authority. To the older generation, this created a climate of uncertainty and fear. People of this generation turned away from the Democratic Party in large numbers to vote for Nixon, who won the presidency over Hubert Humphrey by about 500,000 votes.

Domestic Policy under Nixon

Nixon opposed most of Johnson's Great Society programs; in his view, they were charitable handouts rather than attempts to provide poor people with the same opportunities as wealthier ones. Under the Great Society, the welfare rolls had swelled to more than double what they had been in 1960. Nixon's first welfare-reform plan was called the Family Assistance Plan, in which adults would work in exchange for a guaranteed minimum salary. The Senate did not pass this plan.

Nixon had four opportunities to appoint new justices to the Supreme Court. All of his choices were conservative—two of them so conservative that the Senate refused to confirm them. In the end, Warren Burger became the new chief justice, and Harry Blackmun, Lewis Powell, and William Rehnquist were confirmed as associate justices. Over the years, both Burger and Blackmun proved to be much more moderate in their decisions than Nixon had anticipated.

Domestic energy policy was tied to foreign policy, because the United States had to import most of the oil it used for gasoline and heat. A cartel called OPEC (the Organization of Petroleum Exporting Countries) determined how much to charge for the oil it exported. Of the twelve OPEC nations, ten were Arab states that deeply resented American support for Israel, a state established by international agreement after World War II as a homeland for tens of thousands of displaced European Jews. The land set aside for the state of

Israel had belonged to the Jews in biblical times, but had been held by Arabs for many centuries; therefore, it was a bitter bone of contention between the two peoples.

In a series of wars between Israel and the Arab nations, the United States sided with Israel. OPEC retaliated by refusing to ship oil to the United States, then by sharply raising the price when they resumed shipping. By December 1973, the price had risen by nearly 400 percent. This caused a severe energy crisis in the United States. Nixon called for the conservation of energy, and also investigated ways in which the United States could become less dependent on foreign oil. Nuclear power plants were one such source of energy, but many Americans were nervous about the possibility of an accident or a leak of harmful radiation.

Nixon supported the creation of the Environmental Protection Agency, long before protecting the environment became fashionable among the general public. He also signed several bills that protected the environment and ordered businesses to contribute to cleaning up the environmental waste and pollution their factories created.

Foreign Policy

In the area of foreign policy, Nixon worked closely with his national security adviser (later secretary of state) Henry Kissinger. Kissinger was one of very few associates whom the president trusted. (See Chapter 29 for Nixon and Kissinger's Vietnam policy.)

By the 1970s, China and the Soviet Union, the world's two largest nations, both ruled by Communist regimes, were at odds with each other. Nixon felt that the time was ripe for reestablishing friendly relations between China and the United States, which had been suspended when China became a Communist state. In 1972, Nixon traveled to China, where he and Chinese premier Zhou Enlai agreed to work together to maintain peace in the Pacific and to develop trade relations between China and the United States. Nixon also agreed to withdraw U.S. troops from Taiwan if the Chinese would do the same in North Vietnam. This development astounded Americans, because it reversed the U.S. policy of supporting the Taiwanese in their long-standing bid for independence from China.

From China, Nixon traveled to the USSR, where he met Soviet leader Leonid Brezhnev. The two leaders signed the SALT (Strategic Arms Limitation

Talks) Treaty, which limited the number of intercontinental nuclear missiles each could have. They also agreed to relax trade restrictions and bring their nations closer to *détente*—a friendly understanding.

Watergate and the *Washington Post*

As he began to plan his reelection campaign in 1971, Nixon developed the ambition, according to Kissinger, of winning "by the biggest electoral landslide in history." Nixon let his close advisers know that he would support and authorize any action, no matter how unethical or illegal, to bring about this result. His paid staffers and supporters reacted with enthusiasm. With Nixon's approval, they disrupted Democratic candidates' speeches and rallies, started riots, made inappropriate and embarrassing statements while posing as Democratic campaigners, and sent out oddly-worded or incoherent mailings on Democratic Party letterhead that made voters, thinking Democrats had written them, withdraw their support. Nixon succeeded in winning the 1972 election by a huge landslide, but he and his supporters destroyed his reputation in the process. The step that brought down the entire house of cards happened several months before the election—a break-in at the Democratic Party's national offices in the Watergate buildings in Washington.

Early in the morning of June 17, 1972, police entered the Watergate and arrested five burglars carrying wiretapping equipment, cameras, and wads of hundred-dollar bills. Because this was a local crime story, the *Washington Post* city editor sent two city reporters, Carl Bernstein and Bob Woodward, to cover it. These two men pursued the story for months, uncovering new leads and evidence of crimes that led straight to the Oval Office. Woodward and Bernstein soon learned that the Committee to Re-elect the President, run by Nixon and his White House staff, had paid the Watergate burglars in cash to break into the offices to look for damaging or embarrassing information that might be used against Democratic candidates.

Woodward had a friend of some years' standing in the upper levels of the federal government; this man, known only as "Deep Throat" to protect his security, became one of the most important sources on the Watergate story. More than 30 years later, a soft-spoken elderly man named W. Mark Felt informed *Vanity Fair* magazine that he was Deep Throat. During the Nixon administration, Felt had served as deputy director of the FBI.

The Watergate coverage reveals an extremely important principle of the free press—that the names of sources must be kept confidential. A reporter must judge whether the source's information is reliable. If it is not reliable, the reporter will not print it. If it is reliable, the reporter must protect the source by quoting him or her anonymously, using a phrase such as "one highly placed source says" or "a source inside the White House stated." This ensures that people who possess damaging information about powerful figures feel free to inform the press without risking their careers or their lives. Woodward and Bernstein extended this protection not only to Felt, but to many White House staffers or former staffers whose positions were much less prominent than his. These clerks, switchboard operators, staffers, and secretaries gave the reporters a wealth of specific details about wrongdoing in the Nixon White House.

In 1791, the United States became almost the only nation in the world to guarantee freedom of the press in its Constitution. The *Washington Post*'s Watergate coverage proves that a free press is one of the basic essentials of a democratic society. It is a necessary check on the power of the government. It proves the validity of Abraham Lincoln's description of "government of the people, by the people, for the people."

The 1972 Election

The Democratic Party was unable to capitalize on the flow of Watergate stories to win the presidential election in 1972. The strongest Democratic candidate appeared to be Senator Edmund Muskie of Maine. The Nixon White House used a conservative New Hampshire newspaper to discredit Muskie. First, the paper published a letter to the editor whose author claimed that Muskie had made derogatory remarks about the French Canadians; the purpose was to turn the large French population of New England against him. (The letter was later revealed to have been a total fabrication written by a Nixon supporter.) Second, the newspaper published a story that made numerous personal slurs against Muskie's wife, Jane. When Muskie made an angry speech in her defense, many voters got the impression that he was too emotional to hold high office; Democratic voters divided their support between Muskie and George McGovern.

Nixon defeated McGovern by a landslide; he carried 49 states. Throughout his campaign, he had denied all knowledge of the Watergate burglary, and White House spokesmen had repeatedly denied all the allegations published in the *Post* and in other newspapers. In fact, Nixon blamed the *Post* for trying to smear his reputation; he even accused the paper of being in the pay of the Democratic Party. However, the stories kept coming; Woodward and Bernstein provided so many specific details of questionable or clearly illegal activity that Congress eventually called for an official investigation. In the end, Watergate burglar James McCord confessed to the Senate that the Watergate break-in had been planned in the Oval Office. In June 1973, presidential aide John Dean testified fully concerning the president's complicity in the burglary and the attempted cover-up. These hearings were nationally televised; for weeks on end, millions of Americans watched in disbelief as the elaborate structure of secrecy Nixon had built around himself collapsed into dust.

The Oval Office Tapes

Nixon continued to deny his involvement in Watergate until a peripheral witness, Alexander Butterfield, mentioned that there was a tape-recording system in the Oval Office. Tape-recording technology had come into existence during the 1930s; it had provided presidents from FDR onward with an ideal means for recording the exact words spoken in important meetings or conversations. FDR, Eisenhower, and Kennedy had all made limited use of a taping system; Lyndon Johnson had embraced it enthusiastically, recording his conversations on a daily basis. Published transcripts of the Johnson tapes provide a fascinating look at the day-in, day-out business of running the Oval Office. Like his predecessors, Nixon used the best technology of the day for a taping system when he became president. Of course, the public—including almost everyone who was summoned to the Oval Office—was completely unaware that there was such a system; only Nixon, a few trusted aides, and the men who installed and maintained the system knew of its existence.

The Senate committee subpoenaed the tapes immediately. Nixon refused to surrender them, claiming "executive privilege"—the president's right to keep his private conversations private. At this point, a new scandal arose: Vice President Spiro Agnew, who had been accused of income-tax evasion, resigned his office as part of a plea-bargaining agreement. Nixon appointed the House minority leader, Gerald Ford of Michigan, in Agnew's place.

Lower courts did not accept Nixon's argument of executive privilege and ordered him to turn over the tapes. When he still refused, the case went to a federal court, which also sided against Nixon. Special Prosecutor Archibald

Cox ordered Nixon to surrender the tapes to the federal grand jury investigating Watergate. Nixon responded by ordering first his attorney general, then his deputy attorney general, to fire Cox. Both men chose to resign rather than obey the president's order; it was left to Solicitor General Robert Bork to fire Cox. This series of events is known as the Saturday Night Massacre.

When Nixon took his case to the Supreme Court, his own appointees ruled against him. Chief Justice Burger, writing the opinion for a unanimous court, stated that the tapes were important evidence in a criminal case, and that therefore Nixon had no right to withhold them. The president's privilege, he wrote, "cannot prevail over the fundamental demands of due process of law in the fair administration of criminal justice."

Deep Throat warned Woodward that some of the tapes contained deliberate erasures. Less than two weeks later, the grand jury confirmed that there was an 18½-minute silence on one of the tapes. All along, Nixon had claimed that the full disclosure of the tapes would prove him innocent of any complicity in the Watergate crimes. The fact that the tapes had been partially erased tended rather to confirm his guilt; even some of his most loyal defenders were beginning to doubt his innocence.

In the first weeks of March 1974, the House Judiciary Committee began to discuss impeachment of the president. Rather than face impeachment, Nixon resigned on August 9, 1974; astoundingly, he claimed that he had "never ducked" responsibility for his mistakes. Gerald Ford then became president.

The Pardon

Ford was a good-humored, affable man, well liked by congressional colleagues from both parties, but the first to admit that he was neither a great intellect nor a particularly skilled politician. In a gesture that shocked the entire country, Ford pardoned Nixon one month after taking office, stating that he intended his pardon of Nixon to be a healing gesture and that he wanted people to try to forget the disgraceful spectacle Nixon had created. In a 2004 interview, Ford spoke more candidly about his motives. He revealed that as soon as he took over the Oval Office, he found himself being forced to spend an enormous amount of time listening to lawyers advise him on the next steps to take with regard to Nixon. Having taken over the presidency in difficult circumstances, and unable to give his full attention to the many other issues of concern to the nation, Ford felt that it was best for the country to close the Nixon case and get on with governing.

Resigning from the presidency had already put Nixon beyond the reach of impeachment; the presidential pardon meant that he could not be tried in civil courts for the crimes of which he was accused. Americans were deeply angry that Nixon had "gotten away with it." Of course, in an important sense, Nixon got away with nothing; only true loyalists who had always supported him believed in his innocence.

The Legacy of Watergate

American politicians had always fought one another, and the fighting had been dirty as often as not. But Nixon took the notion of dirty fighting in politics to a new level. No other candidate for president, of any political party, had ever made a systematic attempt to destroy and discredit the opposition by underhanded techniques: lying, stealing, wiretapping telephones, and investigating the private lives of his opponents. For any candidate to do such things in a campaign was appalling; for an incumbent president to do them, or order them done, was unthinkable.

Hundreds of hours of Oval Office conversations from the Nixon years have been transcribed from the tapes and published in the years since Watergate. These transcripts make it possible for Americans to make up their own minds about Richard M. Nixon.

CHAPTER 30 QUIZ

1. The Supreme Court ruled that President Nixon had to give the Oval Office tapes to the federal grand jury on the principle of _____
   A. executive privilege.
   B. due process of law.
   C. separation of powers.
   D. popular sovereignty.

2. Ford's pardon of Nixon protected Nixon from _____
   A. impeachment.
   B. being tried by a civil court.
   C. resignation from the presidency.
   D. having to obey a grand jury subpoena.

3. As a result of a meeting between Nixon and Soviet leader Brezhnev, the two nations agreed _____
   A. to limit their stockpiles of nuclear weapons.
   B. to sign an alliance with China.
   C. to defend one another if either one was attacked.
   D. to withdraw their troops from Vietnam.

4. Carl Bernstein and Bob Woodward are important figures in history because they _____
   A. broke into Democratic Party headquarters in the Watergate buildings.
   B. exposed crimes committed by the Nixon White House in the national press.
   C. revealed the existence of a tape-recording system in the Oval Office.
   D. posed as Democratic campaigners for the purpose of sabotage.

5. Why did Edmund Muskie lose support in the 1972 presidential election?
   A. because he did not have a large enough power base
   B. because he did not suggest a solution to the war in Vietnam
   C. because Republican sabotage provoked him into an emotional display
   D. because the Democrats had no other candidates

6. Nixon resigned the presidency specifically in order to _____
   A. fulfill a bargain he had made with Gerald Ford.
   B. support former Vice President Spiro Agnew.
   C. avoid impeachment for high crimes committed while in office.
   D. avoid being tried in the civil courts.

7. Nixon offered to _____ if Zhou Enlai would agree to withdraw Chinese troops from Vietnam.
   A. defend China if it were invaded by hostile troops
   B. broker a peace agreement between China and the Soviet Union
   C. cut back the American stockpile of nuclear weapons
   D. withdraw U.S. troops from Taiwan

8. Which best describes the Arab nations' attitude toward the United States during the Nixon years?
   A. friendly because the United States was a major purchaser of Arab oil
   B. resentful because of consistent U.S. support for Israel
   C. hostile because the United States was trying to develop alternative sources of power
   D. cordial because of the U.S. role in liberating North Africa during World War II

9. Nixon most probably owed his election in 1968 to the fact that _____
   A. he spent more money than his opponents.
   B. he offered a promise of peace and stability.
   C. he appealed to the younger generation.
   D. he had a great deal of experience in politics.

10. The term *counterculture* refers to which of the following?
    A. the lifestyle of alienated American young people
    B. negative campaigning and dirty tricks
    C. persistent press coverage using anonymous sources
    D. environmental legislation

Chapter 31

The Cold War Ends, 1976–1991

In 1976, the year of the U.S. bicentennial, Democrat Jimmy Carter defeated incumbent President Ford in a close election. Carter had no experience of Washington politics—a point in his favor among voters who were sick of Washington. Despite major achievements in foreign policy, Carter was considered an ineffective president and served for only one term.

In the 1980 election, Ronald Reagan of California was an attractive enough candidate to win many Democratic voters. He promised to balance the federal budget, but instead ran up the federal highest deficits in history. His successor George Bush continued Reagan's policies, bringing the nation to what seemed to many to be the brink of another Great Depression. Rising prices, rising unemployment, widespread buying on credit, and stock market fluctuations all contributed to ruining the national economy.

The Cold War ended during the Reagan–Bush years, and with it ended the long-standing hostility between the United States and the now-defunct Soviet Union.

CHAPTER OBJECTIVES

- Describe the major achievements of the Carter administration.
- Discuss economic policy under President Reagan.
- Identify the Moral Majority and describe its social viewpoint and political influence.
- Explain how the Cold War ended, and identify the key figures and the roles they played.

Chapter 31 Time Line

- 1973   *Roe v. Wade*
- 1976   Jimmy Carter elected president
- 1977   Congress creates Department of Energy
- 1978   Panama Canal treaties

    Camp David Accords
- 1979   Three Mile Island nuclear reactor failure

    Soviet Union invades Afghanistan
- 1980   Ronald Reagan elected president

    Polish workers strike for the right to form unions
- 1984   Reagan reelected
- 1985   Mikhail Gorbachev becomes premier of Soviet Union
- 1986   "Iran Contra" scandal
- 1988   George Bush elected president
- 1989   Berlin Wall comes down
- 1991   Soviet Union breaks up

    East and West Germany reunited

    Persian Gulf War

The Presidency of Jimmy Carter

Gerald Ford served out the remainder of Nixon's term and ran for reelection in 1976. In a fairly close election, he lost to Democrat Jimmy Carter, the former governor of Georgia. The crimes committed by Nixon and many of his aides, Ford's subsequent pardon of Nixon, and the shaky state of the economy led many people to vote for Carter.

In contrast to the colorful Democratic personalities who had preceded him in office—FDR, Truman, Kennedy, and Johnson—Carter evoked memories of Woodrow Wilson. Both men were quiet, scholarly, and soft-spoken and had no experience of national politics. This "outsider" status made Carter attractive to voters who had had enough of Washington insiders after Watergate. Carter was also unimpeachably honest. However, he exhibited little understanding of the mood of the nation, and did not know how to assuage many of the everyday concerns of Americans. At a time when the nation badly needed a confident, strong leader, Carter did not give an impression of either strength or confidence.

Domestically, Carter's presidency was largely unsuccessful. The nation was in the grip of a social and economic malaise that the White House could not shake. Prices, which had been relatively steady for many years until the time that Nixon took office, continued to rise. In 1979, OPEC raised the price of oil by 50 percent, leading to another energy crisis and to more long lines of cars at gas stations. Carter argued that the United States needed to depend more on solar and nuclear energy and less on foreign oil; just at that time, a nuclear reactor at Three Mile Island in Pennsylvania failed, forcing the evacuation of tens of thousands of people from the area. Few Americans would have confidence in nuclear power for some time afterward.

Carter was more successful as a foreign policy president. He urged the Senate to ratify a series of treaties giving the Panamanians full control of the Panama Canal. This move was popular among the voters and also among Latin American countries, most of which had regarded the United States warily and suspiciously for many years. Carter also condemned the South African policy of apartheid, or "separateness"—racial segregation like the Jim Crow laws in the former Confederacy. Carter's outspoken opposition to apartheid strengthened international respect and regard for the United States.

Carter's greatest achievement was his brokering of a peace treaty between Egypt and Israel, which had been at war for 30 years. In September 1978, Egyptian President Anwar al-Sadat and Israeli Prime Minister Menachem Begin sat down with Carter at Camp David, the presidential retreat in Maryland, to negotiate. The result of the Camp David Accords was a formal peace treaty between Egypt and Israel.

The Election of 1980

In 1980, Democratic voters were divided between Carter and Senator Edward Kennedy, the younger brother of John F. and Robert F. Kennedy. Carter was chosen as the Democratic candidate, but lost in November to Ronald Reagan of California.

Carter lost the election for several reasons. First, even die-hard Democratic voters felt that Carter was an ineffective leader. His achievements were not glamorous, and he had often stumbled, or appeared to stumble, over difficult decisions. Democrats who were disillusioned with Carter were ready to cross party lines to vote for a better alternative. Second, Reagan had an appealing personality; his earlier career as a movie actor made him comfortable in front of the camera, and his manner was always pleasant and good-humored. Third, Reagan campaigned on promises that appealed to almost all voters: to balance the federal budget, cut taxes, and "get government off the backs of the American people."

A political movement called the New Right, spearheaded by a fundamentalist religious group called the Moral Majority, united behind Reagan and proved to be his strongest base of support. Reagan and the Moral Majority shared several views, notably their opposition to three things: abortion, gun control, and equal rights for women. The Moral Majority's support of Reagan over Carter was ironic, given that President Carter was an evangelical Christian and Reagan was not; however, Carter and the New Right did not see eye to eye on social policies.

In 1973, the Supreme Court had decided a famous case called *Roe v. Wade*. An unmarried pregnant woman, using the pseudonym Jane Roe to protect her privacy, had sued the district attorney of Texas, where abortion was illegal unless a doctor stated that it was necessary to save a woman's life. The Court decided 7 to 2 in favor of Roe that during the first three months of pregnancy, the government had no right to prevent a woman from having an abortion. The state did have the right to outlaw abortion during the last six months of a pregnancy, unless a doctor determined that abortion was necessary to protect the mother's life and health.

Beginning in the Reagan era, with the emergence of the Moral Majority and the New Right, abortion became almost as politically divisive an issue as slavery had been 100 years earlier. In general, Democratic Party candidates have supported the decision made in *Roe v. Wade*: that the only person who has the right to make the decision to abort or to have a baby must be the mother, not the state. This position has become commonly known as pro-choice. Most Republican candidates take the view that from the moment of conception, the fetus is a human life, and that no one, including the mother, has the right to terminate that life. This view is commonly called pro-life.

Reaganomics

"Reaganomics" was the name that people gave to Reagan's theory of trickle-down or supply-side economics. Reagan did not invent this economic philosophy; it had originated as a practice during the early days of big business and industry. Like many conservatives before him, Reagan believed in removing regulations on big business. His thinking followed this path: Without regulations, businesses can increase their profits. Increased profits lead to higher wages. Higher wages mean that people have more money to spend. More spending means economic growth and prosperity.

The major flaw in the theory of supply-side economics is the idea that wages go up when businesses profit. Because the only purpose of any business is to increase its profits, owners do not raise wages unless they are forced to do so. This means that profits never "trickle down" to the lower middle class or the workers; they watch prices go up while their incomes stay the same. However, by 1983, Reagan's policies had resulted in a substantial drop in inflation and a stock market boom. For those who were well-off to begin with, the Reagan years meant great prosperity.

Under President Reagan, Congress cut spending on social programs. This meant that poor and working-class Americans suffered by being deprived of benefits they badly needed for survival. Unemployment was high across the nation, especially in the old manufacturing centers in the Midwest and in all cities. Spending and buying on credit grew. The economy in the 1980s was somewhat reminiscent of the 1920s, when spending had been reckless and had rested on a very shaky foundation of unpaid debts.

Reagan had promised to balance the federal budget, but his business-friendly policies had the opposite effect. The federal deficit soared under Reagan and also under his successor George Bush. By the time President Bush left office in 1992, the deficit stood at $291 billion. Bush had been forced to take the unpopular step of raising taxes to try to boost government revenue and offset the deficit, but the deficit was so immense that the higher taxes accomplished little. The United States had also begun to import far more than it exported, and both Reagan and Bush were unsuccessful in trying to persuade Japan and other foreign nations to buy more U.S. products.

In 1981, Reagan nominated Sandra Day O'Connor of Texas to be the first female Supreme Court justice. O'Connor was nominally a conservative, but in time she gained a reputation as a moderate. She came to be considered the "swing" vote on the Court: the one who might vote with either the liberal or the conservative justices, depending on the merits of the individual case.

Iran Contra

In 1979, Nicaragua underwent a revolution when rebels called Sandinistas deposed dictator Anastasio Somoza. When President Reagan took office, he cut off all U.S. aid to Nicaragua, claiming that the Sandinistas were funded by the Soviet Union. This had the effect of strengthening the ties between the Sandinistas and the Soviets. Therefore, Reagan decided to throw the support of the United States to the Contras, a rebel army trained and paid by the CIA. He hoped that the Contras would defeat the Sandinistas.

Even though Reagan was a popular president and argued that a Contra victory would bring democratic government to Nicaragua, the public was generally disapproving of the United States intervening in civil unrest in another nation. Memories of the losing struggle in Vietnam's civil war were too raw. In 1984, Congress passed the Boland Amendment, which banned the White House, the CIA, and all other government agencies from aiding the Contras.

In 1986, the American public learned that the Reagan White House had secretly sold weapons to Iran and used the money to aid the Contras. Under the Boland Amendment, this was illegal. Responding to public outrage, Reagan ordered an investigation. He was cleared of any role in the crime, but investigation revealed that others, notably Lieutenant Colonel Oliver North, had sent millions of dollars made in Iranian arms sales to the Contras. Some of Reagan's aides resigned, and criminal charges were filed against North and Admiral John Poindexter. They were convicted, but the conviction was later overturned on a technicality.

The End of the Cold War

The Cold War had dragged on for forty years, with no real move by either side toward a settlement or a significant lessening of tension. Reagan's solution to the Cold War was to build up American nuclear defenses. He believed that a mighty American nuclear arsenal would frighten the Communist nations into abandoning the Cold War. The Strategic Defense Initiative, nicknamed Star Wars after a popular science-fiction movie of the time, was a space-based missile defense system.

As things turned out, the United States took no direct action to end the Cold War. However, Reagan's military buildup had forced the Soviets to follow his example, and this brought the Soviet economy to the brink of ruin. It certainly had an effect on the Soviet Union's ability to spend money on controlling all of Eastern Europe. Apart from this, and from providing an example of a working republic with a capitalist economy, the United States did not play any role in ending the Cold War. It was ended by Soviet leader Mikhail Gorbachev and by the people of Eastern Europe.

By the 1980s, many Eastern European nations had had more than enough of being forced to live under Communist governments that were under Soviet control. Beginning around 1980, soaring prices led Polish laborers to stage a series of strikes and to demand the right to form trade unions. The Polish government gave in to the workers' demands in September, and the workers formed Solidarity, which began as a national council to coordinate independent trade unions, and became a major political force in the country. Solidarity members created a list of demands that made it clear they wanted real reform, not just higher wages: a union's right to strike, freedom for dissenters being held in prison, and the lifting of censorship. Dockworker Lech Walesa, who headed Solidarity, would later become the president of a democratic Poland.

In 1985, Mikhail Gorbachev became the head of the Soviet Union. Born in 1931 to a peasant family in the North Caucasus region, Gorbachev was well aware that major political changes were necessary; he knew that the Soviet Union could not keep pace with American military spending. To remedy the economic and social problems of the USSR, Gorbachev instituted *glasnost* (openness) and *perestroika* (a restructuring of the economy and society). *Glasnost* was intended to encourage open debate within the Soviet Union; Gorbachev believed that the economic and social problems the country faced demanded input from all segments of society, not just Communist Party members. He relaxed censorship and instituted policies that encouraged writers and intellectuals to speak out about society's problems and suggest their own solutions.

Perestroika called for increases in foreign trade and reductions in military spending. During a 1987 meeting, Reagan and Gorbachev signed the Intermediate-Range Nuclear Forces Treaty, which eliminated all medium-range nuclear missiles from Europe. This made Gorbachev very unpopular with the Soviet military, which was convinced that this action made the USSR vulnerable to attack.

In 1988, Gorbachev thoroughly reorganized the Soviet government, making it more representative and giving greater power to a legislature that for years had existed only as the premier's rubber stamp. The era of one-party rule in the Soviet Union was over; non-Communists were allowed to run for office at the national, republic, and local levels in 1989.

In July 1988, a severe economic slump and Gorbachev's own awareness of the changed atmosphere in Eastern Europe caused him to announce that the Soviet Union would withdraw from any interference in the self-government of other nations. Eastern Europe would have to take care of itself from now on; the Soviet Union could no longer afford to control and monitor nations outside its own borders.

In 1989, the Berlin Wall fell. People all over the world watched television, astounded, as young Germans attacked the wall on both sides with sledgehammers and pickaxes, clambering to the top and pulling their friends up to dance and cheer alongside them. Berliners poured freely through the Brandenburg Gate in both directions for the first time since 1961. During the following weeks, border restrictions throughout Eastern Europe were removed, and easterners could once again travel freely to the West. In 1990, East and West Germany were officially and formally reunited under one government. After nearly 50 years, the Iron Curtain had come down.

The map opposite shows the changes in Central and Eastern Europe after the fall of the Iron Curtain. Compare this to the map in Chapter 26.

The Breakup of the Soviet Union

The USSR had created the conditions that led to the Cold War; fittingly, it was the last European nation to let go of Communist rule. In 1991, Communist Party leaders attempted a coup against Gorbachev, who had been losing popularity as a result of a severe economic crisis and the Communist Party's

Post-Cold War Europe in 1991

dismay at its loss of influence in Europe. In addition, the Baltic republics had been agitating for self-determination.

The actual coup attempt was an inept failure that only embarrassed the plotters; however, it gave the western Soviet republics the opportunity to seize their independence. Gorbachev realized that he could no longer hold the Soviet Union together. In late 1991, the Soviet republics became independent nation-states; all except Latvia, Lithuania, and Estonia formed an association known as the Commonwealth of Independent States (CIS). This association was intended as a successor to the USSR, which was officially dissolved on December 31. Members of the CIS are independent, self-governing nations united for purposes of security, economics, internal and external trade, and justice.

The breakup brought an end to the long-standing enmity between the Soviet Union and the United States. President Bush hailed the moment in history as the beginning of a new world order "in which freedom and respect for human rights find a home among all nations." The end of the Cold War left the United States as the world's only remaining superpower.

CHAPTER 31 QUIZ

1. **President Jimmy Carter brokered a peace treaty between _____ at Camp David in 1978.**
   A. Israel and Egypt
   B. Egypt and the Soviet Union
   C. the Soviet Union and the United States
   D. the United States and Israel

2. **The term *apartheid* refers to _____ in South Africa.**
   A. economic policy
   B. racial segregation
   C. restructuring of the government
   D. official scandals

3. **In *Roe v. Wade*, the Supreme Court ruled that a woman had the right to have an abortion without government interference _____**
   A. in the first three months of pregnancy.
   B. at any time during pregnancy.
   C. only in cases of rape or incest.
   D. only in cases where the mother's life was at risk.

4. **Which best describes the results of Reagan's economic policies?**
   A. high unemployment and a rising federal debt
   B. low unemployment and a rising federal debt
   C. high unemployment and a falling federal debt
   D. low unemployment and a falling federal debt

5. **Memories of _____ made most Americans oppose U.S. intervention in Nicaragua.**
   A. the energy crisis
   B. the Camp David Accords
   C. World War II
   D. the Vietnam War

6. **The United States helped to end the Cold War by** _____
   A. keeping up with the USSR in the space race.
   B. sending covert aid to the Contras in Nicaragua.
   C. increasing military defense spending.
   D. negotiating with East Germany to bring down the Berlin Wall.

7. _____ **was the last European nation to abandon Communist rule.**
   A. East Germany
   B. Poland
   C. The USSR
   D. Hungary

8. **Why did the Reagan White House send aid to the Nicaraguan Contras?**
   A. to help them defeat the Sandinistas
   B. to help them in a coup against the dictator
   C. to ensure fair democratic elections
   D. to ensure the return of representative government

9. **Reagan's theory of supply-side economics did not work as promised because** _____
   A. businesses did not increase their profits.
   B. increased profits did not lead to higher wages for the workers.
   C. higher wages did not lead to more consumer spending.
   D. more consumer spending did not improve the economy.

10. **President Bush tried to offset the federal deficit by** _____
    A. balancing the federal budget.
    B. raising taxes.
    C. cutting military spending.
    D. regulating big business.

PART III EXAM

1. Which nation did not fight on the side of the Allied/Entente Powers during World War I?
   A. Austria
   B. Britain
   C. France
   D. Italy

2. All of these except _____ contributed greatly to the new freedom in women's behavior during the 1920s.
   A. women's winning the right to vote in 1920
   B. women's experience as ambulance drivers, nurses, and so on, during World War I
   C. women's support for Prohibition
   D. women's having succeeded on the job while the men they replaced were serving in World War I

3. During the imperialist era at the turn of the nineteenth century, the United States did not attempt to acquire African colonies because _____
   A. it already had a sizable African population.
   B. European nations had already colonized most of Africa.
   C. Africa was not a good source of natural resources.
   D. it already had favorable trade relationships with African nations.

4. The primary purpose of Lyndon Johnson's Great Society programs was _____
   A. to bring economic and educational opportunity to the poorest Americans.
   B. to ensure gender and racial equality in all aspects of the economy and society.
   C. to register all American adults age 18 and over to vote.
   D. to reduce pollution and chemical waste and protect the natural environment for the future.

5. In the twentieth century, _____ did more than any other U.S. president to achieve full civil rights for black Americans.
   A. Eisenhower
   B. Kennedy
   C. Johnson
   D. Nixon

6. _____ was established after World War II as an international peacekeeping organization.

   A. The Quadruple Alliance
   B. The League of Nations
   C. The United Nations
   D. The Warsaw Pact

7. Under the Nixon administration, the United States made important progress in relations with _____

   A. China and India.
   B. India and the Soviet Union.
   C. the Soviet Union and China.
   D. South Africa and India.

8. The Black Power movement was organized around the principle(s) of _____

   A. nonviolent resistance.
   B. separatism and violent resistance.
   C. integration and equal treatment.
   D. overthrowing the U.S. government.

9. Which New Deal program was intended to protect the people against any repetition of the Great Depression?

   A. the Federal Deposit Insurance Corporation (FDIC)
   B. the Tennessee Valley Authority
   C. the Civilian Conservation Corps
   D. the Works Progress Administration (WPA)

10. The United Nations is best described as _____

   A. an international peacekeeping organization.
   B. an agreement for the mutual defense of allied nations.
   C. a peace treaty signed at the end of World War II.
   D. an economic union among the nations of Europe.

11. The administration of Woodrow Wilson is notable for all the following except _____

   A. tariff reduction.
   B. reform of the banking system.
   C. overturning of antitrust legislation.
   D. extension of voting rights to women.

12. **The Great Migration that occurred between about 1915 and 1930 involved** _____
    A. forced relocation of southeastern American Indians to the Midwest.
    B. young men from China, Mexico, and the eastern United States seeking gold in California.
    C. midwestern tenant farmers heading to California to pick fruit.
    D. African Americans traveling north in search of well-paid factory jobs.

13. **All of these contributed to the election of President Richard Nixon in 1968 except** _____
    A. deep divisions in the Democratic Party.
    B. Nixon's promise that he had a plan to end the Vietnam War.
    C. Nixon's promise that he would restore American society to stability.
    D. strong support for Nixon among voters under age 25.

14. **Eleanor Roosevelt is historically noted for her championship of** _____
    A. states' rights.
    B. judicial review.
    C. equality for African Americans.
    D. executive privilege.

15. **The Jones Acts of 1916 and 1917 gave greater self-governing rights to** _____
    A. Puerto Rico and the Philippines.
    B. Hawaii and Alaska.
    C. African Americans.
    D. American women.

16. **The terms** *bread line*, *Okie*, **and** *Hooverville* **are all associated with** _____
    A. the Jazz Age.
    B. the Great Depression.
    C. the Cold War.
    D. the Great Society.

17. **The USSR installed nuclear missiles in Cuba in order to** _____
    A. expand its power base.
    B. make an ally of Cuba.
    C. intimidate the United States.
    D. fulfill a U.N. requirement.

18. The term *apartheid* refers to _____ in South Africa.
    A. political corruption
    B. racial segregation
    C. an artistic and literary movement
    D. European colonization

19. At Yalta in 1945, the Soviet Union promised the United States that it would
    _____ after victory was declared in Europe.
    A. be the first to march into Berlin
    B. join U.S. troops in the war with Japan
    C. hold free elections in Moscow
    D. establish communism throughout Eastern Europe

20. The Nixon-era scandals collectively known as "Watergate" are historically
    important because they prove that _____ is essential to a
    democratic society.
    A. a federal police force
    B. an integrated school system
    C. a military draft
    D. a free press

21. Most Progressive Era legislation was designed to benefit _____
    A. farmers.
    B. the urban working class.
    C. the middle class.
    D. big business and industry.

22. _____ functioned as a peaceful and positive reflection of Cold
    War hostility between the United States and the Soviet Union.
    A. The founding of the United Nations
    B. The funding of the Marshall Plan
    C. The signing of the Warsaw Pact
    D. The race to land the first astronaut on the moon

23. What was the outcome of the Vietnam War?
    A. North and South Vietnam united under Communist rule.
    B. North and South Vietnam united under democratic rule.
    C. North Vietnam remained Communist; South Vietnam became a republic.
    D. Vietnam was absorbed into the USSR as a socialist republic.

24. The *Roe v. Wade* decision states that the government cannot interfere with a woman's right to abort her pregnancy _____
   A. during the first three months of pregnancy.
   B. at any time.
   C. if the abortion is necessary to save the mother's life.
   D. if the woman was the victim of incest or rape.

25. The publication of the Pentagon Papers revealed that the White House _____
   A. had a secret tape-recording system in the Oval Office.
   B. had not been open with the public about the war in Vietnam.
   C. had a secret plan to end the Cold War by increasing military spending.
   D. hoped to contain the spread of Communism throughout the world.

26. The final push for direct U.S. involvement in World War I happened because _____
   A. Germany declared war on American allies Britain and France.
   B. German U-boats sank the *Lusitania* when more than 100 Americans were on board.
   C. Woodrow Wilson, who supported U.S. involvement, had just been reelected.
   D. Germany issued a direct written threat against the United States.

27. Key players on the Chicago White Sox agreed to throw the 1919 World Series because _____
   A. the White Sox owners and management treated them like indentured servants.
   B. they knew that they would probably lose the series anyway.
   C. the gangsters threatened to kill them if they did not accept the bribe.
   D. they hoped to be traded to better teams after the season.

28. In 1945, _____ became the only nation that has ever fired a nuclear weapon at an enemy.
   A. the Soviet Union
   B. Japan
   C. Germany
   D. the United States

29. What was the purpose of the Berlin Airlift?
   A. to unite the three Allied zones of Berlin into one free city called West Berlin
   B. to provide food and supplies to West Berlin in defiance of a Soviet blockade
   C. to bomb strategic locations in Berlin during the last year of World War II
   D. to help East Germans defect to West Berlin

30. **Which two forms of government amount to exactly the same thing?**
    A. communism and fascism
    B. communism and anarchism
    C. fascism and republicanism
    D. democracy and fascism

31. **The Panama Canal was built with the purpose of _____**
    A. improving trade relations between nations.
    B. making shipping faster and more efficient.
    C. achieving self-rule in Panama.
    D. gaining a U.S. victory in the Spanish-American War.

32. **Sandra Day O'Connor is historically significant because she was _____**
    A. a founder of the National Organization for Women (NOW).
    B. a labor union activist during the Progressive Era.
    C. the first female Supreme Court justice.
    D. the first female admiral in the U.S. Navy.

33. **During the Spanish-American War, the United States gained influence over all these places except _____**
    A. Cuba.
    B. Mexico.
    C. Puerto Rico.
    D. the Philippines.

34. **The term *muckraker* refers to _____**
    A. an investigative journalist.
    B. a temperance advocate.
    C. a suffragist.
    D. a World War I infantry soldier.

35. **Which best describes the purpose of the North Atlantic Treaty Organization?**
    A. to eliminate nuclear missiles from the world
    B. to make communism illegal throughout the West
    C. to provide for the defense of any member nation that was attacked
    D. to maintain international peace

36. _____ marks the moment in history when the United States and the USSR were closest to fighting a nuclear war.
   A. The Bay of Pigs invasion
   B. The Cuban Missile Crisis
   C. The building of the Berlin Wall
   D. The fall of Saigon in 1975

37. Which war ended with political conditions the same as they had been at the start?
   A. World War I
   B. World War II
   C. the Korean War
   D. the Vietnam War

38. The United States influenced the outcome of the Cold War by _____
   A. increasing nuclear defense spending.
   B. providing financial aid to Iron Curtain nations.
   C. helping to form the European Union.
   D. achieving friendly relations with China.

39. Clarence Darrow is famous in history for his key role in _____
   A. Prohibition.
   B. the Scopes trial.
   C. the Harlem Renaissance.
   D. the New Deal.

40. Months of _____ was the primary cause of the Dust Bowl.
   A. unusually high temperatures
   B. heavy snows
   C. almost no rainfall
   D. tornadoes

41. The War Powers Act of 1973 states that the president _____
   A. may take any necessary steps to defend U.S. troops against the enemy.
   B. must seek congressional approval to commit troops to a war for more than 60 days.
   C. has full power to oversee and manage troops once Congress has formally declared war.
   D. cannot take any foreign policy action involving the use of troops without Congress's consent.

42. _____ provided the impetus for the constitutional amendment that lowered the voting age from 21 to 18.
    A. The military draft
    B. The women's movement
    C. The Great Society programs
    D. The unionization of industrial workers

43. Which best describes President Truman's foreign policy in regard to the Soviet Union?
    A. to convert Iron Curtain nations from communism to democracy
    B. to bring about regime change in the Soviet Union
    C. to prevent communism from spreading any farther than it already had
    D. to stage an all-out nuclear war

44. All of the following characterize American society in the period 1945–1960 except _____
    A. a largely white migration from the cities to the new suburbs.
    B. a rise in the number of college students from middle- and working-class backgrounds.
    C. massive antiwar demonstrations and the development of the counterculture.
    D. the purchase of a television set and a car.

45. On the home front, Americans showed support for World War I by doing all these things except _____
    A. growing their own vegetables and fruit in "victory gardens."
    B. doing without meat or bread on certain days of the week.
    C. purchasing government-issued war bonds.
    D. digging trenches for the soldiers' shelter and protection.

46. The term *speakeasy* refers to _____
    A. a "yellow journalist" during the Progressive Era.
    B. an antiwar demonstrator during the Vietnam era.
    C. a nightclub or bar that sold alcoholic drinks during Prohibition.
    D. the Oval Office tapes that were a bone of contention during the Watergate era.

47. Which best explains why West Berlin became the symbolic heart of the Cold War struggle?
    A. It was the largest city in Europe.
    B. It was the only free city behind the Iron Curtain.
    C. It demonstrated the failure of capitalism.
    D. It refused to accept Marshall Plan aid.

48. **The Tet Offensive refers to** _____
    A. the U.S. bombing of Cambodia.
    B. a massive North Vietnamese attack on U.S. troops.
    C. an attack on U.S. warships in the Gulf of Tonkin.
    D. a cease-fire agreement signed by North Vietnam and the United States.

49. **Under the** _____ **administration, the United States brokered a major peace agreement between Egypt and Israel.**
    A. Johnson
    B. Nixon
    C. Ford
    D. Carter

50. **Which best describes the illegal actions taken in the 1980s scandal known as "Iran Contra"?**
    A. The United States sold guns to Iran and used the money to aid the Nicaraguan Contras.
    B. The United States sold guns to the Nicaraguan Contras and used the money to aid Iran.
    C. The United States created and trained a Nicaraguan rebel force called the Contras.
    D. The United States created and trained a Nicaraguan rebel force called the Sandinistas.

Final Exam

1. **The Louisiana Purchase was important because** _____

   A. it led to the discovery of the Northwest Passage.

   B. it doubled the size of the United States.

   C. it established permanent friendship between the United States and the American Indians.

   D. it was the last time the United States purchased territory for a cash payment.

2. **Which was the first nation to establish settled colonies in North America?**

   A. England

   B. France

   C. Germany

   D. Spain

3. **Iron Curtain nations refused to accept Marshall Plan aid because** _____

   A. they blamed Germany for destroying the European economy.

   B. there was too much distrust between the former Allied and Axis nations.

   C. they knew they would never be able to repay the United States.

   D. Stalin refused to allow any ties between his satellites and his only strong national rival.

4. Jim Crow laws in the South violated _____

   A. the constitutional right to the equal protection of the laws for all citizens.

   B. the "separate but equal" principle established by the Supreme Court.

   C. the constitutional right of all citizens to peaceably assemble.

   D. the principle of judicial review established by the Supreme Court.

5. _____ established the principle of "separate but equal" facilities for black Americans.

   A. *Gideon v. Wainwright*

   B. *Plessy v. Ferguson*

   C. *Dred Scott v. Sanford*

   D. *Brown v. Board of Education*

6. On what grounds did the Supreme Court declare in 1857 that antislavery laws were unconstitutional?

   A. the Fifth Amendment protection of rights to private property

   B. the Second Amendment guarantee of the right to bear arms

   C. the constitutional requirement that U.S. citizenship was limited to people born in the United States, or born to U.S. citizens

   D. the statement in the Declaration of Independence that all men were created equal

7. Civil Rights movement leaders generally advocated _____ as the most effective weapon against Jim Crow laws.

   A. taking important cases to court

   B. exercising the right to vote

   C. petitioning the government

   D. peaceful demonstrations

8. _____ provided the final push that made the United States declare war on Germany in 1917.

   A. The sinking of the *Lusitania*

   B. The publication of the Zimmerman telegram

   C. The assassination of Archduke Franz Ferdinand and Archduchess Sophie

   D. The execution of the Schlieffen Plan

9. _____ sets out the structure of the U.S. government and the individual rights of the citizens.

A. The Declaration of Independence

B. The Constitution

C. The Bill of Rights

D. The Treaty of Paris

10. The term *Harlem Renaissance* refers to _____ during the Jazz Age.

A. a literary and artistic movement

B. urban renewal

C. desegregation

D. a voter registration drive

11. Which best describes the common thread that linked the writers of the "Lost Generation"?

A. the desire to expose corruption in government and big business

B. disillusionment with ideals such as chivalry and romance

C. celebration of the growth of African-American culture

D. the desire to provide lighthearted escapist fare to victims of the Depression

12. The development of _____ gave the working class some leverage over business owners for the first time in history.

A. communism

B. steam power

C. the railway

D. labor unions

13. When Black Codes were passed throughout the old Confederacy after the Civil War, the U.S. government responded by _____

A. asking the Supreme Court to arbitrate the disagreement.

B. sending troops to occupy the South to supervise compliance with the law.

C. establishing the Freedmen's Bureau.

D. establishing a federal program to encourage freedmen and women to move north.

14. **Britain and France went to war in North America over conflicting claims to** _____

   A. the Ohio River Valley area.

   B. the city of New Orleans, Louisiana.

   C. territory west of the Mississippi River.

   D. the colonies along the Atlantic coast.

15. **Which major figure of the Enlightenment first suggested a government of multiple branches with checks and balances?**

   A. René Descartes

   B. Baron de Montesquieu

   C. Jean-Jacques Rousseau

   D. Voltaire

16. **The Confederacy was at a disadvantage in a war of attrition because** _____

   A. its army had smarter commanding officers.

   B. it hoped for support from foreign allies.

   C. it had a smaller population of able-bodied men.

   D. it could not make use of its industry.

17. **With which goal was the Republican Party formed in 1857?**

   A. to limit European immigration

   B. to fight for women's rights

   C. to end the expansion of slavery

   D. to encourage the settlement of the West

18. **Henry Clay's American System, proposed in the early 1800s, included all the following provisions except.**

   A. a national bank.

   B. going off the gold standard.

   C. protective tariffs on imports.

   D. a national transportation system.

19. **How did their experiences with American Indians help the colonists in the Revolutionary War?**

    A. The American Indians had taught the colonists about democratic government.

    B. The American Indians had helped the colonists manufacture bows and arrows.

    C. The American Indians had showed the colonists how to fight like guerrillas.

    D. The American Indians had taught the colonists the value of controlling the high ground.

20. **Which basic constitutional principle did Richard Nixon violate as president?**

    A. equality of all citizens under the law

    B. executive privilege and the right to privacy

    C. a ban on unreasonable search and seizure

    D. the right to petition the government

21. _____ is notorious in American history for creating public hysteria that forced the United States into declaring war on Spain in 1898.

    A. Upton Sinclair

    B. William Randolph Hearst

    C. Ida B. Wells

    D. Ida Tarbell

22. **The era of Prohibition gave rise to all these new slang terms except** _____

    A. speakeasy.

    B. muckraker.

    C. bootleg.

    D. bathtub gin.

23. **What was the most important purpose of the Berlin Wall?**

    A. to prevent the Berlin Airlift from succeeding in its object

    B. to prevent Iron Curtain nations from accepting Marshall Plan aid

    C. to prevent West Germans and other Western Europeans from defecting to East Germany

    D. to prevent citizens of East Germany and other Iron Curtain nations from defecting to the West

24. **Panama gave the United States perpetual sovereignty over the Panama Canal Zone in exchange for** _____

    A. U.S. support in Panama's war for independence.

    B. a $10 million cash payment and a further annual payment of $250,000.

    C. the promise of U.S. neutrality in the war between Panama and Colombia.

    D. control of the shipping lanes that passed through the canal.

25. **The Articles of Confederation failed for all these reasons except** _____

    A. they gave more power to the states than to the central government.

    B. they created a legislature exactly like the British Parliament.

    C. they did not create executive or judicial branches of government.

    D. they did not give the central government the right to raise taxes.

26. **The Monroe Doctrine, the Roosevelt Corollary, and the Good Neighbor Policy all relate to the relationship between the United States and** _____

    A. Western Europe.

    B. Communist Eastern Europe.

    C. Central and South America.

    D. China and Japan.

27. **In the days leading up to the American Revolution, the British Parliament singled out the colony of** _____ **for punishment.**

    A. Massachusetts

    B. Pennsylvania

    C. Virginia

    D. New York

28. **After the Civil War, the primary goal of the old guard of the Confederacy was to** _____

    A. rebuild the southern economy along modern lines.

    B. restore southern society to the way it had been before the war.

    C. take revenge on the victorious North by any available means.

    D. collaborate with black southerners in a major program of social reform.

29. One consequence of the War of 1812 was a lasting alliance between the United States and _____

    A. Britain.

    B. France.

    C. Canada.

    D. Mexico.

30. _____ is known to history as the father of the U.S. Constitution.

    A. George Washington

    B. Benjamin Franklin

    C. James Madison

    D. John Adams

31. All these political leaders were victims of assassins' bullets in the Civil Rights/Vietnam War era except _____

    A. Martin Luther King, Jr.

    B. Medgar Evers.

    C. Malcolm X.

    D. Lyndon Johnson.

32. The Gettysburg Address served as an important reminder of all these ideas except _____

    A. that the United States was founded on the principle of the equality of all men.

    B. that the U.S. government could function only by the consent of the people.

    C. that the Union was fighting for the cause of human freedom.

    D. that government compromises had caused the situation that led to the war.

33. Which European nation emerged from World War II as a great world power?

    A. Britain

    B. France

    C. Poland

    D. the Soviet Union

34. _____ was the central issue over which the Mexican War was fought.

    A. Territorial rights

    B. Indian rebellion

    C. Protective tariffs

    D. Slavery

35. The Black Panthers and the Black Power movement broke from the mainstream Civil Rights movement because their leaders did not support _____

    A. peaceful resistance.

    B. Great Society programs.

    C. women's rights.

    D. the Democratic Party.

36. The government established the Department of Agriculture to help Plains farmers address the issue of _____

    A. factory inspections.

    B. tax regulations.

    C. irrigation.

    D. Native-American relations.

37. Parliament responded to the Boston Tea Party by passing _____

    A. the Bill of Rights.

    B. the Intolerable Acts.

    C. the Stamp Act.

    D. the Declaration and Resolves.

38. Which nation did not participate in the peace conference held at Versailles in 1919?

    A. France

    B. Germany

    C. Italy

    D. Russia

39. All these women played a significant role in the fight for women's suffrage except _____

    A. Alice Paul.

    B. Susan B. Anthony.

    C. Gertrude Stein.

    D. Carrie Chapman Catt.

40. The Great Society programs achieved which of the following?

    A. They ended segregation in the public schools.

    B. They increased voter registration throughout the old Confederacy.

    C. They raised millions of Americans' incomes above the poverty level.

    D. They provided government health insurance for all Americans.

41. Which accurately describes the U.S. textile-manufacturing industry between the Industrial Revolution and the Civil War?

    A. The South grew cotton and shipped it north for spinning and weaving.

    B. The South grew cotton, then spun and wove it into cloth in southern factories.

    C. The North raised sheep, sheared them, and spun and wove their wool into cloth.

    D. The North shipped southern cotton to Britain to be made into cloth.

42. The New Deal programs were designed to combat _____

    A. organized crime.

    B. isolationism.

    C. Communism.

    D. the Great Depression.

43. _____ was a notable figure in the U.S. Congress during the nineteenth century for achieving compromises on divisive issues.

    A. John Quincy Adams

    B. Henry Clay

    C. Thomas Hart Benton

    D. Lyndon B. Johnson

44. **The term *Viet Cong* refers to** _____

    A. North Vietnamese fighters who supported Ho.

    B. the Army of South Vietnam.

    C. South Vietnamese fighters who supported Ho.

    D. U.S. troops in combat in Vietnam.

45. **What was the main purpose of the Monroe Doctrine?**

    A. to establish alliances between the United States and European powers

    B. to express American support for European colonial ambitions in the West

    C. to imply that the United States would fight any further European attempt to colonize in the West

    D. to acquire colonies of its own in Central and South America

46. **John Brown's goal is best described as** _____

    A. the abolition of slavery throughout the United States.

    B. a halt to the expansion of slavery beyond the states where it already existed.

    C. a reasonable compromise between the North and the South.

    D. the secession of the free North from the slaveholding South.

47. **The USSR and the United States nearly reached the point of nuclear war during** _____

    A. the Cuban Missile Crisis.

    B. the Strategic Arms Limitation Talks.

    C. the partition of Germany into four zones of occupation.

    D. the signing of the Warsaw Pact.

48. **American women age 21 and over gained the right to vote with the passage of the Nineteenth Amendment during** _____

    A. the 1910s.

    B. the 1920s.

    C. the 1930s.

    D. the 1940s.

49. Congress repealed the Tonkin Gulf Resolution in response to _____

    A. the bombing of Cambodia.

    B. the Tet Offensive.

    C. the fall of Saigon.

    D. the press coverage of the Vietnam War.

50. On what grounds did the colonists oppose various acts of Parliament during the 1760s and early 1770s?

    A. that the colonies were an independent sovereign nation

    B. that the acts were aimed at specific individual colonies

    C. that the acts were illegal attempts to regulate Colonial trade

    D. that the colonists were not represented in Parliament

51. The Pentagon Papers are significant because they _____

    A. disproved the theory that the Kennedy assassination was the result of a conspiracy.

    B. revealed that there was a tape-recording system in the Oval Office.

    C. proved that the White House had lied to the public about the Vietnam War.

    D. demonstrated that the presidential election of 1972 was rigged.

52. The doctrine of nullification states that _____

    A. the Supreme Court has the power to determine whether a law is unconstitutional.

    B. no state is bound to obey a federal law that it considers unconstitutional.

    C. the federal government can force states to obey reasonable laws that apply equally to all states.

    D. if a certain number of states ratify a constitutional amendment, it becomes law.

53. During the Progressive Era, the Seventeenth Amendment made the system for electing _____ more democratic.

    A. the president

    B. members of the Senate

    C. members of the House

    D. Supreme Court justices

54. _____ is historically significant for her multivolume autobiography dealing with westward migration and frontier life in the 1870s and 1880s.

   A. Edith Wharton

   B. Emily Dickinson

   C. Zelda Fitzgerald

   D. Laura Ingalls Wilder

55. The Iroquois changed sides during the French and Indian War because _____

   A. the French army betrayed them.

   B. the British army treated them with more respect.

   C. the tide of war had turned in favor of the British.

   D. the tide of war had turned in favor of the French.

56. Which best explains why communism, as it was practiced, was not satisfactory to the peoples of Eastern Europe?

   A. It left them feeling constantly vulnerable to foreign invasion.

   B. It refused them basic freedoms that they demanded as a human right.

   C. It was a corrupt system of government.

   D. It was a barrier to economic progress.

57. The term *Iron Curtain* refers to _____

   A. the U.S. policy of containment of communism after World War II.

   B. the border between democratic Western Europe and Communist Eastern Europe.

   C. the concrete barrier that the East Germans built around West Berlin.

   D. the American insistence on European noninterference in the Western Hemisphere.

58. Andrew Jackson is the first U.S. president who can be described as _____

   A. a southern gentleman.

   B. a New England university graduate.

   C. a military hero.

   D. a common man.

59. **All these factors contributed to the end of the cattle boom in the Great Plains except** _____

   A. a series of severe blizzards in the winter of 1886–1887.

   B. falling prices resulting from the beef supply outpacing the demand.

   C. continual clashes between sheep ranchers and cattle ranchers.

   D. the new practice of fencing off formerly open grazing land with barbed wire.

60. **The Fugitive Slave Act of 1850 included all these provisions except** _____

   A. it rescinded a long-established ban on importing slaves from Africa.

   B. it established special commissions to hear cases of disputed ownership of a slave.

   C. it declared that slave status was permanent.

   D. it declared that any slave who had escaped to freedom before 1850 was no longer free.

61. **With the election of** _____ **, the Democratic Party took over the populist platform that the Republican Party had previously been identified with.**

   A. Abraham Lincoln

   B. Theodore Roosevelt

   C. Franklin D. Roosevelt

   D. Andrew Jackson

62. **What was the purpose of the Marshall Plan?**

   A. to rebuild Europe after the destruction of World War II

   B. to create an international peacekeeping organization

   C. to establish a friendly understanding between the United States and the USSR

   D. to establish a homeland for displaced European Jews after the Holocaust

63. **During the French and Indian War, the British army alienated the colonists by** _____

   A. refusing to make much effort on the battlefield against the French and Indians.

   B. failing to treat George Washington and the Colonial troops as comrades and allies.

   C. not spending enough money to provide the necessary weapons and reinforcements.

   D. arguing in favor of a peace treaty that would have favored the French position in North America.

64. **Theodore Roosevelt coined the term *muckraker* to refer to** _____

    A. labor organizers.

    B. factory workers.

    C. investigative journalists.

    D. combat veterans.

65. **Why did the United States take part in the Korean War?**

    A. to contain the spread of Communism

    B. to prevent the establishment of a strong, united Korea

    C. to demonstrate American military power to the Soviet Union

    D. to restore the Japanese to power in Korea

66. **Eli Whitney is a notable historical figure for his** _____

    A. role in the creation of the Federal Reserve System.

    B. invention of the cotton gin.

    C. authorship of the Bill of Rights.

    D. opposition to Jim Crow laws in the South.

67. **The Alien and Sedition Acts of 1798 marked the first time that the U.S. government had to decide between conflicting issues of** _____

    A. appeasement and aggression toward a foreign nation.

    B. freedom and slavery.

    C. proportional and equal representation.

    D. individual liberty and national security.

68. **Japan attacked the United States in 1941 with the goal of** _____

    A. annexing the United States.

    B. reducing the United States to the status of a second-rate power.

    C. retaking various U.S. colonies in the Pacific.

    D. achieving revenge for the provisions of the Versailles Treaty of 1919.

69. The term *Northwest Territory* refers to an area including the present-day states of _____

    A. Oregon and Washington.

    B. Maine and Vermont.

    C. North and South Dakota.

    D. Ohio and Illinois.

70. The Farmers' Alliance of the 1870s was similar to _____

    A. a labor union.

    B. a corporation.

    C. a trust.

    D. a monopoly.

71. _____ was the turning point in the war between the United States and Japan.

    A. The bombing of Hiroshima and Nagasaki

    B. The Battle of Iwo Jima

    C. The Bataan death march

    D. The Battle of Leyte Gulf

72. What did the Mayflower Compact and the Iroquois Confederacy have in common?

    A. Both were peace treaties between American Indians and European settlers.

    B. Both were exercises in representative government.

    C. Neither was produced by a patriarchal society.

    D. Neither contains democratic principles or ideas.

73. In 1890, Democratic presidential candidate William Jennings Bryan supported _____

    A. the return of the United States to the gold standard.

    B. the minting and circulation of silver coins.

    C. the elimination of the income tax.

    D. the elimination of regulation of big business.

74. At the end of the Cold War, the United States was left as _____

    A. the world's last superpower.

    B. the world's largest nation.

    C. the world's greatest creditor nation.

    D. the world's policeman.

75. The *Federalist Papers* urged the people and the state legislatures to support
    ratification of _____

    A. the Fugitive Slave Act.

    B. the Civil Rights amendments.

    C. the Constitution.

    D. the Bill of Rights.

76. In the 1870s, the Republican Party split into two factions over the issue
    of _____

    A. protective tariffs.

    B. Reconstruction.

    C. civil-service reform.

    D. women's suffrage.

77. The term *Great Awakening* refers to _____

    A. the proliferation of new technologies (elevator, typewriter, and so on) in the late
       nineteenth century.

    B. the backlash against communism behind the Iron Curtain in the 1980s.

    C. the awareness in the British colonies that the time had come for independence from
       Great Britain.

    D. major Christian religious revivals that swept the United States in the late eighteenth
       and early nineteenth centuries.

78. The Dutch founded the colony of _____, but lost it to the British in 1664.

    A. Pennsylvania

    B. New York

    C. Delaware

    D. Maryland

79. **In what way were the 1980s economically similar to the 1920s?**

   A. Americans bought on credit and ended up in debt.

   B. Both decades ended in massive economic depressions.

   C. The White House operated the government on a balanced budget.

   D. Prices and unemployment rose steadily.

80. **The settlement-house movement began in the 1880s with the purpose of _____**

   A. marching and demonstrating to arouse support for women's suffrage.

   B. lobbying Congress to pass a national minimum-wage law.

   C. establishing territory where American Indians could settle permanently on reservations.

   D. welcoming and helping working people and immigrants in city neighborhoods.

81. ***The Grapes of Wrath* is historically important because it dramatizes the experience of _____**

   A. migrant workers during the Great Depression and the Dust Bowl.

   B. flappers during the Jazz Age.

   C. Vietnam veterans returning home.

   D. black people winning the fight during the Civil Rights era.

82. **The political concept of *perestroika* is best described as _____**

   A. an openness to political discourse from all social ranks.

   B. a restructuring of government and society.

   C. the universal right of an adult to vote.

   D. the right of a head of state to choose the national religion.

83. **The term *nativist* refers to the belief that the United States should _____**

   A. establish liberal policies toward American Indians.

   B. curtail certain civil rights of foreign-born Americans and immigrants.

   C. set specific quotas on immigration to the United States from certain countries.

   D. establish an African republic to which slaves could emigrate to gain their freedom.

84. **These are all basic goals of the New Deal except** _____
    A. to reorganize the banking system to prevent another Great Depression.
    B. to provide immediate relief for those who had lost their jobs and savings.
    C. to restore the national economy to stability.
    D. to provide full civil rights for African Americans in the old Confederacy.

85. **Which best describes the position of the Antifederalist Party?**
    A. It believed that a too-strong central government would become tyrannical rather than representative.
    B. It thought that the legislative assembly should represent states not equally, but according to their population.
    C. It supported ratification of the Constitution as written in 1787.
    D. It feared that larger states would be under-represented in the legislature because all states had the same number of senators.

86. **The War on Poverty is associated with which president?**
    A. Lyndon Johnson
    B. Richard Nixon
    C. Gerald Ford
    D. Jimmy Carter

87. **During the Gilded Age, the upper social class comprised families who** _____
    A. had recently made fortunes in business and industry.
    B. had been in the United States for several generations and had inherited their money.
    C. had achieved renown in artistic and intellectual circles.
    D. had ties to important people in politics and government.

88. **In which decade were American Indians granted U.S. citizenship?**
    A. 1780s
    B. 1860s
    C. 1920s
    D. 1960s

89. **Intolerance of religious self-determination characterized the British colonies of _____**

    A. Massachusetts and Plymouth.

    B. Maryland and Virginia.

    C. Connecticut and Rhode Island.

    D. New York and New Jersey.

90. **As a result of _____, the United States greatly improved its national highway system.**

    A. the Square Deal

    B. the New Deal

    C. the New Frontier

    D. the Era of Good Feelings

91. **Business owners have always opposed the existence of labor unions because _____**

    A. labor unions are a check on the owner's power.

    B. labor unions are unconstitutional.

    C. labor unions have historically made unreasonable demands.

    D. labor unions argue for less government regulation of businesses.

92. **When the Democrats came out strongly in favor of _____ in the 1960s, Democratic voters throughout the South changed their allegiance to the Republican Party.**

    A. civil rights

    B. segregation

    C. the war in Vietnam

    D. deregulating big business

93. **The Northwest Ordinance banned _____ throughout the Northwest Territory.**

    A. settled American-Indian communities

    B. slavery

    C. heavy industry

    D. U.S. expansion

94. _____ is historically significant for his role in the Great Awakening.

    A. Benjamin Franklin

    B. George Whitefield

    C. William Lloyd Garrison

    D. Andrew Jackson

95. What was the most important reason for the Europeans' success in establishing dominance over the native populations in the Americas?

    A. They had deadlier weapons.

    B. There were more of them.

    C. They were physically healthier and stronger.

    D. They were more familiar with the local geography.

96. Reconstruction of the old Confederacy ended when _____

    A. the White House withdrew the occupying federal troops.

    B. the Black Codes were overturned.

    C. the Voting Rights Act was passed.

    D. the Civil Rights amendments were passed.

97. A *corporation* is best defined as a business in which _____

    A. one or two owners run things with the help of a small staff.

    B. a board of trustees runs several large businesses as one organization.

    C. owners sell shares of stock to investors and pay them a percentage of the profits.

    D. the government determines wages and prices.

98. Which U.S. president played the greatest role in the Civil Rights movement?

    A. Dwight D. Eisenhower

    B. John F. Kennedy

    C. Lyndon B. Johnson

    D. Richard M. Nixon

99. All these wars resulted in the United States gaining new territory or new colonies except _____

    A. the Spanish-American War.

    B. the War of 1812.

    C. the Mexican War.

    D. the Korean War.

100. All these factors except _____ enabled Europeans to subdue and dominate the American Indians.

    A. European greed for ownership of land

    B. Indians' lack of immunity to European diseases

    C. superior European weapons

    D. Indians' greater knowledge of the terrain

Afterword

The United States since the Fall of Communism

A typical U.S. history survey course will end with the fall of Communism in 1988–1991. The course is called *history*, not *current events*, because it deals with the past and not the present. However, it is a good idea to arm yourself with knowledge of developments in American politics, economics, and society since 1991. This afterword describes some of the trends and issues that the United States is trying to address.

Federalism

There is still tension between the states and the national government over which has the greater authority. Since the 1990s, three issues have been special bones of contention between the two: abortion rights, the right to legal marriage, and acceptance or rejection of a national health-insurance system. As of this writing, more and more states are restricting abortion rights while at the same time expanding the right to legal marriage. The future of health insurance in the United States is still impossible to determine.

Immigration

Immigration continues to have a tremendous impact on the American economy; many immigrants enter the United States illegally and work without proper documentation. Because they are here illegally, many must accept less than the federally required minimum wage for work, and many are paid under the table, thus avoiding income tax but also missing out on benefits such as Social Security. The vast majority of current immigrants to the United States are Latin Americans, due to the geographical proximity of their native countries to the U.S.

Immigration has also had a significant cultural impact. The United States is entirely made up of immigrants and their descendants; therefore, the new wave of immigrants is simply continuing a tradition. However, there is one significant difference between the current wave of Latin American immigrants and all previous groups: they resist assimilation into the American culture. Instead of the new immigrant group assimilating, the culture is changing to meet the needs of the immigrants. This is most noticeable in the way governments and businesses almost always provide information and customer assistance in Spanish as well as English. Something of a nativist backlash against this has developed among the millions of Americans who are not Hispanic.

Foreign Relations

Alliances during and after the two World Wars firmly established a close and friendly connection between the United States and Western Europe. This changed soon after Saudi terrorists attacked the United States in September 2001. American foreign policy immediately became aggressive—so much so that the initially sympathetic European states began to view it with alarm. Although European countries sent troops to the Iraq War, some enthusiastically (i.e., Britain) and others reluctantly, the European Union as a whole would have preferred a more restrained response. A 2008 change of leadership in the White House has gone some way toward mending the transatlantic friendships, and the United States has pledged to bring all troops home by the end of 2011. In an unexpected international development known as the Arab Spring, the early months of 2011 saw a wave of uprisings and democratic revolutions in a number of Middle Eastern nations. It is impossible to predict what the near future holds for U.S. foreign policy, particularly in the Middle Eastern region.

In addition, Europe and the United States no longer have a monopoly on nuclear weapons. China, India, Israel, North Korea, and Pakistan all possess strategic nuclear weapons—a fact that European heads of state must constantly keep in mind. Mutual hostility between India and Pakistan and between North and South Korea is particularly evident as of this writing; since nuclear war might very possibly wreak destruction across the globe, all nations must use care in negotiations.

Religious Divisions

At one time, the United States was bitterly divided over the issue of slavery. Today, it is as bitterly divided over the issue of faith. One side advocates a more Christian society; the other advocates a society that treats all faiths equally or that is secular.

People on both sides of the issue argue that the First Amendment supports their views. Christians point to the phrase, "Congress shall make no law . . . prohibiting the free exercise [of religion]." Non-Christians point to the phrase, "Congress shall make no law respecting an establishment of religion."

The division between groups who advocate a more Christian society and those who want a religiously diverse or secular society has become the most politically divisive issue of the day. The Republican Party actively courts the support of the "religious right," while the Democratic Party takes the opposite position. It is impossible to predict how the division will be resolved.

Racism

In 2008, Barack Obama became the first African-American president of the United States. This was a highly important step in African-American progress toward equal treatment in American society. President Obama was well aware of the symbolic importance of his election; in his inaugural address, he referred to himself as "a man whose father less than 60 years ago might not have been served in a local restaurant." In a great measure of how far the United States had come since the Civil War and the days of the Civil Rights movement, press commentary during the election campaign did not primarily focus on either the race or the gender of the candidates (Obama's closest Democratic competitor for election was a woman, Senator Hillary Rodham Clinton)—it focused only on their approach to the issues of the day.

Answer Key

CHAPTER 1

QUIZ

1. C   2. B   3. D   4. C   5. A   6. B   7. B   8. C   9. D   10. D

CHAPTER 2

QUIZ

1. D   2. C   3. B   4. A   5. C   6. D   7. A   8. C   9. D   10. A

CHAPTER 3

QUIZ

1. A   2. C   3. D   4. B   5. A   6. D   7. B   8. A   9. A   10. D

CHAPTER 4

QUIZ

1. C   2. A   3. C   4. D   5. C   6. B   7. A   8. C   9. B   10. A

CHAPTER 5

QUIZ

1. D   2. C   3. A   4. C   5. B   6. B   7. C   8. D   9. B   10. D

CHAPTER 6

QUIZ
1. C 2. A 3. D 4. B 5. D 6. A 7. A 8. D 9. A 10. B

CHAPTER 7

QUIZ
1. B 2. C 3. D 4. A 5. A 6. C 7. B 8. A 9. C 10. D

CHAPTER 8

QUIZ
1. C 2. B 3. A 4. C 5. C 6. D 7. B 8. D 9. D 10. A

CHAPTER 9

QUIZ
1. D 2. C 3. C 4. D 5. A 6. C 7. C 8. A 9. D 10. A

PART 1 EXAM

1. B 2. D 3. C 4. B 5. B 6. A 7. D 8. B 9. C 10. D 11. B 12. D
13. B 14. A 15. B 16. B 17. A 18. A 19. C 20. D 21. C 22. B 23. B
24. B 25. C 26. B 27. C 28. D 29. A 30. B 31. C 32. C 33. A 34. C
35. A 36. B 37. A 38. B 39. C 40. B 41. D 42. B 43. D 44. B 45. A
46. C 47. A 48. C 49. A 50. C

CHAPTER 10

QUIZ
1. C 2. B 3. A 4. D 5. B 6. A 7. C 8. D 9. B 10. B

CHAPTER 11

QUIZ
1. A 2. A 3. C 4. B 5. C 6. B 7. C 8. C 9. B 10. B

CHAPTER 12

QUIZ
1. B   2. A   3. C   4. B   5. C   6. B   7. B   8. D   9. D   10. A

CHAPTER 13

QUIZ
1. A   2. A   3. C   4. D   5. C   6. C   7. D   8. D   9. B   10. B

CHAPTER 14

QUIZ
1. B   2. C   3. A   4. A   5. D   6. C   7. D   8. A   9. A   10. A

CHAPTER 15

QUIZ
1. C   2. A   3. D   4. A   5. B   6. C   7. B   8. B   9. D   10. A

CHAPTER 16

QUIZ
1. A   2. D   3. B   4. C   5. B   6. D   7. C   8. B   9. A   10. B

CHAPTER 17

QUIZ
1. C   2. B   3. A   4. C   5. D   6. C   7. B   8. D   9. D   10. A

CHAPTER 18

QUIZ
1. C   2. B   3. A   4. B   5. B   6. D   7. C   8. C   9. A   10. B

CHAPTER 19

QUIZ
1. C   2. A   3. B   4. D   5. A   6. B   7. D   8. B   9. A   10. A

PART 2 EXAM

1. B   2. C   3. C   4. A   5. B   6. D   7. B   8. C   9. B   10. C   11. B   12. D
13. D   14. A   15. D   16. B   17. B   18. B   19. B   20. B   21. A   22. C   23. B
24. B   25. D   26. D   27. A   28. B   29. B   30. D   31. A   32. A   33. D   34. B
35. B   36. B   37. B   38. B   39. A   40. C   41. A   42. A   43. C   44. A   45. D
46. A   47. C   48. C   49. C   50. D

CHAPTER 20

QUIZ
1. C   2. D   3. B   4. A   5. B   6. C   7. C   8. D   9. A   10. B

CHAPTER 21

QUIZ
1. D   2. D   3. A   4. C   5. B   6. B   7. C   8. B   9. C   10. D

CHAPTER 22

QUIZ
1. C   2. B   3. B   4. C   5. B   6. C   7. D   8. C   9. A   10. D

CHAPTER 23

QUIZ
1. A   2. D   3. C   4. C   5. A   6. C   7. B   8. C   9. D   10. B

CHAPTER 24

QUIZ
1. B   2. A   3. B   4. A   5. D   6. B   7. A   8. C   9. C   10. B

CHAPTER 25

QUIZ
1. B   2. D   3. D   4. A   5. C   6. C   7. C   8. C   9. A   10. D

CHAPTER 26

QUIZ
1. A   2. D   3. C   4. D   5. B   6. C   7. C   8. A   9. A   10. D

CHAPTER 27

QUIZ
1. A   2. C   3. B   4. A   5. C   6. D   7. A   8. C   9. D   10. D

CHAPTER 28

QUIZ
1. D   2. D   3. C   4. B   5. A   6. B   7. B   8. C   9. D   10. B

CHAPTER 29

QUIZ
1. D   2. C   3. B   4. B   5. A   6. D   7. C   8. D   9. A   10. B

CHAPTER 30

QUIZ
1. B   2. B   3. A   4. B   5. C   6. C   7. D   8. B   9. B   10. A

CHAPTER 31

QUIZ
1. A   2. B   3. A   4. A   5. D   6. C   7. C   8. A   9. B   10. B

PART 3 EXAM

1. A   2. C   3. B   4. A   5. C   6. C   7. C   8. B   9. A   10. A   11. C   12. D
13. D   14. C   15. A   16. B   17. C   18. B   19. B   20. D   21. B   22. D   23. A
24. A   25. B   26. D   27. A   28. D   29. B   30. A   31. B   32. C   33. B   34. A
35. C   36. B   37. C   38. A   39. B   40. C   41. B   42. A   43. C   44. C   45. D
46. C   47. B   48. B   49. D   50. A

FINAL EXAM

1. B   2. D   3. D   4. A   5. B   6. A   7. D   8. B   9. B   10. A   11. B   12. D
13. B   14. A   15. B   16. C   17. C   18. C   19. C   20. A   21. B   22. B   23. D
24. A   25. B   26. C   27. A   28. B   29. A   30. C   31. D   32. D   33. D   34. A
35. A   36. C   37. B   38. D   39. C   40. C   41. A   42. D   43. B   44. C   45. C
46. A   47. A   48. B   49. A   50. D   51. C   52. B   53. B   54. D   55. C   56. B
57. B   58. D   59. C   60. A   61. C   62. A   63. B   64. C   65. A   66. B   67. D
68. B   69. D   70. A   71. D   72. B   73. B   74. A   75. C   76. C   77. D   78. B
79. A   80. D   81. A   82. B   83. B   84. D   85. A   86. A   87. B   88. C   89. A
90. B   91. A   92. A   93. B   94. B   95. A   96. A   97. C   98. C   99. D   100. D

Bibliography and Sources for Further Reading

Books

General Works on U.S. History

Fischer, Claude S. *Made in America: A Social History of American Culture and Character.* Chicago: University of Chicago Press, 2010.

Gilbert, Martin. *The Routledge Atlas of American History*, 4th ed. New York: Routledge, 2002.

Hochman, Stanley, and Eleanor Hochman. *The Penguin Dictionary of Contemporary American History*, 3rd ed. New York: Penguin Books, 1997.

Wexler, Alan, illus. Molly Braun. *Atlas of Westward Expansion.* New York: Facts on File, 1995.

Chapter 1: Settlement and Colonization

Dolin, Eric Jay. *Fur, Fortune, and Empire: The Epic History of the Fur Trade in America.* New York: W. W. Norton and Company, 2010.

Kupperman, Karen. *The Jamestown Project.* Cambridge, Mass.: Belknap Press/Harvard University Press, 2009.

Perdue, Theda, and Michael D. Green. *North American Indians: A Very Short Introduction.* Oxford, U.K.: Oxford University Press, 2010.

Philbrick, Nathaniel. *Mayflower: A Story of Courage, Community, and War.* New York: Penguin Books, 2007.

Weber, David J. *The Spanish Frontier in North America.* New Haven, Conn.: Yale University Press, 1992.

Chapters 2–3: British Colonies

Hall, David D. *Worlds of Wonder, Days of Judgment: Popular Religious Belief in Early New England.* Cambridge, Mass.: Harvard University Press, 1990.

Lambert, Frank. *Inventing the "Great Awakening."* Princeton, N.J.: Princeton University Press, 2001.

LaPlante, Eve. *American Jezebel: The Uncommon Life of Anne Hutchinson, the Woman Who Defied the Puritans.* New York: Harper, 2005.

McCusker, John J. *The Economy of British America 1607–1789.* Chapel Hill: University of North Carolina Press, 1991.

Silver, Peter. *Our Savage Neighbors: How Indian War Transformed Early America.* New York: W. W. Norton and Company, 2009.

Starkey, Marion. *The Devil in Massachusetts: A Modern Inquiry into the Salem Witch Trials.* New York: Anchor Books, 1969.

Taylor, Alan. *The Divided Ground: Indians, Settlers, and the Northern Borderland of the American Revolution.* New York: Vintage Books, 2007.

Chapters 4–6: The French and Indian War and the American Revolution

Borneman, Walter R. *The French and Indian War: Deciding the Fate of North America.* New York: Harper Perennial, 2007.

Chernow, Ron. *Washington: A Life.* New York: Penguin Books, 2010.

Greene, Jack P., ed. *Colonies to Nation: A Documentary History of the American Revolution.* New York: W. W. Norton and Company, 1975.

Silverman, Kenneth. *A Cultural History of the American Revolution.* New York: Columbia University Press, 1976.

Wheeler, Richard, ed. *Voices of 1776: The Story of the American Revolution in the Words of Those Who Were There.* New York: Meridian Books, 1972, 1991.

Chapters 7–8: The Articles of Confederation and the U.S. Constitution

Cappon, Lester J., ed. *The Adams–Jefferson Letters.* Chapel Hill: University of North Carolina Press, 1988.

Franklin, Benjamin. *The Autobiography of Benjamin Franklin.* New Haven, Conn.: Yale University Press, 1964.

Morison, Samuel Eliot. *Sources & Documents Illustrating the American Revolution and the Formation of the Federal Constitution 1764–1788.* London: Oxford University Press, 1975 (originally published in 1923).

Chapters 9–12: Establishing a New Nation; the Early Nineteenth Century; Religion and Reform

Bergon, Frank, ed. *The Journals of Lewis and Clark.* New York: Penguin Books, 1989.

Forbes, Robert Pierce. *The Missouri Compromise and Its Aftermath: Slavery and the Meaning of America.* Chapel Hill: University of North Carolina Press, 2009.

Howe, Daniel Walker. *What Hath God Wrought: The Transformation of America, 1815–1848*. New York: Oxford University Press, 2009.

Koeppel, Gerard. *Bond of Union: Building the Erie Canal and the American Empire*. New York: Da Capo Press, 2009.

Langguth, A. J. *Union 1812: The Americans Who Fought the Second War of Independence*. New York: Simon & Schuster, 2007.

Weightman, Gavin. *The Industrial Revolutionaries*. New York: Grove Press, 2007.

Wood, Gordon S. *Empire of Liberty: A History of the Early Republic 1789–1815*. New York: Oxford University Press, 2009.

Chapters 13–15: Expansion and Sectionalism; the Civil War

Foner, Eric. *The Fiery Trial: Abraham Lincoln and American Slavery*. New York: W. W. Norton and Company, 2010.

Genovese, Eugene D. *Roll, Jordan, Roll: The World the Slaves Made*. New York: Vintage Books, 1976.

Johnson, Susan Lee. *Roaring Camp: The Social World of the California Gold Rush*. New York: W. W. Norton and Company, 2001.

Lincoln, Abraham. *Selected Speeches and Writings*. New York: Library of America/Vintage Books, 1992.

Mayer, Henry. *All on Fire: William Lloyd Garrison and the Abolition of Slavery*. New York: W. W. Norton and Company, 2008.

McGinty, Brian. *John Brown's Trial*. Cambridge, Mass.: Harvard University Press, 2009.

Merry, Robert W. *A Country of Vast Designs: James K. Polk, the Mexican War and the Conquest of the American Continent*. New York: Simon & Schuster, 2009.

Waugh, Joan. *U. S. Grant: American Hero, American Myth*. Chapel Hill: University of North Carolina Press, 2010.

Woodworth, Steven E. *Manifest Destinies: America's Westward Expansion and the Road to the Civil War*. New York: Knopf, 2010.

Chapter 16: Reconstruction to 1877

DuBois, W. E. B. *Black Reconstruction in America 1860–1880*. New York: Free Press, 1998 (originally published in the 1930s).

Foner, Eric. *Reconstruction: America's Unfinished Revolution 1863–1877*. New York: Harper & Row, 1988.

Franklin, John Hope. *Reconstruction After the Civil War*, 2nd ed. Chicago: University of Chicago Press, 1994.

Litwack, Leon F. *Been in the Storm So Long: The Aftermath of Slavery*. New York: Vintage Books, 1980.

Stampp, Kenneth. *The Era of Reconstruction, 1865–1877*. New York: Vintage Books, 1967.

Steward, David O. *Impeached: The Trial of President Andrew Johnson and the Fight for Lincoln's Legacy*. New York: Simon & Schuster, 2009.

Chapter 17: Westward Movement/Expansion to 1898

Brown, Dee. *Bury My Heart at Wounded Knee: An Indian History of the American West*. New York: Holt, 2007 (originally published in 1970).

Cumings, Bruce. *Dominion from Sea to Sea: Pacific Ascendancy and American Power*. New Haven, Conn.: Yale University Press, 2010.

Miner, Craig. *A Most Magnificent Machine: America Adopts the Railroad, 1825–1862*. Lawrence: University Press of Kansas, 2010.

Nugent, Walter. *Habits of Empire: A History of American Expansion*. New York: Knopf, 2008.

Chapters 18–20: The Gilded Age, the Call for Reform, and the Progressive Era

Brands, H. W. *American Colossus: The Triumph of Capitalism 1865–1900*. New York: Doubleday and Company, 2010.

Foner, Philip S. *History of the Labor Movement in the United States*. 10 vols. New York: International Publishers, originally published 1947–1994.

Josephson, Matthew. *The Robber Barons: The Great American Capitalists 1861–1901*. New Brunswick, N.J.: Transaction Publishers, 2010.

Morris, Edmund. *Theodore Rex*. New York: Random House, 2002.

Painter, Nell Irvin. *Standing at Armageddon: A Grassroots History of the Progressive Era*. New York: W. W. Norton and Company, 2008.

Wertheimer, Barbara Mayer, ed. *We Were There: The Story of Working Women in America*. New York: Pantheon Books, 1977.

Chapter 21: The United States Becomes a World Power

McCoy, Alfred, and Francisco Scarano, eds. *Colonial Crucible: Empire in the Making of the Modern American State*. Madison: University of Wisconsin Press, 2009.

O'Toole, G. J. A. *The Spanish War: An American Epic, 1898*. New York: W. W. Norton and Company, 1986.

Silbey, David J. *A War of Frontier and Empire: The Philippine-American War 1899–1902*. New York: Hill and Wang, 2008.

Swanberg, W. A. *Citizen Hearst: A Biography of William Randolph Hearst*. New York: Charles Scribner's Sons, 1961.

Chapter 22: World War I

Fussell, Paul. *The Great War and Modern Memory*. Oxford, U.K.: Oxford University Press, 1975.

Keegan, John. *The First World War*. New York: Vintage Books, 2000.

Wilkerson, Isabel. *The Warmth of Other Suns: The Epic Story of America's Great Migration*. New York: Random House, 2010.

Chapter 23: The Jazz Age

Hiltzik, Michael. *Colossus: Hoover Dam and the Making of the American Century*. New York: Free Press, 2010.

Leuchtenberg, William. *The Perils of Prosperity, 1914–32*, 2nd ed. Chicago: University of Chicago Press, 1993.

Mencken, H. L. *A Religious Orgy in Tennessee: A Reporter's Account of the Scopes Monkey Trial*. New York: Melville House, 2006.

Okrent, Daniel. *Last Call: The Rise and Fall of Prohibition*. New York: Scribner Books, 2010.

Shindo, Charles J. *1927 and the Rise of Modern America*. Lawrence: University of Kansas Press, 2010.

Chapter 24: The Great Depression

Agee, James, and Walker Evans. *Let Us Now Praise Famous Men*. Boston: Houghton Mifflin Company, 1941.

Dickstein, Morris. *Dancing in the Dark: A Cultural History of the Great Depression*. New York: W. W. Norton and Company, 2010.

Kempton, Murray. *Part of Our Time: Some Ruins and Monuments of the Thirties*. New York: New York Review Books, 1998 (originally published in 1953).

Kennedy, David. *Freedom from Fear: The American People in Depression and War 1929–1945*. New York: Oxford University Press, 2001.

Chapter 25: World War II

Beevor, Anthony. *D-Day: The Battle for Normandy*. New York: Penguin Books, 2010.

———. *The Fall of Berlin 1945*. New York: Penguin Books, 2002.

Gilbert, Martin. *The Second World War: A Complete History*, rev. ed. New York: Holt, 2004.

Keegan, John. *The Second World War*. New York: Penguin Books, 2005.

Spector, Ronald. *Eagle Against the Sun: The American War with Japan*. New York: Vintage Books, 1985.

Swanston, Alexander. *The Historical Atlas of World War II*, updated ed. New York: Chelsea House Publishers, 2010.

Tillman, Barrett. *Whirlwind: The Air War Against Japan 1942–1945*. New York: Simon & Schuster, 2010.

Watt, Donald Cameron. *How War Came: The Immediate Origins of the Second World War 1938–1939*. New York: Pantheon Books, 1989.

Chapters 26–27: The Cold War and the New Frontier

Dobbs, Michael. *One Minute to Midnight: Kennedy, Khrushchev, and Castro on the Brink of Nuclear War*. New York: Vintage Books, 2009.

Freedman, Lawrence. *Kennedy's Wars: Berlin, Cuba, Laos and Vietnam*. Oxford, U.K.: Oxford University Press, 2000.

Furet, François. *The Passing of an Illusion: The Idea of Communism in the Twentieth Century*. Chicago: University of Chicago Press, 1999.

Taylor, Frederick. *The Berlin Wall: A World Divided, 1961–1989*. New York: Harper Perennial, 2006.

Chapter 28: The Great Society and the Civil Rights Movement

Friedan, Betty. *The Feminine Mystique.* New York: Dell Publishing, 1983 (originally published in 1963).

Garrow, David. *Bearing the Cross: Martin Luther King, Jr. and the Southern Christian Leadership Conference.* New York: Vintage Books, 1993.

Gillette, Michael L. *Launching the War on Poverty: An Oral History,* 2nd ed. New York: Oxford University Press, 2010.

Gitlin, Todd. *The Sixties: Years of Hope, Days of Rage,* rev. ed. New York: Bantam Doubleday Dell, 1993.

Holsaert, Faith S., et al, eds. *Hands on the Freedom Plow: Personal Accounts by Women in SNCC.* Chapel Hill: University of North Carolina Press, 2010.

James, Rawn, Jr. *Root and Branch: Charles Hamilton Houston, Thurgood Marshall, and the Struggle to End Segregation.* London: Bloomsbury Press, 2010.

Reporting Civil Rights, Part One: American Journalism 1941–1963. New York: Library of America/Vintage Books, 2003.

Reporting Civil Rights, Part Two: American Journalism 1963–1973. New York: Library of America/Vintage Books, 2003.

Sugrue, Thomas J. *Sweet Land of Liberty: The Forgotten Struggle for Civil Rights in the North.* New York: Random House, 2009.

Chapter 29: The Vietnam War

Fitzgerald, Frances. *Fire in the Lake: The Vietnamese and the Americans in Vietnam.* Boston: Back Bay Books, 2002 (originally published in 1973).

Karnow, Stanley. *Vietnam: A History.* New York: Penguin Books, 1997.

Mailer, Norman. *Miami and the Siege of Chicago: An Informal History of the Republican and Democratic Conventions of 1968.* New York: Signet Books, 1968.

Reporting Vietnam, Part One: American Journalism 1959–1969. New York: Library of American/Vintage Books, 1998.

Reporting Vietnam, Part Two: American Journalism 1969–1975. New York: Library of American/Vintage Books, 1998.

Sheehan, Neil. *A Bright Shining Lie: John Paul Vann and America in Vietnam.* New York: Vintage Books, 1989.

Chapter 30: Watergate

Bernstein, Carl, and Bob Woodward. *All the President's Men.* New York: Simon & Schuster, 1974.

———. *The Final Days.* New York: Simon & Schuster, 1976.

McCarthy, Mary. *The Mask of State: Watergate Portraits.* New York: Harcourt Brace Jovanovich, 1974.

Perlstein, Rick. *Nixonland: The Rise of a President and the Fracturing of America.* New York: Scribner, 2009.

Chapter 31: The Reagan Era and the End of the Cold War

Hayward, Steven F. *The Age of Reagan: The Conservative Counterrevolution 1980–1989*. New York: Three Rivers Press, 2010.

Hitchcock, William I. *The Struggle for Europe: The Turbulent History of a Divided Continent, 1945 to the Present*. New York: Anchor Books, 2003.

Taylor, Frederick. *The Berlin Wall: A World Divided, 1961–1989*. New York: Harper Perennial, 2006.

The Internet

The Internet can be a useful, even superb, tool for research—**when used with caution!** It is rich in texts of original primary source documents, many of which are difficult to find in print.

However, the secondary source material that can be found online varies greatly in quality. Anyone can post anything he or she wishes on the Internet; it does not have the fact-checking, quality-control process that goes into the publication of nonfiction books. Therefore, the student is cautioned to use good judgment when consulting online secondary sources in the field of American history; and no matter how impressive an Internet site appears, it is always best to confirm the information in a print source.

Relevant Works of Literature

This is a highly selective list of novels and plays dealing with many of the central issues and events in U.S. history. Many of these works were written in the times they describe.

Of course, the student should not rely on fiction for exact accuracy of facts and dates. However, reading historical fiction and drama can enormously enrich a student's understanding of a period. Great historical fiction can bring an era to life and provide a vivid picture of a time and place.

The Salem Witch Trials

Arthur Miller, *The Crucible*

The French and Indian War

James Fenimore Cooper, *The Last of the Mohicans*

The American Revolution

Walter Edmonds, *Drums Along the Mohawk*
Kenneth Roberts, *Arundel*

The Industrial Revolution

Rebecca Harding Davis, *Life in the Iron Mills*

American Slavery

Toni Morrison, *Beloved*
Harriet Beecher Stowe, *Uncle Tom's Cabin*

The Civil War

Russell Banks, *Cloudsplitter*
Stephen Crane, *The Red Badge of Courage*
Upton Sinclair, *Manassas*

Westward Expansion

Willa Cather, *My Ántonia*

The Rise of Industry

Sinclair Lewis, *The Jungle*
Booth Tarkington, *The Magnificent Ambersons*

The Rise of Big Business

John Dos Passos, *The 42nd Parallel* (from the trilogy *U.S.A.*)
Theodore Dreiser, *The Titan*
Upton Sinclair, *The Money Changers*

World War I

Willa Cather, *One of Ours*
John Dos Passos, *Nineteen Nineteen* (from the trilogy *U.S.A.*)
Erich Maria Remarque, *All Quiet on the Western Front*

The 1920s

John Dos Passos, *The Big Money* (from the trilogy *U.S.A.*)
F. Scott Fitzgerald, *The Great Gatsby*
Sinclair Lewis, *Elmer Gantry*

The Scopes Trial

Jerome Lawrence and Robert Edward Lee, *Inherit the Wind*

The Great Depression and the Dust Bowl

John Steinbeck, *The Grapes of Wrath*

World War II in Europe

Joseph Heller, *Catch-22*
Kurt Vonnegut, *Slaughterhouse-Five*

World War II in the Pacific

James Jones, *From Here to Eternity*
James A. Michener, *Tales of the South Pacific*

Post-World War II Era

August Wilson, *Fences*
August Wilson, *Two Trains Running*
Sloan Wilson, *The Man in the Gray Flannel Suit*

The Sixties Counterculture

James Rado, Gerome Ragni, and Galt MacDermot, *Hair*

Vietnam War

Graham Greene, *The Quiet American*
William Lederer and Eugene Burdick, *The Ugly American*

Index